IMMIGRATION LAW

AND

PROCEDURE
IN A NUTSHELL

THIRD EDITION

By

DAVID WEISSBRODT

Briggs and Morgan Professor of Law
University of Minnesota

ST. PAUL, MINN.
WEST PUBLISHING CO.
1992

COPYRIGHT © 1984, 1989 WEST PUBLISHING CO.
COPYRIGHT © 1992 By WEST PUBLISHING CO.
                        610 Opperman Drive
                        P.O. Box 64526
                        St. Paul, MN 55164–0526

Library of Congress Cataloging-in-Publication Data

Weissbrodt, David S.
    Immigration law and procedure in a nutshell / by David Weissbrodt.
—3rd ed.
        p.   cm. — (Nutshell series)
    Includes bibliographical references (p.   ) and index.
    ISBN 0–314–01070–X
    1. Emigration and immigration law—United States. I. Title.
II. Series.
KF4819.3.W4   1992
342.73'082—dc20
[347.30282]   92–22646
                                                         CIP

ISBN 0–314–01070–X

 TEXT IS PRINTED ON 10% POST
CONSUMER RECYCLED PAPER

Weissbrodt, Imm. 3rd NS
1st Reprint—1994

PREFACE

This brief text is designed to assist students in obtaining an overview of the material which might be expected to be found in a course on immigration law and procedure.

When the first edition of this Nutshell was written, there did not yet exist a standard casebook on immigration law and it was unclear what substance belonged in a course on immigration law and procedure. At that time only a few law schools considered immigration law worthy of a course. Since that time many major law schools have decided to offer immigration law courses and three principal coursebooks have been published: Thomas Alexander Aleinikoff & David Martin, Immigration: Process and Policy (2d ed. 1991); Richard Boswell, Immigration and Nationality Law: Cases and Materials (1991); and Stephen Legomsky, Immigration Law: Cases, Materials and Problems (1992). It was gratifying to see that several parts of this Nutshell were reprinted in two of those coursebooks.

This Nutshell presents the information which a student should want to know about the immigration process as it functions in the United States. With the enactment of the Immigration Act of

1990 and the Technical Amendments of 1991, immigration law and procedures have undergone significant change. In addition to those legislative changes, political upheaval throughout the world has made immigration a far more visible and controversial issue—leading, in turn, to a constantly evolving body of decisions and laws. To reflect these changes and make them as comprehensible and accessible as possible, the third edition has been reorganized into six parts.

The *first* part—chapters 1 through 4—provides a general overview of the history, constitutional source, and institutional structure of immigration law. In addition to tracing the evolution of immigration law and history in the U.S., the first part traces the increasing recognition of the federal power to regulate immigration and describes the federal agencies and congressional committees responsible for the formulation and implementation of immigration law.

The *second* part—chapters 5 through 7—discusses the various standards and application procedures for immigrant, nonimmigrant, and student visas. It should be noted, however, that this Nutshell does not attempt to serve as a manual for practitioners.

In part *three*, chapters 8 and 9 explain the grounds for requiring an alien to depart from the United States and the procedures for deportation and exclusion.

In the *fourth* part, chapters 10 and 11 discuss refugee and asylum issues and summarize international law as it relates to immigration. While extradition is connected to immigration law, the third edition omits the subject of extradition which had been discussed in the first two editions.

Because immigration law is ultimately founded upon the relationship between the individual and the state, part *five*—chapters 12 and 13—focuses on citizenship and the rights of aliens in the United States.

Part *six*—chapters 14 through 17—identifies several ethical issues which immigration lawyers confront and which may help to clarify for students the nature of the immigration process. Chapters 16 and 17 contain a brief conclusion and a bibliography.

The author wishes to thank several present and former law students who assisted in the preparation of this Nutshell. The students who assisted with the first and second editions are identified in those editions. For their contributions to individual chapters of the third edition, many thanks to Carolyn Anderson, Kathy Cima, James Fong, Lisa Koble, James Lee, Alexander Lockwood, Meredith McQuaid, Philomena Nzegge, Peter-Christian Olivo, Jaci Sauer, William Stock, Hsi-An Wu, and Su-Hwa Yu. The author wishes particularly to thank Michael Korengold for his help in revising all chapters of the present third edition. Lyonette

Louis-Jacques provided very helpful bibliographical assistance—especially on the last chapter. Ellen Lane, Marcia McGovern, Tam Murphy, and Mary Thacker did excellent secretarial work to make the third edition possible.

I am also grateful to H. Sam Myers, a distinguished immigration lawyer in Minneapolis, who generously took time from his busy law practice and from his presidency of the American Immigration Lawyers Association during 1991–92 to review the manuscript and to give much assistance. In addition, Michelle A. Egan, Senior Immigration Examiner, Immigration and Naturalization Service in the St. Paul District Office, gave me very useful comments on the citizenship issues in chapter 12. The author, of course, must take ultimate responsibility for what remains in this book and what the Nutshell format required to be deleted.

DAVID WEISSBRODT

Minneapolis, Minnesota
May, 1992

EXPLANATORY NOTES

I have attempted to follow the format of other Nutshell volumes. Accordingly, cases have been cited only where they represent relatively significant landmarks or where they clarify significant issues. The text ordinarily contains only the name of the case, the court of decision, and the date. The student will find the full citation in the Table of Authorities, which follows the Outline. Due to limitations of space and format, some cases are omitted where they would have supported statements in the text and one case is often cited where many others would have been usable as authority.

Immigration law is considerably based upon statutes and regulations. Hence, the text contains frequent references to the principal statutes and regulations, but for reasons of space the citations have been abbreviated in the text. Where both a statute and regulation appear relevant, only the statute is cited. The Table of Authorities contains fuller references to cases, statutes, regulations, and other relevant material.

Because the Nutshell format does not admit footnotes, this volume often omits references to secondary material and other sources, even where such citations clearly exist. The bibliography in the last chapter attempts to redress this problem by listing at least most of the principal sources for the use of the serious student who may want to read more.

OUTLINE

Page

XXIII

*

TABLE OF CASES

References are to Pages

TABLE OF CASES

XXXVII

*

TABLE OF OTHER
AUTHORITIES

UNITED STATES

UNITED STATES CONSTITUTION

TABLE OF OTHER AUTHORITIES

UNITED STATES CONSTITUTION

UNITED STATES CODE ANNOTATED

7 U.S.C.A.—Agriculture

8 U.S.C.A.—Aliens and Nationality

18 U.S.C.A.—Crimes and Criminal Procedure

XLII

XLIII

TABLE OF OTHER AUTHORITIES

UNITED STATES CODE ANNOTATED

28 U.S.C.A.—Judiciary and Judicial Procedure

30 U.S.C.A.—Mineral Lands and Mining

42 U.S.C.A.—The Public Health and Welfare

43 U.S.C.A.—Public Lands

50 U.S.C.A.—War and National Defense

50 U.S.C.A.App.—War and National Defense

TABLE OF OTHER AUTHORITIES

UNITED STATES CODE ANNOTATED

50 U.S.C.A.App.—War and National Defense

STATUTES AT LARGE

STATUTES AT LARGE

TABLE OF OTHER AUTHORITIES

STATUTES AT LARGE

POPULAR NAME ACTS

IMMIGRATION ACT OF 1990

TABLE OF OTHER AUTHORITIES

IMMIGRATION ACT OF 1990

IMMIGRATION AND NATIONALITY ACT

XLVIII

IMMIGRATION AND NATIONALITY ACT

TABLE OF OTHER AUTHORITIES

IMMIGRATION AND NATIONALITY ACT

L

TABLE OF OTHER AUTHORITIES

IMMIGRATION AND NATIONALITY ACT

LI

TABLE OF OTHER AUTHORITIES

IMMIGRATION AND NATIONALITY ACT

TABLE OF OTHER AUTHORITIES

IMMIGRATION AND NATIONALITY ACT

LIII

TABLE OF OTHER AUTHORITIES

IMMIGRATION AND NATIONALITY ACT

TABLE OF OTHER AUTHORITIES

IMMIGRATION AND NATIONALITY ACT

IMMIGRATION AND NATIONALITY ACT

TABLE OF OTHER AUTHORITIES

IMMIGRATION AND NATIONALITY ACT

TABLE OF OTHER AUTHORITIES

IMMIGRATION AND NATIONALITY ACT

TABLE OF OTHER AUTHORITIES

IMMIGRATION AND NATIONALITY ACT

TABLE OF OTHER AUTHORITIES

CODE OF FEDERAL REGULATIONS

TABLE OF OTHER AUTHORITIES

CODE OF FEDERAL REGULATIONS

TABLE OF OTHER AUTHORITIES

CODE OF FEDERAL REGULATIONS

TABLE OF OTHER AUTHORITIES

CODE OF FEDERAL REGULATIONS

TABLE OF OTHER AUTHORITIES

CODE OF FEDERAL REGULATIONS

TABLE OF OTHER AUTHORITIES

CODE OF FEDERAL REGULATIONS

FEDERAL REGISTER

EXECUTIVE ORDERS

OPERATING INSTRUCTIONS

TABLE OF OTHER AUTHORITIES

INTERNATIONAL INSTRUMENTS

TABLE OF OTHER AUTHORITIES

REFUGEE CONVENTION OF 1951

UNITED NATIONS CONVENTION

UNIVERSAL DECLARATION OF HUMAN RIGHTS

TABLE OF OTHER AUTHORITIES

TREATISES AND MISCELLANEOUS

ABA MODEL CODE OF PROFESSIONAL RESPONSIBILITY
Disciplinary Rules

Ethical Considerations

ABA MODEL RULES OF PROFESSIONAL CONDUCT

TABLE OF OTHER AUTHORITIES

ABA MODEL RULES OF PROFESSIONAL CONDUCT

OPINION OF THE ATTORNEY GENERAL

IMMIGRATION LAW

AND

PROCEDURE
IN A NUTSHELL

THIRD EDITION

*

CHAPTER 1

HISTORY OF U.S. IMMIGRATION LAW AND POLICY

§ 1–1 COLONIAL IMMIGRATION

Because an immigrant is defined by *Black's Law Dictionary* as one who leaves a country to settle permanently in another to live, one tends to think of United States immigration as dating from the nation's inception. Most anthropologists, however, believe that the first newcomers to the region that is now the United States entered from Asia over 20,000 years ago across the land bridge where the Bering Strait now lies. These people first settled the western regions, and distinct cultural groups lived in areas spanning to the Atlantic Ocean before any European explorers or later settlers arrived.

In settling the English colonies, immigrants arrived freely and were at first welcomed by other Europeans already settled. Immigration was limited principally by the cost of travel, diseases, and conflict with indigenous inhabitants. Yet by 1640, the population of the colonies had reached approximately 25,000. Population records can only suggest the rate of increase because no immigration records were kept.

The newcomers to the colonies in the years before the American Revolution came from many places and for diverse reasons. Most Europeans—English, French, German, Dutch, Spanish, and Portuguese—came for eco-

1

nomic reasons or to avoid religious persecution in their homelands.

Unfortunately, some of these immigrants began to encounter that same hostility and persecution in the colonies. The Quakers set themselves apart in Pennsylvania and the Scotch–Irish Presbyterians moved west to settle the Mississippi frontier when they received a cold reception in the East. Others, like the French Huguenots, assimilated more easily. Some religious restrictions were adopted by individual colonies attempting to exclude Quakers and Catholics or to subject them to discriminatory taxes. The colonial restrictions were somewhat effective in discouraging immigrants.

Others came involuntarily as punishment or under servitude. Slaves from Africa were forcibly brought. Children were kidnapped from English slums and sold for American labor. English judges were empowered to send both vagrants and felons to the colonies as punishment. These groups also met with disfavor and colonial restrictions; colonies began legislating to exclude "paupers" and "criminals" as early as 1639. Those restrictions excluding "public charges" embraced not only people sent by English courts but also the poor and the diseased who came voluntarily. Southern colonies especially tried to restrict criminals, because that region had received the greatest influx of the 50,000 sent under penal sanction during the fifty years before the Revolution.

These restrictions illustrate the hostility felt towards newcomers by colonists who had just arrived themselves. Although aimed primarily at those banished from England and at public charges who would be added to relief rolls, these restrictions were also a product of religious and national rivalries imported from Europe. The colonies were generally unable to check the influx of migrants, for they lacked both legal authority and a centralized administrative structure. In addition, immigration was still favored to the extent that the colonies needed more people for labor and security. To outsiders, the New World held great promise. Accordingly, by the year 1776, the population of the colonies stood at about 2,500,000, or 100 times the 1640 figure.

The colonial immigration restrictions may have influenced the later legislation of the United States on this subject. In fashioning its laws, the federal government eventually excluded the same general classes of immigrants as did the colonies. The federal legislation also used certain colonial sanctions on immigrants, such as head taxes on individuals and deportation of undesirable aliens.

§ 1–2 EARLY U.S. IMMIGRATION POLICY

Although colonial attitudes continued after the American Revolution, extensive federal legislation dealing with immigration was not enacted for some time, primarily for two reasons. First, for almost a hundred years, it was unclear whether the federal government was even intended by the Constitution to have power to regulate immigration. Second, the United States officially favored unrestricted immigration for about the same period of time after the nation's birth.

The locus of power over the subject of immigration was not definitively identified in any early proclamation of the new government. Under the Articles of Confederation, each state apparently determined its own immigration policy, but there was confusion over the status of prior colonial enactments. The United States Constitution, adopted in 1789, granted Congress broad power to regulate foreign commerce in Article I, section 8, but it was not clear whether foreign commerce included immigration. Not until 1875 did the U.S. Supreme Court in *Henderson v. City of New York* (Sup.Ct.1875) declare state restrictions on immigration to be unconstitutional, as an infringement on the federal power over foreign commerce.

During this long period of uncertainty, Congress did not attempt to invoke its power to regulate immigration, but largely passed a series of acts regulating naturalization and a few other non-restrictive pieces of legislation. Congress adopted the first such law in 1790, liberally granting citizenship to immigrants. Subsequent legislation, however, required increasingly longer periods of residency as well as the renunciation of former allegiances and titles of nobility. In 1798 Congress authorized the President to expel "dangerous" aliens, but that act expired without extension after two years. A new Naturalization Act in 1802 re-established the provisions of a 1795 act, creating a five-year residency requirement for citizenship. In addition, the "passenger acts" of 1819, 1847, 1848, and 1855 set certain minimum space and provisions standards for overseas vessels. Further, the Constitution specifically permitted the adoption of a law forbidding the importation of slaves after 1808 and such a law came into effect that year.

Apart from piecemeal legislation, the first one hundred years of the nation's existence can be characterized as a period of unrestricted immigration. The spacious frontier and the need for labor were the primary reasons for this unrestrictive policy. No official records were kept of immigration until 1820, but it is estimated that 250,000 immigrants arrived in the United States between 1790 and 1820. From 1820 to 1880, while the issue of power over immigration was being debated, over 10 million people arrived.

Discontent with the open immigration policy increased with the rate of immigration and with change in the composition of immigrants. Between 1820 and 1880, political conditions and economic devastation brought over 2.8 million Irish immigrants to the United States. German Catholic immigrants came in large numbers during the European depressions of the 1840's. In a predominantly Protestant country, the Catholic Irish and Germans were not well accepted. The anti-Catholicism that had prevailed in colonial days resurfaced. Several groups, including social reformers, Protestant evangelicals, the Nativists, the Order of the Star–Spangled Banner, and the Know–Nothing Party, campaigned for legislation halting immigration and prohibiting even naturalized immigrants from participating in the nation's political process. These groups were somewhat successful at the state level, but failed at the federal level because the Irish and Germans constituted a large voting block. Politicians at the national level actively sought the vote of these and other newly arrived groups. Hence, federal policy, and apparently the majority of the nation, continued to favor immigration.

Eventually, the Civil War drowned the protests of groups like the Know–Nothings. The need for labor in both North and South was magnified during these war years; an 1864 Act even facilitated immigration by validating contracts pledging future wages in payment for overseas passage.

§ 1–3 RESTRICTION BEGINS: EXCLUDING THE UNWANTED

After the Civil War, federal law began to reflect the growing desire to restrict the immigration of certain groups. The facilitating act of 1864 was repealed in 1868, and in 1875 Congress passed the first restrictive statute. That statute, borrowing from earlier colonial legislation, barred convicts and prostitutes from admission. These limits were the first of many "quality control" exclusions based on the nature of the immigrants themselves. The list of unacceptable types of immigrants would continue to grow in subsequent enactments.

The 1875 Act also attempted to solve the new problem faced by the western states. Westward expansion demanded huge numbers of laborers for work in the mines and on the railroads. Imported Chinese labor had been used since about 1850, and tension between the Chinese workers and the settlers of European descent ran high. Chinese labor depressed wage scales and some Chinese women were being imported as prostitutes. The Chinese did not assimilate and the European groups would not tolerate the cultural differences. In response, Congress adopted a law outlawing so-called "coolie labor" contracts and immigration for lewd and immoral purposes. Many Chinese, however, continued to immigrate voluntarily or were routed through Canada. Hence, in 1882 Congress took stronger action in the Chinese Exclusion Act, the nation's first racist, restrictive immigration law, and one of several acts in the 1880's aimed at stemming the tide of Chinese immigration. The act suspended all immigration of Chinese laborers for ten years and forbade any court to admit Chinese to citizenship. The act was extended in 1902 and later made permanent. (Not until 1943 was it finally repealed so that Chinese could become citizens.)

Congress had finally decided by the 1880's that immigration was fully appropriate for federal control. The Act of 1882 may be considered the first general federal immigration act. It continued to base restrictions on quality controls; in addition to the 1875 exclusions of "convicts" and "prostitutes," it barred "lunatics," "idiots," and those "likely to become public charges." The act also for the first time imposed a head tax on every arriving immigrant. The tax served the express function of raising revenues to defray administrative expenses. Congress also did not want the poor of other nations to be added to the government relief rolls; the tax served the underlying function of deterring the immigration of people unable to pay. In several subsequent statutes, the head tax was raised from fifty cents to two dollars, making the barrier relatively substantial at that time.

Despite these limits, over 5.2 million immigrant aliens arrived in the 1880's. Immigration was seen as a threat to the U.S. economy, and Congress began expanding the list of "undesirable classes," hoping both to upgrade the type of immigrants and to limit overall entry. An 1891 act added the "diseased," "paupers," and "polygamists" to the list of excludable persons. It also forbade advertising in foreign countries which encouraged immigration to America. In addition, immigrants were required to take medical examinations to determine whether they were "diseased." A few years later, special boards of inquiry were established to decide other questions of admissibility under the "quality" restrictions. The 1891 law established the Bureau of Immigration, the forerunner of the present Immigration and Naturalization Service (INS). The Bureau was responsible for inspecting entrants at the 24 ports of entry to the U.S.

Immigration did abate somewhat in the 1890's, totalling 3.6 million—a reduction of over 1.5 million from the previous decade. There was a sharp increase in immigration, however, at the turn of the century, and Congress tried to stem the flow by excluding more classes of immigrants. In 1903, a new law excluded epileptics, the "insane," "beggars," and "anarchists." In 1907 the "feebleminded," the tubercular, and those persons with a mental or physical defect which "may affect" their ability to earn a living were added to the list. During this period, Japanese immigration was restricted by a 1907 agreement negotiated between the United States and Japan. Although the cumulative list was long, these quality controls were not easily enforced. Moreover, at that time the Bureau of Immigration and Naturalization had only 1,200 employees in the U.S. to process arriving immigrants and enforce the entry restrictions. Nonetheless, almost 8.8 million immigrants were admitted by the Bureau in the first decade of the 1900's.

More than the huge numbers concerned Congress, however. The type of person immigrating was changing. In the 1880's, 72% of immigrants to the U.S. came from northern and western Europe. In contrast, during the 1900–10 decade, 71% came from countries in southern or eastern Europe. These "new immigrants" were Latins, Slavs, and Jews, who were considered "inferior" by the predominantly Anglo–Saxon population. Much like the Chinese who preceded them by several decades, the "new immigrants" were slow to assimilate, living together in urban ethnic neighborhoods. The Anglo–Saxons feared that their predominance was threatened and pressured Congress for more restrictive measures.

Because the earlier "quality control" exclusions did little to stem the flow of immigrants, those groups favoring restrictions on immigration began to advocate literacy as an entrance requirement. In 1907, after several failed attempts to pass a literacy bill, Congress established a joint congressional-presidential commission to study the impact of immigration on the United States. In 1911 the Commission published its findings. It concluded that twentieth century immigration to the U.S. was significantly different from earlier immigration and that the new immigration was dominated by the so-called "inferior" and "less desirable" groups. As a result, the Commission concluded that the United States no longer benefited from a liberal immigration policy and should impose further entry restrictions. The Commission recommended a literacy test as one such restriction.

In 1917, over President Wilson's veto, Congress responded. The 1917 Act was clearly aimed at restricting immigration of various nationalities. One important purpose of the act was to limit immigration from southern and eastern Europe, which was accomplished by barring people unable to read. Because the new immigrants were largely illiterate, the impact of literacy tests limited that region's immigration more than any other. The act also raised the head tax to eight dollars, providing yet another obstacle.

In addition, Congress addressed the growing concern over foreign "anarchists" in the 1917 Act. This group had been excluded by an earlier law of 1903 that had been enacted in response to President McKinley's assassination. In 1917, Congress apparently focused on the anti-alien mood prevalent during World War I. This sentiment led to subsequent enactment of the Anarchist Act of 1918, which more specifically defined "anarchists."

The last major exclusion of the 1917 Act prohibited all immigration of Asians from countries within specified latitudes and longitudes. Many similar racist exclusions had been proposed in Congress that year, and the Asiatic Barred Zone survived as an undebated amendment to the 1917 Act. Congressional attempts to prevent blacks from immigrating to the U.S. were defeated, however, due in large part to intensive lobbying by the NAACP.

The literacy entrance requirement and the nervousness surrounding World War I about the ability to assimilate foreign born persons resulted in an Americanization movement. Beginning in 1919 many states established Americanization programs to ensure that immigrants would learn English. Industry joined the movement by establishing similar programs for workers. By 1923, the Bureau of Naturalization reported 252,808 immigrants in 6,632 programs across the country.

§ 1–4 THE QUOTA LAWS

World War I naturally limited immigration by making shipping less available, but after its end, immigration began to grow. The country favored an isolationist policy and wanted to protect its own labor force from the anticipated post-war flood of refugees from Europe. Dissatisfied with its latest set of quality exclusions, Congress implemented numerical controls. Enacted first as a temporary measure, the 1921 Quota Law marked a major shift in the U.S. approach to immigration control. The law limited immigration of each nation to 3% of the number of foreign-born persons of that nationality residing in the U.S. as of the 1910 census. The total quota was 357,000, but because few foreign-born persons from the South and East of Europe lived in the U.S. in 1910, that region's total quota was 45,000 less than that from the North and West of Europe. The effect of the quota allotments was to restrict immigration from the disfavored regions; the northern and western countries of Europe did not even fill their quotas under this law. Fortunately for the restricted group, Congress established certain "non-quota" exceptions. For example, the law permitted a person to be admitted to the United States as an immigrant if the individual had lived in the Western Hemisphere for one year (later changed to five years). Hence, by temporarily living in a Western Hemisphere country, many avoided the quotas.

In 1924, Congress further restricted immigration by reducing the immigration quota from 3% of foreign-born persons under the 1910 census to 2% of the foreign-born under the 1890 census. This change cut the total quota to 164,667 and made the southern and eastern quotas proportionately even smaller than before. Again, people from those regions had to use the non-quota provisions to enter the U.S. Although under the 1924 Act only Western Hemisphere natives were non-quota, Europeans and others used another provision exempting spouses of U.S. citizens from the quotas. Consequently, sham marriages became a popular way of circumventing the quota law.

Despite the restrictive 1924 Act, immigration from the southern and eastern countries of Europe equalled entries from the northern and western countries, thereby defeating the restrictive purposes of Congress. In addition to marital fraud, the quota and quality restrictions resulted in increased surreptitious border crossing. Moreover, although Europe was the targeted region, immigration from the Western Hemisphere began to climb in the 1920's, presenting border control problems. In response, the Bureau created the Border Patrol in 1924, hiring 45 men to guard the country's 8,000 miles of land and sea borders. Total immigration in the years 1924–29 reached 1.5 million.

In 1929, as provided by the 1924 Act, a new quota took effect. The "national origins formula" used the ethnic background of the entire U.S. population, rather than the first generation immigrant population, as its base for calculating national quotas. Because the U.S. population was still predominantly Anglo–Saxon, the national origins quota restricted the newer immigrant groups more severely than the foreign-born formula of the previous quota laws. The national origins quota allotted 85% of the total quota of 150,000 to countries from the North and West of Europe, while the South and East received only 15% of that total quota.

The effect of the national origins formula, however, cannot accurately be measured. Soon after it took effect, the U.S. economy collapsed. The Great Depression limited immigration; only one-half million immigrated to the U.S. during the 1930's. In 1932, at the height of the Great Depression, emigration far exceeded legal immigration. Only 35,576 entered the country in that year, while over 100,000 left. The potential for immigration increased during those years, however, with the growth of highways and increased airplane traffic. By 1938, there were 186 ports of entry into the U.S. On June 14, 1940, the INS was transferred from the Department of Labor to the Department of Justice.

One of the most tragic consequences of the U.S. restrictive immigration policy fell upon refugees trying to flee Europe before World War II. In 1939, Congress defeated a bill that would have accommodated 20,000 children fleeing from Nazi Germany—despite the availability of willing sponsor families—because the number of children would have exceeded the quota allocated to German nationals. In 1940 the State Department did permit consuls outside of Germany to issue visas to German refugees when the German quota was unfilled, but this and other measures were inadequate to help the vast majority of victims of Nazi persecution.

World War II brought an economic upswing, and immigration increased in response, bringing the total of entrants in the 1940's to one million. The United States once again needed labor from abroad and negotiated with Mexico for a temporary worker program to satisfy the country's wartime employment needs. Congress also repealed the ban on Chinese immigration, largely due to the wartime alliance of the United States with China. Congress established a small quota for Chinese immigrants and also permitted Chinese immigrants to be naturalized as U.S. Citizens.

As the United States became painfully aware of the Nazi atrocities and the fate of the refugees it had refused, there was a short period of liberalization of the strict quota laws. President Truman issued a directive in 1945, admitting 40,000 war refugees. Under the War Brides Act of 1945 and the Fiancees Act of 1946, about 123,000 alien spouses, children, and fiancées of WW II military personnel were admitted to the U.S. The Displaced Persons Act of 1948 admitted 400,000 war refugees from Austria, Germany, and Italy to the U.S., but these admissions "mortgaged" their countries' quotas, sometimes limiting or closing off all immigration from a country for several years thereafter.

The work of the INS had burgeoned by the late 1940's. By 1949, the U.S. had 416 ports of entry by land, sea, and air at which the INS annually made about 90 million inspections of immigrants, nonimmigrants and returning citizens for compliance with entry requirements. The Border Patrol force remained stable at about 1,100, yet its total apprehensions of deportable aliens tripled in three years from 100,000 in 1946 to 300,000 in 1949.

In contrast to its liberalizing legislation, Congress soon afterwards acted to restrict another group. Anti–Communism rose after WW II and particularly during the war in Korea. As a result, national security legislation received high priority in Congress. The Internal Security Act of 1950 amended the 1918 Anarchists Act. The exclusions, however, were expressly directed this time at Communists; the act broadly defined the excluded group, barring anyone "likely to" engage in "subversive activity."

At the same time, however, Congress continued to legislate in the area of refugee admissions. In 1953 Congress passed the Refugee Relief Act, which admitted an additional 214,000 refugees. Although designed primarily to facilitate the admission of refugees fleeing from Eastern European countries dominated by the Soviet Union, the act also included provisions to prevent the admission of undesirable aliens. Similar measures were passed in 1956 and 1957 to assist the entry of Hungarians and others fleeing from communism as well as persons fleeing from countries in the Middle East. The 1960 Refugee Fair Share Law established a temporary admission and assistance program for those World War II refugees and displaced persons who remained in camps under the mandate of the United Nations High Commissioner for Refugees.

§ 1–5   THE 1952 ACT AND LATER AMENDMENTS

The Immigration and Nationality Act of 1952 (INA) consolidated previous immigration laws into one coordinated statute. As amended, the 1952 Act provides the foundation for immigration law in effect today.

In the 1952 Act Congress retained, over President Truman's veto, the controversial national origins quota. The 1952 quota was calculated differently than the original national origins quota and established a 150,000 person limit on immigration from the Eastern Hemisphere. Congress exempted the Asia–Pacific Triangle from this quota, because so few people from that region lived in the U.S. as a consequence of the Barred Zone law of 1917; the quota would have been grossly inequitable in that respect. Instead, a modest quota of 2,000 was established for that area. Congress also retained the detailed "quality control" exclusions found in earlier legislation and added several new ones. Within the quota system, four types of entrance preferences were established. First preference was given those entrants with skills or experience needed by the U.S. economy. Those with close family relations to U.S. citizens or resident aliens received lower preferences. This ordering was changed by amendment in 1965, but it should be noted that spouses of U.S. citizens were not and are still not subject to the quota or preference system.

Several aspects of the 1952 Act drew heavy criticism. The national origins quota, based on the 1920 census, was a blatant form of racial and ethnic discrimination. Also, despite some increased procedural safeguards for aliens, the 1952 Act did not provide them procedural due process.

The 1952 Act presented the INS with new and complex laws to enforce, yet Congress did not supply the Service with increased personnel or appropriations to perform its new work. Moreover, the early 1950's saw a large increase in deportable alien apprehensions aimed at the expulsion of Mexicans from the U.S. The Border Patrol, still about 1,000 strong, apprehended 800,000 deportable aliens in 1952; in 1954, that number increased to one million. Because of "Operation Wetback" 90% of those apprehended came from Mexico. It is believed that this expulsion included U.S. citizens of Mexican descent who were not given an opportunity to establish their claim to citizenship.

During the 1950's, Congress made several minor revisions in the 1952 Act, and over 2.5 million immigrated to the U.S. The number of people entering the U.S.

increased in the 1960's, reflecting the growing availability of all means of travel. To facilitate the necessary inspections, in 1963 the INS consolidated duties at ports of entry with several agencies. Hence, one officer performed the duties of the INS, Customs, U.S. Public Health Service, and the Bureau of Plant Quarantine at the Mexican border. This joint approach eased the workload somewhat, for in 1964 the INS made 178 million inspections, almost twice the 1949 figure, yet total INS personnel had only increased from 6,900 to 7,058. In 1966, 200 million persons—immigrants, non-immigrants, and returning citizens—were inspected at over 400 ports of entry. Total immigration for the 1960's was 3.3 million.

The criticized national origins formula was not abolished until 1965 when President Johnson successfully urged enactment of former President Kennedy's program of immigration reform. The 1965 amendments replaced the national origins formula with a limit of 20,000 on each country in the Eastern Hemisphere and an overall limit of 170,000 for that hemisphere. The law established a quota of 120,000 for the Western Hemisphere, without preferences or country limits—to take effect in 1968.

The 1965 amendments abolished the old four-preference system and established in its place a seven-preference system for close relatives and those immigrants with needed occupational skills from the Eastern Hemisphere. Again, spouses of U.S. citizens were permitted to immigrate without reference to the quota or preference system. Under the preference system, unmarried children of U.S. citizens received highest preference; second preference was granted to spouses and unmarried children of permanent resident aliens. The preference for immigrants of "exceptional ability" and those in "the professions" was changed from first to third. Other relatives of citizens and aliens received the fourth and fifth preferences. Sixth preference was given to needed workers. Seventh preference was allocated to refugees.

The abolition of the national origins formula was in large part the result of a pervasive attitudinal change. Anti–Catholic, –Asian, and –Semitic sentiment decreased as the civil rights movement stimulated an increased tolerance of racial and ethnic differences. Unfortunately, there remained strong prejudice against people of color. After World War II, the proportion of Spanish-speaking immigrants increased, and much prejudice was directed toward these newcomers from Mexico as well as Central and South America. Although the 1952 Act did not place a numerical limit on immigration from these areas, Congress included the Western Hemisphere quota of 120,000 in the 1965 amendments as a compromise for abolishing the national origins system. As a result, there was a steadily growing backlog of Latin American applicants forced to wait several years for a visa.

In 1976, a new law was passed which applied the Eastern Hemisphere preference system to the Western Hemisphere. Hence, both hemispheres were subject to the 20,000 per country limit and the seven preference system. The law, however, did retain separate annual limits—120,000 for the Western and 170,000 for the Eastern Hemisphere—and a special 600 visa ceiling for colonies and dependencies.

A 1978 amendment established a world-wide quota of 290,000 and applied the same per country limits and seven preference system to both hemispheres. This worldwide ceiling eliminated the hemisphere consideration and allowed visas to go where the need was greatest. The 20,000 per country limit, however, was a serious restraint on immigration from a few countries such as Mexico.

Meanwhile, the INS staff became increasingly overworked. The number of deportable aliens, which fell in the 1950's, climbed rapidly in the 1960's and 1970's, as did the number of total entries. In 1972, one half million deportable aliens were apprehended. By 1977, that annual figure had doubled. The Border Patrol had grown to a force of 2,400, still too few to guard the borders properly. The Immigration Service estimated that, between undetected border crossings and violations of legal entry conditions, millions of undocumented aliens were living in the U.S. in 1974. In 1973, 250 million persons were inspected at about 1,000 ports of entry. By 1979, 274 million were inspected annually, and the Border Patrol apprehended one million deportable aliens. That year, the INS employed almost 11,000 personnel under a 300 million dollar budget.

In March 1980 Congress dealt with the issue of refugees. The 1980 Refugee Act broadened the definition of refugees to accord with the international definition in the Convention and Protocol relating to the Status of Refugees. Further, the Refugee Act set an annual maximum of 50,000 refugees through the year 1982, but permitted the Administration, in consultation with Congress, to set the number of refugees to be admitted each year after 1982. The initial numerical limits in the Refugee Act were undermined, however, by the deluge of Cuban refugees soon after its enactment. More than 100,000 Cubans arrived in the U.S. in the spring of 1980—mostly via the port of Mariel. Eventually, the Carter Administration concluded that the influx of "Mariel" Cubans was not within the contemplation of the Refugee Act and asked for special legislation to deal with the problem. The 1980 Act reduced the worldwide immigrant quota from 290,000 to 270,000 to offset partially the separate allocation for refugees.

In 1981 Congress adopted another series of amendments to the immigration law, which *inter alia,* eliminated the permanent exclusion of aliens who had been deported and permitted these deportees to return without permission five years after deportation. Also, a person convicted of a single minor marihuana offense could obtain a waiver of excludability. There were a number of other amendments concerning foreign medical graduates, congressional reporting requirements as to visas issued, exchange visitors, and treaty investors. But these minor changes did not address the national perception that the U.S. had lost control of its borders and required a much more thorough revision of immigration law.

The Immigration Marriage Fraud Amendments of 1986 amended the INA to deter immigration-related marriage fraud. The 1986 Fraud Amendments imposed a two-year conditional residency requirement on alien spouses and "sons and daughters" before they could obtain permanent resident status on the basis of a "qualifying marriage" to a U.S. citizen or permanent resident alien. See § 5–3.1 for a discussion of the distinction between the term "children" and "sons and daughters." To obtain permanent status, the couple must have filed a petition within the last 90 days of the conditional status period. The INS could then interview the couple to ascertain that (a) the "qualifying marriage" was not entered into "for the purpose of procuring an alien's entry as an immigrant"; (b) the marriage had not been judicially annulled or terminated, other than through the death of a spouse; or (c) a fee or other consideration other than attorney's fees was not given for the filing of the alien's petition. If these conditions were not met, the alien spouse could have the conditional basis removed from the permanent residence status. In 1990 Congress amended those provisions to permit waiver for cases of battered spouses or children as well as other hardships.

The 1986 Fraud Amendments also imposed criminal penalties for immigration-related marriage fraud of not more than five years and/or not more than $250,000 in fines. In addition, the 1986 Fraud Amendments explicitly made marriage fraud an additional ground for deportation as well as a perpetual bar to future immigration. Furthermore, the Fraud Amendments restricted adjustment of the alien's status based on a marriage undertaken while exclusion or deportation proceedings were pending. The Fraud Amendments required that an alien, who seeks immigration status based upon a marriage to a U.S. citizen or lawful permanent resident initiated after the commencement of deportation or exclusion proceedings, must have resided for a period of two years outside the United States before being eligible to acquire legal status based upon the marriage.

§ 1–6 THE 1986 IMMIGRATION REFORM AND CONTROL ACT (IRCA)

In 1980 the United States Census Bureau counted 2,047,000 undocumented aliens in the country. Based on the Bureau of Census' experience in miscounting other segments of the population, the Bureau had estimated that there were 5,965,000 undocumented aliens in the country on census day April 1, 1980. As the INS attempted to confront these problems with inadequate resources, it was criticized for inefficient internal operations, misconduct, and a general inability to control the flow of undocumented immigration.

Thirty-four years had passed since the enactment of the last major immigration reform, when Congress finally adopted in 1986 the Immigration Reform and Control Act (IRCA). IRCA was not easily adopted, having been unsuccessfully attempted in three previous congressional sessions. It represented a political compromise between three interests—(1) those people seeking to deter illegal immigration by discouraging unauthorized employment in the U.S.; (2) those seeking a one-time amnesty for aliens who, for years, had been locked out as illegal immigrants; (3) those who wished to insure that penalizing employers for illegally hiring aliens would not encourage discriminatory employment practices. Ultimately, the act which was adopted focused almost exclusively on illegal immigration. The act was a partial response to the 1981 recommendations of the Select Committee on Immigration and Refugee Policy chaired by (Rev.) Theodore M. Hesbergh, then President of the University of Notre Dame. IRCA dealt with the major problem of undocumented aliens by imposing sanctions on employers, and at the same time legalizing the status of undocumented entrants who had arrived prior to January 1, 1982. Because Congress was concerned that employer sanctions would result in discrimination in the workplace, IRCA included provisions prohibiting discrimination on the basis of national origin or citizenship status. IRCA also provided the INS with significant new resources to enforce the immigration laws. Furthermore, in response to the demand for foreign agricultural labor, IRCA created a program which grants temporary and permanent resident status to qualified agricultural workers. Despite these major provisions and a number of less important ones, IRCA did not substantially restructure the immigration law as it pertains to immigrant and nonimmigrant visas.

The employer sanction provisions of the act penalize a "person or other entity" who hires, recruits, or refers for a fee for employment in the United States an alien, knowing the alien is unauthorized, or who employs any individual without complying with the act's employment verification system. Employers will also be sanctioned, if after lawfully hiring an alien, the employer continues to employ the alien knowing the alien has since become unauthorized. Those sanctions, however, do not apply to employees hired, recruited, or referred before November 6, 1986. Violating employers are subject to civil fines, injunctive relief, and criminal penalties of up to $3,000 and/or six months' imprisonment for a pattern or practice of violations. Civil fines, which are imposed per illegal alien, range from $250 to $2,000 for the first offense and increase in severity for subsequent offenses. Employers were forbidden from shifting their liability for fines to employees, even illegally employed aliens. In a reversal of previous law, the felony of "harboring" an illegal alien was made applicable to circumstances involving employment. IRCA explicitly preempts all state criminal statutes concerning the employment of illegal aliens, leaving unaffected only areas such as licensing or laws regarding "fitness to do business." Interestingly, to this day there are not sanctions against aliens who accept illegally employment other than the threat of deportation.

A significant obstacle to earlier immigration reform was the concern that employer sanctions would result in widespread discrimination against persons who looked or sounded "foreign." IRCA attempts to resolve this potential problem by prohibiting employment discrimination on the basis of national origin or citizenship status. IRCA states that it is an unfair immigration-related employment practice for a person or other entity employing four or more persons to discriminate against any individual other than an unauthorized alien, with respect to employment or discharge, on the basis of the individual's national origin or citizenship status. President Reagan addressed employer concerns about their inability to verify an employee's identity, authorization, and national origin without appearing to discriminate in their hiring practices, by announcing that these anti-discrimination provisions would be interpreted to require actual discriminatory intent and not simply a disparate impact resulting from employment practices.

Improvement of enforcement and services is a corresponding major goal of IRCA. The act asserts that essential elements of the program of immigration control: (1) increased border patrol as well as other enforcement activities of the INS to deter unlawful entry of aliens into the U.S. and (2) increased the examinations and other service activities of the INS to ensure prompt, efficient adjudication of petitions and applications. To facilitate achievement of these goals, the act increased appropriations for the INS and the Executive Office of Immigration Review (EOIR), increased community outreach programs and in-service training programs, increased the Border Patrol for fiscal years 1987 and 1988 by fifty percent or more from the 1986 level, and sought to improve other immigration and naturalization services.

In exchange for the increased enforcement provisions of IRCA, Congress offered a broad amnesty for many of the undocumented aliens already present in the country. IRCA directed the Attorney General to grant lawful temporary resident status to qualified aliens. Those persons who qualified as temporary resident aliens could then become lawful permanent residents. Since the legalization provisions were intended as a one-time, limited opportunity for aliens to receive amnesty, however, they provided for rather stringent application deadlines.

Aliens must have applied for legalization within one year from May 5, 1987. The alien must have established that s/he entered the United States before January 1, 1982, and that s/he resided unlawfully and continuously in the United States from that date through the date the application was filed. If the alien entered the United States as a nonimmigrant before January 1, 1982, the alien must have established that her/his authorized stay expired before that date or that the alien's unlawful status was known to the government as of that date. On March 30, 1988, a U.S. District Court held that the phrase "known to the Government" meant known to the U.S. government, not just to the INS, as the INS had maintained. The U.S. Court of Appeals, however, vacated this judgment for lack of jurisdiction and ripeness. *Ayuda, Inc. v. Thornburgh* (D.C.Cir.1989).

Legalization applicants also must have established that they had been continuously physically present in the United States since November 6, 1986, except for "brief, casual, and innocent" absences. In *Gutierrez v. Ilchert* (N.D.Cal.1988), the court struck down the provisions of 8 C.F.R. § 245a.1(g) defining the phrase "brief, casual, and innocent" as meaning only an absence authorized in advance by the INS. Applicants must furthermore have established that they: 1) meet most of the requirements of immigrant admissibility to the United States; 2) have not been convicted of any felony or of three or more misdemeanors committed in the United States; 3) have not assisted in any form of persecution; and 4) are registered or registering for the draft, if required to do so.

If an alien succeeded in establishing the above qualifications, s/he should have been granted temporary residence. After 18 months of temporary residence, the alien must then have applied for adjustment to permanent resident status during the one year period beginning with the 19th month of temporary resident status. If the alien failed to apply during this period, the alien lost temporary resident status and once again became undocumented. In order to qualify for permanent resident status, the alien must have established that s/he had continuously resided in the United States since the date temporary resident status was granted (except for certain authorized absences). Applicants must again meet most of the grounds of admissibility to the United

States, must not have been convicted of any felony or of three or more misdemeanors committed in the United States, and must also meet minimal English and civics requirements.

IRCA required strict confidentiality in the legalization program. The act provided for "qualified designated entities"—voluntary organizations experienced in preparing applications for adjustment of status—to receive and forward legalization applications to the INS, but also permitted the alien to apply directly to the INS. Information contained in the files and records of the "qualified designated entity" relating to an alien's application was confidential. The INS could have access to such information only with consent of the alien. The INS could use information contained in a legalization application only for the purpose of making a determination on the application or for imposing penalties for false statements. INS access to this information was also limited to INS officers with no deportation responsibilities, thereby allowing nonqualifying applicants to avoid the risk of deportation. The act prescribed criminal penalties for both (1) misuse of such information and (2) the filing of an application with false information.

Adverse financial impact upon the states was a substantial concern in adopting IRCA. For this reason, IRCA included extensive provisions disqualifying newly legalized aliens (except Cuban/Haitian entrants) from receiving most federal public welfare assistance for five years. Appropriations were also included to compensate state and local governments for other public assistance and medical benefits conferred upon newly legalized aliens, as well as for the costs of incarcerating undocumented aliens and "Mariel" Cubans.

IRCA also established a separate program for granting temporary and permanent status to qualified agricultural workers. This program was the result of agribusiness pressure for greater availability of such farm workers. The act sought to provide a one time supplement to the supply of available agricultural workers by granting temporary legal resident status to workers who have worked at least 90 days between May 1, 1985, and May 1, 1986. Adjustment to permanent resident status is then permitted for qualified temporary workers. The act, however, also allows for a replenishment of workers for four years (1990–1993) if the secretaries of agriculture and labor determine that there is a shortage of agricultural workers, based on anticipated need minus the supply of workers for that year.

Beginning in 1986, Congress began to act on growing constituent concern over the difficulty of immigration from Eastern Hemisphere countries, most notably, Ireland and Italy. This situation was generally thought to have arisen with the repeal of the Western Hemisphere quota in 1965 accompanied by a steady increase in immigration from Asia, Africa, and the Middle East. In Section 314 of IRCA and in Section 3 of P.L. 100–658 (the Immigration Amendments of 1988), Congress created what came to be known as the NP–5 and the OP–1 programs respectively.

The NP–5 program created a "first-come-first-served" worldwide mail registration program benefiting aliens from 36 countries whose immigrant visa availability were adversely affected by the unification of the worldwide quota system in 1965. This program, in effect, "gave away" 30,000 immigrant visas, between fiscal years 1987 and 1988, to earliest-registered aliens and their immediate families, requiring them only to meet the nationality, health, and morals qualifications of immigration laws. This program was extended to cover 30,000 more NP-5 registrants over fiscal years 1989 and 1990.

The OP-1 program was a pure lottery based on a one-time registration program without the facets of early or multiple filings that were characteristic of the NP-5 program. It benefited natives of 162 countries which used less than 25 percent of their maximum quota entitlement in fiscal year 1988.

The significance of these programs is their underlying policy of expanding immigration to countries other than the Eastern Hemisphere sources which have increasingly affected our immigration over the past several decades.

Other less important IRCA provisions increased the quotas for colonies (most significantly Hong Kong) from 600 to 5,000 immigrant visas annually; provided for adjustment of status to special immigrant status for certain G-4 nonimmigrants (officers and employees of international organizations and their family members) who have resided in the U.S. for certain periods; established a three-year pilot program for waiving tourist visas for nationals from certain countries; authorized a number of additional nonpreference visas for fiscal years 1987 and 1988; required reports to Congress on certain provisions of the act; authorized the promulgation of rules to implement the act; established the Commission for the Study of International Migration and Cooperative Economic Development; and established federal responsibility for deportable and excludable aliens convicted of crimes.

It may be useful to examine the success of IRCA's major provisions, (1) imposing employer sanctions, (2) including anti-discrimination provisions, and (3) establishing an amnesty program for the legalization of many undocumented aliens.

The implementation of the employer sanction provisions of IRCA received mixed reviews. Surveys taken by the General Accounting Office in the three years following IRCA's passage offered inconsistent evidence as to whether employers were aware of and complying with their obligations under the new law. See INA § 274A(j)(1). While one survey reported that the vast majority of responding employers had learned of their obligations under the new law, others reported that a large percentage or even a majority believed that the INS had not adequately informed employers of their obligations and that most businesses did not understand their responsibilities. Social service agencies responded that about nine percent of their clients had unjustly lost their jobs because their employers were inadequately informed of the law.

The majority of survey respondents stated that they would comply with the act's employment verification system; but of this group intending to comply, a majority had not actually done so. A small percentage indicated that they did not intend to comply with the act.

IRCA's anti-discrimination provisions did not succeed in eradicating concern about discrimination in the workplace. The majority of respondents believed that IRCA had already resulted in discrimination against workers with a foreign appearance. Almost one-third of large companies surveyed predicted that requiring new employees to provide race, nationality, and age information would result in more discrimination in the future. Reports indicate that discrimination against Hispanics and Asians has been particularly severe.

IRCA's legalization program received a relatively disappointing response. The INS had originally estimated that between two and four million aliens would apply for amnesty. By early 1988, less than 1.2 million applications had been filed. In response, the INS sought innovative means to encourage aliens to apply for amnesty, such as inserting 80,000 amnesty program reminders into tortilla packages in Texas. The INS sent letters to aliens granted temporary resident status, asking them to encourage and help their friends, relatives, and neighbors to apply for amnesty. In a last-minute attempt to encourage applications before the May 4, 1988, deadline, the INS liberalized the legalization process. Beginning April 4, amnesty applicants could file a completed I–687 form and filing fee, and provide supporting documentation or medical information up to 60 days later.

Significant barriers to broader participation in the amnesty program included the aliens' fear of the INS, the high application fee, family unity problems, problems of obtaining required documentation, and sluggish INS program implementation and publicity efforts.

In April 1988, the House of Representatives narrowly approved an extension of the May 4, 1988, deadline for aliens to apply for legalization. Proponents argued that extension was necessary because of the delayed implementation of the amnesty program, the numerous changes in requirements which resulted in confusion, and the continuing fear of the INS among undocumented aliens. The Senate, however, ended any hope of extension by failing to pass a motion to close debate on the extension proposal, thereby preventing the Senate from voting it. Opponents of extension argued that amnesty had gone far enough and that extension would give the wrong impression. They claimed that extension would encourage millions of aliens to cross the border illegally in the future, on the assumption that the U.S. could not enforce its immigration laws. By the May 4, 1988, deadline, 1.4 million people had applied for amnesty.

§ 1–7 THE IMMIGRATION ACT OF 1990

In 1990, Congress passed a series of amendments to the Immigration and Nationality Act, collectively referred to as the Immigration Act of 1990 ("1990 Act" also known as "IMMACT 90"). Like the INA of 1952, the 1965 Amendments, and IRCA, IMMACT 90 is a landmark in immigration legislation. The statute significantly modifies many of the INA's provisions, and leaves virtually no area of the previous law untouched. Primarily, IMMACT 90 reforms the rules pertaining to the *legal* entry of foreign nationals. It augments the regulations enacted by IRCA (see § 1–6), which focused primarily on illegal immigration. Because of the breadth of IMMACT 90's provisions, specific changes are treated in their proper context throughout this book. This section presents a synopsis of the most prominent changes enacted in the 1990 Act and the less important Immigration Technical Amendments Act of 1991.

§ 1–7.1 Overall Increase in Worldwide Immigration

The most visible feature of IMMACT 90 is the increase by approximately 35% in the numerical limitation system, or overall immigration allowed. IMMACT 90 establishes an annual limit for worldwide immigration of 700,000 for three years, after which it decreases to 675,000. Because other provisions of the 1990 Act allow immigration of groups not counted in the 700,000, and a separate law permits as many as 125,000 refugees to be legally admitted, the actual worldwide immigration limit is closer to 800,000.

The groups benefiting from this increase illustrate congressional priorities, and reflect a moderately optimistic belief in the country's capacity to absorb new immigrants. The 1990 Act increases the allocation for both family-related and employee-related immigration. In addition, the new law creates a separate basis by which "diversity" immigrants, that is, nationals of countries previously under-represented by visa issuance since 1965, can gain entry. The 1990 Act eliminates the nonpreference category which had been unavailable due to excessive visa demand since late 1976. All-in-all, of the 700,000 annual allotment, 465,000 are available to family-sponsored immigrants, 140,000 for employment-based immigrants, and 55,000 for diversity visas.

a. Family–Sponsored Immigration

Beginning October 1, 1991, all family-sponsored immigration is limited to approximately 480,000 annually for two years, after which the yearly limit drops to 465,000. The relatively large percentage of the overall limit allocated to family-related immigration reflects the continued commitment to family unity as a primary goal of immigration policy. The 1990 Act does not dramatically increase the total number of visas for family-sponsored immigration, however. Currently, family-preference visas are allocated to 216,000 persons, while 200,000 visas not figured in the quota are granted to immediate relatives (*i.e.*, spouses, minor children, and parents of U.S. citizens).

The 1990 Act accounts for both family-preference visas and immediate relatives of U.S. citizens in the new limit; hence, the new law increases potential family-related immigration by approximately 65,000 annually.

It is anticipated that visas for immediate relatives of U.S. citizens will continue to increase. The 1990 Act provides, however, that the other family-preferences are guaranteed a minimum of 226,000 visas annually, irrespective of the demand for visas to immediate relatives. In addition, the "cap" of 480,000 discussed above may be "pierced" as the result of provisions of the new act that permit this figure to be supplemented by any visas from the employment-related categories which may be unused in a previous fiscal year. See INA § 201(c)(ii). The four family-preference categories in the previous law remain essentially unchanged. In addition, the 1990 Act codifies a "family fairness" policy which gives work authorization and indefinite stay of deportation for the spouses and minor children of aliens granted amnesty under IRCA.

b. *Employment–Related Immigration*

Responding to fears concerning the U.S. work force's ability to compete in the global economy, the 1990 Act significantly changes the allotments of employment-related visas. The new law replaces the old third and

sixth preferences (which distinguish between professional and skilled employees) with five new classifications
totalling 140,000 visas per year. The first employment-
based preference category allocates 28.6% of the total
number of employment-based visas (currently 40,000)
for "priority workers," that is, aliens with an extraordinary potential for contribution to their fields. This
category includes noted professors, researchers, and
multinational executives, as well as individuals who
have attained widespread acclaim.

The second employment-based preference category allocated another 28.6% of the employment-based visas
for professionals with advanced degrees or aliens with
exceptional ability in science, the arts, or business.
Hence, the new second preference largely covers the old
third preference for professionals. The new third employment-based preference class allots 28.6% for skilled
workers or professionals with baccalaureate degrees, as
well as other unskilled workers. The new category
combines the balance of the old third preference with
the old sixth preference which included "other unskilled
workers." The new law allows a maximum of 10,000
visas for this group. The fourth employment-related
category allocated 10,000 visas for certain religious
workers and employees of the U.S. mission in Hong
Kong.

The "Employment Creation" fifth preference encourages the immigration of aliens who will invest at least
$1 million in a business that benefits the U.S. economy
and employs at least 10 U.S. citizen workers or current
permanent residents. This preference provides for up
to 10,000 visas. Unused visas "spill up" to the first
priority category with further visas "spilling down" to

the second and third categories. The Attorney General may lower the required investment to $500,000 if the business is located in an area of high unemployment, or raise it up to $3 million if the business is located in an area of high employment. The present regulations contain an upper limit of $1 million on the investment and a lower limit of $500,000 for areas of high unemployment. The investor is granted a conditional permanent residence for two years, after which s/he can petition for the condition's removal. This provision was criticized for allowing wealthy foreign nationals to "buy their way in." Its supporters contend, however, that the previous law curtailed foreign investment by impeding a company's principal investor from gaining Labor Department certification and point to the employment creation facet of the new status as of considerable benefit to the U.S. economy.

The new employment-based preference system places a high priority on educational attainment, or excellence in a profession. To illustrate: an outstanding offer of employment and labor certification are not required for applicants with extraordinary ability (first preference class). Multinational managers and executives are also exempt from the certification requirement. Unfortunately, because employers are often unwilling to wait for labor certification to employ low-skilled workers, and because of the low allocation of 10,000 visas, the 1990 Act may offer limited opportunities for individuals without skills or the benefit of formal education.

The 1990 Act does not substantially change the Labor Department's certification process which requires showing that no qualified U.S. workers are available to work in the position sought. One revision requires that notice of filing for labor certification be given to the union representative of the affected employees in the potential place of employment. The act also replaces the current Schedules A & B with a pilot program in which the Labor Department must determine whether labor shortages or surpluses exist in ten occupations.

(1) DIVERSITY VISAS

Because the families of immigrants who arrived in the U.S. two or more generations ago no longer qualify for family-related visas (see § 1–2), several of the countries which figured most prominently in this nation's immigration history are today "under-represented." Section 132 of the 1990 Act establishes a mail-in lottery, known as the AA–1 program to address the problem of under-representation by allocating 40,000 "diversity" visas (55,000 beginning in 1994) to nationals from "adversely affected" countries. Of the visas available in this category, 40% are designated for natives of Ireland. Significantly, this allotment creates the first visas by which foreign nationals can immigrate without an immediate relative to sponsor them and without a job for which there is a labor shortage. Because applicants are selected on a random basis, the diversity visa is an unpredictable way for a foreign national to gain entry.

(2) INHABITANTS OF HONG KONG

Motivated by the impending return of Hong Kong to the People's Republic of China, the 1990 Act allows for separate means of aiding Hong Kong residents who may want to immigrate to the U.S. The provision increases the allocation for immigration from Hong Kong to 10,-

000 (from 5,000) for the first three years of the act, after which the level rises to 20,000. Other provisions benefit employees of certain U.S. businesses in Hong Kong, and employees of the U.S. mission there. In addition, the new law extends visas issued to Hong Kong residents until January 1, 2002, allowing them to immigrate if conditions after 1997 so dictate, while providing them with the security to stay in the meantime.

(3) REFUGEES AND TEMPORARY STATUS

The 1990 Act alters the process of attaining permanent residence for refugees. One year after an alien has been granted asylum in the U.S., s/he can apply for permanent residence. The 1990 Act increases the resident visa allotment to 10,000 annually (from 5,000); moreover, aliens who had previously qualified are granted permanent residence by a special provision. The new law also offers "Temporary Protected Status" (TPS) to aliens prevented from returning to their home countries because of war, disaster, or other unstable circumstances. In the interim, the Attorney General is required to provide employment authorization for these aliens. The Attorney General determines which countries are "protected." El Salvador received designated TPS status from the statute itself. Other countries have also been given TPS designation.

§ 1–7.2 Nonimmigrant Provisions

The 1990 Act modifies some of the INA's provisions pertaining to aliens who seek entry for a temporary period of time or for a limited purpose. The new law adds four categories of nonimmigrants to the previous 13 visas. Hence, the 1990 Act defines 18 nonimmigrant categories, identified as A through R visas. The visa waiver pilot program benefiting foreign travelers, previously applicable to eight countries, may now be extended to any country by the Attorney General and Secretary of State. The new law also modifies visa categories for crewmembers (D), traders (E), temporary workers (H), and intracompany transferees (L).

The 1990 Act establishes four new nonimmigrant categories. Category O nonimmigrants must have attained great achievements or possess extraordinary ability in the arts, sciences, education, business, or athletics, provided the alien seeks entry to work within their field of expertise. Category P includes aliens who perform as athletes or entertainers, or are members of a performance group, again provided the alien seeks entry to perform within this discipline. Category Q provides for international cultural exchange programs and participants, while category R grants entry to aliens within certain religious occupations.

§ 1–7.3 Naturalization

Until the 1990 Act, the federal district court had the ultimate responsibility for naturalization upon a recommendation by the INS and for administration of the oath of allegiance to new U.S. citizens. Under the 1990 Act, the INS made the actual determination on naturalization and the district director administered the oath. The Immigration Technical Amendments Act of 1991, however, left the naturalization decision with the INS, but returned most oaths of allegiance to the federal district court. The courts are more conveniently located for the administration of oaths and better able to handle the problems of changing names which often occur with acquisition of U.S. citizenship.

The 1990 Act also provides that an alien denied naturalization by the INS may seek *de novo* judicial review. In addition, the 1990 Act effectively overrules three Supreme Court determinations denying naturalization to Philippine veterans of World War II (*See INS v. Hibi* (Sup.Ct.1973); *United States v. Mendoza* (Sup.Ct.1984); *INS v. Pangilinan* (Sup.Ct.1988)), naturalizing Filipinos who performed honorably in World War II.

§ 1–7.4   Grounds for Exclusion

Prior to the 1990 Act, there were more than 34 separate grounds for exclusion, many of which had complex rules and subdivisions. Some of these provisions were considered obsolete. For example, as a result of the McCarran–Walter Act of 1952, individuals could be excluded for beliefs or party membership, rather than a specific act. The 1990 Act attempts to address this problem, but by no means enacts provisions that will significantly narrow the grounds for exclusion.

a.   Health–Related Exclusion

The health-related provisions were modified to exclude only aliens with communicable diseases that threatened public health. This determination is to be made by the Secretary for Health and Human Services. Moreover, the 1990 Act attempts to bring the health-related grounds for exclusion up to date with modern medical knowledge and procedure. A meaningful illustration of the 1990 Act's reforms is the elimination of the exclusion of gay men and lesbians. Further, the waiver for close relatives was expanded, thus diminishing the number of family-sponsored aliens excluded for health reasons.

b. Crime–Related Exclusion

The substantive rules of criminal exclusion were not significantly modified by the 1990 Act. For aliens under 18 years of age, minor criminal conduct is not a ground for exclusion, provided the alien was convicted at least five years prior to her/his application. One significant revision reduces the number of discretionary waivers by requiring the criminal conviction to have occurred at least 15 years prior to application.

c. Security as a Grounds for Exclusion

The 1990 Act bars any alien who has engaged in terrorist activities, adding this ground for exclusion to espionage, sabotage, or violent overthrow of the U.S. government. Further, the Secretary of State may bar any alien who would adversely affect the foreign policy of the United States. Critics of these provisions contend that the new law places too much discretion with the Secretary of State. Moreover, they fear that the term "terrorism" will be construed broadly or for political reasons.

d. Communists

The 1990 Act limited the exclusion of members of the Communist or another totalitarian party. This exclusion is no longer applicable to nonimmigrants, and involuntary membership is excused. In addition, membership is excused if it was terminated at least two years prior to application (five years if the country is still controlled by a totalitarian dictatorship, *e.g.,* China). Again, a discretionary waiver is permitted for close relatives and if the waiver is in the public interest.

e. Exclusion for Misrepresentation

The 1990 Act retains the exclusion for misrepresentation (extended by the Immigration Marriage Fraud Act) with two modifications. First, the waiver for close relatives is expanded by changing the term "child" to "son or daughter," which includes adult married children. Second, if the misrepresentation occurred more than 10 years prior to the application, waiver is permitted. Unfortunately, a ten year bar may still be excessive.

§ 1–7.5 Grounds for Deportation

a. Marriage Fraud

The 1990 Act substantially modifies three provisions of the Immigration Marriage Fraud Act. First, and most significant, the new law recognizes marriages entered into while deportation or exclusion proceedings are pending. The new law, however, requires "clear and convincing evidence" that the marriage was undertaken in good faith and not for the purposes of evading immigration laws. Second, when a marriage is terminated within two years of the conditional grant of residence, the alien spouse can petition for removal of the condition, regardless of who initiated the divorce. Third, discretionary waiver of the conditional residence requirement is available if the alien spouse or her/his child was the victim of battery or abuse.

b. National Security Concerns

The 1990 Act eliminates the provision for deporting members of the Communist party or other "subversive" organizations. Like the related ground for exclusion, the act does prescribe deportation for aliens who have engaged in terrorist activity or who pose a threat to national security. Again, the Secretary of State enjoys considerable discretion in determining whether an alien threatens foreign relations.

§ 1–7.6 Summary of Technical Amendments of 1991

The Immigration Technical Corrections Act of 1991 clarified, defined, and modified various provisions in the 1990 Act. Although all relevant corrections will be treated in their proper context in this book, some significant modifications should be mentioned here. For example, the 1991 Act translated numerical allocations of employment-related visas to percentages for determining visas remaining from other categories that haven't been exhausted.

The considerable political battle which was fought over restricting the H–1B status continued in the Technical Amendments. The procedural requirements for prospective U.S. employers of H–1B workers were loosened somewhat and foreign-educated medical doctors' ability to be employed in the U.S. under the authority of H–1B visa status was clarified and defined.

Several other corrections clarified whether relatives of the principal alien are charged against the numerical limits of various categories through which that alien sought entry. The diversity program and application process were changed significantly to become more of a pure lottery; Temporary Protected Status was modified, for example, to cover stateless residents of the countries selected. As to immigration enforcement, murder was made a permanent bar to a finding of good moral character; the INS no longer is required to stay the deportation of an alien convicted of an aggravated felony pending the determination of a petition for review; and no security grounds can be waived for legalization applicants.

The technical corrections returned to the federal district courts and state courts the authority to administer oaths of allegiance for the purposes of naturalization provided that the oath is administered within 45 days from INS approval of the naturalization application. These provisions go under the heading, "Judicial Naturalization Ceremonies Amendments of 1991." The technical corrections fill in several of the gaps that the 1990 Act left ambiguous. Again, the corrections are better understood in the context of the provisions they modify.

§ 1–7.7 Further Reform

The 1990 Act establishes a commission to examine how immigration affects our society, to analyze how the immigration laws function, and to compute the demographics of the immigrant population. The commission is an example of the 1990 Act's attempt to educate lawmakers on immigration policy and suggest directions for the future. The new law thus provides flexibility for future changes beyond the limits of the 1990 Act and the technical corrections of 1991.

It is uncertain whether Congress will respond to periods of recession and increased unemployment by cutting immigration. It is also unclear how efforts to establish a free trade zone with Canada, Mexico, and eventually other countries in the Western Hemisphere will affect U.S. immigration policy.

§ 1–8   MORAL AND POLICY ISSUES OF IMMIGRATION

Immigration transforms the demographic profile of the U.S. population, particularly in large cities. Fears of overcrowding, unemployment, scarcity of resources, and fears of cultural fragmentation make the politics of immigration extremely complex. Immigration law is the principal means by which the country not only determines who will gain access to the limited resources and opportunities in the U.S., but also what will be the national and cultural identity of the U.S.

The argument in favor of free immigration—that is, an "open-door" policy of admission—asserts that fears are greatly exaggerated that the U.S. national and cultural identity will be destroyed by immigration. The United States functions best as a heterogeneous, diverse population, and is expansive enough to absorb many new immigrants. Contrary to fears about job security, immigration is a necessary ingredient in plans for future U.S. economic growth and an enlarged workforce. In fact, even the influx of unskilled workers—often the group most feared for the potential to sap the country's social programs and resources—aid U.S. economic growth by filling jobs that many U.S. citizens and permanent residents do not want.

There is a moral component to the argument in favor of free immigration as well. Given the U.S. tradition as a country of immigrants, it is difficult to comprehend how current citizens—almost all of whom have benefited from immigration—can claim any right to exclude future immigrants. Also, family reunification is the core of much of our immigration policy and is based upon a fundamental respect for the right to be with one's loved ones. Moreover, immigration law is only as effective as its enforcement. Weak enforcement and illegal immigration mock the actual numerical limits that are enacted. Some scholars argue that the U.S. should adopt an immigration policy commensurate with the country's capacity for enforcement, or at least, legally recognize the actual number of aliens who enter the U.S.

The argument against free immigration—that is, for maintaining a restrictive immigration policy—have figured prominently in the history of U.S. immigration law. These reasons are often based upon a fear that increased immigration will compromise the U.S. standard of living. This argument posits that the very reasons immigrants have historically been attracted to the United States—*e.g.,* the "American Dream"—are themselves vulnerable if the country becomes overcrowded.

Specifically, the arguments against a free or even more lenient immigration are as follows: First, xenophobia plays a strong role in persons who seek to protect the cultural identity of the U.S.; the English-only movement is one example. Second, individuals who oppose freer immigration argue that there are finite resources and jobs; accordingly, U.S. citizens and lawful permanent residents should not have to compete with immigrants for them. Third, advocates of a restrictive immigration policy argue that there must be limits somewhere—certainly, the U.S. cannot allow the whole world to come here. Once the need for some limits is recognized, the U.S. ought to structure those limits in a realistic and pragmatic way that will be most advantageous to the future of the U.S. Fourth, some scholars argue that the U.S. should commit its resources to helping countries in need so that potential immigrants will be encouraged to remain in their developing countries. This perspective contends that immigration is a drain on other countries' human resources. All countries would benefit if these potential immigrants remained in their country of origin.

The tension throughout the debate comes from the fact that the U.S. is largely a nation of immigrants who did not inherit this land by divine right, but rather, by an open immigration policy and by taking the land from the indigenous inhabitants. It appears to be an act of selfishness, if not moral ingratitude, to bar future groups seeking to immigrate. In addition, U.S. citizens like to believe that our nation helps the world's needy, sharing the plentiful resources that this country enjoys. U.S. immigration policy turns on this moral inquiry: what is the U.S. obligation to those people in need of a better place to live, and where should the lines be drawn?

Some political forces have played upon the nation's fears that open borders will exacerbate domestic problems such as crime, drugs, urban violence, unemployment, and homelessness. They remain unconvinced that freer immigration is a pragmatically or morally persuasive policy.

The 1990 Act, like most immigration legislation, is a compromise; this middle-ground appears to be the destination for our immigration policy. The 1990 Act recognizes that immigration policy is a tool to help the

United States compete internationally. The 1990 Act principally benefits those immigrants who will most help the U.S., as immigrants have throughout the nation's history. But the act's selectivity illustrates the unanswered, if not unaddressed, moral and policy issues regarding the right to exclude others.

CHAPTER 2

THE SOURCE AND SCOPE OF THE FEDERAL POWER TO REGULATE IMMIGRATION AND NATURALIZATION

The broad power of the federal government to regulate the exclusion, expulsion, and naturalization of aliens has its roots in the early history of the United States. Modern statutes, Supreme Court decisions, and federal agency regulations attest to the plenary nature of this power. This chapter examines the source of the power over immigration, the limits such federal power impose on state attempts to regulate aliens, and the allocation of this power among the three branches of the federal government—Congress, the courts, and executive agencies.

§ 2–1 THE SOURCE OF THE FEDERAL POWER

Throughout the history of the United States the Supreme Court has upheld all manner of federal statutes regulating immigration. States, in contrast, have been precluded from passing legislation that directly impinges on this area of federal dominion. The Supreme Court's basis for action is clear when the area regulated is naturalization. Article 1, section 8, clause 4, of the United States Constitution specifically grants Congress the power to establish a "uniform Rule of Naturalization." By expressly allocating this power to Congress, the Constitution prevents the confusion that would result if individual states could bestow citizenship. The Constitution does not, however, explicitly provide that the power to exclude or expel aliens rests with the federal as opposed to state governments. Hence, in the early immigration cases the Supreme Court faced the problem of identifying the source of the federal government's exclusive and plenary power over immigration.

§ 2–1.1 The Foreign Commerce Power

In the earliest cases, the Court looked to the federal power over foreign commerce. When states demanded fees from foreigners wishing to debark at state ports, the foreign commerce clause was invoked to ban such action in the *Passenger Cases* (Sup.Ct.1849). The Court invalidated state immigration fees even though Congress had yet to implement any relevant federal regulations. The Court reasoned that foreign affairs and foreign commerce were exclusively controlled by Congress even when the power had not been exercised. In the *Head Money Cases* (Sup.Ct.1884), the Court upheld a federally imposed tax on foreign immigrants, again with direct citation to the foreign commerce power. As congressional action began to reach beyond taxation to other forms of regulation, however, the Court sought a broader ground for decision.

§ 2–1.2 National Sovereignty

The Court eventually found the source of the federal power to regulate immigration in a combination of international and constitutional legal principles. *The Chinese Exclusion Case* (Sup.Ct.1889) was the first case to hold that the federal power to exclude aliens is an incident of national sovereignty. The Court reasoned that every national government has the inherent authority to protect the national public interest. Immigration is a matter of vital national concern. Furthermore, it is the role of the federal government to oversee matters of national concern, while it is the province of the states to govern local matters. Hence, the Court found that the inherent sovereign power to regulate immigration clearly resides in the federal government. Subsequent cases reinforced national sovereignty as the source of federal power to control immigration and consistently reasserted the plenary and unqualified scope of this power. *Fong Yue Ting v. United States* (Sup.Ct.1893) explicitly held that the power to deport aliens rests upon the same ground as the exclusion power and is equally "absolute and unqualified."

§ 2–1.3 Constitutional Provisions

Early cases also cite specific constitutional provisions to support the inference that the federal government possesses complete power over international relations. In *Nishimura Ekiu v. United States* (Sup.Ct.1892) the Supreme Court cites the foreign commerce power; the power to establish a uniform rule of naturalization; the power to declare war and provide and maintain armies and navies; and the power to make all laws necessary and proper. The *Fong Yue Ting v. United States* (Sup. Ct.1893) case adds the power to define and punish piracies, felonies committed on the high seas, and offenses against the law of nations; as well as the presidential power to make treaties, to appoint ambassadors, and to select other public ministers and consuls.

The Migration and Importation Clause in Article I, § 9, clause 1 of the Constitution has also been considered a potential grant of power to Congress. This clause provides: "The Migration or Importation of such Persons as any of the States now existing shall think proper to admit, shall not be prohibited by the Congress prior to the year one thousand eight hundred and eight." The specific limit on congressional power before 1808 could be construed to imply that after 1808, Congress would have power over migration and importation. The prevailing interpretation, however, is that this clause was simply intended to bar any attempts by Congress to stop the slave trade before 1808.

The War Power, found in Article I, § 8, clause 11, also could be cited as a potential source of federal control over immigration. The War Power gives Congress the authority to "declare war." The War Power authorized the exclusion and expulsion of enemy aliens. In the Alien and Sedition Acts, for example, Congress granted this power to the President. The Supreme Court upheld the constitutionality of these provisions in *Ludecke v. Watkins* (Sup.Ct.1948).

Later cases clarified, however, that these constitutional provisions are not the source of an implied right of the federal government to regulate aliens, but only demonstrate that the federal government is the national government and therefore the keeper of the inherent sovereign power to regulate international affairs.

§ 2–1.4 Delegated Versus Inherent Power

In *United States v. Curtiss–Wright Export Corp.* (Sup. Ct.1936), the Court clearly distinguished between powers delegated to the federal government in the Constitution and inherent sovereign powers. Delegated powers were carved from the general mass of legislative powers previously governed by the states. The inherent sovereign powers were, however, transferred from Great Britain to the union of states when the U.S. declared its independence. These powers were thus vested in the national government before the Constitution was written and exist without regard to any constitutional grant. It has been suggested that the apparently limitless scope of federal authority over immigration results from this undefined and undefinable source. The Supreme Court has upheld every exercise of this power and has consistently termed it "plenary and unqualified."

Other theorists suggest sources of federal immigration power that lie somewhere between the explicitly delegated powers of the Constitution and the inherent powers. The "Rule of Necessity," for instance, suggests that because federal power over immigration is *necessary* to the successful operation of the Constitution, this power may be interpolated into the Constitution.

Structural arguments have also been used to justify the exclusive federal immigration power. These arguments draw an inference of power from the structure of the Constitution as a whole, rather than from individual clauses. The Constitution's primary goal is to create a system of government for the nation, and a process through which its citizens establish the rules governing people within the territory. Under this premise, two structural arguments emerge.

First, the power to regulate immigration is essential to a nation's self-preservation. In order to be a sovereign nation, a people must have control over its territory. Without such control, a nation would be unable to govern itself and its borders effectively, and as a result, would be subject to the sovereignty of other nations. The power to regulate immigration is therefore inherent in the Constitution's creation of a sovereign nation.

Second, the power to regulate immigration is essential to the process of national "self-definition." Through the governmental process, a nation's citizens determine the values espoused by the nation, and hence, formulate the nation's identity. By determining who will comprise the nation and participate in creating the nation's identity, immigration laws constitute the process of self-definition itself. Decisions about who may enter a country say much about a nation. Although the process of national self-definition may be characterized as racist, discriminatory against outsiders, and otherwise unjust, it is an essential characteristic of a sovereign nation. These theories of self-preservation and self-definition mandate broad federal powers over immigration.

In addition, the constitutionally "implied" power of the executive over foreign affairs has been cited by scholars to authorize federal control over immigration. In *The Chinese Exclusion Case* (Sup.Ct.1889) (see § 2–1.2), Justice Field stated that the Foreign Affairs Power is the foundation for all federal control over immigration. Moreover, this power has been cited as a basis for invalidating state statutes that attempt to regulate immigration. *See, e.g., Chy Lung v. Freeman* (Sup.Ct.1875).

Today the source of the federal government's power to control international affairs generally, and immigration in particular, is accepted without question. For example, during the Iranian hostage ordeal of 1979–81, the U.S. Court of Appeals for the D.C. Circuit upheld the Attorney General's authority to order all Iranian students in the United States to report to INS offices and demonstrate the lawfulness of their presence in the country. *Narenji v. Civiletti* (D.C.Cir.1979). Many cases refer to these powers as constitutional when, in fact, the powers are drawn from a more ancient foundation. The practically unlimited scope of the federal power over aliens may possibly be traced back to the undefined nature of its source.

§ 2-2   THE SCOPE OF THE FEDERAL POWER

§ 2-2.1   Plenary Congressional Power

To date there have been no successful challenges to federal legislation that excludes classes of aliens from this country or deports resident aliens. Federal immigration power thus appears limitless. Indeed, the Supreme Court has stated: "[O]ver no conceivable subject is the legislative power of Congress more complete." *Fiallo v. Bell* (Sup.Ct.1977), *Kleindienst v. Mandel,* (Sup. Ct.1972), and *Oceanic Steam Nav. Co. v. Stranahan* (Sup.Ct.1909). Extreme judicial deference bears witness to the truth of this statement.

Both the Constitution and the U.N. Charter have been dismissed as grounds for opposing federal immigration power. The federal courts and immigration authorities have without much consideration rejected an assertion in *Hitai v. INS* (2d Cir.1965), *Vlissidis v. Anadell* (7th Cir.1959), and *Matter of Laurenzano* (BIA 1970) that the immigration quota system is inconsistent with the U.N. Charter. The Supreme Court has upheld the constitutionality of federal statutes that exclude aliens on the basis of race (*Chinese Exclusion Case* (1889)) and political belief (*Kleindienst v. Mandel* (Sup.Ct.1972)). Moreover, excluded aliens have no constitutional right to a hearing. *Shaughnessy v. Mezei* (Sup.Ct.1953).

Even where the First Amendment and Equal Protection rights of U.S. citizens were jeopardized, in *Mandel,* the courts refused to assure the superiority of constitutional rights over the federal immigration power. One district court, found that aliens have First Amendment rights not to be deported for political activity, but the U.S. Court of Appeals reversed for lack of standing and ripeness. *American–Arab Anti–Discrimination Committee v. Thornburgh* (9th Cir.1991). See § 13–4.5, *infra.*

Federal courts have both invalidated and sustained the detention of aliens convicted of aggravated felonies without the opportunity for a predetention hearing under the Fifth and Eighth Amendments. The Supreme Court also refused to reach the issue of whether the Equal Protection principles inherent in the Due Process Clause of the Fifth Amendment protected a class of undocumented Haitians detained without parole. Instead, the Court ruled that the aliens' claims were to be judged under nondiscriminatory federal statutes and regulations. *Jean v. Nelson* (Sup.Ct.1985). In *Fernandez–Roque v. Smith* (11th Cir.1984), however, the U.S. Court of Appeals for the Eleventh Circuit held that Cuban nationals found excludable had no constitutionally-based liberty interest in challenging denial or revocation of parole. In *Garcia–Mir v. Meese* (11th Cir.1986), the same court further held that unadmitted Mariel Cuban parolees did not have any other Due Process liberty interest entitling them to parole revocation hearings, nor were they entitled to such hearings on the basis of international law. Similarly, deportation orders are consistently upheld despite a myriad of conceivable constitutional challenges. Courts inclined to limit Due Process restrictions have cited *Mathews v. Diaz* (Sup.Ct.1976).

In *McNary v. Haitian Refugee Center* (Sup.Ct.1991), the Supreme Court held that challenges to the constitutionality of the practices, procedures, and policies of the INS are proper subjects for judicial review. Hence, the Court distinguished between judicial review of individual applications and review of the process by which the INS makes such determinations. In 1992, the U.S. Court of Appeals held in *Haitian Refugee Center v. Baker* (11th Cir.1991) that aliens who were detained on the high seas and, hence, had never presented themselves at a U.S. border, had no right to judicial review of INS decisions under the Administrative Procedure Act. Moreover, the court held that these aliens had no individual right of action, unless they qualified for refugee status. Further, the court held that the refugee center and their attorneys had no First Amendment claim for gaining access to those detained aliens. The Supreme Court denied certiorari over the objections of Justice Blackmun, who complained that this challenge to the U.S. procedures for determining whether a group faces political persecution should not go unheard by the Court. See §§ 8–3.1, 9–2.4, *infra*.

Hence, the federal legislative decision to exclude or expel an alien is presently final—not subject to effective judicial scrutiny. Cases sustaining the broad authority of Congress over immigration have relied upon *Fiallo v. Bell* (Sup.Ct.1977). Thus far, the courts have largely resisted prodding by scholars and litigants to place some limits on the federal power over this subject matter.

Some scholars have argued that the plenary power Congress enjoys is susceptible to abuse, often at the expense of fundamental human rights. These critics argue that Congress' current plenary power over immigration is an outdated manifestation of repression arising from racism, past wars, and cold war tensions.

§ 2–2.2 Permissible and Impermissible State Regulations

States may not usurp the federal power over immigration. State attempts to regulate concurrently in a field already occupied by a federal statute have been struck down under the doctrine of preemption. In *Hines v. Davidowitz* (1941), for example, the Court held that the Federal Alien Registration Act preempted the Pennsylvania alien registration provisions. Under the preemption doctrine, federal law in a specific area may preclude even consistent state regulations.

The courts will also invalidate state statutes which conflict with federal policy. This ground has been coupled with the Equal Protection Clause to invalidate state discrimination against aliens. In the nineteenth and early twentieth centuries, the Supreme Court allowed states to pass laws discriminating against aliens. In 1915, however, the case of *Truax v. Raich* (Sup.Ct. 1915) reversed this trend. *Truax* rested on the dual ground of equal protection and exclusive federal control over immigration. The Court overturned an Arizona statute restricting alien employment. In addition to being a denial of equal protection, the statute ran contrary to the implied intent of Congress that aliens allowed into the country under federal immigration laws would be free to pursue a livelihood. Similarly, the Court rejected state laws restricting fishing rights of aliens denied naturalization in *Takahashi v. Fish and Game Com'n* (Sup.Ct.1948), and length of residency requirements for aliens seeking welfare in *Graham v. Richardson* (Sup.Ct.1971). In each of these cases, the Court perceived a conflict between the burdensome state regulation and the decision by federal authorities to grant residency privileges to the affected aliens.

In a somewhat different vein, the Court in *Nyquist v. Mauclet* (Sup.Ct.1977) invalidated a New York law that made commencing naturalization procedures a prerequisite to receiving financial assistance for higher education. Although the *Mauclet* case relied heavily on the Equal Protection Clause for its outcome, the Court noted that encouraging naturalization is an illegitimate purpose for discrimination in light of federal dominion over that field. It seems then that even where state statutes do not directly conflict with federal policy covering the same subject, the state statute may still be struck down if it meddles in immigration policy.

The mere existence of the federal immigration power does not, however, automatically preclude state regulations affecting aliens. The Supreme Court so held in *De Canas v. Bica* (Sup.Ct.1976). In *De Canas* the Court upheld a California statute prohibiting an employer from knowingly employing an alien who is not entitled to lawful residence in the U.S. if such employment would have an adverse effect on lawful resident workers. Writing for the majority, Justice Blackmun stated "the Court has never held that every state enactment which in any way deals with aliens is a regulation of immigration and thus per se preempted by this constitutional immigration power, whether latent or exercised."

In finding that the Immigration and Nationality Act (INA) did not preempt the California statute, the Court noted that the nature of the subject matter does not compel a conclusion of exclusive federal control. Furthermore, the INA does not evince a congressional intent to occupy the field totally. The Court distinguished previous preemption cases in the immigration field on a number of grounds. First, the California statute did not cover ground specifically addressed by the INA. (Such a federal statute, however, was adopted in 1986.) Second, Congress seemed at that time to authorize concurrent state legislation in the area regulated by the state law. Third, the federal interest is not as predominant in a "situation in which state law is fashioned to remedy local problems, and operates only on local employers and only with respect to individuals whom the federal government has already declared cannot work in this country." Finally, the previous cases overturned statutes which "imposed burdens on aliens lawfully within the country that created conflicts with various federal laws." *De Canas* indicates that the gaps in the federal regulatory scheme governing aliens may be filled by the states so long as the state regulations do not run afoul of federal policy. Lower courts have thus upheld state and local regulation in certain areas such as enforcement of the criminal provisions of federal immigration law. *Gonzales v. City of Peoria* (9th Cir.1983). The Immigration Reform and Control Act of 1986, as well as the Immigration Act of 1990, evinces federal preemption of a far broader range of immigration-related activity, including state laws regulating the employment of aliens.

In a related area the Supreme Court also has upheld state probate laws which incidentally and indirectly affect foreign relations. *Clark v. Allen* (Sup.Ct.1947) called into question a state statute which conditioned a nonresident alien's right to inherit property upon the existence of a reciprocal right of U.S. citizens to inherit property in the alien's nation. The statute's opponents claimed it was an incursion into an area of exclusive federal control. The Court labeled that claim "far fetched" and held such laws are valid unless they conflict with a federal law or statute.

Of course, if states use their probate laws to implement foreign policy, they enter a forbidden field. Hence, in *Zschernig v. Miller* (Sup.Ct.1968) the Court struck down an Oregon statute requiring an alien entitled to inherit property to show that his/her government would allow the receipt of such property without confiscation. The provision necessarily mandated judicial inquiry into the current status of political rights in foreign countries. Such inquiries are the exclusive responsibility of the federal government. A state may not cross the line between incidental and direct effects on either immigration or foreign policy.

It is clear that the scope of federal immigration power is not so broad as to preclude all state statutes touching the field. While state statutes may be preempted, the *De Canas* case holds that the unexercised federal power over immigration is not by itself a bar to state regulations which single out aliens. State statutes that do not discriminate against resident aliens should be analyzed under the preemption doctrine to determine if they conflict with congressional intent or govern an area already exclusively covered by federal law.

§ 2–3 THE FUNCTIONS OF THE THREE BRANCHES OF THE FEDERAL GOVERNMENT IN REGULATING IMMIGRATION

§ 2–3.1 The Legislature

The plenary and unqualified power of the federal government to regulate immigration, naturalization, and related foreign policy belongs to Congress. The possible international consequences of decisions in this area have made the federal judiciary extremely reluctant to substitute its judgment for the legislature's. Justice Jackson articulated the Court's position in *Harisiades v. Shaughnessy* (Sup.Ct.1952): "[A]ny policy towards aliens is vitally and intricately interwoven with contemporaneous policies in regard to the conduct of foreign relations, the war power, and the maintenance of a republican form of government. Such matters are so exclusively entrusted to the political branches of government as to be largely immune from judicial inquiry or interference." Subsequent decisions echo this sentiment. Since the judiciary poses no obstacle, Congress has been historically free to "exclude aliens altogether or prescribe the terms and conditions upon which they may enter and stay in this country." *Lapina v. Williams* (Sup.Ct.1914). Accordingly, it appears the legislative branch wields the full measure of the federal plenary power over immigration. See chapter 4, *infra*.

§ 2–3.2 The Judiciary

The Supreme Court has stopped short of abdicating all responsibility for immigration law. The Court has reserved a narrow ground for review which is worth examining for hints of possible future trends.

a. Exclusion Decisions

Aliens who are outside the national boundaries of the United States have no constitutional rights and as a practical matter have absolutely no basis for challenging their exclusion from this country. Although the Supreme Court has not quite deemed exclusion cases non-justiciable under the political question doctrine, the extreme degree of deference the Court gives to legislative determinations on this issue make the ground of review so narrow as to be practically nonexistent. Indeed, earlier cases evince a complete "hands off" attitude by the courts. It is only later cases which refer to a narrow ground of review.

Fiallo v. Bell (Sup.Ct.1977) illustrates the Court's gingerly approach to exclusion cases. A federal statute governing immigration preferences made it more difficult for illegitimate children and fathers to be reunited in this country than illegitimate children and mothers. See § 5—2.1. U.S. citizens and resident aliens disadvantaged by the statute challenged it on equal protection grounds. In a footnote, Justice Blackmun, for the majority, explicitly rejected the government's contention that admission of aliens is not an appropriate subject for review: "our cases reflect acceptance of limited judicial responsibility under the Constitution even with respect to the power of Congress to regulate the admission and exclusion of aliens...." Having once established the reviewability of this type of case, however, Blackmun applied a standard of review that is, as dissenter Justice Marshall noted, "toothless." The Court acknowledged that the statute discriminates on the basis of sex and that the fathers have no opportunity to prove a close relationship in order to overcome the statutory presumption. Blackmun flatly stated, "[T]he decision nonetheless remains one solely for the responsibility of the Congress and wholly outside the power of this Court to control." After the Court's decision, Congress did resolve the problem raised in this case by providing that illegitimate children can obtain the same immigration benefits from the natural father as from the natural mother "if the father has or had a bona fide parent-child relationship." INA § 101(b)(1)(D).

Federal courts have reserved a narrow ground of review in a few cases: *Hill v. INS* (9th Cir.1983) (although the power of Congress is plenary, exclusion of homosexuals is improper without a medical certificate of psychopathic personality, sexual deviation, or mental defect); *Allende v. Shultz* (1st Cir.1988) (government impermissibly denied visa to widow of former Chilean president invited to speak in U.S. on the basis of general harm to foreign policy created by her presence); *Abourezk v. Reagan* (D.C.Cir.1986) (when alien is a member of Communist or anarchist organization, government may exclude alien based on projected engagement in activities prejudicial to public interest, only if reason for threat to public interest is independent of membership in proscribed organization); and *Harvard Law School Forum v. Shultz* (D.Mass. *vacated without opinion* 1st Cir.1986) (Law School forum entitled to preliminary injunction prohibiting Secretary of State from refusing travel permission to a P.L.O. member without a "facially legitimate and bona fide reason" for the INS decision). All of these court decisions presaged legislative actions in 1990 which removed restrictions on the immigration of homosexuals and eased the issuance of nonimmigrant visas to members of the Communist party and other controversial visitors.

b. Resident Alien Cases

Resident aliens possess recognized constitutional rights. When pitted against the federal power to regulate immigration, however, these rights provide a little protection. Deportation proceedings must observe procedural due process. *Japanese Immigrant Case* (Sup.Ct. 1903). The Court does not, however, examine the adequacy of the fair hearing Congress prescribes. *Id.* Although in early deportation cases the Court refused to recognize substantive Due Process guarantees, recent cases indicate this practice may change. In *Galvan v. Press* (Sup.Ct.1954) the Court at least looked at the congressional classification making Communists deportable and found "it was not so baseless as to be violative of due process and therefore beyond the power of Congress." Similarly, in *Mathews v. Diaz* (Sup.Ct.1976) the Court implicitly applied equal protection analysis to a federal statute which discriminated between two classes of aliens. The Court upheld the classification as rational. Although these cases provide no direct precedent for reversing a deportation order, they do indicate that congressional power in this area may some day fail to support a completely arbitrary act or classification.

In fact, the Supreme Court has on more than one occasion expressed in dicta regret in not being able to afford some measure of protection to resident aliens. For example, in *Galvan v. Press* (Sup.Ct.1954), Justice Frankfurter remarked:

"[C]onsidering what it means to deport an alien who legally became a part of the American community, and the extent to which, since he is a 'person' an alien has the same protection for his life, liberty and property under the Due Process Clause as is afforded to a citizen, deportation without permitting the alien to prove that he was unaware of the Communist Party's advocacy of violence strikes one with a sense of harsh incongruity. If due process bars Congress from enactments which shock the sense of fair play—which is the essence of due process—one is entitled to ask whether it is not beyond the power of Congress to deport an alien who was duped into joining the Communist Party, particularly when his conduct antedated the enactment of the legislation under which his deportation is sought. And this is because deportation may ... deprive a man 'of all that makes life worth living.' "

The weight of authority backing the government's plenary power to deport was too great to push aside with the mere invocation of "fair play," however, and the Court held Due Process was satisfied in this case. These judicial rumblings may yet produce results.

Deportation is not a criminal penalty. Hence, deportation orders cannot be challenged as a violation of the *ex post facto* clause when past conduct which was not illegal when committed, is the basis for a deportation order (*Mahler v. Eby* (Sup.Ct.1924); *Harisiades v. Shaughnessy* (Sup.Ct.1952)). For the same reason denial of bail (*Carlson v. Landon* (Sup.Ct.1952)), double jeopardy (*United States v. Ramirez–Aguilar* (9th Cir.1972)), speedy trial (*Argiz v. INS* (7th Cir.1983)), and cruel and unusual punishment (*Fong Yue Ting v. United States* (Sup.Ct.1893)) challenges are of no avail.

c. Naturalization Cases

As with exclusion and deportation, the Supreme Court accords great deference to the naturalization guidelines set by Congress. In *United States v. Ginsberg* (1917) the Court stated "An alien who seeks political rights as a member of this nation can rightfully obtain them only upon the terms and conditions specified by Congress. Courts are without authority to sanction changes or modifications; their duty is rigidly to enforce the legislative will...." In cases involving classifications in the naturalization process, the Court has given a near absolute presumption of validity to distinctions drawn by Congress.

As discussed above, all phases of immigration, including the regulation of resident aliens and naturalization, are guided by the legislative branch. In all cases the judiciary has refused to second guess federal legislation, although the courts retain the power of review. See chapter 4, *infra.*

d. Asylum Cases

The Supreme Court also defers to Congress on issues involving asylum. The problem has been reconciling the nation's commitments under the Protocol relating to the Status of Refugees with Congress' expressions of substantive and procedural rights under the Refugee Act of 1980. In *INS v. Cardoza–Fonseca* (Sup.Ct.1987) the Supreme Court used its power of review to determine the standard to be applied in granting asylum. Specifically, the Court held that a refugee seeking asylum pursuant to § 208(a) of the INA must show only a "well-founded fear of persecution" in his/her country of origin, and not a "clear probability" of persecution, as is required for withholding of deportation under § 243(h) of the INA. The Court had earlier decided in *INS v. Stevic* (Sup.Ct.1984) that the "well-founded fear" standard did not govern § 243(h) applications for withholding of deportation.

In rejecting the "clear probability" test, Justice Stevens made it clear that the Court was within its boundaries. He wrote,

"... courts must respect the interpretation of the agency to which Congress has delegated the responsibility for administering the statutory program.... But our task today is much narrower, and is well within the province of the judiciary. We do not attempt to set forth a detailed description of how the well-founded fear test should be applied. Instead, we merely hold that the Immigration Judge and the BIA were incorrect in holding that the two standards are identical."

Hence, while generally deferring to Congress, the Court will take an indirect role in shaping immigration policy by ruling on issues of statutory interpretation, including whether INS regulations are consistent with the intent of legislation.

Critics have also charged that persons seeking asylum are victims of discrimination on the basis of their nationality. In particular, persons from El Salvador and Guatemala have alleged that they have not been given fair adjudications of their asylum claims. In a significant, and perhaps far-reaching settlement, the Department of Justice agreed to re-adjudicate up to 150,000 asylum claims; further, all Salvadorans and Guatemalans in this country since October 1990 are protected from deportation and receive work authorization. *American Baptist Churches v. Thornburgh* (N.D.Cal. 1991). As many as half a million people may be affected by the settlement.

§ 2–3.3 The Executive

As in other areas of the law, the function of executive agencies in the field of immigration is to enforce the legislation passed by Congress. Once Congress determines which classes of aliens will be denied admission or expelled, the executive decides who fits within each class. Since the executive has no inherent power over immigration, it must stay within the grant of authority defined by the statute. Any unauthorized executive decisions are illegal and the courts may overturn them. *Mahler v. Eby* (Sup.Ct.1924).

Congress need not, however, give the agencies detailed direction. The courts have not hesitated to uphold broad delegations of power to the enforcement agency. *Jay v. Boyd* (Sup.Ct.1956). In general, Congress need only delineate basic policy. Agencies then have relatively free rein in creating procedures to implement the policy. Congress also may make the executive decisions final, thereby precluding review by the courts of agency factual findings. The structure of the federal executive agencies which administer and enforce the immigration laws is discussed in chapter 3.

In 1983, an issue surfaced concerning the division of power between the executive and legislative branches which pertains to deportation regulations. Congress had reserved the power of one house of Congress to veto any individual decision by the INS to suspend deportation. The House of Representatives exercised this veto in the case of an East Indian from Kenya and the alien, who was thus to be deported, challenged the congressional action as a violation of constitutional separation of powers. The Supreme Court held in the landmark decision of *Immigration and Naturalization Service v.*

Chadha (Sup.Ct.1983) that such legislative veto provisions violated the constitutional requirement that, before becoming law, all bills must pass both the House and the Senate, and be presented to and signed by the President.

Finally, Congress may not give the executive the power to impose punishment for crimes. The courts alone may exercise this power and the procedures must comply with the constitutional requirements for all criminal prosecutions. Deportation is not considered criminal punishment, however, even when triggered by illegal acts.

CHAPTER 3

ADMINISTRATIVE STRUCTURE
OF IMMIGRATION LAW

There are five major departments of the executive
branch of the federal government involved in the immigration process: The Department of State, the Department of Justice, the Department of Labor, the Department of Health and Human Services, and the United
States Information Agency. Congress has a role in the
immigration process which is discussed in chapter 4.

§ 3–1 THE DEPARTMENT OF STATE

For most aliens the immigration process begins
abroad in the over 200 U.S. consulates and embassies,
which are a part of the Department of State. In order
to obtain the visa necessary to travel to this country, an
alien must file an application at the U.S. consulate in
her/his country of last residence. A common example
is the B–2 tourist visa, which is usually obtained abroad.
In contrast, for example, if an alien wishes to enter the
U.S. as an immediate relative or fiancé(e) of a U.S.
citizen, or under almost all employment-sponsored temporary visa statuses, a petition must first be filed by the
sponsoring relative or employer for such classification
with the Immigration and Naturalization Service (INS)
in the United States. A U.S. citizen or permanent
resident residing abroad may also file family petitions
at INS offices abroad. If the INS grants the petition, it

notifies the U.S. embassy or consulate in the alien's country of last residence, and the visa is sought by the alien following a separate application process.

Consular officers make the decision whether to grant or refuse a visa and this decision is subject to very limited review. Although the Immigration and Nationality Act (INA) delegates general visa documentation responsibility to the Department of State, it excludes from the Secretary of State's broad authority "those powers, duties, and functions conferred upon the consular officers relating to the granting or refusal of visas." INA § 104(a)(1). The Department of State, however, conducts a highly discretionary informal review system in which each visa refusal is reviewed by a second consular officer. The second consular officer may disagree with the first officer's decision and issue the visa, but s/he cannot mandate that the visa be granted by the first officer. If a dispute does arise between consular officers, the matter may be referred to the Visa Office of the Department of State in Washington, D.C. The Visa Office will issue an advisory opinion. Although technically only binding as to legal questions, the Visa Office advisory opinion is usually followed.

Consular decisions denying visas to aliens not yet present in the United States are generally held to be neither administratively nor judicially reviewable. *See, e.g., Li Hing of Hong Kong, Inc. v. Levin* (9th Cir.1986); *Ventura–Escamilla v. INS* (9th Cir.1981). Several courts, however, have asserted a narrow ground of review in visa denial cases. See *Abourezk v. Reagan* (D.C.Cir.1986) (plaintiffs were entitled under the Administrative Procedure Act to judicial review of agency action denying a visa, due to the absence of "clear and convincing evidence" of congressional intent to the contrary) and *Allende v. Shultz* (D.Mass.1985) (U.S. citizens claiming denial of visa for Chilean speaker violated their First Amendment rights of free speech and association were entitled to judicial review because "[t]he exercise of judicial review, though necessarily limited in scope, is particularly appropriate in cases ... which involve fundamental rights of U.S. citizens.").

Even receipt of a visa, however, does not ensure admission to the United States. The immigration officer at the U.S. border or port of entry (referred to as an "inspector") may either disagree with the consular officer or conclude that the alien has given false information to the consular officer, and in either case, hold the alien for an exclusion hearing. Fortunately, such situations seldom occur. An interesting illustration of INS efforts to avoid exclusion hearings at the border for entering aliens can be seen in the "preinspection" procedures or "interdiction" programs where INS officials examine aliens either in their country of departure or on the high seas.

The Department of State's role extends beyond issuing visas. The Department of State supervises embassy adjudications of citizenship questions when a person outside the U.S. claims to be a U.S. citizen. It issues advisory opinions on refugee and asylum petitions, and supervises consular actions in other matters which might affect the relationship of the U.S. government with other countries. The Department of State also provides consular services for U.S. citizens abroad, such as for persons with lost passports or a need for other documents, as well as for U.S. citizens arrested in a foreign country.

§ 3–2 THE DEPARTMENT OF JUSTICE

The Attorney General has the power of administering and enforcing the INA, and "all other laws relating to the immigration and naturalization of aliens." INA § 103(a). This power does not include those duties expressly delegated to other officials or agencies, such as the Department of State. *Id.* The Attorney General is authorized to delegate his responsibilities to agencies within the Department, such as the INS and the Executive Office of Immigration Review. INA § 103.

§ 3–2.1 The Immigration and Naturalization Service

Although the INA does not state specifically which duties are to be delegated to a particular agency, the Attorney General delegates most duties to the Immigration and Naturalization Service (INS). The INS, which has general jurisdiction over aliens in the U.S., handles visa petitions, adjustments from nonimmigrant to immigrant status, citizenship adjudications, and deportations for aliens present in this country. As previously mentioned, the INS also inspects aliens at the border before entry into the U.S. and excludes persons who are not admissible.

The Commissioner of Immigration and Naturalization heads the INS. The Commissioner is appointed by the President, normally on the recommendation of the Attorney General, and with the consent of the Senate. INA § 103(b). Four Associate Commissioners and the General Counsel assist the Commissioner; all are located in the INS central office in Washington, D.C.

The central office deals almost exclusively with administrative matters, such as budgeting and policy formulation. Given this administrative function, an attorney handling an immigration case involving an individual alien would not normally deal with the central office. In some instances, however, such as when the attorney believes that a district office is not complying with national policy, the central office may be contacted for assistance and even advisory opinions. For example, there is a division referred to as the Administrative Appeals Unit which handles administrative appeals from certain decisions of lower adjudicatory officers.

There are four INS regional offices, which are located in Burlington, Vermont; Fort Snelling, Minnesota; Laguna Nigel, California; and Dallas, Texas. These offices constitute the intermediate administrative level of the INS. Each region has a Regional Commissioner. Like the central office, the regional offices are concerned primarily with administrative issues. The regional offices provide administrative coordination for the 34 district offices. There are also several district offices abroad, which have a very limited scope of responsibility.

The level of the INS primarily responsible for implementing the immigration laws is the district office. Each district office has a district director and several assistant directors. The district offices are divided into units which focus on investigation, examination, deportation, administration, and records/information. The district counsel advises the district and acts as their advocate. The investigative division in each district includes officers who enforce the immigration law in the interior of the country by locating undocumented aliens, investigating fraud and smuggling operations, and engaging in other enforcement activities. The examination unit is comprised of officers who engage in border inspections and adjudications. The officers responsible for inspections examine documents presented by entering citizens and aliens at the approximately 200 ports of entry within the U.S.

The Border Patrol prevents illegal entries into the U.S. and detains or expels undocumented aliens already present. The Patrol's officers report to the central office and are not under the supervision of the district directors.

The adjudication division of each INS district office reviews petitions for adjustment of status, visa extension, immigrant visas for overseas relatives, and for various other benefits under the INA. Immigration officers have broad discretion in deciding whether an application is complete, accurate, credible, and in compliance with statutory and regulatory requirements. The district director has the authority to initiate investigations, deportations, orders to show cause, and arrest warrants, as well as to set bail in connection with deportation hearings.

For the past several years, the INS has embarked upon an intensive program to centralize its adjudication functions into what are known as Regional Service Centers. The INS hopes that eventually almost all adjudications will be heard at those regional centers. A large number of petitions for immigrant and nonimmigrant status are sent to one of the four Regional Service Centers, where a high-volume of applications can be decided without any personal contact with the applicant. The centers are located in St. Albans, Vermont; Lincoln, Nebraska; Laguna Nigel, California; and Dallas, Texas. In most regions, the applicant sends her/his petition directly to the appropriate center. INS officers at these centers decide the cases almost in a "vacuum." They cannot be reached by phone, but will respond to written inquiries. This approach renders the application process highly documentary and not susceptible to personal advocacy.

§ 3–2.2 The Executive Office of Immigration Review

The INS does not have complete control over every alien's fate. The immigration courts and the Board of Immigration Appeals are independent from the INS. Together they constitute the Executive Office of Immigration Review (EOIR). The EOIR is an administrative body, not a court under Article 1 or 3 of the Constitution.

a. The Immigration Courts

Immigration judges (identified in the statute, and still in many regulations, as "special inquiry officers," INA § 101(b)(4)) preside primarily over exclusion and deportation hearings. They may also participate in other adjudications such as proceedings to rescind adjustments of status under INA § 246, hearings to withdraw approval of schools for attendance by nonimmigrant students, 8 CFR § 214.4, and challenges brought by aliens ordered to remain in the country under the provisions of 8 C.F.R. §§ 215, 215.4, 215.5. Decisions made by immigration judges are final unless appealed to the Board of Immigration Appeals. 8 C.F.R. §§ 3.36, 3.37.

Until 1983, immigration judges were a part of the INS. These judges were senior immigration officers who held hearings in addition to their enforcement

responsibilities.   Concerns about the neutrality of
judges with enforcement responsibilities prompted Due
Process challenges to these hearings. In 1950, the Supreme Court ruled that the Administrative Procedure
Act (APA) demands a separation of functions between
immigration judges and enforcement officials. *Wong
Yang Sung v. McGrath* (Sup.Ct.1950). Shortly thereafter, Congress passed a provision exempting immigration adjudications from the APA separation-of-functions
requirements. Under the INA, Congress again expressly provided that immigration judges could also serve as
enforcement officials. INA § 242(b). The act, however,
did prohibit an immigration judge from presiding over a
case on which s/he had previously acted as prosecutor
or investigator. *Id.* The Supreme Court found no Due
Process violation under these new provisions. *Marcello
v. Bonds* (Sup.Ct.1955).

While due process arguments failed, the desire for
professionalism within the INS and the need for more
predictable, rational adjudication resulted in changes.
Beginning in 1956, the INS required immigration judges
to have law degrees. In 1962, the INS began to employ
a staff of trial attorneys to present the government's
case; it became standard practice for a trial attorney or
other INS officer to appear in almost every deportation
and exclusion proceeding.

Despite these reforms, immigration judges remained
dependent on INS district directors for budgeting and
administrative matters. In 1983, the Department of
Justice resolved this problem by removing immigration
judges from the INS and placing them under the direct
supervision of the Associate Attorney General in the

newly created Executive Office of Immigration Review. See 8 C.F.R. § 3.

b. *The Board of Immigration Appeals*

Unlike the immigration courts, the Board of Immigration Appeals (BIA) has never been a part of the INS and has always been directly accountable to the Attorney General. In fact, the BIA was not created by the INA, but pursuant to regulations promulgated by the Attorney General. The Board consists of five permanent members appointed by the Attorney General, and, since 1988, two temporary immigration judges. Under this new system, cases are usually heard by a panel comprised of two permanent BIA members and one temporary immigration judge. Important matters, however, may still be heard by the five permanent members sitting *en banc.*

Most appeals to the Board are from immigration judges' decisions on deportation and exclusion. See 8 C.F.R. § 242.21 and 8 C.F.R. § 3.1(b)(1), (2). The Board also hears appeals from other decisions of immigration judges, such as those decisions relating to bonds, parole, or detention of an alien; the imposition of fines and penalties on carriers; and rescission of adjustment of status. The Board also reviews certain decisions of INS district directors, including determinations made on immigrant visa petitions based on family relationship. 8 C.F.R. § 3.1(b). The Attorney General may review certain decisions of the Board which the Chair or a majority of the Board believe should be referred to the Attorney General for review, as well as those decisions which the Commissioner of the INS requests be referred for review, and those decisions which the Attorney General directs the Board to refer to her/him. 8 C.F.R. § 3.1(h).

c. The Administrative Appeals Unit

Most decisions made by immigration judges are reviewable by the BIA. Most decisions issued by district offices and Regional Service Centers, however, can be appealed to the Administrative Appeals Unit (AAU), a group of appellate examiners located within the office of the Associate Commissioner for Examinations in Washington, D.C. There are exceptions to these usual routes of appeal; for example, the AAU also has limited authority to hear appeals from immigration judge decisions. Hence, a practitioner is advised to consult the regulations to determine which route of appeal—the BIA or AAU—is appropriate. See 8 C.F.R. §§ 3.1(b), 103.1(f).

§ 3–2.3 Asylum Adjudication

In 1990, the INS issued regulations creating a new system for processing asylum applications and authorizing the installation of a documentation center to collect and disseminate information on worldwide human rights conditions. 8 C.F.R. § 208.1(c).

Under this new system, a newly-created corps of asylum officers reports directly to the INS Central Office for Refugees, Asylum, and Parole (CORAP) in Washington, D.C., rather than to the INS district offices. Hence, the asylum officers have been separated from INS enforcement functions. Under the new regulations, the asylum officers are to be trained in international relations and international law, and will be briefed about human rights from the new documentation center. 8 C.F.R. § 208.1.

Asylum officers adjudicate most applications for asylum and petitions for stays of deportation. 8 C.F.R.

§ 208.2. An alien seeking asylum, not arising out of a deportation or exclusion proceeding, applies to the district director, who then forwards the application to an asylum officer. After a nonadversarial interview and an examination of supporting documents, the asylum officer determines whether the applicant has established refugee status. There is no right of appeal from a decision of an asylum officer, though an unsuccessful applicant can renew an asylum petition during a subsequent exclusion or deportation proceeding.

§ 3–2.4 Other Units

Passage of the Immigration Reform and Control Act of 1986 (IRCA) led to the creation of two additional units dealing with employment discrimination within the Department of Justice. The first, the Office of Chief Administrative Hearing Officer (OCAHO), hears allegations of employer violations—particularly the employment of certain unlawful aliens and employer discrimination on the basis of national origin or citizenship status. The second new unit, the Office of Special Counsel for Immigration–Related Unfair Employment Practices is empowered to investigate and bring charges under the employer sanctions provisions of IRCA.

§ 3–3 THE DEPARTMENT OF LABOR

Aliens wishing to immigrate to the U.S. based upon an offer of permanent employment by a U.S. employer must first obtain certification from the Department of Labor that the employment may not be performed by a qualified, willing U.S. worker and that it will not adversely affect U.S. wages or working conditions. The labor certification program is a stark reminder that one of Congress' aims in controlling immigration is to protect the U.S. labor force. Under the 1990 Act, labor certification is required for immigrants in the second employment-related preference class (members of the professions holding advanced degrees and aliens of exceptional ability), the third (skilled workers, professionals, and other workers), as well as for H–2 nonimmigrant visas. The Department of Labor will grant certification if it determines that there are insufficient qualified and willing U.S. workers available where the alien will be employed and that the alien's employment will not have an adverse impact on wages or working conditions of similarly employed U.S. workers. INA § 212(a)(14). For a further discussion of the procedure to obtain a labor certificate, see § 5–5.1, *infra.*

While the Department of Labor ultimately grants the labor certification, the state employment service office where the job will be located is substantially involved in the procedure. 20 C.F.R. § 656.21(a). In Minnesota, for example, the Minnesota Department of Economic Security makes the initial review as to the local prevailing wage rate for the job, considers the availability of persons within the geographic area for the type of job being sought, and takes into account other factors. A prospective employer must follow a supervised recruitment procedure. Usually the employer must advertise for the position, including a detailed job description stating the prevailing wage and hours. In addition, the 1990 Act requires a showing by the applicant-employer that notice of the individual application for labor certification has been given to the union or bargaining representatives. Where no union exists, the employer must post the notice at the workplace. If the Department of Economic Security is satisfied that there are no qualified, willing U.S. workers for the position and that employing the alien will not adversely affect U.S. labor, the labor certification is sent to the regional office of the Department of Labor for final review. The Department of Labor then examines the certification to ensure that all statutory and regulatory provisions are met. Once all applicable provisions are met, the Labor Department grants certification. Denials of labor certification may occur for a number of reasons including position requirements which are not normal to the occupation or justified by business necessity, improper recruitment procedures, or bad faith of the employer in reviewing U.S. worker applicants. Denials may be appealed by the prospective employer to the Board of Alien Labor Certification Appeals (BALCA), an appellate process which can last two years.

For some occupations the Department of Labor does not make an independent decision on each application for labor certification. Instead, it uses two schedules of occupations. Schedule A contains a list of occupations for which the Department has determined that there are insufficient workers and for which the employment of aliens would not adversely affect wages or working conditions. Examples of Schedule A occupations include nurses, certain members of the medical profession, and persons following certain religious callings. 20 C.F.R. § 656.10. In addition, immigrants within the first employment-related preference class ("priority workers") are exempt from the certification requirement.

In contrast, Schedule B occupations are those jobs for which the Department has determined that there are sufficient U.S. citizens and permanent resident workers, upon which alien employment would have an adverse impact. This group mainly includes unskilled workers such as janitors, salespeople, and drivers. 20 C.F.R. § 656.11.

Schedule A applications may be submitted directly to the INS or to a U.S. consular office abroad. 20 C.F.R. § 656.22. Certification is granted without further processing if the INS determines that the alien does, indeed, have a Schedule A occupation. No certification is available for Schedule B occupations unless a rare special waiver is obtained. 20 C.F.R. §§ 656.11, 656.23.

The 1990 Act creates a pilot program in which the Secretary of Labor must publish a list of ten occupations with labor shortages or surpluses. This program ostensibly will replace the two Schedules; it is expected, however, that this new list will not differ significantly from the occupations previously included. It does suggest a congressional interest in relying upon scheduled occupations to a greater extent in order to stem the increasing number of individual labor certifications.

§ 3–4 THE DEPARTMENT OF HEALTH AND HUMAN SERVICES

The Department of Health and Human Services also plays a role in the administration of immigration law. The Department's Public Health Service has doctors abroad and at ports of entry to give medical exams before visas are issued and to arriving aliens. These doctors play a significant role in the immigrant process by determining whether an alien's physical or mental condition is within the grounds for exclusion.

§ 3–5 THE UNITED STATES
INFORMATION
AGENCY

The United States Information Agency (USIA) is responsible for cultural and educational exchange programs, sending U.S. citizens to other countries, and encouraging thousands of foreign nationals to visit the U.S. Those aliens enter the U.S. under the nonimmigrant status for "exchange visitors" (J–1). Unlike most of the other nonimmigrant visas, aliens entering the U.S. on a J nonimmigrant visa must generally meet a two-year foreign residency requirement before they seek immigration status.

The Fulbright program is one example of an exchange arrangement overseen by the USIA. The USIA (formerly the International Communications Agency) promulgates all of the regulations concerning exchange visitor programs, including employment-related provisions. See § 6–10 *infra* for a detailed discussion of J nonimmigrant visas.

CHAPTER 4

THE CONGRESSIONAL ROLE IN THE IMMIGRATION PROCESS

§ 4–1 INTRODUCTION

Members of the U.S. Senate and House of Representatives are important actors in the formation of immigration law and policy. They draft and approve legislation that, with Presidential signature, becomes the foundation of U.S. immigration law. But Congress performs other vital immigration functions as well. In cases of extreme hardship, private legislation may be passed providing lawful permanent residence or even citizenship for an individual alien. Senators and Representatives are available to take up the case of an alien who may be having administrative problems with the Immigration and Naturalization Service. Both houses of Congress hold oversight hearings in which they examine the internal workings of the INS and other agencies. Furthermore, particularly in the area of refugees, the executive branch must regularly consult with Congress.

This chapter will address each of these congressional immigration activities. While all of them are important, private legislation receives the most extensive treatment, primarily because of the technical rules governing that process.

§ 4–2 LEGISLATION

The most obvious responsibility of Congress in the immigration area is considering public legislation. Congress took virtually no action in this regard until passing its first general immigration statute in 1882. Over the next 70 years, Congress passed a variety of restrictive immigration laws. In large part these laws were aimed at excluding Asians, criminals and the diseased from the U.S.

In 1952 Congress passed the Immigration and Nationality Act of 1952 (also known as the Walter–McCarran Act). This legislation consolidated and revised many of the earlier immigration statutes. To this day the Walter–McCarran Act remains the foundation of U.S. immigration law.

That view does not indicate that Congress has failed to pass significant immigration legislation since 1952. Major reforms occurred in 1965, 1980, 1986 (the Immigration Reform and Control Act), and most recently, the Immigration Act of 1990. The Immigration Reform and Control Act of 1986 offers an example of congressional action to establish an amnesty program for some of the hundreds of thousands of undocumented aliens in the U.S., to impose criminal sanctions on employers of aliens not eligible for legalization, and to provide for stricter border control in the future. Moreover, the 1990 Act illustrates Congress' attempt to update family immigration quotas in light of increasing demand, modernize grounds of exclusion, toughen laws related to alien criminal offenses, and to create a more globally competitive workforce while trying to protect the U.S. labor market.

§ 4–3 PRIVATE LEGISLATION

§ 4–3.1 The Theory

Private legislation provides another way for Congress to contribute in the immigration area. Private legislation, through a private bill, may be introduced specifically to benefit an individual alien or group of aliens. These bills most often provide relief for adopted children and foreign medical graduates. In effect, through this process, an alien is asking that he or she be exempted from the general immigration laws. In conjunction with this request, Congress acts as a tribunal of last resort—primarily through the House Subcommittee on Immigration, Refugees, and International Law and the Senate Subcommittee on Immigration and Refugee Policy. Congress is hesitant to provide many exceptions to the general immigration laws, however, believing that to do so would undermine their effectiveness. Former House Subcommittee Chairman Mazzoli, in introducing the House procedures and policy for private bills in the 99th Congress, spoke to this practice: "Since the Subcommittee acts as a court of equity in deciding whether to grant special relief in private immigration cases, it must reserve affirmative action to those of extraordinary merit and posing heavy hardship."

The constitutional rationale for private bills has never been adequately developed. Some members of Congress view this process as one in which individuals are able to use the First Amendment to petition for a redress of grievances. Complaints that private bills violate the separation of powers were rejected in *Paramino Lumber Co. v. Marshall* (Sup.Ct.1940), in which the Supreme Court found that such measures did not intrude into judicial matters.

§ 4–3.2   The History of Private Legislation

Private immigration bills have traditionally served a number of useful purposes. As mentioned already, they are a way for Congress to provide some flexibility in situations where the strict application of immigration law would produce harsh or unjust results. Also, a number of private bills pertaining to similarly situated aliens may lead to legislation amending the immigration law from which hardship is emanating. For example, before the Immigration and Nationality Act of 1952, the number of Asian spouses of U.S. citizens allowed to enter the country was restricted by quota. When U.S. servicemen were stationed in the Far East, marriages between the servicemen and Asian spouses resulted in a multitude of private bills granting non-quota status to the individual Asian spouse. The increased number of private bills relating to Asian spouses of U.S. servicemen led to public legislation which granted non-quota status to spouses of U.S. servicemen irrespective of ancestry. This public legislation in turn was incorporated into the Immigration and Nationality Act of 1952, which treats equally all spouses of U.S. citizens.

This transformation from private bill exceptions to immigration law is justified on the theory that "it is unfair and improper to extend the benefit of legislative relief solely to a few selected individuals who are in a position to reach the Congress for redress of their grievances. It is felt that humanitarian approach should be extended to an entire defined class of aliens rather than to selected individuals." House Report No. 1199, 85th Congress, 1st Session.

In a similar manner, private legislation is occasionally amended to create a public law during congressional deliberations. For example, a private bill in 1978 to exempt an elderly alien from the English literacy requirement of INA § 312 for naturalization was passed by the Senate. The House amended the private bill to provide for a waiver of the requirement for all aliens over fifty years of age who have been living in the United States for periods totalling at least twenty years after lawful admission for permanent residence. The Senate concurred in the amendment, the President signed the bill, and again, the exception became law.

While keeping these benefits in mind, it is important to understand that very few privately introduced immigration bills ever gain congressional approval. For example, in the 77th Congress (1941–42), 22 of 430 private immigration bills were passed, and in the 98th Congress (1983–84), that number was 33 of 454. Given these statistics, one may question the feasibility of a private bill for most aliens seeking relief from deportation or other benefits.

In the past, however, the introduction of these bills was almost as important as their passage. Formerly, the mere introduction of a private immigration bill would automatically cause the INS to halt deportation activity during the bill's pendency. See *United States ex rel. Knauff v. McGrath* (2d Cir.1950). After a private bill was introduced, the House or Senate Judiciary Committee would request a report from the INS on the alien who was the subject of the bill. According to Operations Instruction 107.1c, a stay of deportation will generally be authorized by the INS when it receives a committee's report request. If a bill is introduced early in a session of Congress, it could effectively gain the alien a stay of deportation for the remainder of the session (up to two years) with no further action being taken. Also, it was not uncommon for a Representative or Senator to reintroduce an expired private bill at the beginning of the next Congress, thereby continuing the stay of deportation.

As the effectiveness of these tactics in delaying deportation became apparent, private legislation grew in popularity. By the 90th Congress (1967–68), 7,293 private immigration bills were introduced; 218 were enacted. Because of this volume, 4,896 of these private bills were still pending at the end of that Congress. These numbers led the House of Representatives to tighten considerably the requirements for the introduction and consideration of private bills. Most significantly, the previously commonplace requests for INS reports on aliens after private bill introduction were restricted to cases involving extreme hardship. An earlier decision, *Roumeliotis v. INS* (7th Cir.1962), had established that there was no right to a stay of deportation in the absence of such a request for a report from the INS.

For a time, the Senate refused to follow the House of Representatives' lead, making the Senate more attractive for those seeking introduction of a private bill. The Senate continued automatically to request an INS report on an alien who was the subject of the private bill, thus producing a stay of deportation. Finally in 1981, the Senate approved rules similar to those enacted by the House of Representatives. These rules were a significant factor in bringing the number of private bills introduced down to 454 in the 98th Congress (1983–84).

§ 4–3.3 How Private Legislation Works Today

a. An Overview

The process begins when a Senator or Representative is persuaded to offer a private bill on behalf of an alien.

The bill is introduced on the floor of the House of Representatives or Senate and is then referred to the applicable Judiciary Committee. From there it is referred to either the Senate Subcommittee on Immigration and Refugee Policy or the House Subcommittee on Immigration, Refugees, and International Law. At this stage the author of the bill normally provides the respective Subcommittee with information on the alien's case and requests that a report be requested from the INS (to stay deportation).

If the Subcommittee approves the private bill, it will then return to the Senate or House Judiciary Committee from which it came. Favorable consideration at the Committee level will send the private bill back to the Senate or House floor. After an affirmative vote, which almost always occurs after Committee and Subcommittee approval, the bill will be referred to the other house of Congress for its review. Normally, this step involves referral to its Judiciary Committee, Subcommittee, and so forth. The exception to this procedure is the case in which the latter body has also taken some action on a similar or identical bill, in which instance its approval may be expedited. After both houses of Congress have approved the private bill, it is sent to the President for signature. Because of the extensive screening and investigation done by Congress on each of these bills, Presidential approval is usually only a pro forma requirement.

As can be seen by this overview, the key to a private immigration bill's passage lies in the action taken by the subcommittees. Meeting their requirements and gaining their approval will often insure favorable consideration by subsequent actors. It is important, therefore, to explore what the subcommittees seek in a private bill.

b.   *The House Subcommittee on Immigration, Refugees, and International Law*

It is appropriate to concentrate on the House Subcommittee since the greater number of private immigration bills originate in the House of Representatives. Also, the House Subcommittee's rules were enacted first and serve as the basis for those now employed in the Senate.

Rule 1 specifies that the *introduction* of a private bill does not stay the deportation of aliens illegally in the United States or those who have overstayed the terms of their visa. Rule 2 provides that all administrative remedies must be exhausted, including suspension of deportation, asylum, and labor certification, before the Subcommittee will consider a private bill. Rule 3 prevents the delays formerly caused by reintroduction of a private bill, despite its having been defeated in the previous congressional session. Additional provisions allow reintroduction in the event new evidence becomes available.

Rule 4, the Subcommittee rule most often cited, provides that the Subcommittee will consider requesting a departmental report (*i.e.*, from the INS) upon receipt of a letter from the author of the private bill. The Rule further states that a Subcommittee report request will only be made to prevent extreme hardship to the beneficiary (when the beneficiary is in this country) or a U.S. citizen. The last portion of Rule 4 provides that when a report is requested from the INS, the INS *may* stay deportation until final action is taken on the private bill. The INS, however, customarily grants a stay of deportation on receipt of such a request. The INS used to make a recommendation on the private bill when submitting the report to the Subcommittee, but no longer does so. Rule 4 has substantially curtailed requests for INS reports and the resulting stays of deportation.

Rule 5 provides that consideration of certain private bills is open to objection unless two-thirds of the Subcommittee approves consideration. Rule 6 establishes Subcommittee quorum rules and Rule 7 limits testimony at private bill hearings to that of the bill's author. Rule 8 forbids private bill consideration while court proceedings are pending on the alien's case and Rule 9 sets forth the requirement that federal agency and/or department reports be received by the Subcommittee before final action is taken on the bill.

Rule 10 sets forth the facts and documents that the author of a private bill must submit to the Subcommittee Chairman before the Subcommittee takes action. While these necessary supporting items are too numerous to mention here, the rule generally requires the author of the private bill to establish the necessary hardship caused by strict application of the immigration law. The Subcommittee staff is available to offer advice on the attainment of necessary materials. The Subcommittee also renders advisory opinions on fact situations that might offer the basis for future private bills. Subcommittee Rules 11–14 deal with procedural requirements that must be met before the private bill is actually considered by the Subcommittee.

Accompanying these Rules is the Subcommittee Statement of Policy, which emphasizes that exceptions to the immigration law are to be granted only in extraordinary cases. The Statement outlines various situations in which immigration relief has been sought in the past and the current prospects that each has for success. Included are situations involving adoption, doctors and nurses, drugs and criminal activity, medical cases, deferred action cases, investors, waivers of exclusion, naturalization, and bills tabled in a previous Congress. The policy section closes with the caveat that those aliens having private bills passed on their behalf must thereafter apply for the appropriate relief within two years.

§ 4–4 MEMBERS OF CONGRESS AS OMBUDSMEN

Senators and Representatives are often asked to help ensure that the various government agencies are responsive to the needs and requests of constituents. Members of Congress typically have staff working solely on assisting constituents in dealing with bureaucratic procedures and/or obstacles. In essence, the member of Congress is the liaison between the constituent and the government agency, often becoming an advocate for the interests of the constituent. Politically, this casework service for constituents is often viewed as vital to the Congressperson's reelection.

Casework in the immigration area often involves the interests of a U.S. citizen who has filed a petition on behalf of an alien relative or prospective employee. A complaint to a Senator or Representative that the INS is giving inadequate treatment to a citizen's petition will normally lead to immediate communication from the Member of Congress or the congressional staff to INS officials. Such communication is often helpful in relieving excessive delays and ensures that the INS is enforcing immigration laws in accordance with congressional intent. Members of Congress may, and often do, request a status report on an INS petition, or request INS review of a particular case. In some instances, the Congressperson will also write a letter in support of an alien, either to the INS directly or to a U.S. embassy abroad. To ensure that a letter of support is warranted, however, the Congressperson will demand extensive information on the status of the alien. A Senator or Representative will also be reluctant to take action which might place an alien applying for an immigrant visa ahead of other deserving applicants.

Finally, another important aspect of the casework process is its function in educating a legislator about the bureaucratic workings of the INS. Consistent problems in particular areas may lead to congressional hearings and investigations. The end result may be legislation which solves the problem.

§ 4–5 OVERSIGHT OF THE INS

Related to, and sometimes a direct result of, constituent casework, is the oversight function of Congress. Under the Legislative Reorganization Act of 1946, oversight is intended to ensure that the various administrative agencies execute the laws related to them in the manner prescribed by Congress. The oversight task is shared by the standing committees and applicable subcommittees. With regard to the INS, oversight is performed by the Judiciary Committees of the Senate and House of Representatives with their respective House Subcommittee on Immigration, Refugees, and International Law and the Senate Subcommittee on Immigration and Refugee Policy.

There are three principal aspects of oversight: investigations, hearings, and reporting requirements. Pursuant to the Legislative Reorganization Act of 1946, Congress investigates how well the laws are being executed and whether administrators are performing effectively. Specific agency investigations, however, are not frequently undertaken.

The focal point of oversight is the hearing process. Hearings are always held to determine the necessary yearly appropriations for the INS. At that time committee members are able to question INS and Department of Justice officials about the operations of their programs. Hearings are also held when new immigration legislation is being considered. For instance, an extensive number of hearings were held over the years leading to enactment of the Immigration Reform and Control Act of 1986. These hearings provide an excellent opportunity for members of Congress to question INS officials about future implementation of the legislation and also to receive input from groups that would be potentially affected.

The oversight process also involves reporting. Legislation often requires the President or the Attorney General to report to the Congress on the progress of certain INS programs. For example, section 402 of the Immigration Reform and Control Act of 1986 required annual Presidential reports to Congress on the implementation of § 274A of the Immigration and Nationality Act (relating to unlawful employment of aliens) during the first three years after its implementation. This requirement was meant to facilitate congressional oversight of the newly established employee verification system. The 1990 Act authorized the President to appoint a commission which will report to Congress on the impact of immigration law.

§ 4–6 EXECUTIVE CONSULTATION WITH CONGRESS

§ 4–6.1 Refugees

The President and Congress have attempted to deal with problems involving refugees several times over the past 40 years. Refugee issues came to the forefront after World War II. In 1948 Congress adopted the Displaced Persons Act which allowed for the admission into the U.S. of some 400,000 aliens. Congress passed several other measures facilitating refugee admission over the next 20 years.

Despite this congressional action, the requests for relief coming from many other refugees were overwhelming. Two notable examples were the demands of Hungarians and Cubans in 1956 and 1960, respectively. The Attorney General paroled these groups to the United States, pursuant to INA § 212(d)(5)(A). This provision gave the Attorney General discretion to parole into the United States temporarily for emergency reasons or for reasons deemed strictly in the public interest any alien applying for admission. As a matter of practice, the Attorney General regularly consults the relevant Committees about the use of the parole provision—particularly where large groups are involved.

Wary of the use of parole, particularly insofar as it bypassed legislative input, Congress created a seventh preference category for refugees as part of the Immigration and Nationality Act Amendments of 1965. This preference category, however, only was open to aliens fleeing persecution in a Communist-dominated country or a country in the Middle East. Six percent of the Eastern Hemisphere immigration quota could be filled by such refugees. In 1976 this preference was also opened to Western Hemisphere refugees, and in 1978 the refugee quota was set at a flat 17,400 aliens per year.

Despite this new preference category, the parole power was used extensively in the late 1960's and 1970's. The primary beneficiaries were hundreds of thousands of Cubans and Southeast Asians. Recognizing that the seventh preference provision was inadequate to meet refugee demand, Congress passed the Refugee Act of 1980. This legislation, codified at INA § 207, repealed the seventh preference provision and required extensive Presidential consultation with Congress in conjunction with setting the yearly refugee quotas. Specifically, a Cabinet-level representative of the President must review the refugee situation with members of the House and Senate Judiciary Committees. Among the information to be provided the Committee members is:

(1) A description of the nature of the refugee situation.

(2) A description of the number and allocation of the refugees to be admitted and an analysis of conditions within the countries from which they came.

(3) A description of the proposed plans for their movement and resettlement and the estimated cost of their movement and resettlement.

(4) An analysis of the anticipated social, economic, and demographic impact of their admission to the United States.

(5) A description of the extent to which other countries will admit and assist in the resettlement of such refugees.

(6) An analysis of the impact of the participation of the United States in the resettlement of such refugees on the foreign policy interests of the United States.

(7) Such additional information as may be appropriate or requested by such members.

For fiscal years 1980–82, the Refugee Act authorized a 50,000 refugee quota unless the President determined after congressional consultation that a larger number was justified by humanitarian concerns or was otherwise in the national interest. INA § 207(a)(1). Since 1982, the refugee quota has been determined entirely through presidential-congressional consultation. In the event of an "unforeseen emergency refugee situation," the President may, after appropriate congressional consultation, expand the admissible number of refugees if such action is justified by "grave humanitarian concerns or is otherwise in the national interest." INA § 207(b). In 1990, for example, the Presidential Determination allowed for the admission of 125,000 refugees.

While the Refugee Act of 1980 has provided a more realistic framework for congressional involvement in the refugee area, it has experienced problems. Soon after its passage in 1980, the Mariel boatlift brought over 100,000 Cubans to the U.S. During the same period thousands of Haitian boat people came to this country. The Carter Administration eventually again resorted to the parole process to handle this influx, later asking for special authorizing legislation from Congress. Section 202 of the Immigration Reform and Control Act of 1986 provided eligibility for permanent resident status for certain Cuban and Haitian entrants who have continuously resided in the United States since before January 1, 1982.

§ 4–6.2   Suspension of Deportation

Until recently, Congress was also a key actor in suspension of deportation proceedings. Pursuant to INA § 244, the Attorney General has the discretion to suspend deportation of an alien and adjust his or her status to that of an alien lawfully admitted for permanent residence in situations where the alien is of good moral character, has been continuously present in the U.S. for a requisite period, and where deportation would cause extreme hardship. The Attorney General was required to report to Congress on the first day of each calendar month in which it is in session with a complete and detailed statement of the facts and pertinent provisions of law in the case.

Before *INS v. Chadha* (Sup.Ct.1983), Congress was authorized to revoke the suspension of deportation through either a resolution or concurrent resolution, depending on the statutory section used for suspension of deportation by the Attorney General. Congress had until the end of the succeeding legislative session to take such action. In *Chadha,* the Supreme Court found this legislative veto provision to be unconstitutional as a violation of the separation of powers doctrine. In the aftermath of *Chadha,* the Immigration and Technical Corrections Act of 1988 repealed the statute which provided for suspension of deportation decisions to be overruled by Congress.

CHAPTER 5

IMMIGRANT VISAS

§ 5–1 INTRODUCTION

All aliens admitted to the United States fall into one of two categories: (1) persons who wish to enter for a limited period of time and usually for a limited purpose (known as "nonimmigrants") and (2) persons who want to become permanent residents of the U.S. (known as "immigrants"). The Immigration and Nationality Act (INA) defines a series of nonimmigrant and immigrant classifications by which aliens may enter the U.S. The INA also provides separate grounds for barring entry ("exclusion") and grounds for removing aliens who have already entered ("deportation") along with the associated procedures for entry, exclusion, and deportation.

Any alien desiring to enter the United States is presumed to be an immigrant and therefore must qualify for one of the classes of immigrant visas or demonstrate that s/he is a nonimmigrant. INA § 101(a)(15). Immigrant visas are divided into two categories: visas subject to numerical limitations and visas which are not. Visas not subject to numerical limitations are granted to immediate relatives (spouses and children) of U.S. citizens, resident aliens returning from temporary visits abroad, and former U.S. citizens (discussed in § 5–4, *infra*). INA § 201(b). Visas subject to numerical limitations are granted to persons who qualify for family-sponsored, employment-related, or diversity immigrant

102

visas. It is presumed that every person entering the U.S. is an immigrant, whose visa is subject to numerical limitations, unless the person can establish entitlement to another classification. INA § 203(f).

§ 5–2   VISAS NOT SUBJECT TO NUMERICAL LIMITATIONS

§ 5–2.1   Immediate Relatives of U.S. Citizens

The 1990 Act authorizes the issuance of 226,000 family-sponsored preference visas, as well as 239,000 visas granted to immediate relatives. If more than 239,000 immediate relatives apply, however, the total family-sponsored immigration will exceed the 465,000 numerical limit. The law does allow "piercing" the 465,000 ceiling if the volume of immediate relatives so requires. This level of immediate relative visas is not expected to occur until the late 1990's. INA § 203(c).

An alien may receive a visa as an immediate relative of a U.S. citizen if the person is a child, spouse, or parent of the citizen. INA § 201(b). To qualify as a "child" of a U.S. citizen, the person must be unmarried, under 21 years of age, and either a legitimate child, stepchild, illegitimate child, adopted child, an orphan adopted abroad, or an orphan coming to the United States to be adopted. INA § 101(b)(1). The legitimate child category includes those children born out of wedlock who were later legitimated (granted full legal status) under the laws of either the child's or the father's residence or domicile. The child must have been under 18 and in legal custody of the legitimating parent or parents at the time of legitimation. Children are most often legitimated through marriage of the child's natural parents. The INS interpreted "legitimated" to include a child born out of wedlock who has been accorded legal rights identical to a child born in wedlock. In *De Los Santos v. INS* (2d Cir.1982), the Court of Appeals upheld this interpretation as consistent with the language and purpose of the INA. The stepchild must have been less than 18 years of age at the time of the marriage creating the relationship. Before 1986, an illegitimate child could qualify for a visa only through the relation to its natural mother, and not through its father. The Supreme Court upheld the constitutionality of this discrimination, affirming the government's broad power to expel or exclude aliens. *Fiallo v. Bell* (Sup.Ct.1977). The Immigration Reform and Control Act of 1986, however, provided that an illegitimate child may qualify for a visa through the relation to its natural mother, or to its natural father "if the father has or had a bona fide parent-child relationship with the person." INA § 101(b)(1)(D).

An adopted child may receive a visa if the child was under 16 years of age at the time of adoption and has resided with the adopting parents for two or more years. A child qualifies as an orphan if both parents have died, disappeared, or abandoned the child, or if the sole or surviving parent is incapable of providing proper care and has in writing irrevocably released the child for emigration and adoption. The orphan must be adopted or be coming to the United States to be adopted by a U.S. citizen and spouse jointly, or by an unmarried U.S. citizen at least 25 years of age. If adopted abroad by an unmarried U.S. citizen, that citizen must have personally observed the child prior to or during the adoption proceedings.

A parent who has any of the relationships described under the definition of "child" meets the statutory definition of a "parent," INA § 101(b)(2), provided the child is not over 21 years old. INA § 201(b). If the child is a citizen by reason of adoption by U.S. citizens, or if the child qualifies as an orphan, the child's natural parents are barred from claiming any rights to a visa because of the child's citizenship. INA § 101(b)(1)(E) & (F).

In order to receive a visa as the spouse of a U.S. citizen, the alien must have a "valid and subsisting marriage" with that citizen. The validity of the marriage is generally determined by the laws of the country where the marriage took place. The INA defines the term "spouse" in the negative by identifying who cannot qualify as a spouse. INA § 101(a)(35). A spousal relationship cannot be created through a proxy marriage unless the marriage has been consummated. Marriages adverse to public health and morals, such as incestuous or polygamous marriages, cannot create the necessary relationship.

Sham marriages, that is, marriages motivated by a desire to confer an immigration benefit, do not provide the requisite relationship, regardless of their validity in the country where the marriage took place. The INS and the Board of Immigration Appeals originally denied spousal petitions when it determined that the parties "did not intend to establish a life together at the time they were married" (*Bark v. INS* (9th Cir.1975)) or that the marriage was "factually dead" or nonviable at the time of petitioning. The Court of Appeals in *Dabaghian v. Civiletti* (9th Cir.1979), however, rejected the "factually dead" test and held that if the marriage is not a sham or fraudulent from its inception, it is valid for adjustment of status purposes until legally dissolved. Subsequent separation of the spouses alone, therefore, should not be the sole basis for denying a spousal petition.

The Immigration Marriage Fraud Amendments of 1986 attempt to deter immigration-related marriage fraud. The Fraud Amendments impose a two-year conditional residency requirement on alien spouses and "sons and daughters" before they may obtain permanent resident status on the basis of a "qualifying marriage" to a U.S. citizen or permanent resident alien, if the marriage is less than two years old at the time of obtaining such status. To obtain permanent status, the couple must file a petition within the last 90 days of the conditional status period. The INS will then interview the couple to ascertain that (a) the "qualifying marriage" was not entered into "for the purpose of procuring an alien's entry as an immigrant"; (b) the marriage had not been judicially annulled or terminated, other than through the death of a spouse; or (c) a fee or other consideration other than attorney's fees was not given for the filing of the alien's petition. INA § 216.

If the Attorney General makes a favorable determination, conditional status is removed and lawful permanent resident status granted. If the Attorney General makes an unfavorable determination, or if the couple fails to file a petition without good cause shown, the conditional resident status is terminated. The alien spouse and children are then deportable. The Attorney General, however, may allow a hardship waiver and grant permanent resident status if the alien demonstrates that extreme hardship would result if s/he were deported. A waiver is also available if the alien can prove that her/his terminated marriage was undertaken in good faith, and that the alien was not at fault for failing to file a proper petition to have the conditional status removed. In addition, the Attorney General may grant a waiver if a good faith marriage resulted in the battery of or "extreme cruelty" to the alien spouse or the couple's child, again assuming the alien was not at fault for failing to file the required petition or appear for a personal interview. INA § 216(c)(4). This provision was designed to remove the incentive for an alien to stay in an abusive relationship in order to maintain an immigration status. Concern, however, was expressed that this waiver provision would be susceptible to fraud. Hence, the alien must provide evidence, including professional evaluations, to support a waiver petition. 56 Fed.Reg. 22635–01.

The Marriage Fraud Amendments seem to suggest that if an alien and U.S. citizen or permanent resident spouse married with the intention of establishing a life together, as required by the pre–1986 standard, but also married, in part, "for the purpose of procuring [the] alien's entry as an immigrant," that alien might be deportable. The words "the purpose" may, however, be read to mean "the sole purpose" in which case the alien would not be deportable.

An alien who marries while in exclusion or deportation proceedings may not obtain immediate relative or preference status by reason of that marriage until the alien has resided outside the United States for two years following the marriage date. INA § 204(h). An exception to this foreign residency requirement applies if the alien establishes by "clear and convincing evidence" that the marriage was undertaken in good faith and not for the purpose of evading immigration laws, and further, that no fee was paid in consideration of the petition. INA § 245(e). The Fraud Amendments impose criminal penalties for immigration-related marriage fraud of not more than five years and/or not more than $250,000 in fines, and make marriage fraud an additional ground for deportation as well as a perpetual bar to permanent residence.

§ 5–3 VISAS SUBJECT TO NU- MERICAL LIMITATIONS

Prior to the 1990 Act, visas subject to numerical limitations were divided into six preference and one nonpreference categories. Any visas remaining after all preference visas were granted were allocated to nonpreference immigrants. Because no nonpreference visas had been issued since 1978, the 1990 Act eliminated the nonpreference category altogether. 1990 Act § 162, *amending* INA § 203.

The 1990 Act increases worldwide immigration levels to 700,000 per year for three years, after which the limit decreases to 675,000 annually. Visas subject to numerical limitations are divided among family-sponsored, employment-related, and, in 1995, diversity immigrants. INA § 201(a). Additional visas are available to the spouses and children of formerly undocumented aliens who benefited from IRCA's amnesty program; this provision is effective through 1994. More visas also are available for certain employees of U.S. businesses operating in Hong Kong, their spouse, and their children. 1990 Act §§ 112, 124, *amending* INA § 203.

Family-sponsored and employment-related immigrant visas are also subject to per-country numerical caps; the 1990 Act creates a series of calculations necessary to determine these limits. See INA § 202. Generally, the per-country ceiling will be at least 25,000, and does not count visas granted to immediate relatives. In an attempt to ease the backlog of second preference admissions (spouses and minor children of permanent resident aliens), particularly from Mexico, the 1990 Act exempts 75% of the second preference limitation for Mexico.

Visas are charged to a country based on the alien's country of birth—even if the alien has become a citizen of another country. INA § 202(b). If charging the alien's visa number to the country of birth would result in separation of the family, in the case of a spouse or child, the visa may be charged to the country of the accompanying spouse or parent. This rule, however, does not apply to aliens born in a country other than the parent's country of residence, or to aliens born in the U.S. The former are charged to the country of their parents' birth and the latter are charged to their country of citizenship or if none, to the country of parental residence. The U.S. Department of State, Bureau of Consular Affairs, publishes a monthly visa bulletin that summarizes the availability of visas subject to numerical limitations, and lists any countries which have filled their allotments.

§ 5–3.1 Preference Visas

Prior to the 1990 Act, visas subject to numerical limitations were divided into six preference categories. The 1990 Act separates family-sponsored immigrant visas from employment-related visas and creates new, though often only slightly modified, categories for each. Family-sponsored immigrants are allotted 226,000 annually with a somewhat flexible maximum of 465,000, while employment-related visas are allocated 140,000 per year (see § 5–3.1, *infra*).

In an effort to avoid separation of nuclear families seeking to immigrate, the law provides that if the spouse or child of an alien granted a family-sponsored, employment-related, or diversity immigrant visa, cannot otherwise gain an immigrant visa, the spouse or child is admitted in the same preference category and the same priority as the principal alien. To obtain this derivative status, however, the spouse or child must be "accompanying" or "following to join" the principal alien. INA § 203(d). A spouse or child acquired after the principal alien obtains permanent resident status, however, is not given this derivative status and must apply under the second preference family-sponsored class, discussed below.

a. Family-Sponsored Preferences

In addition to the minimum of 226,000 family-sponsored immigrant visas, any unused employment-related visas from the previous fiscal year are available in this category. The four family-sponsored preference categories are as follows:

First Preference—Unmarried sons and daughters of U.S. citizens—23,400 visas plus any unused visas from the other family-sponsored preference classes.

Second Preference—Spouses, children, and unmarried sons and daughters of lawful permanent resident aliens—minimum of 114,200 visas. Separate numerical limits exist for:

    A. Spouses and children—87,934 (77% of the visas under this preference);

B. Unmarried sons and daughters (at least 21 years old)—26,266 (33% of the visas issued under this preference).

Third Preference—Married sons and daughters of U.S. citizens—23,400 plus any unused visas from the first and second family-sponsored preference categories.

Fourth Preference—Brothers and sisters of U.S. citizens, if the citizen is at least 21 years old—65,000 plus any unused visas from the first, second, and third family-sponsored preference categories.

The use of the term "sons and daughters" in the family-sponsored preference classes is designed to avoid the statute's definition of "child," since "children" of U.S. citizens are exempt from numerical limitations as immediate relatives. Hence, a son or daughter is a "child" of the petitioner who has passed the age limits for the definition of child. The term "unmarried" used in the first and second preference classes is defined as the marital state of the alien at the time of the visa issuance, regardless of any previous marriage. INA § 101(a)(39). The term "brothers and sisters" used in the fourth family-sponsored class is undefined, but may be derived from the defined term "children" from common "parents."

b. Employment–Related Preferences

The 1990 Act allocates 140,000 visas, plus any unused family-sponsored visas, to employment-related immigration. Prior to the 1990 Act, only 54,000 employment-related visas were available. Hence, the 1990 Act dramatically increases the visas available for employment-related immigration, and allocates them among the following five preference categories:

First Preference—Priority Workers—28.6% (40,000 at present) of the total worldwide level plus any unused visas from the fourth and fifth employment-related preference categories. INA § 101(a)(44). Priority workers consist of:

    A. Persons of "extraordinary ability" in the sciences, arts, education, business, or athletics;

    B. Outstanding professors and researchers;

    C. Certain multinational executives and managers.

Second Preference—Professionals holding advanced degrees, or persons of exceptional ability in the sciences, arts, or business—28.6% (40,000 at present) of the total worldwide level plus any unused visas from the first preference category. Unless waived by the Attorney General, an alien seeking to enter the U.S. under a second employment-related visa must have proof of a job offer.

Third Preference—Skilled workers in short supply, professionals holding baccalaureate degrees, and other workers in short supply—28.6% (40,000 at present) of the total worldwide level plus any unused visas from the first and second employment-related preference categories; not more than 10,000 visas can go to "other workers" from this preference category.

Fourth Preference—Certain Special Immigrants—7.1% (10,000 at present) of the total worldwide level. This category includes the special immigrants detailed in § 5–4, *infra.* Principally, this preference category is comprised of religious workers, as well as former employees of the U.S. government and international organizations. The numerical allotment for special immigrants is expected to be sufficient for the next several years. INA § 101(a)(27)(C) through (J).

Fifth Preference—Employment Creation Visas— 7.1% (10,000 at present) of the total worldwide level. This preference category is comprised of investors who will create at least ten U.S. jobs by investing in a new commercial enterprise benefiting the U.S. economy. The minimum required investment is $1 million, though it may be as little as $500,000 if the investment is in a rural area, or an area of high unemployment. If the commercial enterprise is located in an area of low unemployment, the required investment may be raised by the INS to $3 million. The INS has issued regulations setting the required investment at $1 million. To avoid fraud, investors are accorded only conditional permanent resident status for two years, after which a review of the investment will be undertaken.

"Extraordinary ability" is defined as a "level of expertise indicating that the individual is one of that small percentage who have risen to the very top of the field of endeavor." 56 Fed.Reg. 60897–01. The 1990 Act requires that the alien's extraordinary ability be reflected through "sustained national or international acclaim" and extensive documentation of the alien's contribution to her/his field. INA § 203(b)(1). The phrase "members of professions" lacks statutory definition, so case law and the regulations must be consulted for any particular profession.

The employment-related preference categories instead focus on the educational attainment of the alien. A profession is generally an occupation which requires a high level of specialization. Likewise, "exceptional ability" means a degree of expertise significantly above that ordinarily encountered in the arts, sciences, or business. For example, an average musician is not included, but one with national recognition is. *Cf. Lee v. INS* (9th Cir.1969). The possession of a degree, diploma, certificate, or license to practice a particular profession is not, by itself, sufficient evidence of exceptional ability. INA § 203(b)(2).

c. Diversity Immigrants

The 1990 Act attempted to regain the flexibility that the nonpreference categories were intended to create under the INA, while at the same time, reverse the drastic reductions in immigration from European countries, particularly Ireland. The 1986 Immigration Reform and Control Act established the NP–5 pilot lottery program, through which persons from "adversely affected" countries, that is, countries contributing disproportionately few immigrants, could gain immigrant visas. Approximately 1.3 million people applied for these 10,000 visas. In 1988, Congress increased the allotment from 10,000 over two years, to 20,000—again in an effort to assist the entry of aliens from "underrepresented" countries.

The 1990 Act establishes a permanent diversity immigration program, which will begin in 1995. The new law uses a complicated formula to determine whether in the previous five years, the alien's country of origin was a "low-admission" country. If so, the alien is eligible for one of the 55,000 visas annually allocated to diversity immigrants. These countries were previously identified under the NP–5 program; under the 1990 Act, aliens seeking entry apply under the AA–1 program. The actual selection process is still a random lottery, and the alien may file only one petition per year. Hence, it is a highly uncertain way to seek an immigrant visa. Furthermore, an alien seeking a diversity visa must have attained a high school education or its equivalent, or have at least two years of work experience in an occupation which requires at least two years of training or experience.

d. Inhabitants of Hong Kong

The 1990 Act also contains several specific provisions aimed at addressing a particular group's needs. One such group is Hong Kong residents who may want to immigrate to the U.S. after the return of Hong Kong to the People's Republic of China. The 1990 Act increases the allocation for immigration from Hong Kong to 10,-000 (from 5,000) for the first three years of the act, after which the level rises to 20,000. 1990 Act § 103. These provisions are also aimed at benefiting employees of the U.S. government and certain U.S. businesses in Hong Kong. 1990 Act § 152. In addition, the new law extends visas issued to Hong Kong residents until January 1, 2002, allowing them to immigrate if conditions after 1997 so dictate, while providing them with the security to stay in the meantime.

§ 5–4 SPECIAL IMMIGRANTS

Special immigrant visas are available to resident aliens returning from temporary trips abroad; former U.S. citizens; ministers of recognized religious denominations, their spouse, and their children; certain religious workers other than ministers seeking to enter the U.S. before October 1994, their spouse, and their children; employees of the U.S. government abroad with 15 or more years of service; certain employees of the

Panama Canal Company or Canal Zone government, their spouse, and their children; certain officers and employees of international organizations, their spouse and their children; graduates of foreign medical schools who are fully licensed to practice in a state and have been practicing in such state since January 1978 or earlier, their spouse, and their children; and certain aliens declared dependent on a juvenile court in the U.S. and deemed eligible for foster care. INA § 101(a)(27).

Until the 1990 Act, immigrant visas issued to special immigrants were not subject to numerical limitations. The new law, however, leaves only those special immigrant visas issued to resident aliens returning from temporary trips abroad and to former U.S. citizens free from numerical limits. INA §§ 201(b)(1), 203(b)(4). The remaining special immigrants are limited to 10,000 visas per year. Aside from the several hundred thousand lawful permanent residents returning from temporary trips abroad, special immigrants use approximately six thousand visas annually. Hence, the 1990 Act's limit should be sufficient for the next several years. The special immigrant group is the subject of frequent legislative modifications, so the possible inclusion or exclusion of any particular alien must regularly be checked against the statutory language.

Commuter aliens, or "green card commuters," are an interesting group included in the special immigrant category. Commuter aliens are those aliens who reside in Mexico or Canada, but who are admitted into the U.S. as immigrants on a daily or seasonal basis for employment. These aliens are placed under the special immigrant category of resident aliens returning from temporary trips abroad. The great majority of these workers commute from Mexico. 8 C.F.R. § 211.5.

§ 5–5   PROCEDURAL REQUIREMENTS

§ 5–5.1   Petitions and Certification

Before a consular officer can issue a visa based on immediate relative status or on one of the family-sponsored or employment-related preference categories, that officer must have received a petition, approved by the INS, on behalf of the applying alien. INA §§ 201(f), 204. For the immediate relative visa and for the family-sponsored preference visas, the petition is filed by the U.S. citizen or resident alien, who claims the requisite relation to the prospective immigrant, on Form I–130 or, for an adopted orphan, on Form I–600. One exception is the Amerasian children provision of the INA, which allows the alien or any person on behalf of the alien to file the petition. Any person fathered by a U.S. citizen, who was born after 1950 and before October 22, 1982, in Korea, Vietnam, Laos, Kampuchea, or Thailand, may file or have filed on her/his behalf a visa petition under the immediate relative or first or third family-sponsored preference categories. INA § 204(f).

Form I–130 is submitted by the relative of the alien to the INS office or Regional Processing Center having jurisdiction over the relative's residence. 8 C.F.R. § 204.1(a)(3)(i). For example, the wife of an alien might submit Form I–130 on behalf of her husband. If the relative resides outside of the U.S., the nearest consulate must be consulted to determine the proper place to file the petition. 8 C.F.R. § 204.1(a)(3)(ii). The petition must be accompanied by proof of the petitioner's U.S. citizenship or permanent resident status and by documents which prove the petitioner's relationship to the alien (*e.g.*, a marriage certificate in the case of a spouse). 8 C.F.R. § 204.2.

The date on which a Form I–130 visa petition is filed with the Attorney General for a family-sponsored or employment-related preference visa is the petitioner's priority date. This date determines when the alien will be considered for visa issuance in relation to others in the same preference category and from the same country. Depending on their preference category, residents from some countries may have to wait over 10 years. Others may not need to wait at all. If an alien's temporary immigration status changes during the waiting period or even if the alien has no temporary immigration status, the alien may keep his original priority date as long as s/he still meets the criteria of the approved petition.

The 1986 Immigration Fraud Amendments attempt to eliminate benefits gained through a second preference petition as a result of a prior sham marriage. A permanent resident spouse who immigrated through marriage to a prior spouse is prohibited from petitioning on behalf of a new alien spouse for five years after attaining permanent resident status. This condition is eliminated if the marriage was terminated because the prior spouse died or the permanent resident can meet the burden of proving that the prior marriage was not fraudulent. INA § 204(a)(2).

If an adopted orphan seeks admission, petition Form I–600 is used and the documents previously mentioned must be submitted along with proof that the child is an orphan. This petition must also include a home study, conducted by an authorized or licensed public adoption agency, recommending that the proposed place of residence is a suitable environment for the orphan. 8 C.F.R. § 204.2.

For employment-related preference categories, the alien or an employer must file a petition on behalf of the alien on Form I–140, before the status will be granted. For aliens with extraordinary ability, the alien or any person on behalf of the alien may file the petition. INA § 204(a)(1)(E). Similarly, diversity immigrants and aliens in the fourth and fifth employment-related preference categories may file their own petitions. INA § 204(a)(1)(E) through (G). An employer must file the petition for an alien seeking immigrant status under second and third employment-related preference categories. INA § 204(a)(1)(D). The Attorney General may waive the job offer requirement for aliens in the second category if the waiver is deemed to be within the national interest. An approved labor certification is required before a second or third employment-related preference petition can be filed with the INS.

The Form I–140 petition is submitted to the INS office in the district where the alien will be employed or to the INS office where the alien will reside. 8 C.F.R. § 204.-1(d)(1). This petition must be submitted with an approved labor certification, unless the alien is the beneficiary of a Schedule A filing or is precertified. 8 C.F.R. § 204.2(i)(4). A second employment-related preference petition must also include documents that prove the beneficiary's special ability, such as diplomas and licenses or records of national or international recognition, including any recognized prizes or awards received. 8 C.F.R. § 204.2(i)(1).

An approved labor certification is required for second and third employment-related preference classes. INA § 212(a)(5). The labor certification will not be issued unless the Secretary of Labor determines that: (a) there are not sufficient qualified workers available at the place where the alien will be employed; and (b) that employment of the alien will not adversely affect wages or working conditions of similarly employed U.S. workers. The labor certification application is initiated on Form ETA 750, which requires a statement from the employer describing the job, qualifications, and wages as well as a statement from the alien of her/his qualifications. The application for labor certification is initially handled by a local state job service office that acts on behalf of the Department of Labor.

The Department of Labor has simplified the certification process by issuing two lists of occupations in 20 C.F.R. § 656, Schedule A (including professions such as doctors, nurses, and ministers) and Schedule B (including unskilled labor such as clerks, janitors, drivers, etc.). If the alien's occupation is included in Schedule A, Form ETA 750 may be submitted directly to the INS or the U.S. consular office abroad along with the preference petition. 20 C.F.R. § 656.22(a). When the INS determines that the occupation is on Schedule A, certification is granted without further process. If the alien's occupation is included in Schedule B, no certification is available, unless a special waiver is obtained from the Department of Labor Regional Certifying Office. 20 C.F.R. § 656.23. Such waivers are very rare. The 1990 Act creates a pilot program in which the Secretary of Labor must publish a list of at least ten occupations with labor shortages or surpluses. Though designed to replace the existing two Schedules, the new list is expected to include the same occupations. The INS' determination of the alien's qualification for Schedule A is final; review is not available.

For occupations not listed on either schedule, Form ETA 750 must be submitted to the local state job service office where the alien will be employed. 20 C.F.R. § 656.21. Along with Form ETA 750, the employer must include documents showing the employer's unsuccessful attempts to find a U.S. worker for the job. The employer must have advertised the job, describing the job with particularity, and offering the prevailing wage rate, working conditions, and requirements for the occupation in the region of intended employment. The employer must also have offered wages and employment terms and conditions as favorable as those offered to the alien. 20 C.F.R. § 656. The validity of these regulations was upheld in *Production Tool Corp. v. Employment and Training Administration* (7th Cir.1982). Furthermore, the employer must document that all U.S. applicants for the job were rejected solely for lawful, job-related reasons. 20 C.F.R. § 656.21(b)(7).

The local state job service office will process the application and forward it to the certifying officer of the Regional Office of the Department of Labor for final determination. If the certifying officer decides to issue a certification, Form ETA 750 will be returned to the employer with an official certification stamp. 20 C.F.R. § 656.28. The INS will then examine the employer's actual visa application. Despite labor certification, the INS may still deny a visa petition because of fraud or misrepresentation by the employer or alien, the alien's inadequate qualifications for the job, or the employer's inability to pay the offered wage.

If the certifying officer decides that the employer's petition does not meet all the requirements, s/he will issue a Notice of Findings, which is a preliminary denial of certification. 20 C.F.R. § 656.24(b). The employer then has 35 days to comply with the requirements or to submit a written argument rebutting the bases of the negative determination. 20 C.F.R. § 656.25(c). If unsuccessful, the certifying officer will issue a Final Determination, denying certification. 20 C.F.R. § 656.25(g). The employer is entitled to a review of the denial by the Board of Alien Labor Certification Appeals, which may take about two years. 20 C.F.R. § 656.26. If the administrative appeal is unsuccessful, judicial review in federal district court is available under the Administrative Procedure Act.

In considering labor certification, the certifying officer has substantial discretion to determine what is required for the "basic job" that the employer wishes to fill and whether the requirements listed in the employer's job description are excessive. For example, the Court of Appeals for the D.C. Circuit in *Pesikoff v. Secretary of Labor* (D.C.Cir.1974) found no abuse of discretion in denying labor certification to a live-in maid, even though there were no maids available in the area who were willing to live in. The Court held that the employer's live-in requirement was an irrelevant personal preference and that it was "well within the Secretary's discretion to ignore employer specifications which he deems ... irrelevant to the basic job which the employer desires performed." The Department of Labor has issued a Dictionary of Occupational Titles which provides the principal source of information for determining the requirements for jobs which may be the subject of labor certification.

Labor certification will be denied if an alien is self-employed or if the employer's application for certification does not clearly show that the job opportunity has been and is clearly open to any qualified U.S. worker. 20 C.F.R. § 656. In *Hall v. McLaughlin* (D.C.Cir.1989), the U.S. Court of Appeals held that no genuine employment relationship exists where the alien and the corporation were inseparable and the alien was indispensable. The court followed a two-part test for determining whether a genuine employment relationship exists. First, the court considered whether the arrangement was a "sham" and inquired whether the corporation was established for the sole purpose of obtaining labor certification for the alien. Second, the court considered the "inseparability" question: "Whether the corporation, even if legitimately established, relies so heavily on the pervasive presence and personal attributes of the alien that it would be unlikely to continue in operation without him." The court reasoned that if the alien is inseparable from the corporation, the corporation will not truly consider hiring a U.S. worker.

The employment position for which the employer seeks labor certification must also be permanent in nature. There is, however, no guarantee that aliens entering under second or third employment-related preference visas will not later change occupations and compete with U.S. workers. In *Yui Sing Tse v. INS* (9th Cir.1979), labor certification was upheld despite evidence of the alien's intent to change his occupation eventually.

All visa petitions are made under oath (INA § 204(a)(1)) and the burden of proof is always on the applicant. INA § 291. The petition may be voluntarily withdrawn at any time. Approval of a petition may be revoked if there is a change in either party's status, such as death, divorce, or loss of the job offer, prior to final decision on an application for permanent residency. 8 C.F.R. § 205.

§ 5–5.2 Visa Application for Aliens Outside the U.S.

After approval of the labor certification and preference petition, the actual visa application process begins for an alien who resides outside the United States. This process takes place at the appropriate U.S. consulate, usually in the consular district where the alien resides. 22 C.F.R. § 42.61. For the consul's initial inquiry, the applicant submits a completed Form OF–222, which is used to determine prima facie eligibility and any need for registration on a waiting list, should the visa class applied for be oversubscribed. 22 C.F.R. § 42.63. If the alien appears ineligible, the consul will inform the alien of any deficiencies in the visa application (*e.g.*, lack of labor certification) so that appropriate steps may be taken to cure the defects.

If the consular officer determines that the applicant is eligible, the consul sends the applicant a notice to assemble and submit the documents required to make the final visa determination (Form OF–169). These documents include biographic data; police, court, prison, and military records; birth and marriage certificates; passports; photographs; and evidence that the alien will not become a public charge while in the U.S. INA § 212(a)(4). When all of this information is assembled, the applicant informs the consulate and is then given the formal visa application, Form OF–230, and a scheduled appointment for the required personal appearance.

22 C.F.R. §§ 42.62–.63. The applicant completes Form OF–230 and brings it, along with all of the assembled documents and the results of a medical examination (22 C.F.R. § 42.66) to the consul at the appointed time. The consular officer reviews the documents, may fingerprint the alien (22 C.F.R. § 42.67), conducts a personal interview, and if all is in order, has the applicant sign the formal application under oath.

The consul then rules on the application, usually the same day. The authority to pass on the eligibility of an applicant belongs exclusively to the consul. INA §§ 104(a), 221(a). The principal consular officer must review any refusal to issue a visa, but there is no formal review available after that. 22 C.F.R. § 42.81. The consulate must inform the applicant of the provision of law or regulation upon which the refusal was based. 22 C.F.R. § 42.81(b). The Department of State may also review a visa denial but, other than in matters of interpretation of law, its opinion to the consul is only advisory. 22 C.F.R. § 42.81(d). The applicant has one year to overcome the objection to the visa on which the refusal was based or else the entire visa application process must be started anew. 22 C.F.R. § 42.81(e). The burden of proof is always on the applicant to establish eligibility. INA § 291.

§ 5–5.3   Visa Issuance and Entry

If the consul rules in favor of the visa applicant, the consul issues a visa from the consular office outside of the U.S. INA § 101(a)(16). The visa consists of a Form OF–155, showing the consul's approval, the applicant's completed Form OF–230, and any documents necessary in determining the applicant's identity, classification, and eligibility. 22 C.F.R. § 42.73(b). The visa is valid for a period of four months (3 years for an adopted child) and may not be extended beyond that time. 22 C.F.R. § 42.72(a) & (b). A new immigrant visa, however, may be issued to immigrants not subject to numerical limitations if they are unable to travel to the U.S. during the four month period, provided they remain qualified for the visa. 22 C.F.R. § 42.74. An immigrant subject to numerical limitations may receive a "replace" visa if the immigrant was unable to travel to the U.S. during the four month period, but only if the replacement visa is issued in the same fiscal year as the original visa and the immigrant's number was not returned to the Department of State for reissuance. 22 C.F.R. § 42.74(b). A special provision of the 1990 Act allows residents of Hong Kong to defer use of their visas until any time before January 1, 2002.

Once the immigrant actually arrives in the U.S., an immigration officer again independently examines the alien's visa eligibility. If the inspecting immigration officer finds the immigrant to be inadmissible, the officer may exclude the alien, in spite of the visa. INA § 221(h). In that case, the alien may be temporarily detained, either aboard the vessel of arrival or in the U.S. while further determination is made. 8 C.F.R. § 235.3. If the immigration officer finds the visa to be in order and the alien to be admissible, the visa is retained by the INS as a permanent record of admission. INA § 240(a). The alien is then issued a Form I–151 (green card) and becomes a permanent resident alien. 8 C.F.R. § 264(1)(b). "Green cards" are now off-white in color, but the older green ones remain valid. Although it is most often thought of as an employment permit, the green card was originally designed to serve as evidence of the alien's status as a permanent resident of the United States.

§ 5–5.4 Permanent Resident Procedures for Aliens Already Inside the U.S.

Aliens who want to immigrate are ordinarily expected to remain outside the United States until their immigrant visas are available. Nonetheless, many aliens enter this country as nonimmigrants and then apply to adjust to immigrant visa status. See INA § 245. In recent years, adjustments of status have accounted for over twenty percent of all numerically limited immigrant visas. The procedures for the visa petitions and labor certificates are precisely the same for aliens in or outside the U.S. If the alien is immediately eligible for an immigrant visa, the alien may apply to the INS office where s/he resides for the preference status and then for adjustment of status from nonimmigrant to immigrant. For several years it was the practice of the INS that if the alien was entitled to be classified under a preference category and to adjustment of status, both applications could be presented in person to the INS office. The alien was entitled to an expedited "one-step visa processing," in which the preference petition was processed immediately, and the adjustment application was processed later. The concurrent processing is not presently available, but may eventually be restarted. Under the present procedure, the INS may need several months to adjudicate the visa petition, after which the adjustment of status application may be processed. The procedures for adjustment of status applications are discussed in the last section of chapter 6 on nonimmigrant visas *infra*.

CHAPTER 6

NONIMMIGRANT VISAS

Nonimmigrant visas constitute the largest number of all visas issued by more than seventeen to one. For example, in 1989 the INS admitted 16,144,500 nonimmigrants to the United States. Most nonimmigrant visas were issued to tourists (12.1 million) and to temporary business visitors (2.5 million). Nonimmigrant visas are divided into eighteen main categories, and one special purpose category for NATO personnel, which will not be considered further. The main categories are given letter designations corresponding fairly closely with the alphabetical and numerical subdivisions of their enabling legislation, INA § 101(a)(15) and 8 C.F.R. § 214.2. Most nonimmigrant visas are not subject to numerical limitation. A significant issue with respect to each nonimmigrant category is whether the nonimmigrant may engage in employment in the U.S. without violating the terms of the visa status.

The 1990 Act changed several of the existing nonimmigrant provisions and added several more. The act created separate nonimmigrant visa status for "aliens with exceptional ability" (category O) and for athletes, artists, and entertainers (categories P, Q, R). The 1990 Act also established nonimmigrant visas for cooperative/coproduction defense workers and for aliens participating in special education training programs for disabled children.

The 1990 Act imposed numerical limitations on a number of categories that were previously unlimited. For example, the law limits temporary visas for professionals to 65,000 (H–1B category); temporary agricultural workers to 66,000 (H–2B); and performing athletes, artists, and entertainers to 25,000 (P–1). The technical amendments of 1991 deleted the numerical limitation for the P–1 classification. These numerical limitations apply only to the principal alien, not to their spouse or children. The eighteen main categories of nonimmigrants are as follows: A, career diplomats; B, temporary visitors for business and pleasure; C, aliens in transit; D, crewmembers; E, treaty traders and investors; F, students; G, international organization representatives; H, temporary workers; I, foreign media representatives; J, exchange program visitors; K, fiancé(e)s or children of U.S. citizens; L, intracompany transferees; M, students in non-academic institutions; N, parents and children of special immigrants; O, aliens with extraordinary abilities; P, entertainers; Q, cultural exchange program participants; and R, religious workers. Each is treated in greater depth below.

§ 6–1   DIPLOMATIC PERSONNEL

A–1 visas are issued to ambassadors, public ministers, career diplomatic, or consular officers, and members of their immediate families. A–2 visas are issued to other foreign government employees and officials as well as their family members. A–3 visas are for personal employees, attendants, and servants of persons holding A–1 and A–2 visas. 22 C.F.R. §§ 41.12, 41.20. A–1 and A–2 visas are valid as long as the Secretary of State extends recognition to the holder. A–3 visas are valid for not more than three years and may be extended in increments of not more than two years. 8 C.F.R. § 214.2(a). Both A–1 and A–2 visa holders may accept employment if permission is granted after submitting Form I–566. 8 C.F.R. § 214.2(a).

§ 6–2 TEMPORARY VISITORS

B–1 visas cover visitors for business purposes and B–2 deal with visitors for pleasure. For example, tourists, prospective F–1 students coming to the U.S. to select a school, and visitors entering the U.S. for medical treatment would receive B–2 visas. Frequently, visitors are issued a multiple purpose B–1/B–2 visa. Both B–1 and B–2 visas are valid for one year and are renewable in six month increments. 8 C.F.R. § 214.2(b). Neither B–1 nor B–2 visa holders may accept employment in the U.S. 8 C.F.R. § 214.1. What constitutes "employment" in violation of the B–1 or B–2 status is sometimes a difficult issue to determine. *See, e.g., Matter of Neil* (BIA 1975).

The Immigration Reform and Control Act of 1986 authorized the development of a three year pilot program to waive B–2 tourist visas for nationals from eight countries which extend reciprocal privileges and have low visa-abuse rates. INA § 217. Aliens entering the U.S. under this program receive a Form I–94W, may remain in the country no longer than 90 days, and are prohibited from adjusting their status to that of immigrant (except as immediate relatives) or to that of any other nonimmigrant classification. INA §§ 245(c), 248(4). Such aliens also waive any right to review or appeal an immigration officer's admissibility determination, or to contest, other than on the basis of an application for asylum, any action for deportation against the alien. INA § 217.

The B–1 visa is often issued when the alien does not fit any of the other nonimmigrant business categories. For the alien, the B–1 is often an easier route to entry than the other categories. Labor certification is not required for B–1 visas and the alien need not file a petition with the INS. In *International Union of Bricklayers and Allied Craftsmen v. Meese* (N.D.Cal.1985), the court held that the INS practice of issuing B–1 visas to skilled and unskilled workers "contravenes both the language and legislative intent of the Act." Those skilled and unskilled workers are explicitly excluded from B–1 eligibility; they must apply instead for H category visas. Hence, in practice, the B–1 visa will not help most workers avoid the labor certification requirement.

§ 6–3　VISITORS IN TRANSIT

The C–1 visa is for continuous travel through the U.S. which involves a layover of eight hours maximum (or the next available transport) and no more than two transfers. C–2 visas are for persons who have a right of transit to the United Nations. The C–3 visa includes foreign government officials in transit. 8 C.F.R. § 214.-2(c). Both C–2 and C–3 visas are valid for 29 days maximum and all C visas are nonrenewable. Holders of C visas may not adjust their status to any other nonimmigrant visa classification. 8 C.F.R. § 248.2(b). No employment is permitted under this visa class. 8 C.F.R. § 214.1(e).

§ 6–4 CREW MEMBERS

The D visa classification is for crewmembers serving in a capacity required for normal operation on board a vessel. The D–1 visa is issued to employees remaining with their vessel; the D–2 is issued to discharged employees who intend to work on another vessel. 8 C.F.R. § 252. D visa holders are prohibited, with few exceptions, from engaging in longshore work in the ports or coastal waters of the U.S.

D visa holders cannot be admitted into the U.S. during a strike or lockout involving the alien's employer. The Attorney General, however, may parole an alien into the U.S. if the entry is in the interest of national security. The alien may also be admitted if s/he worked for the employer throughout the year preceding the labor dispute. Both the D–1 and D–2 visas are valid for a maximum of 29 days and are non-renewable. 8 C.F.R. § 252.1(d). Holders of this visa are not allowed to adjust their status to any other visa. INA § 248.

§ 6–5 TREATY TRADERS
AND INVESTORS

E–1 visas are for treaty traders and their spouses and children, while E–2 visas are for treaty investors and their spouses and children. These nonimmigrants are entitled to enter the U.S. pursuant to treaties of commerce existing between the U.S. and the alien's country. Under the 1990 Act, aliens from countries lacking a treaty with the U.S. are still eligible for E treaty alien status if that country grants reciprocal benefits to U.S. nationals. Examples include Australia, Canada, and Sweden. This visa is somewhat unusual in that it does not require a petition to be filed with the INS before application is made at the embassy or consulate.

Certain managers, executives, or employees possessing essential skills who work for organizations, individual investors/traders, or companies (otherwise meeting the requirements for E classification) may also be admitted as E–1 and E–2 visa holders, with their families. They must be entering the U.S. either to engage in substantial trade in goods or services (E–1) including trade in services or trade in technology, or to develop an enterprise involving substantial amounts of capital. INA § 101(a)(15)(E). "Substantial" trade refers to both the volume of trade in goods or services conducted and the monetary value of the transactions. "Substantial Trade" is defined as trading activities with the U.S. that comprise more than 50% of the alien's total business transactions in the U.S., and proof of a continued course of international trade. 56 Fed.Reg. 50349–02. Proof of numerous transactions, although each is of small monetary value, might establish the requisite continuing course of international trade. 9 Foreign Affairs Manual of State Department § 41.51 n. 4.2 (1988). *Matter of Walsh and Pollard* (BIA 1988) held that no minimum dollar amount is required to meet the substantiality requirement. Applicants have strengthened their case for this visa by showing that the investment will lead to the employment of several U.S. citizens and permanent residents. Under the 1990 Act, employment creation *immigrant* visas are available to individuals who invest at least $1 million and create ten U.S. jobs. Hence, the threshold for an E–1 most likely will be consistent with this amount. E–2 status is generally denied if the expected return on the alien's investment will provide a living only for the alien and her/his family. E–1 and

E–2 visa holders are permitted employment authorization consistent with the purposes for which they were admitted. Although family members of E visa holders are not permitted to be employed, in a unique policy, this rule will not be enforced if they work without authorization, as would be the case with family members of most other nonimmigrants. Both E–1 and E–2 visas are valid for one year and are renewable indefinitely, as long as the alien continues in the same capacity for which the visa was granted. 8 C.F.R. § 214.2(e).

§ 6–6 ACADEMIC STUDENTS

The F–1 visa is for the academic student, who enters the U.S. temporarily solely to pursue a full course of study at an established academic high school, college, university, seminary, conservatory, or language school. F–2 visas are for the spouse and children of the student. INA § 101(a)(15)(F). Both visas are normally granted for the duration of status as a student or for the time necessary to complete the course of study. 8 C.F.R. § 214.2(f)(5). A student who has been in academic status for eight consecutive academic years or who has remained in one educational level for an extended period of time must apply for an extension of stay to continue studies beyond this time. 8 C.F.R. § 214.2(f)(7). See chapter 7 for a complete discussion of all aspects of student visas.

§ 6–7 INTERNATIONAL ORGANIZATION REPRESENTATIVES

This class of visas is subdivided into five separate groups. G–1 is for principal representatives of governments, recognized *de jure* by the U.S., to an international organization, their staff, and their family members. G–2 covers other accredited representatives of foreign governments to international organizations, their staff, and their family members. G–3 includes aliens who would qualify for G–1 or G–2, except that their government is not recognized *de jure* by the U.S.; G–3 also includes their family members. G–4 visas are for officers and employees of international organizations and their family members, and G–5 is for the attendants, servants, and personal employees of G–1, G–2, G–3, and G–4 visa holders, as well as members of their immediate families. INA § 101(a)(15)(G). All G visas are normally issued for one year and are renewable. Only family members of the G–4 class may accept employment in the U.S. subject to approval of the INS. 8 C.F.R. § 214.-2(g)(2). The Immigration Reform and Control Act of 1986 authorized the adjustment to special immigrant status for certain G–4 nonimmigrants who had resided and been physically present in the U.S. for specified periods of time, including: unmarried sons and daughters of officers or employees of international organizations, retired employees of international organizations and their spouses, and surviving spouses of deceased employees of such organizations. INA § 101(a)(27)(I). The 1986 Act affords nonimmigrant status under a N–visa category to certain parents and children of aliens given special immigrant status. INA § 101(a)(15)(N). See § 6–14.

§ 6–8 TEMPORARY WORKERS

H nonimmigrant visas are designed principally to help employers meet an immediate and temporary need for labor. The 1990 Act made a number of changes to this nonimmigrant visa category.

Aliens entering the U.S. temporarily to perform services as registered nurses are classified as H–1A nonimmigrants. Each alien seeking H–1A status must have the Secretary of Labor certify that an unexpired attestation is on file as to each facility, other than a private household worksite, for which the alien will work as a nurse. INA § 101(a)(15)(H)(i).

Prior to the 1990 Act, the H–1B category consisted of professionals and persons of exceptional ability in the sciences and arts. Under the 1990 Act, however, the H–1B classification was redefined to include aliens working in "specialty occupations." To qualify as a member of a specialty occupation, the alien's job must require theoretical and practical application of a highly specialized body of knowledge. In addition, to satisfy credential requirements, an alien seeking an H–1B nonimmigrant visa must either:

(1) obtain a state license to practice in the occupation, if such a license is required to practice;

(2) have attained a bachelor's or higher degree in the specific specialty; or

(3) have attained experience in the specialty equivalent to the completion of the bachelor's degree, as well as positions of expertise which demonstrate specialty.

The 1990 Act's allowance of experience as a substitute for a formal degree is the culmination of an earlier trend within the INS which discouraged such equivalencies. *Compare Matter of Portugues do Atlantico Information Bureau, Inc.* (BIA 1984) with 8 C.F.R. § 214.2.

The 1990 Act for the first time subjects H–1B visas to a numerical limit of 65,000 annually. In a requirement somewhat similar to the nurse (H–1A) classification, H–1B visa holders are also required to have a Labor Condition application filed with the Secretary of Labor by the proposed employer. The application consists of assertions of the employer that the wages to be paid equal or exceed the prevailing average for the occupation, that the position's working conditions will not have an adverse effect on similarly situated U.S. workers, and that no labor dispute or lockout exists at the place of employment. A copy of this application must be conspicuously posted at the principal place of business. A complaint procedure exists to permit adversely affected parties to challenge these assertions. Civil penalties, backpay awards, and debarment from filing other immigration petitions may be assessed for successful complaints. An H–1B visa holder's admission is limited to three years.

Often, aliens seeking H visa status (and other nonimmigrant categories) wish to immigrate to the U.S. Because most nonimmigrant visas require an intention to return to the alien's home country (sometimes referred to as "nonimmigrant intent"), many aliens have had either to hide their intent, or postpone their plans. The 1990 Act recognizes the propriety of this "dual intent." First, the act removes the requirement that H visa holders have a foreign residence with no intent to abandon. INA § 101(a)(15)(H). Second, aliens seeking H–1B visa status are exempted from the presumption of immigrant intent that usually accompanies the application process. INA § 214(b). Third, the act explicitly allows the H nonimmigrant to seek permanent resident status, without affecting the terms of the H visa. INA § 214(h).

H–1 visa holders are admissible for an initial period of not more than three years. H–2 visa classification covers any alien coming to the U.S. temporarily for work of a temporary nature and includes seasonal workers of all types. The Immigration Reform and Control Act of 1986 (IRCA) created a "H–2A" nonimmigrant visa classification for temporary agricultural workers. Perishable crop growers complained that the procedures for obtaining H–2 workers were too slow and unpredictable for their industry. They feared that, because of their dependence upon undocumented alien workers, implementation of the employer sanction provisions of IRCA would put an end to some of their operations. In response, IRCA provided for expedited procedures for approving grower requests for foreign agricultural workers and for review of denied applications. The employer, however, must still first make an effort to recruit domestic workers. INA § 216.

The H–2B nonimmigrant visa category is specifically for aliens entering temporarily to fill a *temporary* position. The 1990 Act limits H–2 visas to 25,000 annually. The employer must attain a temporary labor certification which is an abbreviated form of the procedure described at § 5–5.1.

The 1990 Act authorizes the Attorney General to provide nonimmigrant status to an alien who enters the U.S. to participate in a special education training program. This program must provide practical training and experience in educating children with physical, mental, or emotional disabilities. INA § 223(a)(2). The alien must not have the intent to immigrate and the visa is valid for a maximum of eighteen months. No more than fifty aliens per fiscal year may enter the U.S. under this classification.

The H–3 visa covers trainees coming to the U.S. for up to two years to receive training not available in the alien's own country, except graduate medical training and training programs designed to provide employment are excluded. H–3 visas include aliens coming to the U.S. to receive training in the education of children with physical, mental, or emotional disabilities. 56 Fed.Reg. 50349–02. H–4 visas are issued to the spouse and children of H–1, H–2, and H–3 visa-holders. Subject to regulatory time limitations, H visas are valid for the duration of the employment period specified by the employer in its approved petition. This period may be extended if required. H–4 aliens may not accept employment in the U.S. unless they are specifically included in the employer's petition (Form I–129B). INA § 101(a)(15)(H); 8 C.F.R. § 214.2(h).

§ 6–9   INFORMATION MEDIA REPRESENTATIVES

This single class visa category (I) includes any representative of foreign press, radio, film, television, or other media provided that U.S. citizens are granted reciprocal privileges by the alien's government. Spouses and children of the representative are included in this visa. I visas authorize admission for the duration of employment. INA § 101(a)(15)(I). 8 C.F.R. § 214.2(i).

§ 6–10   EXCHANGE VISITORS

J–1 visas are issued to aliens accepted to participate in exchange visitor programs designated by the United

States Information Agency (USIA). 22 C.F.R. § 41.-65(a)(1). J–1 nonimmigrants include students, scholars, trainees, teachers, professors, research assistants, specialists, or leaders in a field of specialized knowledge or skill. INA § 101(a)(15)(J). J–2 visas are for the alien's spouse and children. These visas are valid for various periods of time depending upon the underlying program duration. J–1 status holders may engage in employment within the U.S. J–2 visa holders may obtain permission from the INS to accept approved employment, but only for their own support and not for the support of the J–1 recipient. 8 C.F.R. § 214.2(j)(1). Certain J visa holders must reside in their own country for two years after completion of their program before they are eligible to apply for permanent resident status, an immigrant visa, or for nonimmigrant visas H and L. This two-year foreign residence requirement applies to J–1 holders who: (1) participated in a program which received financing from the U.S. government or from the alien's government; (2) are nationals or residents of countries designated by the United States Information Agency as clearly requiring the services of persons engaged in the alien's field of specialized knowledge or skill (such specializations are published in the form of a skills list); or (3) came to the United States or obtained a J visa in order to receive graduate medical training. INA § 212(e). J visa holders who have received graduate medical training are ineligible to change their status to that of any other nonimmigrant classification. Other J visa holders subject to the two-year foreign residency requirement may not change their visa to any other nonimmigrant visa except A or G before complying with the requirement. INA § 248. Waivers of this requirement may be sought in cases where (1) a hardship can be demonstrated to a U.S. citizen or permanent resident spouse, parent, or child of the status holder; (2) fear of persecution on account of nationality, race, religion, political opinion, or membership in a particular social group; (3) where the alien's home country does not object to the grant of a waiver; or (4) if an interested U.S. governmental agency requests that the waiver be granted. The J–1 visa holder may apply for a waiver of the two-year foreign residency requirement through the USIA. INA § 212(e).

§ 6–11 FIANCÉE OR FIANCÉ OF U.S. CITIZEN

The K (fiancé or fiancée) visa is a special, short term visa, valid for ninety days, for an alien who is coming to the U.S. solely to conclude a valid marriage with a U.S. citizen. The U.S. citizen must first file a petition, Form I–129F, with the INS in the district where the citizen resides. 8 C.F.R. § 214.2(k). The approved petition is forwarded to the U.S. consulate where the alien applies for the K visa. Before the visa is approved, the alien must submit to a medical examination. 22 C.F.R. § 41.-113. This is the only nonimmigrant visa for which a medical examination is required. The K visa is treated as if it were an immigrant visa, since the alien will generally become a permanent resident alien. The K–1 visa is issued to the principal alien and the K–2 visa is for any accompanying children. The K visa does authorize employment during the ninety day period. If the alien fails to marry the U.S. citizen within ninety days of entry, s/he must depart the U.S. INA § 214(d). Holders of a K visa may not adjust their status to any other nonimmigrant visa classification.

The Immigration Marriage Fraud Amendments of 1986 sought to prevent marriage fraud with respect to K nonimmigrants by requiring the alien fiancé(e) and the U.S. citizen to "have previously met in person within 2 years before the date of filing the petition, [and] have a bona fide intention to marry...." INA § 214(d). The Attorney General, however, may waive the personal meeting requirement. *Id.* The Fraud Amendments also prohibit adjustment to permanent resident status of K nonimmigrants prior to their marriage, when they become eligible for immediate relative status. INA § 245(d).

§ 6–12   INTRA–COMPANY TRANSFEREES

This classification was intended to help multinational corporations facilitate employee transfers. This visa allows companies to transfer employees temporarily to the U.S. in order to aid or initiate business operations in the U.S. The employer must first submit a petition, Form I–129L, to the INS district where the alien will be employed. 8 C.F.R. § 214.2(*1*)(2). The alien must have been employed for at least one year by the firm outside the U.S. and must be employed in a managerial or executive capacity, or have specialized knowledge of the company's product or procedures in international business markets. INA § 101(a)(15)(L). The person who qualifies receives an L–1 visa valid during the period petitioned for, up to a maximum of five years. Employers may file a blanket petition for intended employees rather than filing individual petitions. Moreover, the L visa holder may possess the dual intent to seek permanent residency while maintaining nonimmigrant status.

See § 6–8, *supra*. The L visa is renewable. The spouse and children may be granted L–2 visas, but are not authorized to engage in any employment.

§ 6–13　VOCATIONAL STUDENTS

M–1 visas are for vocational or nonacademic students, who enter the U.S. temporarily to pursue a full course of study at an established or recognized vocational or other nonacademic institution. INA § 101(a)(15)(M). M–2 visas are for the spouse and children of the M–1 student. Both visas are normally granted for the period of time necessary to complete the course of study plus thirty days, or for one year, whichever is less, and are renewable. 8 C.F.R. § 214.2(m). M–2 visa holders may not accept employment during their stay in the U.S. Temporary employment for practical training may be authorized for M–1 students after completion of studies. The student's school must certify that the proposed employment is recommended for the purpose of practical training, is related to the student's course of study, and is unavailable to the student in her/his home country. 8 C.F.R. § 214.2(m)(14).

§ 6–14　RELATIVES OF EMPLOYEES OF INTERNATIONAL ORGANIZATIONS

The Immigration Reform and Control Act of 1986 created the N visa category for certain relatives of G–4 employees of international organizations. INA § 101(a)(15)(N). N visas are given to the parents of G–4 aliens accorded special immigrant status under INA §§ 101(a)(27)(I)(i), but only if and while the alien is a child. The children of these parents granted N visas and of G–4 aliens accorded special immigrant status under INA §§ 101(a)(27)(I)(ii), (iii), and (iv) are also given N visas.

§ 6–15   ALIENS WITH EXTRAORDINARY ABILITY

Created by the 1990 Act, O–1 visas are for aliens with "extraordinary ability," as demonstrated by sustained national or international acclaim, in the sciences, arts, education, business, or athletics. This visa is a variation of a class of aliens formerly included within the H–1B category. Moreover, O–1 visas are issued to aliens who have an extensively documented record of extraordinary achievement in motion pictures or television. The alien must seek entry to work in her/his area of expertise and the Attorney General must determine that the alien's entry will result in substantial prospective benefit to the United States.

O–2 visas are for aliens seeking entry solely to accompany and assist the artistic or athletic performance of an admitted O–1 visa holder. An alien seeking an O–2 visa must be an integral part of the performance and have a foreign residence with no intent to abandon it.

An O–3 visa is issued to the spouse and children of an alien with either an O–1 or O–2 visa, provided they are accompanying or following to join the principal alien. O visas are valid for the period specified by the Attorney General, usually the duration of the event for which the alien is admitted.

§ 6–16 INTERNATIONALLY RECOGNIZED ATHLETES AND ARTISTS, ETC.

The 1990 Act also established the P nonimmigrant category to cover a former subclass of H–1B workers. P–1 visas are for athletes who perform or compete at an internationally recognized level, or are members of an internationally recognized entertainment group. The alien must have had a sustained and substantial relationship for at least one year with such a group, and must provide functions integral to the group's performance to qualify for a P–1 visa.

P–2 visas are issued to aliens who perform as artists, entertainers, or as an integral part of an entertainment group associated with an exchange program between a U.S. organization and an organization in a foreign state. INA § 101(a)(15)(P)(iii). P–3 visas are for artists or entertainers performing in a "culturally unique" program. The principal alien entering under P visa status may be accompanied or followed by her/his spouse and children, who receive P–4 visas.

P visas are valid for as long as the Attorney General specifies, but usually last for the duration of the competition, event, or performance for which the alien is admitted. Individual athletes may enter for an initial period of up to five years, which may then be extended for another five years. Under the 1990 Act, P–1 and P–3 visas were subject to a numerical limit of 25,000 annually for each category. That numerical limit, however, was deleted by the technical amendments of 1991.

The 1990 Act also established Q nonimmigrant visas for participants in international exchange programs and R visas for religious workers and their children.

§ 6–17 CANADIAN BUSINESS TRAVELERS AND THEIR FAMILIES

The United States–Canada Free Trade Agreement, ratified in 1988, establishes special provisions for the temporary admission of Canadian business visitors, traders, investors, professionals, intra-company transferees, and their families wishing to enter the United States. U.S. citizens traveling to Canada receive reciprocal rights of entry. The agreement, and the occupational schedules which have been promulgated to implement it, facilitate entry by expediting the admission of particular occupational groups. Pursuant to these regulations, specified Canadian business travelers are admitted under the classification symbol B–1 "TC," status holders. Their spouses and children are eligible for B–2 visitor visas for periods of one year, which may be extended for additional periods of a year.

§ 6–18 PROCEDURAL REQUIREMENTS FOR NONIMMIGRANT VISAS

Any alien desiring a nonimmigrant visa must apply using the specific procedures for the particular visa sought. These procedures may be broadly divided into three classes: (1) Applications which require no prior contact with anyone in the U.S. (visas A, B, C, D, E, G, I, and O); (2) applications which require proof of acceptance in an authorized program (visas F, J, M, Q, and visas for special education trainees); and (3) applications which require approved petitions that provide the basis for the alien's presence in the U.S. (visas H, K, L, P, and R).

In the first class, where no prior U.S. contact is needed, the alien begins the application process by submitting Form OF–156 to the U.S. consular office where the alien resides. The consular officer has the discretion to accept applications from aliens who do not reside in the consular district, but are physically present there. 22 C.F.R. § 41.110. In such cases, the consular officer may examine the alien's reasons for not applying to the consulate where the alien resides. The application is normally made in person, although the consular officer may waive this requirement. 22 C.F.R. § 41.114. The consular officer may also require additional documents to verify the alien's purpose in requesting the visa. Supporting documents will usually concern the alien's eligibility to enter the U.S. and the alien's intention to depart at the end of the intended stay. 22 C.F.R. § 41.111. The alien's intention to depart from the U.S. and return is usually established by the alien's job, residence, and/or family in the alien's country. If the application is for a temporary visitor (B) or a student (F or M) visa, the consul may also require that a bond be posted to insure the alien's departure from the U.S. INA § 221(g). The visa is usually issued on the same day application is made and is in the form of a stamp in the alien's passport. 22 C.F.R. § 41.124.

If the visa desired is in the second class (F, J, and M visas), the alien must also present an acceptance form from the school or program. For the student (F and M) visa, Form I–20 is executed by an accredited school where the student will study. 22 C.F.R. § 41.45; 8 C.F.R. § 214.2(f)(1). The exchange visitor must present Form IAP–66, executed by the program sponsor, indicating the applicant's participation in an approved program. 22 CFR § 41.65. If the consulate is satisfied that the applicant has sufficient funds to cover expenses while in the U.S. and that the applicant has the necessary knowledge of the English language, a visa will be granted. 22 C.F.R. §§ 41.45(a) & 41.65(a).

Visas in the third class (H, K, L, P, and R) require that the applicant be a beneficiary of an approved petition Form I–129 submitted by the prospective employer for the H visa, by the prospective employer for the L visa, and by the prospective spouse for the K visa. Certain prospective employers of L visa applications may file a blanket petition rather than separate, individual petitions. If the consular officer finds the supporting documents in order and the alien eligible in all other respects, the visa will be granted.

The consular officer may require additional proof of the applicant's eligibility for any visa if the officer is not satisfied with the initial application or knows or has reason to believe that the applicant is ineligible for such visa. If the added proof is still deemed insufficient after review, the consulate may deny the visa application, informing the applicant of the grounds for refusal. 22 C.F.R. § 41.130. The Department of State cannot overrule the consulate's decision so long as the decision was based on the application of law to facts. INA §§ 104A & 221(a). Although there is generally no judicial review available, several courts have reserved a narrow ground of review in visa denial cases. *See, e.g., Abourezk v. Reagan* (D.C.Cir.1986), *Allende v. Shultz* (D.Mass.1985). See also § 3–1.

Upon entry to the U.S., the alien holding any nonimmigrant visa will be subject to inspection by an immigration officer and will receive a Form I–94 indicating the length and terms of their stay.

§ 6–19   ADJUSTMENT OF STATUS TO IMMIGRANT

Generally, all nonimmigrant visa holders who are in the U.S. may apply to have their visa status adjusted to permanent residence status, with the exception of crew member (D) visa holders. INA § 245. In order to receive an adjustment of status, the alien must file an adjustment of status (Form I–485) with the INS district office where the alien resides. 8 C.F.R. § 245.2. The alien must have been inspected and admitted or paroled into the U.S., must meet standard eligibility requirements for an immigrant visa, and an immigrant visa must be immediately available at the time the application is filed. INA § 245(a). Additionally, the alien must not have either (1) been in an unlawful status anytime after November 6, 1986, since entering the U.S. or (2) on or after January 1, 1977, accepted any unauthorized employment while present in the U.S. as a nonimmigrant, unless the alien is an immediate relative of a U.S. citizen, the alien is a graduate of a foreign medical school licensed to practice in the U.S. since 1978, or unless the violation was technical in nature and not the fault of the alien. INA § 245(c).

CHAPTER 7

NONIMMIGRANT VISAS: STUDENTS

§ 7–1 INTRODUCTION

The F–1 visa is for the academic student, who must be entering the U.S. temporarily and solely to pursue a full course of study at an established academic high school, college, university, seminary, conservatory, or language school. An F–1 visa does not apply to a student who wishes to attend a vocational or nonacademic program. A student who intends to enroll in such a program may enter only on an M visa.

Unlike many of the other nonimmigrant visas, an F visa frequently entails a stay in the United States which spans a number of years. The regulations for F visas, at 8 C.F.R. § 214.2(f), address some of the issues which are likely to arise during a student's stay in the United States.

§ 7–2 APPLYING FOR THE F–1 VISA

Once the student has been accepted into an academic program, the institution in which s/he will enroll completes a Certificate of Eligibility for Nonimmigrant (F–1) Student Status, Form I–20A–B and sends it to the student. The student applies for the F–1 visa by presenting the I–20A–B and a nonimmigrant visa application to a United States consulate in the student's home coun-

150

try. The student should also be prepared to present documentation which will show: (a) that the student will have sufficient funds available to support her- or himself during the entire proposed course of study; and (b) that the student is maintaining a residence abroad to which the student intends to return on completion of her/his studies in the United States. Moreover, the student must provide persuasive documentation showing the student's intention to return to her/his home country. A job offer or proof of demand for the student's skills usually suffices. Once the visa is issued, the student may apply at a port of entry for admission to the United States.

§ 7–3 FAMILY OF THE STUDENT

F–2 visas are for the spouse and minor children of the student. The spouse and children may accompany the student into the United States or they may follow to join the student. If family members are accompanying the student, they do not need an I–20A–B of their own to apply for the F–2 visa, because they are included on the student's I–20A–B. If they are following the student, they will need an I–20A–B. It can be either a new one or a reproduced copy of the student's original I–20A–B which bears an original endorsement by the designated school official verifying that the information on the form is still current. 8 C.F.R. § 214.2(f)(3). The F–2 spouse and children of an F–1 student may not, under any circumstances, accept employment. 8 C.F.R. § 214.2(f)(15).

§ 7–4 DURATION OF STATUS

Persons holding F–1 and F–2 visas are generally admitted for the "duration of status" as a student. "Duration of status" is defined as the period during which the student is pursuing a full course of study in any educational program or is receiving authorized practical training, plus sixty days within which to depart from the United States. 8 C.F.R. § 214.2(f)(5). An F–1 student who continues from one educational level to another, from one educational program to another, and/or from one school to another, remains in status as long as the proper procedures are followed. 8 C.F.R. § 214.-2(f)(5).

There are limitations to the flexibility allowed the student. When a student begins an educational program, the school must state when the student is expected to complete the particular program of study. The student remains in status as long as s/he is making normal progress toward completing her/his educational objective. 8 C.F.R. § 214.2(f)(7). If a student wishes to transfer to another school but has not pursued a full course of study at the school which s/he was last authorized to attend, the student must apply to the INS for reinstatement to student status. If the student is granted reinstatement, s/he may attend the new school. 8 C.F.R. § 214.2(f)(8).

If a student is unable to complete her/his degree objective by the date on her/his I–20, s/he must apply to the school for an extension of stay. 8 C.F.R. § 214.-2(f)(7). The school may grant an extension to a student who has maintained student status and whose inability to complete by the date on the I–20 is caused by "compelling academic or medical reasons." 8 C.F.R. § 214.-

2(f)(7)(iii). Examples of legitimate academic reasons are change of college major and unexpected research difficulties; illnesses must be documented. Delays caused by academic problems (academic probation, suspension) are not acceptable reasons for extension. The school notifies INS of the extension on a Form I–538, submitted with a new I–20A–B showing the new completion date.

An F–1 student is considered to be in status during summer vacation if the student is eligible and intends to register for the upcoming term. If the school operates on the trimester or quarter system, the student may take any term as a vacation, as long as the student takes only one term a year, is eligible and intends to register for the next term, and has completed the equivalent of a complete academic year before taking the vacation. A student remains in status if s/he is forced to interrupt or reduce her/his course of study because of illness or other medical condition, provided the student returns to a full course of study upon recovery. A student will also retain F–1 status for sixty days after completion of her/his last academic program. Upon expiration of this sixty day period, the student must leave the United States. 8 C.F.R. § 214.2(f)(5).

§ 7–5 FULL COURSE OF STUDY

The conditions necessary to satisfy the full course of study requirement vary depending on the academic program involved. For postgraduate or postdoctoral study, research at a college or university, or undergraduate or postgraduate study at a night school, conservatory, or religious seminary, full course of study is a program certified as such by the school. 8 C.F.R. § 214.2(f)(6)(i).

An undergraduate student must generally take twelve semester or quarter hours per term, unless fewer hours are required for the student to complete the course of study in the current term. 8 C.F.R. § 214.2(f)(6)(ii). A primary or high school student must take at least the minimum number of hours per week required by the school for normal progress toward graduation. 8 C.F.R. § 214.2(f)(6)(v).

A student may drop below the required number of hours for a full course of study if advised to do so by a designated school official for valid academic reasons. Valid academic reasons include: (a) English language difficulties; (b) unfamiliarity with U.S. teaching methods or reading requirements; and (c) improper course level placement. The designated school official's advice to drop below a full course of study is subject to review by the INS. 8 C.F.R. § 214.2(f)(6). In practice, however, school officials exercise discretion in finding valid academic reasons based on other circumstances such as health problems or the fact that the student is working on a thesis.

§ 7–6 EMPLOYMENT

The 1990 Act significantly modified employment options previously available to F–1 students. An F–1 student may work on-campus up to 20 hours per week while school is in session and while enrolled as a full-time student. A student must be in F–1 student status for nine consecutive months before seeking off-campus employment authorization.

§ 7–6.1   On–Campus Employment

An F–1 student pursuing a full course of study is also permitted to engage in on-campus employment as long as the employment will not displace a United States resident. The student may not engage in any on-campus employment for more than twenty hours per week, except during vacation times, or after the course of study has been completed. "On campus" includes employment by commercial firms which provide services for students on campus, such as a bookstore or food service company. 8 C.F.R. § 214.2(f)(9).

The 1990 Act expanded the definition of on-campus employment to include off-campus locations which are affiliated with the school. 8 C.F.R. § 214.2(f)(9). This arrangement was designed to permit graduate students to conduct research at off-campus locations under the supervision of their professors. The INS requires that employment by an organization whose affiliation with the school is based on a contract be an integral part of the student's educational program and be commensurate with the level of study. 8 C.F.R. § 214.2(f)(9). Employment with on-campus commercial firms (such as a company constructing a school building) which do not provide direct student services are classified as off-campus employment.

On-campus employment pursuant to the terms of a scholarship, fellowship, or assistantship is permitted and is deemed a part of the academic program of a student otherwise taking a full course of study. Hence, students assigned teaching or research responsibilities pursuant to the terms of a scholarship or fellowship may carry a reduced course load. Note, however, that the student's total employment may never exceed 20 hours per week while school is in session.

§ 7–6.2 Off–Campus Employment

The F–1 student must apply to the INS for permission to engage in off-campus employment, unless the employment is pursuant to the student's alternate work/study program. In response to intense lobbying by McDonald's and other corporations, the 1990 Act created a three-year pilot program under which the Attorney General may allow students to work off-campus for an employer who complies with Department of Labor regulations meant to protect U.S. workers. To be eligible, the student must meet the following conditions:

(1) the student must have had F–1 student status for at least one academic year and maintained good academic standing during that time;

(2) the proposed employer must attest to the academic institution and the Secretary of Labor that the employer has recruited U.S. workers for the position for at least sixty days without success;

(3) the proposed employer must attest that s/he will pay the student prevailing wages for that position; and

(4) the student cannot be employed for more than twenty hours per week, except during vacation. 8 C.F.R. § 214.2(f)(9)(ii).

The Department of Labor regulations for the labor attestation are found at 20 C.F.R. § 655. The pilot program is now the only available off-campus work authorization aside from practical training. Congress has directed the INS to submit a report before April 1,

1994, on the effect of F–1 student employment on prevailing wages and a recommendation on whether to extend the program. Critics of the program predicted the Labor Department's complicated attestation requirements would limit the number of employers willing to participate in the program, and initial experience has shown this prediction to be correct.

§ 7–7 PRACTICAL TRAINING

Practical training is an authorized period of temporary employment which allows the student to obtain work experience related to the student's course of study but not available to the student in her/his home country. A student who is engaged in authorized practical training remains in status for the duration of the training. There are two types of practical training available: curricular and post-completion. Practical training is available to F–1 students who have been lawfully enrolled on a full-time basis for a minimum of nine consecutive months. 8 C.F.R. § 214.2(f)(10). Exceptions to the nine months requirement are provided for students enrolled in graduate studies which require immediate participation in curricular practical training. 8 C.F.R. § 214.2(f)(10).

§ 7–7.1 Curricular Practical Training

Curricular practical training is employment prior to completion of studies, and is only permitted if the institution requires an internship or other field experience, for a particular degree in that field. 8 C.F.R. § 214.-2(f)(10). The 1990 Act does not consider curricular practical training to include unsponsored employment directly related to the student's area of study.

The school may authorize the student for employment if satisfied that the work qualifies as curricular practical training and must then notify the INS by filing a Form I–538 with the data processing center in Kentucky. In practice, many foreign student advisors interpret the concept of "internship" liberally to permit foreign students an opportunity to gain work experience. A student who receives one year or more of full-time curricular practical training is ineligible for post-completion practical training. 8 C.F.R. § 214.2(f)(10).

§ 7–7.2   Post–Completion Practical Training

Following completion of the academic program, INS regulations provide that a student is eligible to apply for 12 months of post-completion practical training. 8 C.F.R. § 214.2(f)(10). Post-completion practical training can be authorized only by the INS, upon recommendation of the school. Prior to the 1990 Act, post-completion practical training was split into two six-month segments; the present regulations, however, provide for a single twelve-month training period.

A student who has been in status for one full academic year and has completed a course of study is eligible to apply. An F–1 student may be authorized to engage in post-completion practical training only once during the duration of student status. 8 C.F.R. § 214(f)(10)(ii).

An F–1 student may request recommendation for practical nonimmigrant status form, along with an I–20A–B Certificate of Eligibility for Nonimmigrant (F–1) Student Status from the school the student wishes to attend, and supporting documentation. The change to

F–1 status is generally granted to persons who show they qualify as students.

A special situation is presented by a change from B–2 visitor for pleasure to F–1 status. The intending student must give a convincing explanation of why s/he did not apply for an F–1 visa at the consulate abroad. Because the B–2 visitor visa is believed to be easier to acquire than the F–1 visa, the INS is skeptical of applications for change from visitor status to student status. The INS tends to suspect that the individual applying for such a change planned all along to study in the United States. It is possible, however, to get a B–2 visitor visa as a "prospective student." The intent to visit educational institutions and to seek admission must be clearly explained to the consulate abroad and should be marked on the B–2 visa. In this case, the INS will be more liberal in granting a change to F–1 status. The nonimmigrant seeking F–1 student status will also need the supporting documentation required of any applicant for an F–1 visa, including proof of financial resources and of the bona fide intent to return home on completion of studies.

§ 7–8 CHANGE OF STATUS TO OR FROM OTHER NON-IMMIGRANT STATUS

An F–1 nonimmigrant student may qualify to adjust status to that of permanent resident either through her/his family or employer. If the student is the spouse, child, or parent of a U.S. citizen, the student may acquire permanent residence through that relative without regard to the availability of visas subject to numerical limitations. In an attempt to deter immigration-related marriage fraud, the Immigration Marriage Fraud Amendments of 1986 impose a two-year conditional residency requirement on alien spouses and children before they may obtain permanent resident status on the basis of a "qualifying marriage" to a U.S. citizen or permanent resident alien. Permanent resident status is subject to verification that the marriage continued as a valid marriage for two years from the date of initial petition for permanent residence. INA § 216. For more information on visas for immediate relatives of U.S. citizens see § 5–2.1. Other relationships to United States citizens and to permanent residents may qualify the student for a family-sponsored or employment-related preference visa, subject to numerical limitations. *See* § 5–3.1. Availability of numerically limited visas may be subject to waiting periods for students from some countries.

A student seeking permanent resident status through an employer will most likely qualify for the second or third employment-related preference for professionals with advanced degrees or aliens of exceptional ability in science, art, or business. The third employment-related category is for professionals with baccalaureate degrees, skilled workers, and other workers. Both of these preference categories require the employer to obtain labor certification, showing that there is no U.S. citizen or resident available who can fill the position. Even if a labor certification is obtained, both preferences may be subject to waiting periods imposed by the numerical limitations on preference visas.

§ 7–9 VIOLATION OF STUDENT STATUS: CONSEQUENCES AND RISKS

§ 7–9.1 Reinstatement to Student Status

If the student has overstayed her/his authorized period of stay or has otherwise violated the conditions of her/his F–1 visa, the INS may consider reinstating the student to F–1 status. Reinstatement is difficult to obtain. The reinstatement will be considered only if the student:

(1) makes a written request for reinstatement, accompanied by a properly completed I–20A–B from the school the student is attending or intends to attend;

(2) can establish that the violation of status resulted from circumstances beyond the student's control or that failure to reinstate the student would result in extreme hardship to the student;

(3) is currently pursuing or intends to pursue a full course of study;

(4) has not engaged in unauthorized off-campus employment;

(5) provides documentary proof of funding to continue in school and maintain full-time status; and

(6) is not deportable on any ground (other than her/his violation of student status). 8 C.F.R. § 214.-2(f)(16).

The INS district director's decision to disallow reinstatement is not subject to review, except pursuant to a declaratory judgment action in a U.S. district court.

§ 7–9.2 Adjustment to Permanent Resident Status

In the past, when a student's request for reinstatement to F–1 status was denied, the student could leave the United States, reapply for a nonimmigrant F–1 visa, and return to the United States without adversely affecting her/his eligibility for adjustment to permanent resident status.

Current regulations, however, make ineligible for adjustment to permanent resident status any alien (other than an immediate relative as defined in INA § 201(b) or a special immigrant described in INA § 101(a)(27)(H)) who has failed (other than through no fault of her/his own for technical reasons) continuously to maintain a legal status since entry into the United States. 8 C.F.R. § 245.1(b). The student's departure and subsequent reentry will not eliminate this bar to adjustment of status. 8 C.F.R. § 245.1(c).

This provision does not prevent any individual from leaving the United States and returning on an immigrant visa. Obtaining a numerically limited visa, however, may be a very lengthy process, depending on the current availability of the desired family-sponsored or employment-related preference category. Even when available, the application process may require many months of consular procedures before the visa interview is granted.

§ 7–9.3 Exclusion

Included in the Immigration Marriage Fraud Amendments of 1986 is an amendment to INA § 212(a)(19) which increases the sanctions applicable to a student who fraudulently or willfully violates the terms of her/his student status. This amendment provides that any alien who fraudulently or willfully misrepresents a material fact in order to procure any benefit conferred by the Immigration and Nationality Act is ineligible to receive a visa and shall be excluded from admission into the United States. Before the 1986 amendment, the language of this provision excluded individuals who obtained a visa or other documentation or sought to enter the United States through the use of fraud or willful misrepresentation. The prior provision did not include as a ground for exclusion or denial of a visa the use of fraud to obtain "other benefit[s] provided under this Chapter." This broad exclusionary provision could prevent a student from re-entering the United States, either as an immigrant or as a nonimmigrant, if that student misrepresented a material fact in order to qualify for immigration benefits such as permission to be employed or permission to take less than a full course of study.

CHAPTER 8

DEPORTATION

§ 8–1 INTRODUCTION

Deportation is the expulsion of an alien who has already entered the United States either legally or illegally. The Immigration and Nationality Act lists five major categories of deportable aliens. Due to the large number of subcategories within each category, however, there are many more grounds for deportation. For example, the first category alone establishes nine classes of aliens excludable at the time of entry. The 1990 Act reduced the number of grounds for deportation in an attempt to make the list comprehensible and more current. The Technical Amendments Act of 1991, however, expanded the grounds for deportation by adding the attempt or conspiracy to commit a crime.

In theory at least, deportation is not a criminal punishment, but is a civil proceeding designed primarily to rid the United States of statutorily defined undesirables. The courts have long recognized the plenary power of Congress to expel and deport aliens. That Congress allows aliens to enter the United States "is a matter of permission and tolerance. The government's power to terminate hospitality has been asserted by this court since the question first arose." *Harisiades v. Shaughnessy* (Sup.Ct.1952).

Even though the courts do not recognize deportation as criminal punishment, they recognize that deportation penalizes the alien. The alien has voluntarily chosen to come to the United States and deportation forces her/him to leave her/his home, job, friends, and in some cases, family. Indeed, deportation may result "in loss of both property and life; or all that makes life worth living." *Ng Fung Ho v. White* (Sup.Ct.1922). Further, a deported alien is barred for five years from entering the United States unless s/he obtains special permission from the Immigration Service to re-enter. INA § 212. Because the consequences of deportation are drastic, the student of immigration law should become familiar with the many and varied aspects of deportation. This chapter examines first, the grounds for deportation and second, the procedures incident to both the prehearing process and the deportation hearing.

§ 8–2 GROUNDS FOR DEPORTING THE ALIEN

§ 8–2.1 General Considerations

The Immigration and Nationality Act—as amended by the 1990 Act—presently contains five major broad categories of deportable aliens. INA § 241(a). The five categories cover (1) aliens excludable at time of entry or adjustment of status, (2) criminal offenses, (3) failure to register and falsification of documents, (4) security and related grounds, and (5) public charge. The various grounds for deportation can be divided into two general classes—aliens deportable for acts committed at or prior to entry and aliens deportable for committing certain prohibited acts since their entry. Before examining these categories in any detail, some general aspects of deportation will be examined.

Deportation applies only to aliens, since only aliens may be deported. According to the INA, an alien is "any person not a citizen or national of the United States." INA § 101(a)(3). Hence, no matter how one obtained citizenship in the United States, s/he is not deportable and need only prove her/his citizenship to avoid deportation. Deportation proceedings may only be commenced against a naturalized citizen after the successful completion of denaturalization proceedings to remove the individual's U.S. citizenship. Aliens who have entered the U.S. whether lawfully or unlawfully, and who remain even with permanent resident status, are subject to deportation. There are several specific classes of aliens exempt from the deportation statutes. Deportation laws do not apply to ambassadors, public ministers, accredited career diplomats, consular officers, and the members of their families. Employees of international organizations such as the United Nations are also exempt from deportation statutes. INA § 102.

Deporting an alien often may result in the "de facto deportation" of the alien's U.S. citizen children. The Third Circuit rejected the claim that deportation of an alien denies her/his child the right, as a U.S. citizen, to continue to reside in the United States. Deportation of the child's parents will merely postpone, but not bar, the child's residence in the United States, if s/he should later choose to live in this country. The court reasoned that Congress did not intend to give such a child the ability to confer immigration benefits on her/his parents. *Acosta v. Gaffney* (3d Cir.1977).

Unlike most statutes regulating conduct, the INA frequently applies retroactively. The INS may deport an alien for conduct which was not a ground for deportation at the time the alien committed the act. For example, a Nazi who legally entered the United States in 1965 may be deported under the provisions of a 1978 amendment to the act, even though s/he has resided in the United States for a number of years. Hence, deportation for acts which were legal when committed does not violate the constitutional prohibition against *ex post facto* laws. *Mahler v. Eby* (Sup.Ct.1924). The INA also does not contain a general statute of limitations, although there are particular statutes of limitation contained within the classes of deportable aliens. For example, an alien who becomes a charge of the state is deportable only if s/he becomes a public charge within five years of her/his entry into the United States. INA § 241(a)(5). Accordingly, the Immigration Service may deport a Greek who becomes a public charge four years after entry, but not an Italian who becomes a public charge five and a half years after entry. Because there is no general statute of limitations, however, the Immigration Service can deport the Greek who became a public charge within five years of entry *at any time*— even though s/he may no longer fit this description.

Like the public charge provision, many of the INA's provisions depend on when the alien entered the United States. Entry is defined by statute to be "any coming of an alien into the United States." INA § 101(a)(13). Since the statute applies to any coming into the United States, aliens who re-enter the United States after a voluntary departure are considered to have entered at that time, even though their initial entry may have occurred many years previous. The re-entry provision can have a negative impact on the alien who voluntarily departs from the United States for a brief period of time. For example, an alien who has legally resided in the United States for ten years develops a condition that will later cause her/him to become a charge of the state. S/he leaves this country for a few months and then re-enters. Because s/he entered the country with the condition, the alien could be deportable even though s/he would not have been if s/he had not left the country. See § 9–2.1, *infra*.

§ 8–2.2 Aliens Deportable for Acts Committed Prior to Entry

The Immigration and Nationality Act provides for the deportation of certain aliens for acts committed prior to or at the time of their entry. The first category of deportable aliens covers the broad grouping of aliens excludable at the time of entry. INA § 241(a)(1). Section 241(a)(1) allows the INS to "look back" at conditions existing at the time of an alien's entry and deport aliens who should not have been allowed to enter the United States. This concept has profound implications. An alien who may not have committed a deportable offense, discussed below, may still be deportable if s/he can be shown to have committed acts which would have amounted to excludable conduct before entry. See § 9–1, *infra*, for a detailed discussion of the exclusion provisions.

An alien may also be deported for entering the United States without inspection or at an undesignated place. INA § 241(a)(1)(B). This section of the INA reflects the government's policy that all aliens, even lawful residents, must pass the scrutiny of immigration officials each time they pass the border. An alien who enters under a fraudulent claim of United States citizenship, thereby avoiding inspection, has entered the United

States without the required inspection and may be deported. *Reid v. INS* (Sup.Ct.1975).

An alien who violates or fails to comply with any of the terms of entry is deportable, as is any alien who fails to maintain the nonimmigrant status that permitted her/his entry. INA § 241(a)(1)(C). An alien who knowingly encourages, aids, or abets another alien to enter the United States illegally may be deported; the Attorney General, however, may waive this provision if the waiver would serve humanitarian purposes, assure family unity, or would be in the public interest. INA § 241(a)(1)(E).

Another category of aliens deportable for violating entry requirements are those aliens involved in marriage fraud. Aliens who marry United States citizens solely to obtain entry into the United States may be deported under the provisions of INA § 241(a)(1)(G). This statute covers annulled marriages and marriages otherwise terminated within two years, unless the alien demonstrates to the satisfaction of the Immigration Service that the marriage was not for the purpose of entering the United States. The INS also has discretion to determine whether any other alien-citizen marriage was fraudulent and if so, to deport the alien.

In addition, a 1978 amendment to the INA updated in the 1990 Act, permits the INS to deport aliens who participated in Nazi activities. According to the act, any alien, who in association with the Nazi party, "ordered, incited, assisted, or otherwise participated in the persecution of any person because of race, religion, national origin, or political opinion" may be deported. INA §§ 241(a)(4)(D), 212(a)(3)(E). This provision has been unsuccessfully challenged as an unconstitutional bill of attainder and *ex post facto* law. The Second Circuit in *Linnas v. INS* (2d Cir.1986) held that the provision is not a bill of attainder because deportation is not punishment. Linnas, who was found to be chief of a Nazi concentration camp, was ordered deported to the Soviet Union, even though he was convicted *in absentia* in the Soviet Union and sentenced to death there for his war crimes. Linnas' argument that his deportation would be unlawful extradition was likewise unsuccessful.

§ 8–2.3 Aliens Deportable for Conduct After Entry

The INS also may deport aliens for engaging in certain prohibited activities after their entry into the United States. Since there is no statute of limitations in the INA, the alien may be deported any time after the prohibited act is committed. Prior to the 1990 Act, a complex and often controversial set of provisions prescribed deportation for membership in the Communist party or affiliation with a subversive organization. The 1990 Act eliminated and simplified those provisions, replacing them with a statute that reflects current national security and safety concerns. INA § 241(a)(4). Prior to the amendments, the statute classified the following as subversives:

1. Anarchists;

2. Aliens advocating or teaching opposition to all organized government;

3. Aliens who are members of or affiliated with the Communist Party or any other totalitarian organization;

4. Aliens, not already covered by the preceding classes, advocating the economic, international, and governmental doctrines of world communism;

5. Aliens advocating the overthrow, by force and violence, of the United States government, or any of its officers;

6. Aliens who write, publish, or distribute materials which are subversive;

7. Aliens who affiliate with persons who write, publish, or distribute subversive literature;

8. Aliens whom the Attorney General believes entered the United States principally or incidentally to engage in activities endangering the welfare, safety, or national security of the United States.

The current law permits deportation for any alien who violates U.S. espionage law, engages in criminal activity that endangers public safety or national security, or engages in any activity whose purpose is to overthrow the U.S. government by force or unlawful means. INA § 241(a)(4)(A). An alien who at any time after entry engages in terrorist activity also is deportable. INA § 241(a)(4)(B). In addition, the Secretary of State has the discretion to recommend for deportation an alien whose presence s/he believes will have serious adverse consequences for U.S. foreign policy.

A second broad category of aliens deportable for conduct which occurs after entry are those aliens convicted of various criminal offenses. INA § 241(a)(2). The first class of general crimes under this provision covers crimes of moral turpitude. Aliens "convicted of a crime involving moral turpitude committed within five years after entry and either sentenced to confinement or confined therefor in a prison or corrective institution, for a year or more, or who at any time after entry is convicted of two crimes involving moral turpitude...." INA § 241(a)(2)(a). The alien must be convicted of the crime—a mere admission of the crime by the alien is not sufficient for deportation. The Board of Immigration Appeals defined a conviction sufficient for deportation as an action of the court considered by the state as a conviction and/or a judicial finding of guilt which removes the case from the category of pending cases. *Matter of L_____ R_____* (BIA 1959).

For purposes of the INA, an alien is considered sentenced only if s/he is sentenced to confinement or is confined in a prison or other corrective institution for a period of a year or more. Sentencing the alien to an alcohol, drug, or other treatment program for a year or more is not a sentence sufficient for deporting the alien. *Holzapfel v. Wyrsch* (3d Cir.1958). The most difficult aspect of deporting aliens for crimes of moral turpitude is defining which crimes involve "moral turpitude." The courts generally agree that crimes of moral turpitude include crimes of violence and crimes "commonly thought of as involving baseness, vileness or depravity." *Jordan v. De George* (Sup.Ct.1951). This definition, however, is nearly as vague and open-ended as "moral turpitude." The Supreme Court in *Jordan* held that the use of the term "moral turpitude" did not render the INA unconstitutionally vague because "the language conveys sufficiently definite warning as to the proscribed conduct when measured by common understanding and practices."

The INS or reviewing court must decide whether the criminal law violated by the alien inherently involves moral turpitude; that is, whether violation of the law under any circumstance would involve moral turpitude. *Matter of R.* (BIA 1954). In practice, the courts have held that the following crimes involve moral turpitude: assault with intent to kill or with a deadly weapon, bigamy, bribery, child beating, conspiracy, counterfeiting, narcotics offenses, forgery, fraud, most types of homicide, larceny, most sexual offenses, and certain misdemeanors, such as larceny. In order to determine if the alien's crime involved moral turpitude, the court can consider only the crime of which the alien was convicted or to which the alien pled guilty—not what the alien actually did or the particular nature of the alien's act.

INA § 241(a)(2)(iii) provides for the deportation of any alien who has been convicted of an aggravated felony at any time after entry. The term "aggravated felony" includes murder, drug trafficking, firearm trafficking, money laundering, crimes of violence for which the term of imprisonment is five years or more, or any attempt or conspiracy to commit such acts. INA § 101(a)(43). This list, which reflects the addition of "crimes of violence" by the 1990 Act, codifies *Application of Barrett* (BIA 1990) which interpreted the aggravated felony definition to apply to state as well as federal offenses. Foreign convictions within this definition cease to qualify as aggravated felonies 15 years after the alien is released from prison. INA § 101(a)(43). An alien convicted of an aggravated felony is "presumed to be deportable from the United States." INA § 242A(c).

Accordingly, the lawyer representing an alien accused of a crime has special considerations to keep in mind.

First, if the alien is accused of a crime of moral turpitude, or an "aggravated felony," the lawyer may want to consider pleading the alien to a lesser offense not involving moral turpitude, with a mandatory sentence of less than one year, and/or not classified as an aggravated felony. Second, the INA also specifies that the moral turpitude or aggravated felony provisions shall not apply in the case of any alien who has subsequent to such conviction been granted a full and unconditional pardon by the President or the governor of the state of conviction. INA § 241(a)(2)(A)(ii). Hence, as a last resort, the lawyer may attempt to obtain a full pardon for the alien. The statute does not provide, however, for offenses involving controlled substances or firearms, nor for an automatic stay of deportation while the alien applies for a pardon and, therefore, for a stay of deportation. The provisions of INA § 241(a)(2)(A) apply only to crimes involving moral turpitude and do not apply to other crimes for which the alien may be deported, for example, drug offenses.

Other sections of the Immigration and Nationality Act allow deportation for conviction of specific crimes. The INS may deport an alien convicted of violating any law or regulation relating to a controlled substance, such as narcotic drugs and marihuana. INA § 241(a)(2)(B). Cf. § 1–5, supra. Moreover, any alien who at any time after entry abuses or becomes addicted to drugs is deportable. INA § 241(a)(2)(B)(ii). Unlike the general moral turpitude category, an alien need not be sentenced in order to be deported for narcotics offenses. Likewise, an alien convicted of possessing or carrying any automatic weapon, semiautomatic, or sawed-off shotgun may be deported. INA § 241(a)(2)(c). Aliens convicted of violating the Selective Service Act, espionage statutes, or certain other statutes dealing with the national defense are subject to deportation if the Immigration Service designates the alien as an undesirable. INA § 241(a)(2)(D).

The INA also provides for the deportation of certain other statutorily defined undesirables. The INS may thus deport a nonimmigrant alien in the United States who violates her/his visa conditions. INA § 241(a)(1)(c). Such violations include overstaying the time limit of the visa or accepting employment without the requisite permission. The Immigration Marriage Fraud Amendments provide for the deportation of aliens accorded permanent resident status on a conditional basis under INA § 216 and who have such status terminated. INA § 241(a)(1)(D). The Immigration Reform and Control Act of 1986 made deportable those aliens lawfully admitted for temporary residence as special agricultural workers under the act, who have failed to meet the employment requirements of such status. INA § 241(a)(1)(c). Finally, those aliens, who in the opinion of the Immigration Service have become public charges within five years of their entry, from causes not affirmatively shown to have arisen after entry, may be deported. INA § 241(a)(5).

§ 8–3 PROCEDURES FOR DEPORTATION

§ 8–3.1 Prehearing Procedure

The INS uses a variety of techniques to investigate the presence of deportable aliens in the United States. The methods used by the INS include inspecting all vehicles and persons at the border and at certain fixed check-points near the border, using roving patrols to stop and question persons in certain vehicles, searching businesses which are alleged to employ deportable aliens, and acting on information obtained through informants. This section examines the scope of the INS' power in conducting prehearing investigations.

a. *Immigration Service Powers Prior to Arrest*

The INA provides that any officer of the Immigration Service may, without a warrant:

(1) Interrogate any alien or person believed to be an alien as to her/his right to be or remain in the United States;

(2) Arrest any alien who in the officer's presence or view is entering or attempting to enter the United States in violation of any law or if the officer has reason to believe the alien is in the United States in violation of any law and is likely to escape if not arrested;

(3) Board and search any vehicle to look for illegal aliens within a reasonable distance from the border. INA § 287(a).

The Code of Federal Regulations defines a reasonable distance from the border to be "100 air miles from any external boundary of the United States." 8 C.F.R. § 287.1(a)(2). The statute appears to confer broad investigatory powers on the INS. The Supreme Court has held that the Immigration and Naturalization Service may use evidence in a deportation proceeding which had been obtained in violation of the Fourth Amendment. Using a balancing test, the Court decided that the likely costs of excluding unlawfully obtained evidence outweigh the likely social benefits. Excluding such evidence would hinder the deliberately simple deportation hearing system, would possibly suppress large amounts of information that had been obtained lawfully, and would "compel the courts to release from custody persons who would then immediately resume their commission of a crime through their continuing, unlawful presence in this country." In the Court's view, the social benefits from excluding such evidence would be minor because exclusion would have little deterrent effect on future Fourth Amendment violations by INS officials. *INS v. Lopez–Mendoza* (Sup.Ct.1984).

(1) OUTSIDE THE TERRITORIAL BOUNDS OF THE UNITED STATES

Ordinarily, the United States has power only over persons and property contained within its territorial bounds, including the territorial waters. One exception is the pre-boarding inspection offices established in foreign countries to inspect aliens before their departure to the United States. Congress has authorized the Attorney General, with the consent of the Secretary of State to detail immigration officers for duty in foreign countries. INA § 103(a). Pre-inspection occurs only when the vessel proceeds directly to this country and eliminates the need for inspection at the border.

In 1981 the President of the United States proclaimed that the entry of undocumented aliens from the high seas would be prevented by the interdiction of certain vessels carrying such aliens. Through Executive Order 12324 of September 29, 1981, the President gave the INS the authority to stop and board vessels which either came from the United States or from foreign nations having agreements with the United States (currently only Haiti), which allowed such stops. Once on board, the INS is authorized by the President to make inquiries of those on board and examine documents to determine the destination and purpose of the vessel. If the Service finds or has reason to believe that an offense is being committed in violation of United States immigration laws, the Executive Order directs the INS to return the vessel and its passengers to the country from which the vessel comes.

The Executive Order apparently extends the INS' authority to the high seas. The D.C. Circuit in *Haitian Refugee Center v. Gracey* (D.C.Cir.1987) upheld the statutory and constitutional authority of U.S. officials to interdict on the high seas aliens who lack visas. The Refugee Center challenged the 1981 agreement between the United States and Haiti permitting U.S. authorities to board Haitian vessels on the high seas to inspect, among other things, the status of the people on board. The court rejected the Center's allegations that the agreement denied the aliens Due Process, on the ground that aliens have no constitutional right to enter the United States. This right of interdiction was upheld in *Haitian Refugee Center v. Baker* (11th Cir.1992) which denied judicial review of INS decisions under these circumstances on the ground that the aliens never presented themselves at the U.S. border. See § 9–2.4.

(2) AT THE BORDER

The INS has the authority to stop all vehicles and persons at the border or its functional equivalent. Because Congress has the unquestioned power to admit or exclude aliens, it can authorize inspection of all persons as they cross the border. *See* INA § 235. Incident to this inspection power at the border, the Immigration Service may board and search any vehicle, including boats and aircraft, which they believe contains aliens. These searches may be legally conducted without a search warrant and can occur at the border or in the territorial waters of the United States. INA §§ 235, 287.

When an alien arrives at the border, the INS is authorized to inspect her/him to determine whether the alien may enter the United States or whether s/he is excludable. INA § 235(a). After this inspection, the examining officer may elect to admit the alien and in practice, nearly all aliens with visas are admitted. If the alien appears excludable, the officer may temporarily detain the alien for further inquiry. INA § 235(b). This procedure is customarily referred to as secondary inspection. The inquiry provides the INS with additional information about the alien's right to enter. Although a detained alien is interrogated by the Service, the Fifth Circuit held in *United States v. Henry* (1979) that no *Miranda*-type warning is necessary unless the questioning becomes custodial in nature.

The immigration officer also may elect to release the alien on parole pending further investigation. Under INA § 212(d)(5), the INS is authorized to parole, temporarily and under such conditions as the Service prescribes, any alien entering the United States. The Service grants parole chiefly as a matter of practicality. Often, time constraints prohibit the Service from making a thorough investigation at the border and parole allows the Service additional time to determine the alien's right to enter the United States. The alien who enters on parole has not "entered," is not admitted, and may be excluded without formal deportation proceedings. Such aliens do have a statutory right to an exclusion hearing (discussed *infra* chapter 9). The Board of Immigration Appeals held in *Matter of Castellon* (1981) that parole is purely discretionary and no administrative review of the decision is possible, although judicial review will lie in a district court for a declaratory judgment or habeas corpus action.

Alternatively, the immigration officer may choose to refer the alien to other immigration personnel. If the officer believes the alien's excludability is easily remedied, s/he may refer the alien to the district director for a waiver of inadmissability. 8 C.F.R. § 235.7. In rare cases, the officer may believe the alien is excludable and can temporarily exclude the alien for security reasons. If so, the officer refers the case to the regional commissioner who determines whether the alien will receive a hearing. INA § 235(c). Again, no administrative appeal from this decision is possible. Finally, after inspecting the alien, the officer may conclude s/he is excludable. The officer must then refer the alien to an immigration judge for a final determination. INA § 235(b). After the officer decides to refer the alien, the Code of Federal Regulations requires the officer to give notice to the alien of the hearing and to advise the alien of her/his right to counsel at no expense to the government. 8 C.F.R. § 235.6(a).

(3) 100 MILES INSIDE THE BORDER

(a) Investigatory Stops for Identification. The Supreme Court applies somewhat different standards to investigatory stops made by roving patrols and at fixed check-points. The Court in *United States v. Brignoni–*

Ponce (Sup.Ct.1975) held that roving patrols may stop vehicles at points away from the border only if they are aware of specific articulable facts that reasonably warrant suspicion that the vehicle contains aliens illegally in the United States. Even though the intrusion resulting from a brief stop is modest, the Court concluded that it is not reasonable under the Fourth Amendment to make random stops. Factors relevant to the existence of a reasonable suspicion include proximity to the border, traffic patterns, previous experience with alien traffic in the area, the driver's behavior, the appearance of the vehicle, and the officer's experience in recognizing the characteristic appearance of foreign nationals. Foreign appearance alone, however, is insufficient to support an inference of illegal presence. The Court applied this standard in *United States v. Cortez* (Sup.Ct.1981), where the Court held that the roving patrol did have a reasonable suspicion. While the Court disapproved of random stops in both *Cortez* and *Brignoni–Ponce,* the Court has indicated in *Delaware v. Prouse* (Sup.Ct.1979) that using patrols to stop every car, or perhaps some other systematic number of cars, may be consistent with the Fourth Amendment.

In addition, the INS can make routine investigatory stops at reasonably located fixed check-points even in the absence of any suspicion that the vehicle contains illegal aliens. The Court in *United States v. Martinez–Fuerte* (Sup.Ct.1976) reasoned that the Service's need to make such stops in order to control the entry of illegal aliens is great and the consequent intrusion on Fourth Amendment rights is limited since motorists are given advance warning of the stop which involves only the briefest detention—usually less than a minute. On balance, the Court supported the INS' right to make investigatory stops at fixed check-points.

(b) Searches. The INS also utilizes vehicle searches as another way of detecting illegal aliens. At areas removed from the border, Congress has empowered the INS to board and search any vehicle to check for illegal aliens without a warrant. *See* INA § 287(a)(3). The courts, however, have limited this power when the officers act without a search warrant. In *Almeida–Sanchez v. United States* (Sup.Ct.1973), the Supreme Court held that a warrantless search of an automobile made by a roving patrol without probable cause or consent violated the alien's right to be free from unreasonable searches and seizures. The Court extended this holding to searches made at fixed check-points in *United States v. Ortiz* (Sup.Ct.1975). In *Ortiz,* the Court concluded that a vehicle search involves a substantial invasion of privacy; and to protect motorists from arbitrary searches, the INS must have probable cause to believe that the vehicle contains illegal aliens before a search is possible. When conducting the search, immigration officers may inspect only those areas of the car where an alien could reasonably hide. In other words, the officer may not, as the Supreme Court observed in *United States v. Ross* (Sup.Ct.1982), open and search small pieces of luggage or other small containers and compartments to look for aliens.

(c) Temporary Detention for Questioning. One step between an investigatory stop for identification and an actual arrest is a forcible detention of a suspected alien for interrogation. While the alien questioned during an investigatory stop is free to leave, an alien forcibly detained is not, even though s/he is not technically under arrest *Yam Sang Kwai v. INS* (D.C.Cir.1969). Immigration officers may forcibly detain persons temporarily when the circumstances warrant a reasonable suspicion that the alien is illegally in the United States. The First Circuit rationalized in *Navia–Duran v. INS*

(1977) that, since a forcible detention falls short of an actual arrest, no *Miranda*-type warning is necessary before questioning the alien. Other circuits endorse this view. Courts will consider, however, the voluntariness of any statement given by the alien in the absence of a *Miranda*-type warning. If the INS coerced the alien, her/his right to Due Process, as guaranteed by the Fifth Amendment, may be violated. The court, as in *Navia–Duran*, may suppress any evidence obtained through coercion during the deportation hearing.

(4) INTERIOR OF THE UNITED STATES

With the exception of areas within 100 miles of the external boundaries of the United States, the INS may not make investigatory stops using roving patrols or fixed check-points. INA § 283(a). The Service may, however, briefly detain aliens for interrogation. Like detentions made near the border, the INS must have a reasonable belief that the alien is illegally present in this country before detaining her/him for interrogation. Special circumstances, however, may permit greater INS authority. The D.C. Circuit Court of Appeals upheld the Attorney General's authority, during the Iranian hostage crisis, to order nonimmigrant Iranian students to report to INS district offices and to demonstrate their lawful status. *Narenji v. Civiletti* (D.D.C. 1979).

The INS may also search vehicles inside the United States if there is probable cause. Of course, the INS may search not only vehicles, but business establishments as well, if they obtain an appropriate search warrant. While immigration officers have substantial authority to search if they have a warrant, the court in *Blackie's House of Beef, Inc. v. Castillo* (D.D.C.1978) held that the authority is limited. First, the warrant must have been properly issued. Second, the search warrant must be issued for persons, not property. As the court said in *Blackie's,* neither the Fourth Amendment nor any statute authorizes immigration officers to use a warrant commanding a search for property as permission to enter a private business establishment to search for illegal aliens employed there. Due to the large number of undocumented aliens in the United States and the difficulties in enforcing the immigration laws, however, the Supreme Court has increasingly applied a relaxed standard of review to alleged Fourth Amendment violations by immigration officers. *See, e.g., INS v. Delgado* (Sup.Ct.1984). If the INS makes the search in retaliation for the alien's union activities, however, a district court has held in *United States v. Turner* (N.D.Cal.1982) that the employer who requests such a search violates the National Labor Relations Act.

(a) Arrests Without a Warrant. The INA empowers immigration officers to arrest, without a warrant, "any alien in the United States, if he has reason to believe that the alien so arrested is in the United States in violation of any such law or regulation and is likely to escape before a warrant can be obtained for his arrest...." INA § 287(a)(2). The Tenth Circuit in *Roa–Rodriguez v. United States* (1969) has limited this authority by holding that a belief that the alien intends to violate her/his entry conditions is insufficient for an arrest. The arresting officer must base her/his belief on something more than mere suspicion. After an arrest made without a warrant, specific administrative procedures for the INS must be followed. Once arrested, the alien is taken before a different immigration officer for questioning unless no other officer is readily available. 8 C.F.R. § 287.3. If the examining officer

determines that a prima facie case exists for deporting the alien, s/he refers the case to an immigration judge.

Even though deportation is a severe penalty, courts have concluded that deportation is civil and not criminal in nature and hence, uniformly agree that a *Miranda* warning at the time of the arrest for deportation is not required. After the INS makes the decision to proceed with deportation, however, section 287.3 of the Code of Federal Regulations requires the arresting officer to advise the alien of (1) the reason for the arrest; (2) the alien's right to counsel at no expense to the government and the availability of free legal service programs; and (3) the alien's right to remain silent. While not technically a *Miranda* warning, in essence, the arresting officer is required to advise the alien of her/his rights as defined by the Court in *Miranda*. Although the statute requires the officer to give the warning only after s/he decides to proceed with deportation, the court may scrutinize any statements given by the alien before the warning from the INS to determine whether the statements were made voluntarily. In addition, the alien must be informed within 24 hours whether s/he will be detained further or released on bond or recognizance.

(b) Arrests With a Warrant. If the INS issues a warrant for arrest, it simultaneously issues an Order to Show Cause why the alien is not deportable. (See § 8–3.2 for a discussion of the Order to Show Cause.) Only INS district directors, deputy district directors, and assistant directors; chief and assistant patrol agents; and directors of the Organized Crime Drug Enforcement Task Force may issue an arrest warrant, and then only if it is necessary to hold the alien in custody. 8 C.F.R. § 242.2. Once issued, the INS must serve the warrant

within a reasonable period of time. *See United States v. Weaver* (4th Cir.1967). Should the INS determine the alien is not deportable, any officer authorized to issue an arrest warrant may cancel it.

The Code of Federal Regulations also requires the arresting officer to inform the alien at the time of her/his arrest of the reason for the arrest and to advise the alien of her/his rights. 8 C.F.R. § 242.2(b). The officer advises the alien of: (1) the right to counsel at no expense to the government; (2) that any statements made may be used against her/him in subsequent proceedings; and (3) whether or not s/he will remain in custody. Arrested aliens are often advised of their rights through Form I–214 which is served on the alien with the arrest warrant. The form lists the *Miranda*-type warning in English; hence, an alien who does not understand English may sign the form without realizing its significance. If the alien is not advised of these rights or fails to understand them, s/he may move to suppress evidence obtained because of the lack of warning. *Navia–Duran v. INS* (1st Cir.1977).

(c) Release on Bond or Personal Recognizance. Once arrested, the INS has discretion either to release the alien or continue the custody. According to the INA, pending a final determination of deportability, any alien arrested may (1) be continued in custody; or (2) be released upon bond in the amount of not less than $500 with security approved by the Attorney General, containing such conditions as the Attorney General may prescribe; or (3) be released on conditional parole. INA § 242(a). The INA also authorizes the INS to revoke the bond or parole at any time if the alien is likely to flee. A lawfully admitted alien convicted of an aggravated felony must demonstrate that s/he does not pose a threat to the community and that s/he will appear

before any scheduled hearings to be eligible for release from custody. INA § 242(a)(2).

In practice, as the Board observed in *Matter of Patel* (BIA 1976) the alien is usually granted release on personal recognizance unless s/he poses a risk to national security or is a bail risk. The INS has discretion to determine whether the alien threatens national security and, as the Fifth Circuit concluded in *Barbour v. District Director* (Sup.Ct.1974), may base its decision on undisclosed security information. The factors considered relevant by the Board in *Patel* to determine whether the alien is a bail risk include prior arrests in this country, convictions in the alien's native country, illegal entry into the United States, participation in subversive activities, employment status, and the presence of relatives in the United States. The bail or parole decision is reviewable by any court of competent jurisdiction. INA § 242(a).

The INA gives the Attorney General the authority to provide for special expedited deportation proceedings for aggravated felons. INA § 242A(a). These special proceedings are to take place at the federal, state, or local correctional facility where the felon is incarcerated. INA § 242A(a). The initiation and completion of deportation proceedings, as well as subsequent administrative appeals should be completed "to the extent possible" before the aggravated felon's release. INA § 242A(d)(1).

The intention of allowing special expedited proceedings for aggravated felons is to have the entire deportation process occur while the alien is serving her/his sentence. In that way the alien can be deported immediately upon release from incarceration with no intervening detention. In keeping with this goal of expediency, the 1990 Act reduced the period during which an aggravated felon can seek judicial review to 30 days. INA § 106(a)(1).

Because Congress recognized the difficulty for an incarcerated felon to secure adequate counsel, witnesses, and other aspects of presenting her/his case, INA § 242A(b) provides that the "Attorney General shall make reasonable efforts to ensure that the alien's access to counsel" is not impaired. INA § 242A(b).

§ 8–3.2 Deportation Hearing

a. Order to Show Cause

The deportation process is officially commenced by the filing with the immigration judge of the Order to Show Cause why the alien is not deportable. 8 C.F.R. § 242.1. Only those officials with power to issue warrants have the authority to issue an Order to Show Cause and then, as the Supreme Court noted in *Abel v. United States* (Sup.Ct.1960), only on the basis of a prima facie showing of deportability. If an alien has been given a reasonable opportunity to be present at a proceeding to determine her/his deportability and s/he fails without reasonable cause to attend, the special inquiry officer may proceed and make a determination "as if the alien were present." INA § 242(b). If the alien fails to appear for a deportation hearing, s/he shall not be eligible for most kinds of relief from deportation. INA § 242B(e). Section 242(b) outlines the basic requirements for the proceedings: (1) the alien must be given proper notice; (2) the alien may choose to be represented by counsel; (3) the alien shall have the opportunity to offer evidence in her/his behalf and examine evidence against her/him; (4) a decision of deportability must be based upon "reasonable, substantial, and probative evidence." INA § 242(b)(1)–(4).

The Code of Federal Regulations lists the specific requirements for an Order to Show Cause. It must contain a statement of the nature of the proceeding, the legal authority under which the proceeding is conducted, a concise statement of the factual allegations informing the alien of the act or conduct alleged to be in violation of the law, and a designation of the charges against the alien and of the statutory provisions alleged to have been violated. 8 C.F.R. § 242.1(b). In addition, the Order to Show Cause lists the time and place when the alien will be required to show cause why s/he should not be deported.

The Code of Federal Regulations also provides for service of the order. The INS may either serve the order by personal service or "routine service" which usually means registered mail. In either case, when the order is served, the Service must inform the alien of the order's contents, of her/his right to counsel, and that any statements made may be used against her/him. 8 C.F.R. § 242.1(c). The Court of Appeals in *Attoh v. INS* (D.C.Cir.1979) held that a failure to give the alien notice of these rights may result in a new hearing.

b. Participants in the Deportation Hearing

Of course, the most obvious party to the proceedings is the alien. (The alien's rights will be discussed in a following subsection.) In addition to the alien, however, the deportation hearing also involves an immigration judge, the trial attorney, the alien's counsel, and if necessary, an interpreter.

(1) IMMIGRATION JUDGE

In 1982, the Attorney General of the United States gave final approval to a plan to reorganize the Board of Immigration Appeals and the immigration judges into the Executive Office of Immigration Review that became part of the Department of Justice effective January 1, 1983. Immigration judges are selected by the Attorney General. The judges may conduct specified classes of proceedings, including exclusion and deportation hearings. INA § 101(b)(4). The INA authorizes the immigration judge to "conduct proceedings under this section to determine the deportability of any alien, and shall administer oaths, present and receive evidence, interrogate, examine, and cross-examine the alien or witnesses, and ... shall make determinations, including orders of deportation." INA § 242(b). The INA allows the immigration judge to serve as both prosecutor and judge, although in practice the judge acts as a prosecutor only when the alien concedes deportability. The Ninth Circuit in *LeTourneur v. INS* (9th Cir.1976) has, however, held that the dual role of the immigration judge is consistent with Due Process.

In addition, the Code of Federal Regulations provides the immigration judge with the authority to consider claims for discretionary relief and to determine the country of deportation. 8 C.F.R. § 242.8(a). As a presiding officer in a deportation hearing, the immigration judge has the authority to hear motions for postponements, rules on the admissibility of evidence, orders the taking of depositions if a witness is not readily available and her/his testimony is essential, and issues subpoenas. 8 C.F.R. §§ 242.13, 242.14, 287.4(a)(2). The immigration judge may not, however, exercise authority in matters exclusively under the control of the district director, including, but not limited to, waivers of inadmissibility, orders to show cause, and extensions of temporary stay. Finally, if the immigration judge considers her/himself unqualified to conduct the hearing, s/he may withdraw pursuant to the provisions of 8 C.F.R. § 242.8(b). According to the Fifth Circuit in *Marcello v. Ahrens* (5th Cir.1954), one such circumstance calling for withdrawal occurs when the immigration judge performed an investigatory function in the case. The alien must request the judge to withdraw if s/he is unqualified or biased and if the judge refuses, the ruling may be questioned on appeal.

(2) Trial Attorney

In cases where the alien does not concede deportability or is unrepresented and incompetent or under 16 years of age, the district director assigns an attorney to the case. 8 C.F.R. § 242.9(b). Pursuant to the INA the trial attorney "shall have authority to present evidence, and to interrogate, examine and cross-examine the alien or other witness in the proceedings." INA § 242(b). In effect, the trial attorney acts as the prosecutor for the government. Calling the prosecutor a trial attorney may be misleading, however, since the prosecutor need not be a lawyer. The Board of Immigration Appeals in *Matter of Reyes–Gomez* (1973) concluded that using laypersons as trial attorneys does not violate Due Process. As the prosecutor, the trial attorney may appeal a decision of the immigration judge and may move for a reconsideration. 8 C.F.R. § 242.9(a).

(3) ALIEN'S COUNSEL

The INA provides that the "alien shall have the privilege of being represented (at no expense to the Government) by such counsel, authorized to practice in such proceedings, as he shall choose." INA § 242(b)(2). The alien is informed of this right several times during the deportation process, including at the time of arrest, when served with the Order to Show Cause, and at the outset of the deportation hearing. As a matter of course, the immigration judge routinely grants one postponement during the hearing to allow the alien to obtain counsel. *See* 8 C.F.R. § 242.13. In certain very rare circumstances, courts have found that Due Process requires that an indigent alien be appointed counsel in a deportation proceeding. The indigent alien has a right to appointed counsel if, in the particular case, the assistance of counsel is necessary to provide "fundamental fairness." *Aguilera–Enriquez v. INS* (6th Cir.1975). The immigration judge must advise the alien of the availability of free legal services for which s/he may qualify. 8 C.F.R. § 242.16(a). The Code of Federal Regulations allows the following persons to represent an alien in deportation proceedings: (1) attorneys who are members in good standing of the highest court of any state, (2) under certain conditions, law students and law graduates not yet admitted to the bar, (3) representatives of accredited organizations recognized by the Board of Immigration Appeals, (4) accredited officials of the government to which the alien owes allegiance, (5) statutorily defined reputable individuals who meet certain criteria, (6) attorneys outside the United States licensed to practice law and in good standing in a court of general jurisdiction of the country in which the attorney resides, and (7) if the Board grants permission, amicus curiae. 8 C.F.R. § 292.1.

(4) INTERPRETER

If the alien does not understand English, an interpreter may form an integral part of the deportation hearing. Although there is no statutorily defined right to have an interpreter present during the hearing, the alien may request an interpreter if s/he does not understand English. According to the Seventh Circuit in *Niarchos v. INS* (7th Cir.1968), a deportation hearing conducted in a language the alien does not understand and without an interpreter present may result in a denial of Due Process. An interpreter in a deportation case is sworn to interpret and translate accurately. 8 C.F.R. § 242.12. If the interpreter appears to be incompetent, the alien may raise the issue on appeal, but the Second Circuit in *United States ex rel. Catalano v. Shaughnessy* (2d Cir. 1952) held that the alien has the burden of proving the incompetence. Another difficulty is that the interpreter usually interprets only direct questions or statements to the alien and the alien's responses; accordingly, the alien may not understand additional testimony, arguments of counsel, and other matters arising in the hearing.

c. *The Alien's Rights During the Deportation Hearing*

The INA provides that all aliens subject to deportation proceedings are entitled to the basic rights inherent in procedural Due Process. INA § 242(b). In 1903, the Supreme Court laid the foundations for this principle in the *Japanese Immigrant Case* (Sup.Ct.1903). Included among those rights are the right to adequate "notice, reasonable under all circumstances, of the nature of the charges against him and of the time and place at which the proceedings will be held."   INA § 242(b)(1).

The INA also provides that the "alien shall have a reasonable opportunity to examine the evidence against him, to present evidence in his own behalf, and to cross-examine witnesses presented by the Government."   INA § 242(b)(3).   The alien may present any evidence that is material and relevant either to the issue of deportability or discretionary relief.   8 C.F.R. § 242.14(c).   The alien also may present either oral testimony or written depositions.   If an essential witness is unavailable to testify, the alien may request the immigration judge to order a deposition.   8 C.F.R. § 242.14(e).   The alien may also apply for a subpoena to compel the presence of a witness at the hearing.   Before the immigration judge may issue a subpoena, the alien must state what s/he expects to prove by the testimony, and must affirmatively show that a diligent effort was made to produce the witness without the subpoena.   8 C.F.R. § 287.4(a)(2).   The alien's right to cross-examine includes the right to examine government witnesses whose testimony was submitted via an affidavit, but, as the Sixth Circuit concluded in *Weinbrand v. Prentis* (6th Cir.1925), the alien must make the request at the time the witnesses' testimony is introduced.

The alien has the right to be present at and participate in the deportation hearing.   According to the INA, however, "[i]f, any alien has been given a reasonable opportunity to be present at a proceeding under this section, and without reasonable cause fails or refuses to attend or remain in attendance at such proceeding, the special inquiry officer may proceed to a determination in like manner as if the alien were present." INA § 242(b). The Board of Immigration Appeals endorsed the fairness of this procedure in *In re S* (1957), subject only to the conditions that the alien was served with the Order to Show Cause and refused to appear without reasonable cause. If the alien is present at the hearing, s/he may choose either to testify or remain silent. The Supreme Court in *Hyun v. Landon* (Sup.Ct.1956), however, affirmed the right of the immigration judge to draw unfavorable inferences from the alien's silence. *See Cabral–Avila v. INS* (9th Cir.1978) (same holding). If necessary, the immigration judge can compel the alien to testify. According to the Seventh Circuit in *Laqui v. INS* (7th Cir.1970), the alien may claim the Fifth Amendment privilege against self-incrimination only if her/his alleged actions constitute a crime.

d. The Hearing

(1) CONDUCT OF THE HEARING

Deportation hearings are open to the public unless the immigration judge excludes the general public or particular individuals in order to protect witnesses, the alien, or the public interest. 8 C.F.R. § 242.16(a). At the outset of the hearing, the immigration judge must advise the alien of her/his rights during the hearing and inquire as to whether s/he waives any of those rights, place the alien under oath, read and explain the allegations of the Order to Show Cause, enter the order as an exhibit in the official record, and ask the alien to plead to the Order to Show Cause. 8 C.F.R. § 242.16. In a procedure analogous to pleading in the criminal context, the alien must either admit or deny the allegations of the Order to Show Cause. If the alien admits the allegations and concedes deportability, as usually occurs, the immigration judge accepts the plea and the hearing moves forward to determine issues of discretionary relief. 8 C.F.R. § 242.16(b). Alternatively, if the alien denies the allegations, the immigration judge requests the INS to assign a trial attorney and continues with both sides presenting evidence. 8 C.F.R. § 242.-16(c).

(2) Evidence

Both the trial attorney and the alien are allowed to present evidence to the deportation hearing. The rules of evidence applicable to criminal proceedings, however, do not apply to deportation hearings. The Supreme Court in *Bilokumsky v. Tod* (1923), noted that a failure to abide by judicial rules of evidence does not render a deportation hearing unfair. Evidence during a deportation hearing is controlled by the Code of Federal Regulations; any type of evidence is admissible so long as it is material and relevant to the issues before the hearing. 8 C.F.R. § 242.14. The regulation allows hearsay evidence if it meets the test of relevancy. Evidence may take the form of depositions and affidavits. If authenticated, tangible evidence is admissible. Either party may call witnesses to testify, but such testimony only will be taken under oath or affirmation administered by the immigration judge.

(3) Ancillary Matters

(a) Additional Charges. In most cases, the alien's deportability is determined by the charges that appear in the Order to Show Cause. The Ninth Circuit con-

cluded in *Madrona Banez v. Boyd* (9th Cir.1956), that incorrect statements or errors in the Order to Show Cause do not, however, render it invalid, if the trial attorney establishes the correct information at the hearing. During the hearing, the trial attorney may lodge additional charges of deportability against the alien. 8 C.F.R. § 242.16(d). The additional charges must be submitted in writing. When submitted, the immigration judge reads and explains the additional charges to the alien. Again, the judge must inform the alien of her/ his right to counsel and must recess the hearing to allow the alien additional time to meet the charges. 8 C.F.R. § 242.16(d). The Second Circuit in *United States ex rel. Catalano v. Shaughnessy* (2d Cir.1952) upheld the procedure of lodging additional charges as consistent with Due Process.

(b) Designation of Country and Application for Discretionary Relief. During the hearing, the immigration judge must provide the alien with an opportunity to designate a country for deportation should s/he be found deportable. INA § 243(a). This designation does not constitute an admission of deportability. After the alien has been given an opportunity to designate a country, the immigration judge names as an alternative country of deportation any country of which the alien is a subject or national in the event that the alien's choice does not accept her/him. INA § 243(a). The same section of the Immigration and Nationality Act sets up a system for determining still another country of deportation should the previous choices fail to accept the alien. Moreover, the Attorney General may disallow a country if s/he determines that deportation would be prejudicial to the interests of the United States.

If the alien believes s/he is eligible for some form of discretionary relief, s/he must apply for it during the hearing. 8 C.F.R. § 242.17. (The types of discretionary relief available to the alien will be more fully discussed in "Relief From Deportation" § 8–4, *infra*.) Again, an application for discretionary relief is not construed as an admission of deportability. The alien may apply for suspension of deportation, voluntary departure, adjustment of status, or other appropriate relief. 8 C.F.R. § 242.17. The immigration judge must inform the alien of her/his apparent eligibility for suspension of deportation or registry, and must allow the alien an opportunity to apply. The judge is not required to inform the alien about other types of available relief.

(c) The Decision

(1) Burden of Proof. The deportation decision must be based on reasonable, substantial, and probative evidence in order to be valid. INA § 242(b)(4). The Code of Federal Regulations provides that "[a] determination of deportability shall not be valid unless it is found by clear, unequivocal and convincing evidence that the facts alleged as grounds for deportation are true." 8 C.F.R. § 242.14(a). The Supreme Court established this standard of proof in *Woodby v. INS* (Sup.Ct.1966). The Second Circuit held in *United States ex rel. Bishop v. Watkins* (Sup.Ct.1947) that initially, the government has the burden of proving, with clear and unequivocal evidence, that the alien is, indeed, an alien. The burden then shifts to the alien to prove the time, place, and manner of her/his entry into the United States. INA § 291. According to the Sixth Circuit in *Brader v. Zurbrick* (6th Cir.1930), the government must then meet and overcome positive evidence of the alien's legal right to be in the United States. If the government fails to meet its burden of proof, the immigration judge must decide for the alien.

(2) Rendering the Decision. The decision of the immigration judge may be either written or oral and must include a discussion of the evidence and findings, unless the alien has conceded deportability. 8 C.F.R. § 242.-18(a). The decision must either direct the alien's deportation, the termination of the proceedings, or the granting of discretionary relief. The order may be in the alternative. 8 C.F.R. § 242.18(c). If the decision is written, a copy must be served on the alien and the trial attorney. Oral decisions, however, must be made with both parties present. 8 C.F.R. § 242.19. The order is final unless there is an appeal. 8 C.F.R. § 242.20. The alien may appeal any decision to the Board of Immigration Appeals, but must do so within ten days of the decision. 8 C.F.R. § 242.21.

§ 8–4 RELIEF FROM DEPORTATION

If the immigration judge finds the alien deportable, the alien may seek relief from deportation before the INS actually executes the deportation order. This section examines two major types of relief available to the alien under a deportation order—appeals, both administrative and judicial; and discretionary relief.

§ 8–4.1 Appeals and Relief

a. Motion to Reopen or Reconsider

An alien may move to reopen or reconsider the decision of the immigration judge by submitting Form I–328 or the judge may do so on her/his own motion. 8 C.F.R. § 242.22. The immigration judge hears the motion unless the alien has already appealed the decision to the Board of Immigration Appeals. The immigration judge may grant the motion only if s/he is satisfied that the evidence sought to be offered is material and was unavailable at the time of the hearing. 8 C.F.R. § 242.22. Hence, if the alien is seeking to have the judge reconsider the same evidence, the judge will deny the motion and the alien must seek alternative routes of review. The judge also may deny the motion because the alien has not established a prima facie case for the underlying substantive relief sought. *INS v. Abudu* (Sup.Ct.1988). A motion to reopen for the purpose of providing the alien an opportunity to apply for discretionary relief that was available during the hearing will be denied unless the alien's right to make the application was not fully explained at the time of the hearing. 8 C.F.R. § 242.22. Likewise, in regard to a belated application for asylum, the judge may hold that the alien has not reasonably explained her/his failure to apply for asylum prior to completion of the initial deportation proceedings, as required by 8 C.F.R. § 208.11. *Abudu.* Furthermore, in cases requesting discretionary relief (asylum, suspension of deportation, and adjustment of status, but not withholding of deportation), the judge may ignore the above concerns and simply decide that even if the application were properly asserted, the alien is not entitled to the discretionary relief. *Id.* The appropriate standard of review of such denials on any of these grounds is abuse of discretion. The Court in *Abudu* stressed that motions to reopen are disfavored in deportation proceedings because "[g]ranting such motions too freely will permit endless delay of deportation by aliens creative and fertile enough to continuously produce new and material facts sufficient to establish a prima facie case." Filing a motion to reopen the hearing will not stay the execution of a pending deportation order. The alien must move separately for a stay of deportation. *Id.*

b. *Administrative Appeals*

An appeal taken from a deportation hearing is heard by the Board of Immigration Appeals (BIA). 8 C.F.R. § 242.21. The BIA is supervised by the Department of Justice and is comprised of a Chairperson and four additional members, all appointed by the Attorney General. 8 C.F.R. § 3.1(a)(1). The BIA has jurisdiction over the following appeals: decisions of the immigration judge in exclusion proceedings, decisions of the immigration judge in deportation proceedings, decisions concerning discretionary relief, decisions involving administrative fines, decisions concerning petitions for immigrant status, decisions relating to bond or parole, decisions of the immigration judge involving recision of an adjustment of status, decisions of asylum officers or applications for asylum or withholding of deportation filed by alien crewmen or stowaways, and decisions of the immigration judge relating to Temporary Protected Status. 8 C.F.R. § 3.1(b).

In deciding the cases that come before it, the Board can exercise the discretion and authority conferred on it by the Attorney General. 8 C.F.R. § 3.1(d). These powers include the right to dismiss summarily any appeal from deportation proceedings if the party fails to substantiate the basis for the appeal. The Board may also dispose of a case by remanding it to the immigration judge, or in rare cases, by referring the case to the Attorney General for a decision. 8 C.F.R. § 3.1(d) & (h). Any decision made by the Board is administratively final although the alien may seek judicial review. 8 C.F.R. § 3.1(d)(2). The Board bases its decisions on the record of the deportation or exclusion hearing, briefs submitted by counsel, and oral argument. 8 C.F.R. §§ 3.1(e), 3.5. Oral arguments are heard only if the petitioner requests an opportunity for an argument. 8 C.F.R. § 3.1(e). Any appeal taken from a deportation hearing, except as to aggravated felons or a motion to reopen, automatically stays execution of a deportation order while the appeal is pending. 8 C.F.R. § 3.6.

c. Judicial Review of Orders of Deportation and Exclusion

The INA authorizes the courts to take jurisdiction over certain decisions appealed from the BIA. *See* INA § 106. The alien has six months from the final order of deportation to file a judicial appeal and such appeal automatically stays execution of the exclusion or deportation order. In deportation cases, the sole method for judicial review is by petition for review in the Court of Appeals. The Eighth Circuit in *Daneshvar v. Chauvin* (8th Cir.1981) held that review of final orders of deportation lies exclusively in the Court of Appeals when deportability is in question and habeas corpus review is available only with respect to the denial of discretionary relief where deportability itself is not an issue. In exclusion cases, the sole method of judicial review is by way of a habeas corpus petition in United States district court. Whenever the alien is being held in custody, habeas corpus is available to review the legality of the custody. INA § 106a(a)(10). The Fifth Circuit Court of Appeals in *United States ex rel. Marcello v. District Director* (5th Cir.1981) held that in enacting INA § 106(a)(10), Congress intended the phrase "held in custody" to mean actual physical custody in the place of detention. Until there is actual physical custody, the alien is required to seek review by direct appeal.

(1) DEPORTATION APPEALS

The Supreme Court in *Foti v. INS* (Sup.Ct.1963) noted that the fundamental purpose behind the petition for review is to reduce the likelihood that the process of judicial review will be used by persons subject to deportation to forestall departure by dilatory practices in the courts. The INA sets forth specific requirements for granting a petition for review. First, the appeal must be taken from a final order of deportation. INA § 106(a). According to the Supreme Court in *Cheng Fan Kwok v. INS* (Sup.Ct.1968), Congress restricted review of deportation orders to those orders entered during proceedings under INA § 242(b). Final orders issued during deportation proceedings and reviewable in the Court of Appeals are as follows: denials of discretionary relief; denials of motions to reopen; and denials of suspension of deportation, withholding of deportation, and voluntary departure.

The Seventh Circuit Court of Appeals held that the district director's denial of a nonimmigrant student's applications for a school transfer and extension of stay was not reviewable in the Court of Appeals because the applications were not submitted pursuant to a proceeding under INA § 242(b) or a motion to reopen such a proceeding. *Kavasji v. INS* (7th Cir.1982). This rule was not altered by the Supreme Court when it held that the Ninth Circuit Court of Appeals had jurisdiction to review a constitutional challenge of the House of Representatives' authority to veto an immigration judge's suspension of deportation. *INS v. Chadha* (Sup.Ct.

1983). Congress argued that the One–House veto authorized by the INA was not a proceeding under § 242(b), and that the Court of Appeals therefore lacked jurisdiction under INA § 106 to review its constitutionality. The Court interpreted the term "final order" in § 106 to encompass all matters "on which the validity of the final order is contingent, rather than only those determinations actually made at the hearing." Because Chadha's deportation was contingent upon the validity of the challenged veto and because Chadha was directly attacking the deportation order, the Court of Appeals had jurisdiction under § 106.

In *Mohammadi–Motlagh v. INS* (9th Cir.1984), the Ninth Circuit confirmed that the *Chadha* decision did not signify a retreat from the narrow construction of § 106 adopted in *Cheng Fan Kwok*. The Court of Appeals in *Mohammadi–Motlagh* found no jurisdiction to review the denial of the alien's request for a school transfer because, in contrast to the purely legal question presented in *Chadha*, the alien's challenge of the district director's decision raised factual questions as to whether discretion was properly exercised.

Second, the INA authorizes judicial review only after the alien has exhausted administrative appeals available to her/him as of right. INA § 106(c). Hence, if the alien has not appealed the decision of the immigration judge to the BIA, s/he may not seek review in the Court of Appeals. The Third Circuit in *Bak v. INS* (3d Cir.1982) concluded that failure to exhaust administrative remedies deprives the Court of Appeals of jurisdiction to consider the case, but referred to a judge-made exception to the exhaustion requirement. Exhaustion is unnecessary if administrative appeal would be "futile."

Administrative appeal would be futile if the BIA is absolutely bound by INS regulations and could not help but render the same decision.

Another potential exception to the exhaustion requirement is an allegation of "a wholesale, carefully orchestrated program of constitutional violations." *Haitian Refugee Center v. Smith* (5th Cir.1982). In *Haitian Refugee Center,* 4,000 Haitians claimed they had been denied Due Process and Equal Protection by accelerated INS deportation procedures instituted to achieve the mass deportation of Haitian nationals seeking political asylum in the United States. The Haitians did not seek reversal of the district director's denial of their claims for asylum. Hence, the Fifth Circuit focused on the distinction between a constitutional challenge and a substantive claim of entitlement. The court held that the exhaustion requirement did not bar the district court from asserting jurisdiction. The Fifth Circuit decided that a pattern or scheme by immigration officials to violate the constitutional rights of aliens is independently reviewable in the district court under its federal question jurisdiction. The court, however, stressed the uniqueness of the case in warning that its holding was not to be construed as permitting a constitutional challenge in the district court based on a procedural ruling in a deportation case with which an alien is dissatisfied.

In addition, INA § 106(c) precludes judicial review in cases where the alien has departed from the United States after entry of the deportation order. The Ninth Circuit in *Mendez v. INS* (9th Cir.1977), however, held that if the government had illegally forced the alien to leave the United States, the court could grant a petition for review.

Finally, the scope of the review power of the Court of Appeals in deportation cases is limited. The court is restricted to questioning whether the manner in which the proceeding was conducted was arbitrary, capricious, or illegal and whether the proceeding comported with the requirements of Due Process. *Biggin v. INS* (3d Cir.1973). The appeals court may review only those issues which were raised during the deportation hearing and which are part of the administrative record. INA § 106(a)(4). The Tenth Circuit in *Pilapil v. INS* (10th Cir.1970), however, concluded that the Court of Appeals could consider constitutional issues raised by the alien on appeal even though they were not raised during the hearing, so long as the facts necessary to decide the issue are part of the administrative record.

d. Discretionary Relief

(1) GENERAL CONSIDERATIONS

The alien under an order of deportation may apply for one or more of the available types of discretionary relief. If granted, discretionary relief eliminates or postpones the execution of the deportation order. The alien must generally apply for discretionary relief during the deportation hearing. *See* 8 C.F.R. § 242.17(e). (The alien may apply for various types of discretionary relief, discussed below, prior to the deportation hearing, *i.e.,* a request for asylum or registry. This section, however, examines discretionary relief only as it applies to the alien during deportation proceedings.) In some circumstances, the alien may apply for discretionary relief after the deportation hearing by moving to reopen the hearing. (See the previous section.) The immigration judge will grant a motion to reopen to apply for discretionary relief only if the circumstances which form the basis of the relief arose after the deportation hearing. 8 C.F.R. § 242.22. Hence, if the alien believes s/he is eligible for any type of discretionary relief, s/he must apply during the deportation hearing or risk being denied the opportunity to apply.

In determining whether to grant the requested relief, the judge undertakes a two step process. First, the judge determines whether the alien is eligible for the particular form of relief. The alien has the burden of proving that s/he meets the statutory requirements. 8 C.F.R. § 242.17(e). Even though the alien may meet the requirements, however, the judge does not necessarily grant the relief. The immigration judge has the discretion to make the final determination as to whether the relief will be granted. Even though the alien may establish her/his eligibility, the Ninth Circuit in *Patel v. INS* (9th Cir.1980), concluded that the judge may deny the requested relief. According to the Second Circuit in *Wong Wing Hang v. INS* (2d Cir.1966), judicial review of such a denial is limited to a determination of whether the agency abused its administrative discretion. The court in *Wong Wing Hang* observed that an abuse of discretion occurs if the denial was made without a rational explanation, departed from established policies in an unexplained manner, or rested on an impermissible basis such as discrimination in an unfair manner against a particular race or group.

(2) TYPES OF DISCRETIONARY RELIEF

(a) Voluntary Departure. According to the INA and Nationality Act, "the Attorney General may, in his discretion, permit any alien under deportation proceedings ... to depart voluntarily from the United States at his own expense in lieu of deportation if such alien shall establish to the satisfaction of the Attorney General that he is, and has been, a person of good moral character for at least five years immediately preceding his application for voluntary departure under this subsection." INA § 244(e). (An alien not yet in deportation hearings also may apply for voluntary departure under INA § 242(b) any time prior to the initiation of proceedings against him or her. 8 C.F.R. § 242.5(b). Relief under this section may be granted by district directors, district officers in charge of investigations, officers in charge, and chief patrol agents. 8 C.F.R. § 242.5(a)(1).) Certain aliens are prohibited from applying for voluntary departure, including those found deportable because of immoral or subversive activities. INA § 244(e). Voluntary departure remains, however, one of the most sought-after types of relief, especially when the alien concedes deportability. The reason behind the popularity of voluntary departure lies in that it avoids the stigma of deportation, enables the alien to select her/his own destination, and most important, facilitates the possibility of immediate return to the United States. An alien granted voluntary departure is not considered deported by the INS and, consequently, may re-apply for admission to the United States after departure. (Those aliens deported may not generally re-enter for five years.)

In order to be eligible for voluntary departure, the alien must prove that s/he meets the statutory requirements. *Hibbert v. INS* (2d Cir.1977). First, an alien granted voluntary departure under INA § 244(e) must show that s/he has the ability to pay her/his own expenses of departing. According to the Ninth Circuit, in *Diric v. INS* (9th Cir.1968), failure to prove an ability to pay the expenses makes the alien ineligible for voluntary departure. (If, however, an alien granted voluntary departure under INA § 242(b) is financially unable to depart at her/his own expense, the government may pay the departure expenses if the Attorney General deems the alien's removal to be in the best interest of the United States. INA § 242(b).) Second, the INA provides that no individual shall be entitled to voluntary deportation if the alien is deported for (1) certain criminal offenses (including crimes of moral turpitude, multiple criminal convictions, aggravated felonies, crimes involving controlled substances, firearms offenses, etc.); (2) persons who have given false testimony for the purpose of obtaining immigration benefits; (3) persons who at any time have assisted in the illegal entry of other aliens to the United States; and (4) persons deported for security reasons relating to espionage, terrorism, foreign policy consequences, and Nazi persecution. INA §§ 242(b), 241(a)(2)–(4).

If the alien meets the statutory requirements, s/he is eligible for voluntary departure. The final administrative decision, however, lies with the immigration judge and is discretionary.

Another form of voluntary departure is "extended voluntary departure." Extended voluntary departure allows aliens from countries with dangerous public order situations to remain in the United States. Extended voluntary departure has been granted during certain periods to aliens from countries such as Afghanistan,

Chile, Cuba, Ethiopia, Iran, Lebanon, Nicaragua, Poland, Uganda, and Vietnam. This policy has been increasingly criticized and challenged on the ground that extended voluntary departure is often granted or denied for improper political reasons. *See, e.g., Hotel & Restaurant Employees Union, Local 25 v. Smith* (D.D.C.1984). At the same time, others have advocated the extension of extended voluntary departure to individuals fleeing the strife in Central America. The practice of extended voluntary departure has been codified and largely replaced, at least for groups of aliens, by Temporary Protected Status under INA § 244a. See §§ 10–2.4–2.5. Extended voluntary departure may still be granted to individual aliens for humanitarian reasons.

(b) Suspension of Deportation. In certain cases, the alien may be eligible for suspension of deportation and adjustment of status to that of an alien lawfully admitted for permanent residence. According to the Ninth Circuit in *Fong v. INS* (9th Cir.1962), the sole purpose of suspension of deportation is to ameliorate the harsh consequences of deportation for those aliens who have been present in the United States for long periods of time. The INA provides that the Attorney General or her/his designated representative may suspend deportation for any alien who applies and meets the requirements. INA § 244(a). The requirements for suspension of deportation differ for aliens deportable for immoral and subversive activities and those persons deportable for other reasons. The former aliens must have been continuously present in the United States for ten years following the commission of the deportable act, must be persons of good moral character for the same amount of time, and must be persons whom the Attorney General believes would suffer exceptional and extremely unusual hardship if deported. INA § 244(a)(2). Aliens

deportable for less serious reasons must meet less rigid eligibility requirements, although it is still difficult to qualify for suspension of deportation. These aliens must have been physically present for seven years or more following the deportable act, must be persons of good moral character, and must be persons for whom deportation would cause extreme hardship. INA § 244(a)(1).

Again, aliens applying for suspension of deportation bear the burden of proving statutory eligibility. 8 C.F.R. § 242.17(e). In determining whether the alien has been continuously present, the BIA in *In re Bufalino* (1965) concluded that the immigration judge must calculate the alien's residence from her/his last deportable act, and not from the time of entry into the United States.

In *INS v. Phinpathya* (Sup.Ct.1984) the Supreme Court construed the continuous physical presence requirement of INA § 244 strictly to forbid suspension of deportation for an alien who had traveled three months outside the United States. The Court noted that Congress had changed the statute from "continuous residence" to limit the scope of discretionary relief from deportation. Following the strict holding of *Phinpathya*, the 5th Circuit denied suspension of deportation to two otherwise eligible aliens who had been continuously physically present in the United States for twelve years except for a one night stay in Mexico. *Sanchez–Dominguez v. INS* (5th Cir.1986). The hardships resulting from *Phinpathya* led Congress to overturn the Court's holding by amending § 244 to allow for "brief, casual, and innocent" absences from the United States which "did not meaningfully interrupt the continuous physical presence." INA § 244(b)(3).

In addition to establishing continuous presence, the alien must also establish that s/he has been a person of good moral character for the same amount of time. Good moral character is determined by the provisions of INA § 101(f). Further, the alien must show that deportation would result in extreme hardship (or in the case of aliens deportable for immoral and subversive activities, exceptional and extremely unusual hardship) "to the alien or to his spouse, parent, or child, who is a citizen of the United States or an alien lawfully admitted for permanent residence." INA § 244(a)(1). The Supreme Court has held that the plain meaning of this statute controls. Hence, consideration of hardship does not extend to other relatives, even if the alien's relationship to that relative is the "functional equivalent" of a parent-child relationship. *INS v. Hector* (Sup.Ct.1986). The BIA has used several factors in determining the existence of unusual hardship, including age of the alien, family ties in the U.S. and abroad, length of residence in the U.S., condition of health, economic and political conditions in the alien's country, financial status, the possibility of adjustment of status, the alien's special assistance to the U.S., immigration history, and position in the community. *Matter of Anderson* (Or. App.1978). The Ninth Circuit in *Villena v. INS* (9th Cir.1980) held that factors which support a finding of extreme hardship include (1) the alien's contribution to her/his community, (2) the effect of the alien's separation from family, including extreme hardship caused to the alien's citizen child by the alien's deportation, and (3) economic hardship to the alien. In addition to the above factors, the BIA in *In re S* (1953), considered the length of residence in the United States and the possibility of obtaining a visa abroad as factors relevant in determining whether the alien would suffer exceptional and extremely unusual hardship.

A claim of extreme hardship must be supported by affidavit or other evidentiary material. The Attorney General and the INS have considerable discretion in determining what constitutes extreme hardship. *INS v. Jong Ha Wang* (Sup.Ct.1981). Furthermore, even if an alien's motion to reopen deportation hearings is based on intervening circumstances demonstrating seven-year residence and extreme hardship, constituting a prima facie case of eligibility for suspension of deportation, the Attorney General has the discretion to deny the motion to reopen. *INS v. Rios–Pineda* (Sup.Ct.1985); *INS v. Abudu* (Sup.Ct.1988). In *Rios–Pineda,* for example, the Court reasoned that the Attorney General can, in exercising his discretion, "legitimately avoid creating a further incentive for stalling by refusing to reopen suspension proceedings for those who became eligible for such suspension only because of the passage of time while their meritless appeals dragged on." The discretionary authority of the Attorney General does not foreclose all judicial review. Such review, however, is limited to a determination of whether there has been an abuse of discretion. *INS v. Abudu* (Sup.Ct.1988); *Ravancho v. INS* (3d Cir.1981).

Until the decision in *INS v. Chadha* (Sup.Ct.1983), congressional approval was required for a suspension of deportation even if the Attorney General had granted it. The suspensions granted under INA § 244(a)(1) were considered approved by Congress if neither the House nor Senate passed a resolution against the suspension within a certain period of time. INA § 244(c). Suspensions authorized under INA § 244(a)(2), however, re-

ceived congressional approval only if both the House
and the Senate passed resolutions favoring the suspension. But, the Supreme Court in *Chadha* concluded
that congressional vetoes of suspensions violated the
separation of powers. When suspension is granted, the
Attorney General records the alien's admission to the
United States as a permanent resident as of the date the
deportation was suspended. INA § 244(d).

(c) Adjustment of Status. Still another type of discretionary relief for which the alien may apply during the
deportation proceedings is adjustment of status. Adjustment relieves certain aliens, whose status would
otherwise entitle them to remain in the United States,
from the hardship and expense of going abroad for long
waits while an immigrant visa is processed. According
to the INA, "[t]he status of an alien who was inspected
and admitted or paroled into the United States may be
adjusted by the Attorney General, in his discretion and
under such regulations as he may prescribe, to that of
an alien lawfully admitted for permanent residence if
(1) the alien makes an application for such adjustment,
(2) the alien is eligible to receive an immigrant visa and
is admissible to the United States for permanent residence, and (3) an immigrant visa is immediately available to him at the time his application is filed." INA
§ 245(a).

Aliens who accept unauthorized employment prior to
filing an application for adjustment of status are, in
general, statutorily ineligible to adjust their status.
INA § 245(c). The Immigration Reform and Control
Act of 1986 (IRCA) amended INA § 245 to add to those
aliens ineligible for adjustment of status any alien (other than an immediate relative of a U.S. citizen) who "is
not in legal immigration status on the date of filing the
application for adjustment of status or who has failed

(other than through no fault of his own for technical reasons) to maintain continuously a legal status since entry into the United States." INA § 245(c). The Immigration Marriage Fraud Amendments of 1986 (IMFA) amended § 245(e) to make ineligible for adjustment of status any alien seeking to receive an immigrant visa on the basis of a marriage entered into during deportation proceedings. The 1990 Act, however, softened this restriction by permitting an adjustment of status based on a marriage during deportation or exclusion proceedings, if the alien can show the marriage was entered in good faith. INA § 245(e). The IMFA also prohibited approval of a petition to grant an alien immediate relative or preference status by reason of a marriage entered into during deportation proceedings until the alien has resided outside the United States for a two-year period beginning after the date of the marriage. INA § 204(g). These amendments substantially limit the availability of adjustment of status as a means to avoid deportation.

In order to be eligible for adjustment of status the alien must show that s/he meets the statutory requirements. First, the alien must show that s/he has been inspected and admitted into the United States. Hence, according to the BIA in *In re Woo* (1966), aliens who enter illegally or on the basis of a willfully false claim of United States citizenship may not adjust their status. Second, the alien must show that s/he is eligible for a permanent resident visa. Since the alien applying for adjustment of status is considered to be "standing on the border," s/he must not be excludable under any of the categories of INA § 212(a). Aliens excludable for any reason are not eligible for adjustment of status. Finally, and most importantly, the alien must show that there is an immigrant visa immediately available to her/him. The BIA concluded in *In re Wang* (1979) that the alien satisfied the requirement of immediate availability when s/he showed that the visa was available when the application was filed—either with the district director before the Order to Show Cause was issued or with the immigration judge after the deportation proceedings commence.

(d) Asylum. Unlike the types of discretionary relief discussed above, the granting of asylum to an alien does not guarantee the alien permanent residence in the United States. (See chapter 10.) Asylum is the granting of temporary residence and the right to work in the United States for the period of time that the alien is entitled to refugee status. According to the Refugee Act of 1980, "an alien physically present in the United States or at a land border or port of entry ... may be granted asylum in the discretion of the Attorney General if the Attorney General determines that such alien is a refugee...." INA § 208(a). Hence, an alien may apply for asylum as a form of discretionary relief either during a deportation or exclusion hearing, so long as s/he meets the requirements of refugee status. The INA defines "refugee" to mean "(A) any person who is outside any country of such person's nationality ... and who is unable or unwilling to return to, and is unable or unwilling to avail himself or herself of the protection of, that country because of persecution or a well-founded fear of persecution on account of race, religion, nationality, membership in a particular social group, or political opinion," or (B) any person within a nationality specifically designated by the President as a refugee. INA § 101(a)(42).

An alien requesting asylum in deportation proceedings may either apply for asylum during or after the deportation hearing. 8 C.F.R. §§ 208.10, 208.11. If the alien applies after the hearing, however, s/he must reasonably explain the failure to apply during the hearing. 8 C.F.R. § 208.11. The alien and the INS present evidence relating to the alien's request for asylum. If the immigration judge grants the requested asylum, the alien is admitted for one year.

After one year, any alien admitted under the provisions of the Refugee Act of 1980 and (1) whose admission has not been terminated in the discretion of the Attorney General, (2) who has been physically present in the United States for at least one year, and (3) who has not acquired permanent resident status must report to the INS for inspection. INA § 209(a). After this inspection or after a hearing in front of an immigration judge, the INS will admit the alien as a lawful permanent resident if the alien is otherwise admissible as an immigrant. *Id.* The Attorney General may terminate the alien's asylum if s/he determines that the alien is no longer a "refugee" under the provisions of the INA. INA § 208.

(e) Withholding of Deportation. Closely related to asylum is the relief known as withholding of deportation. The INA provides that "[t]he Attorney General shall not deport or return any alien (other than an alien described [as a Nazi]) to a country if the Attorney General determines that such alien's life or freedom would be threatened in such country on account of race, religion, nationality, membership in a particular social group, or political opinion." INA § 243(h)(1). Aliens who assisted in the persecution of others, who were convicted of a crime dangerous to the community of the United States, who committed a serious nonpolitical crime before entering the U.S., or who otherwise represent a threat to the national security are not eligible for withholding of deportation. INA § 243(h)(2). Although

similar in nature to asylum, withholding of deportation differs in that the alien may request withholding of deportation only as part of a deportation hearing, while s/he may request asylum at any time.

While the BIA has previously concluded that withholding of deportation is not available in exclusion proceedings, the 1981 amendments to the Act supersede the Board's previous position. In *In re Cenatice* (1977), the Board held that an alien being excluded could not apply for withholding of deportation because s/he was not "within the United States" as required by the previous wording of the Act. Since the INA now explicitly makes the act applicable to aliens being returned to their native country, withholding of deportation applies to exclusion as well as deportation.

The Supreme Court held in *INS v. Stevic* (Sup.Ct.1984) that an alien seeking to avoid deportation pursuant to this section of the INA must establish a clear probability of persecution. According to the BIA in *Matter of McCullen* (1980), if the immigration judge determines that the alien meets the statutory requirements, the decision to grant withholding of deportation is mandatory. Asylum leads within one year to permanent residence; withholding of deportation, however, only grants the alien temporary residence in the United States and only for so long as the alien's life or freedom is threatened.

(f) Stay of Deportation. The alien may apply for a stay of deportation by submitting Form I–246. 8 C.F.R. § 243.4. The application is made to the district director of the INS. Such a stay is temporary and is granted at the discretion of the district director. Although it is commonly used in connection with a motion to reopen or reconsider, the alien under a deportation order may

also move for a stay pending an application for permanent residence and in other exceptional circumstances.
A pending application for immigration status, however,
does not entitle an alien to a stay of deportation; instead, the stay remains a discretionary matter. *Arm-
strong v. INS* (9th Cir.1971). If granted, the district
director may impose such conditions as s/he decides are
appropriate and s/he sets a specific time limit for the
stay. 8 C.F.R. § 243.4. An application for a stay does
not relieve the alien from strict compliance with an
outstanding order of deportation. *Id.* The district director's decision on the application is not appealable,
although the alien may renew the application before the
BIA. *Id.*

(g) *Other Discretionary Relief.* In addition to the
above types of discretionary relief, there are three other
forms of relief that will not be as extensively discussed.
The first, registry, is available to aliens who entered the
United States prior to January 1, 1972. Registry is the
creation of a record of lawful admission for permanent
residence when the record is not otherwise available.
INA § 249. In addition to proving that s/he entered
prior to the specified date, the alien must also show that
s/he has been a continuous resident of the United
States, is a person of good moral character, and is
otherwise eligible for citizenship. *Id.* The sole and
limited purpose of registry is to ameliorate the harsh
consequences of deportation for those persons who have
been long term residents of the United States.

A second type of discretionary relief which is available to aliens is defined under INA § 212(c). According
to this section of the INA, "[a]liens lawfully admitted for
permanent residence who temporarily proceeded abroad
voluntarily and not under an order of deportation, and
who are returning to a lawful unrelinquished domicile
of seven consecutive years, may be admitted in the

discretion of the Attorney General without regard to the provisions" of INA § 212(a), other than (3)(A)–(3)(E) except for 3(D). Although the express provisions of the INA require that the alien must have left the country to apply for this relief, the Second Circuit in *Francis v. INS* (2d Cir.1976) concluded that any alien who had lived here for at least seven years could apply for relief even though s/he had never left the country. Further, even if the alien meets the statutory requirements, the BIA concluded in *In re Marin* (1978) that the granting of the relief is still discretionary.

"Deferred action status" or "non-priority status" is yet another form of discretionary relief. The deferred action program is not created by statute but is an intra-agency administrative guideline contained within the Operations Instructions of the INS. District directors place aliens under deferred action status when the directors determine that "adverse action would be unconscionable because of the existence of appealing humanitarian factors." O.I. 242.1a(22). Once placed under this status, the alien is informed that the INS will take no action to disturb her/his immigration status or that the alien's departure from the United States has been deferred indefinitely. *Id.*

In *Nicholas v. INS* (9th Cir.1979), the Ninth Circuit Court of Appeals found that, although the Operations Instruction create no substantive rights, they clearly and directly affect substantive rights—the ability of an individual to continue residence in the United States. The discretion allowed by the instructions should therefore be subject to review. The court held that the decision of an INS district director upon an application for non-priority status will stand unless it "so departs from an established pattern of treatment of others similarly situated without reason, as to be arbitrary and capricious, and an abuse of discretion."

After *Nicholas* the INS amended its Operations Instructions to indicate that deferred action does not create an entitlement and to specify the factors to be used in making deferred action determinations, including the likelihood of ultimately removing the alien and the presence of sympathetic factors. O.I. 242.1a(2).

(h) Estoppel. Occasionally, the conduct of the United States government is a substantial cause of an alien's deportability, such as when an alien relies on false information given by a government employee. In these cases the courts have been quite reluctant to estop the government from deporting the alien. Despite opportunities to do so, however, the Supreme Court has not completely ruled out the doctrine of estoppel in deportation cases. In holding that an 18–month delay on the part of the INS in processing the alien's adjustment of status application falls short of affirmative misconduct in *INS v. Miranda* (Sup.Ct.1982), the Court was not required to reach the question of whether affirmative misconduct in a particular case would estop the government from enforcing the immigration laws.

Similarly, in most cases where the estoppel issue has been addressed by a lower court the decision has turned on whether affirmative misconduct occurred. The courts usually have held that there was no affirmative misconduct and therefore no estoppel was appropriate. A few lower courts, however, have held the government was estopped from deporting the alien as a result of the government's affirmative misconduct. In *McLeod v. Peterson* (3d Cir.1960), the alien would have complied with the continuous presence requirement for suspension of deportation had the INS not erroneously informed him that he was ineligible for nonquota status and advised him that his voluntary departure from the United States would aid his wife in making the necessary application for his legal re-entry. The Third Circuit Court of Appeals ignored the alien's departure and held that he had complied with the requirement of five years presence. In *Corniel–Rodriguez v. INS* (2d Cir. 1976), U.S. consular officers in the Dominican Republic violated 22 C.F.R. § 42.122(d), by failing to warn an alien who was issued a visa as an unmarried minor child of a special immigrant that she would forfeit her exemption from the labor certification requirement for entry if she married before admission to the United States. This violation of a regulation by the consular officers precluded deportation of the alien despite the alien's marriage three days before her departure from the Dominican Republic.

The estoppel doctrine also has been addressed in immigration cases outside the deportation context. *See, e.g., Montana v. Kennedy* (Sup.Ct.1961) (refusal of a U.S. consular officer to issue a passport to a pregnant U.S. citizen to enable citizen to re-enter the U.S., at a time when the U.S. did not require passports for citizens to return to the U.S., was not misconduct such that the government was estopped from denying the child's U.S. citizenship when born abroad); *INS v. Hibi* (Sup.Ct. 1973) (the government's failure after World War II to publicize fully the statutory right of Filipino servicemen to apply for naturalization and to provide a naturalization representative in the Philippines at all times during the period of eligibility did not rise to the level of affirmative misconduct); *INS v. Pangilinan* (Sup.Ct. 1988) (Supreme Court rejected applicability of estoppel doctrine to claims about the same situation in the Philippines as in *Hibi*); *Podea v. Acheson* (2d Cir.1950) (alien did not lose his U.S. citizenship by serving in a foreign army and swearing allegiance to a foreign sovereign after an erroneous State Department ruling that the alien had already lost his U.S. citizenship because of certain prior acts).

CHAPTER 9

EXCLUSION

Exclusion is the denial of entry or admission of an alien attempting to enter the United States. Ordinarily, the consular official who must determine the alien's eligibility for a visa considers whether any of the grounds for exclusion apply. Even if s/he determines that none do, however, an INS official can still make a contrary determination at the border when the alien actually attempts to enter the U.S.

§ 9–1 GROUNDS FOR EXCLUSION

An alien seeking to gain entry into the United States must avoid any of the grounds for exclusion as detailed in INA § 212(a). Aliens fitting one or more of the classes listed in this section, shall be "ineligible to receive visas and ... shall be excluded from admission into the United States." INA § 212(a).

The 1990 Act simplified what was previously considered an unnecessarily complex and outdated classification scheme. Before the 1990 changes, the INA listed 34 classes of exclusion, all of which functioned as bases for deportation as well. Section 212(a) as it now stands instead divides the classes into nine categories: health-related grounds; criminal and related grounds; security and related grounds; public charge proscription; labor certification requirements; illegal entrant proscription;

documentation requirements; ineligibility for citizenship; and miscellaneous. Until the 1990 changes, even the most archaic classes remained intact; *e.g.,* the exclusion of homosexuals as one class and "paupers, professional beggars, or vagrants" as another. The 1990 Act eliminated both classes.

§ 9–1.1　Health–Related Grounds

Section 212(a) begins with grounds for exclusion based on the alien's physical or mental health. Aliens who have a "communicable disease of public health significance" are excluded as are those persons with a "physical or mental disorder and behavior associated with the disorder that may pose ... a threat to the property, safety, or welfare of the alien or others." INA § 212(a)(1)(A). Moreover, a drug addict or abuser is excludable under this section. INA § 212(a)(1)(A)(iii).

One controversial issue is whether section 212(a) excludes people who have tested positive for the Human Immunodeficiency Virus (HIV), the virus believed to cause Acquired Immune Deficiency Syndrome (AIDS). Such medical tests are only required of individuals seeking to remain permanently in the U.S. People testing HIV–positive originally were excluded under an appropriations bill rider in 1987. The 1990 Act then incorporated the reference to "communicable diseases of public health significance." In response, the Department of Health and Human Services (HHS) promulgated proposed regulations that restricted this class to diseases whose public health significance resulted from their contagious nature. Because AIDS/HIV cannot be spread through casual contact, it was apparently removed from the list of exclusions, leaving the exclusion for health-related grounds limited to carriers of tuberculosis and similar communicable diseases.

The HHS proposal generated considerable criticism, particularly from conservatives in Congress and the Bush administration. In May 1991 the INS implemented the 1990 Act by defining "communicable diseases of public significance" to exclude from the United States persons who have tested positive for HIV, as well as tuberculosis, syphilis in its infectious stage, gonorrhea, leprosy, and several other diseases. Under INA § 212(g), however, the Attorney General may waive an exclusion for health-related reasons on behalf of any alien who is the spouse, unmarried son or daughter, or parent of a U.S. citizen or permanent resident. In addition, INA § 212(d) authorizes a waiver for nonimmigrants, which would allow persons who have tested positive for HIV to attend conferences in the U.S. and visit this country.

§ 9–1.2 Criminal and Related Grounds

Section 212(a)(2) renders excludable any alien who has committed a "crime involving moral turpitude" but provides exceptions for minor offenses and crimes committed by juveniles. See *grounds for deportation* for a detailed discussion of how courts have defined "moral turpitude." The INA excludes aliens violating laws relating to controlled substances, or aliens reasonably believed by a consular or immigration official to be engaged in drug trafficking. INA § 212(a)(2)(C). In addition, an alien participating in a prostitution enterprise or other serious criminal activity in the U.S. for which s/he had asserted immunity from prosecution is excludable. INA § 212(a)(2).

§ 9–1.3   Security and Related Grounds

Prior to the 1990 Act, the national security grounds for exclusion were extremely detailed—excluding anarchists, Communists, subversives, and individuals who advocated overthrow of the government through violent means. The Supreme Court upheld this provision against a First Amendment challenge in *Kleindienst v. Mandel* (Sup.Ct.1972). The Court reasoned that aliens have no constitutional right to enter the United States, and U.S. citizens have no right to have aliens enter the country so that ideas may be exchanged. Essentially, Congress' plenary power to control immigration supercedes a citizen's right to receive information under the First Amendment.

Section 212(a)(3), as modified by the 1990 Act, excludes aliens believed to seek entry "solely, principally, or incidentally" to engage in activities which violate espionage laws or whose purpose it is to overthrow the U.S. government by unlawful means. INA § 212(a)(3)(A). Any alien who has engaged in terrorist activity, or is believed likely to do so in the future is excludable. INA § 212(a)(3)(B). The INA specifically states that a member of the Palestine Liberation Organization will be considered engaged in terrorist activity for the purposes of exclusion. INA § 212(a)(3)(B)(i)(II). *See United States v. P.L.O.* (S.D.N.Y.1988).

The D.C. Circuit held in *Abourezk v. Reagan* (D.C.Cir. 1986) that the government's exclusion of an anarchist or a Communist party member must be based on projected engagement in activities prejudicial to the public interest, and such perception must be independent of the fact of membership alone in an organization.

Any alien who the Secretary of State believes will have adverse foreign policy consequences may be excluded. Excludability for membership in a totalitarian or Communist party is waived if the alien was an involuntary member or terminated her/his membership at least two years prior to the date of application for entry into the U.S. INA § 212(a)(3)(D). Finally, any alien who participated in or was affiliated with the Nazi government is excludable. INA § 212(a)(3)(E).

§ 9–1.4 Other Grounds for Exclusion

Any alien who is believed likely to become a public charge is excludable at the time of application. INA § 212(a)(4). In *Matter of Kohama* (1978), the Associate Commissioner of Examinations decided that an immigrating couple who had no means of support other than their reliance on their daughter and son-in-law, could not properly be excluded as likely to become public charges. The daughter and son-in-law submitted depositions and other evidence of their ability and willingness to support the couple. The court held that such evidence was sufficient to overcome the belief that they would become charges of the state.

Section 212(a)(5) reiterates the criteria for labor certification, without which an alien immigrating under § 203(b) is excludable. Any alien who has been previously deported within five years, excluded within the last year, or deported for an aggravated felony within 20 years, is excludable. INA § 212(a)(6). Any alien who has made a material misrepresentation of fact in the application process is excludable, as are stowaways and aliens who have aided or abetted the illegal entry of other aliens. INA § 212(a)(6).

Section 212(a)(7) spells out the documentation requirements for an alien seeking entry. An unexcused failure to possess the travel documents renders the alien excludable. The alien at the time of application must have a valid immigrant visa, re-entry permit, border crossing identification card, other valid entry document, and an unexpired passport. INA § 212(a)(7). Immigrants permanently ineligible for citizenship are excludable, as are those who departed from the United States solely to evade the draft. INA § 212(a)(8). Further, any alien entering the U.S. to practice polygamy is excludable. INA § 212(a)(9).

§ 9–2   PROCEDURAL PROCESS

There are two types of proceedings by which an alien may be required to depart the United States: deportation hearings and exclusion hearings. Deportation hearings, which are discussed in § 8.–3.2, are employed to remove an alien who has already entered the United States. Exclusion hearings apply to aliens outside the United States—that is, persons who have not yet entered and are seeking admission.

§ 9–2.1   Entry and Re–Entry

Some courts have held that "entry" has not occurred until physical presence is accompanied by freedom from official restraint. Although aliens may be physically present, they will not have made an "entry" into the U.S. until they are free from this restraint. *United States v. Oscar* (9th Cir.1974). In *Matter of Lin* (BIA 1982), the court concluded that an entry involves physical presence, inspection, and admission.

Whether there has been "entry" becomes the key question in determining whether the nonimmigrant alien is entitled to deportation or exclusion hearings. The "re-entry doctrine" holds that the word "entry" in the INA refers to any coming into the U.S., not simply the *first* entry of the alien. Hence, a permanent resident alien may be subject to the grounds of exclusion every time s/he leaves and returns to the United States.

In *United States ex rel. Volpe v. Smith* (Sup.Ct.1933) the Supreme Court upheld the deportation of an alien who, after 24 years of residence in the U.S. following a lawful entry, was held to be excludable on his return from a brief visit to Cuba. The Court's restrictive view concluded that "entry" included any coming of an alien from a foreign country whether such coming was the alien's first entry or not. The Court in *Rosenberg v. Fleuti* (Sup.Ct.1963) departed from this rigid application, recognizing that an alien does not make an "entry" upon his return to the United States where he had no intent to leave, or did not in fact leave the country voluntarily. Hence, an innocent, casual, and brief excursion outside the United States was not intended as a departure disruptive of the resident alien's status, and the alien should not be subject to the conditions of an entry.

§ 9–2.2 Parole

Immigration officers may elect to release an alien on parole pending further investigation. Parole allows an alien to travel away from the border and detention facilities while remaining subject to exclusion proceedings. The alien who enters on parole is not officially admitted and may be excluded without any formal deportation proceedings. Parole can be used for a variety of reasons, such as preventing the separation of families. The court in *Leng May Ma v. Barber* (Sup.Ct.1958) held that a parolee still has not satisfied the criteria for "entry," *i.e.,* freedom from official restraint.

§ 9–2.3   The Exclusion Hearing

In an exclusion hearing, the alien must prove her/his right to enter the United States. INA § 291. Exclusion proceedings commence with the issuance of the Notice to Applicant for Admission Detained for Hearing, Form I–222. 8 C.F.R. § 236.2(a). Unlike the Order to Show Cause used in deportation proceedings, the Notice does not necessarily contain specific allegations. The hearing is closed to the public, although the alien may request that it be opened. 8 C.F.R. § 236.2(a). During the hearing, the alien is entitled to many attributes of procedural Due Process just as the alien who is subject to deportation. *See* INA § 236; 8 C.F.R. § 236.2(a). An alien who is excluded may not, however, designate a place of deportation, but is returned to the country where the alien boarded the vessel of arrival. INA § 237. Most forms of relief for deportation are not applicable to exclusion proceedings, but the alien may seek asylum or withholding of deportation under INA § 243(h). *See* § 8–4.1, ch. 10.

In *Landon v. Plasencia* (Sup.Ct.1982) the Supreme Court reaffirmed that a permanent resident, who had been outside the United States for a few days and was attempting to return, must be entitled to procedural Due Process in any exclusion hearing. The Court particularly questioned whether Due Process was accorded when 1) it was unclear whether the government or the alien had the burden of proof, 2) the alien received only 11 hours notice of the charges and the hearing, and 3) the alien was allowed to waive the right to counsel without being informed of the availability of free legal services.   An alien seeking initial admission to the U.S. does not, however, have the constitutional right to Due Process beyond the procedures afforded by statutes and regulations.

Unlike the deportation context, the alien can challenge an exclusion order only by petitioning for a writ of habeas corpus.   INA § 106(b).   The Supreme Court in *Brownell v. We Shung* (Sup.Ct.1956) upheld a habeas corpus petition as the proper method of review of exclusion orders.   According to the Third Circuit in *Hughes v. United States* (3d Cir.1924), the district courts are limited to a determination of whether the government's evidence adequately supported the immigration judge's decision.   Although judicial review usually lies for agency determinations, in *Peña v. Kissinger* (S.D.N.Y.1976) the court, citing *Mandel*, held that exclusion orders are a congressionally-mandated exception.

§ 9–2.4   Interdiction

In the wake of political and economic upheavals in Haiti, large numbers have fled their country and sought entry into the United States.   Pursuant to a 1981 agreement between Haiti and the U.S., the Coast Guard intercepted vessels carrying these Haitians, interviewed them briefly as to their reasons for wanting to enter the U.S., and forcibly repatriated almost all of them.   The interdiction agreement provides that those aliens who apparently qualify for refugee status will not be returned to Haiti.   It should be noted that Haiti is the only country with which the U.S. has an interdiction agreement. In *Haitian Refugee Center v. Gracey* (D.C.Cir.1987) the D.C. Circuit upheld the validity of the interdiction. See §§ 2–2.1, 8–3.1.

During fall-winter of 1991–92, more than 16,000 Haitians were intercepted on the high seas and were taken to the U.S. Naval Base at Guantanamo Bay in Western Cuba. They were questioned as to whether they had a prima facie claim to asylum status. Except for a very brief period the Haitians had no access to lawyers. They also had no right to appeal. Although some Members of Congress have sought Temporary Protected Status (TPS) for the Haitians, the Bush administration has refused to stop enforcement of the agreement. The interdiction and interview procedures were challenged in federal court; their claims were initially sustained in federal district court.

Nonetheless, the U.S. Court of Appeals for the Eleventh Circuit held in *Haitian Refugee Center v. Baker* (11th Cir.1992) that aliens who were detained on the high seas and, thus, had never presented themselves at a U.S. border, had no right to judicial review of INS decisions under the Administrative Procedure Act. Moreover, the court concluded that these aliens had no private right of action, unless they qualified for refugee status. Further, the court stated that the Refugee Center and their attorneys had no First Amendment claim for gaining access to the detained aliens. The Supreme Court denied certiorari over the objections of Justice Blackmun, who argued that this challenge to the U.S. procedure for determining whether a group of aliens faces political persecution deserved a hearing by the Supreme Court.

While the courts provided no relief to the Haitians interdicted on the high seas and taken to Guantanamo, the litigation may have increased the number of Haitians found to have prima facie claims to refugee status. Over 35 percent of the Haitians were eventually found to have prima facie claims and were to be transported to the U.S. for adjudication of their asylum cases. Almost all of the others were transported back to Haiti.

In May 1992 the Bush administration ordered the Coast Guard to return any Haitians leaving their country in boats without an inquiry as to whether they qualify for asylum. The U.N. High Commissioner for Refugees and the Haitian Refugee Center challenged this measure as a violation of the U.S. government's obligations under the Protocol relating to the Status of Refugees.

CHAPTER 10

REFUGEES AND ASYLUM

An alien may be considered for refugee or asylum status in the United States if the alien has a well-founded fear of persecution in his/her home country. To be eligible for either refugee or asylum status, the applicant must qualify as a refugee, as defined by INA § 101(a)(42). The asylum applicant is already present in the United States or at its borders, whereas refugee status may be sought from outside of the United States. Refugee or asylum status, along with occasional lotteries (see chapters 1 and 5), constitute the only significant avenues for immigrating to the United States for individuals without family ties or employment opportunities in the U.S. Refugee and asylum status differ in several other aspects, as discussed below.

§ 10–1 REFUGEES

The President has the power under INA § 207 to admit as refugees those aliens who are outside the United States and who qualify for refugee status. The President, after consultation with Congress and before the beginning of the fiscal year, is permitted to set a worldwide refugee admission ceiling for the year at such number as the President determines is "justified by humanitarian concerns or is otherwise in the national interest." INA § 207(a)(2). The President must also allocate this number among refugees from regions of the

world which are of special humanitarian concern to the
United States. In the event of an "unforeseen emergency refugee situation," the President may, after appropriate consultation with the relevant congressional committees, expand the admissible number of refugees if
such action is justified by "grave humanitarian concerns
or is otherwise in the national interest." INA § 207(b).

For example, President Bush has set the refugee
admission ceiling for fiscal year 1992 at 142,000, almost
doubling the figure for 1988. The President allocated
the total number regionally as follows: Africa, 6,000;
East Asia, 52,000; former Soviet Union, 61,000 (including 10,000 funded by the private sector); Eastern Europe, 3,000; Near East/South Asia, 6,000; Latin America and the Caribbean, 3,000; undesignated, publicly
funded, 1,000; and undesignated, funded by the public
sector, 10,000. In the last few years, several hundred
Cubans have been admitted through the undesignated
allocation as a result of funding by the Cuban American
National Foundation. Also, unused allocations may be
transferred to regions where needed.

Like an asylum applicant, an applicant for refugee
status must meet the definition of a refugee contained
in INA § 101(a)(42), which includes the possession of a
"well-founded fear of persecution on account of race,
religion, nationality, membership in a particular social
group, or political opinion." While the applicable standard is the same, the refugee applicant applies from
abroad, whereas the asylum applicant applies while
present in the United States or at its border. Applicants for refugee status are subject to numerical limitations, but no such limitations are imposed upon asylum.

In addition to meeting the statutory definition of refugee, the alien must be generally admissible as an immigrant under INA § 212(a), must not be firmly resettled in any other country, and must be determined to be of special humanitarian concern to the United States. INA § 207(c). Several of the exclusion provisions of INA § 212(a) do not apply to refugees, including those provisions relating to labor certification, self-sufficiency, valid entry documents and visas, literacy, and foreign medical graduates. The Attorney General may, for humanitarian purposes, to assure family unity, or when it is otherwise in the public interest, waive other exclusion provisions. INA § 207(c)(3).

Each refugee applicant, however, must be sponsored by a responsible person or organization which will guarantee transportation for the applicant from his/her present abode to the place of resettlement in the United States. 8 C.F.R. § 207.2(d). Churches, community organizations, and other voluntary agencies often fill this role.

To apply for refugee status, the alien must complete Form I–590 (Registration for Classification as a Refugee). Applicants 14 years of age or older also must submit Form G–325C (Biographic Information) and Form FD–258 (Applicant Card). 8 C.F.R. § 207.2. The alien must file these completed forms, along with supplementary statements and documentary evidence, at an INS office outside the United States. The alien then will be interviewed by an immigration officer to determine eligibility, and a medical examination will be performed. 8 C.F.R. § 207.2(b) and (c).

Waiting lists are maintained for each designated refugee group of special humanitarian concern. The date on which the alien's application was filed determines the alien's position on the waiting list. The Attorney General may, however, adopt appropriate criteria for selecting refugees and assigning priorities for each designated group based on considerations of family reunification, close association with the United States, compelling humanitarian concerns, and public interest factors. 8 C.F.R. § 207.5.

If the alien's application is approved, the alien must enter the United States within four months. 8 C.F.R. § 207.4. Spouses and children (unmarried and under the age of 21) accompanying or following to join a refugee may be admitted if not otherwise entitled to admission, and if they have not participated in the persecution of others. Spouses and children are charged against the numerical limitation under which the refugee's entry was charged. 8 C.F.R. § 207.1(e).

Once in the United States, the alien retains refugee status for one year. Whereas asylum status may be terminated during this period if conditions improve in the alien's home country, making asylum unnecessary, refugee status is not conditional in this respect. INA §§ 207(c)(4), 249(a). After one year the refugee is eligible to apply for an adjustment of status to lawful permanent residence. The alien must return to the INS for an inspection and examination in order to determine admissibility. INA § 209(a)(1). Although INA § 209(a) provides for the adjustment of status of those aliens *admitted* to the United States under § 207, a refugee may be removed from the United States through exclusion rather than deportation proceedings if it is subsequently determined that the alien was not in fact a refugee within the meaning of § 101(a)(42) at the time

of the alien's "admission." INA §§ 207(c)(4), 209(a). If
the alien is found to be admissible, permanent resident
status will be granted and made effective as of the date
the alien arrived in the United States. INA § 209(a)(2).
While there is an annual numerical limitation of 10,000
on adjustment of status for asylees, there is no numerical limitation on adjustment of status for refugees. INA
§ 209(b). *See* O.I. 209.3K.

§ 10–2 ASYLUM

An alien who is present in the United States or
arrives at its border may apply for asylum if the alien
qualifies as a refugee. INA § 208. A refugee is defined
in INA § 101(a)(42)(A) as "any person who is outside
any country of such person's nationality or ... any
country in which such person last habitually resided,
and who is unable or unwilling to return to, and is
unable or unwilling to avail himself or herself of the
protection of that country because of persecution or a
well-founded fear of persecution on account of race,
religion, nationality, membership in a particular social
group, or political opinion." Asylum can provide relief
from exclusion as well as deportation and a grant of
asylum may lead to permanent residence. Moreover,
there is no waiting period before one qualifies.

§ 10–2.1 Burden and Standard of Proof in Asylum Cases

The burden of establishing eligibility as a refugee is
on the applicant. 8 C.F.R. § 208.13. The applicant
must show that s/he has a well-founded fear of persecution in the home country on account of race, religion,
nationality, membership in a particular social group, or

political opinion. The requirement of a "well-founded fear," however, has not been clearly defined. In *INS v. Stevic* (Sup.Ct.1984) and *INS v. Cardoza–Fonseca* (Sup. Ct.1987) the Supreme Court established the standard of proof which the INS must apply in considering asylum applications and examined the procedures available for review if such applications are denied. Stevic was a Yugoslavian citizen who was ordered deported from the United States; while his motion to reopen his deportation was pending before an immigration judge, he applied for asylum. The immigration judge denied the reopening and an appeal to the Board of Immigration Appeals was dismissed. The Board noted that "[a] motion to reopen based on a ... claim of persecution must contain prima facie evidence there is a clear probability of persecution to be directed at the individual [alien]." The Board concluded that Stevic had failed to prove that he would be singled out for persecution if he returned to Yugoslavia.

Stevic sought review in the U.S. Court of Appeals of the Board's denial of his motion to reopen the deportation proceedings on the asylum matter; the appeal was consolidated with his appeal from the denial of his habeas corpus petition in the federal district court concerning an earlier motion to seek withholding of deportation on the basis of INA § 243(h).

The Court of Appeals for the Second Circuit held that when the United States acceded to the United Nations Protocol relating to the Status of Refugees in 1968, and later adopted the Refugee Act of 1980, it intended to establish a more generous standard in evaluating asylum claims than the " 'clear probability' that an individual will be singled out for persecution" approach used by the Board of Immigration Appeals.

The Supreme Court granted certiorari and concluded from an analysis of legislative history and statutory language that the well-founded fear standard is more generous than the clear probability of persecution standard applicable to the withholding of deportation under INA § 243(h). The Court defined the clear probability of persecution standard as inquiring whether it is more likely than not that the alien would be subject to persecution. Hence, although in *Stevic* the Court specifically addressed only withholding of deportation under § 243(h) and did not precisely define the well-founded fear standard, the Court suggested through dicta that "so long as an objective situation is established by the evidence, it need not be shown that the situation will probably result in persecution, but it is enough that persecution is a reasonable possibility."

In *INS v. Cardoza–Fonseca* (Sup.Ct.1987) the Supreme Court directly addressed the standard of proof applicable to applications for asylum under § 208(a). Cardoza–Fonseca was a Nicaraguan citizen who overstayed her nonimmigrant visa. When the INS commenced deportation proceedings, Cardoza–Fonseca requested withholding of deportation pursuant to INA § 243(h) and asylum pursuant to § 208(a). To support her asylum claim, she attempted to show a "well-founded fear of persecution" upon her return to Nicaragua with evidence that her brother had been tortured and imprisoned because of his political activities in Nicaragua. Cardoza–Fonseca claimed that she, too, would be tortured if forced to return, because the Sandinistas knew she had fled Nicaragua with her brother and would want to interrogate her about her brother's whereabouts. Because of the status of her brother, the Nicaraguan government would become aware of her own political opposition to the Sandinistas.

At the deportation hearing, the immigration judge applied the § 243(h) "more likely than not" standard of proof to Cardoza–Fonseca's § 208(a) asylum claim. The judge held that she was not entitled to asylum because she had failed to establish "a clear probability of persecution." The Board of Immigration Appeals (BIA) affirmed the decision. The Court of Appeals reversed, holding that the § 208(a) "well-founded fear" standard is more generous than the § 243(h) clear probability standard in that § 208(a) requires only a showing of past persecution or "good reason" to fear future persecution. The Court of Appeals remanded the case to the BIA, to be evaluated under this standard.

The Supreme Court affirmed the judgment of the Court of Appeals, holding that the § 243(h) clear probability standard does not govern asylum applications under § 208(a), and that "the reference to 'fear' in the § 208(a) standard obviously makes the eligibility determination turn to some extent on the subjective mental state of the alien." The Court, however, declined to give concrete meaning to the term "well-founded fear," leaving this task to the process of case-by-case adjudication.

If the asylum applicant has satisfied the § 243(h) clear probability standard as to withholding of deportation, the alien has *a fortiori* satisfied the more generous "well-founded fear" standard governing asylum claims. *Hernandez–Ortiz v. INS* (9th Cir.1985). In *Hernandez–Ortiz*, the alien's evidence of threats or acts of violence against members of her family in El Salvador showed a clear probability that her life would be threatened by return to El Salvador, and that the threat of persecution was related to the alien's political opinion. Having established a clear probability of persecution, the alien had *a fortiori* established a well-founded fear of persecution, thereby entitling her to asylum status.

The Ninth Circuit has held that in order to establish a well-founded fear of persecution, there must be clear evidence of a specific individualized threat to the alien or the alien's family members. *Mendez–Efrain v. INS* (9th Cir.1987). The Ninth Circuit held that evidence of the tragic and widespread danger of violence and human rights violations affecting all Salvadorans was insufficient to establish a well-founded fear of persecution, without clear evidence of specific individualized threat to the alien or his family members. The same court, however, pointed out in *Hernandez–Ortiz* that an alien's residence in a country where the lives and freedom of a large number of people are threatened does not lessen the significance of evidence of specific threats to the alien's life or freedom.

Under the 1990 regulations, the applicant for asylum can sustain the burden of proving a well-founded fear of persecution if s/he establishes that a pattern or practice of persecution exists in his/her country on account of race, religion, nationality, or political opinion and s/he establishes his/her inclusion or identification with one such persecuted group. 8 C.F.R. § 208.13(b)(2).

The Ninth Circuit has determined that an applicants' petition for asylum must satisfy both a subjective and an objective component. Subjectively, the applicant must show that his/her fear is genuine. The objective component requires a showing by credible and specific evidence in the record of facts that would support a reasonable fear of persecution. *Arriaga–Barrientos v. INS* (9th Cir.1991).

In a 1992 case, the Supreme Court held that a guerrilla organization's coercion to join its organization does not necessarily constitute persecution on account of political opinion for the purposes of INA §§ 101(a)(42) & 208. *INS v. Elias–Zacarias* (Sup.Ct.1992). In that case, Jairo Jonathan Elias–Zacarias testified during deportation proceedings that he was subject to persecution if he returned to his native Guatemala. He described how guerrillas had forced their way into his home and requested that Elias–Zacarias and his parents join their organization. They refused, and the guerrillas promised to return. Elias–Zacarias testified that he believed joining the organization would subject him to retaliation by the government.

In his opinion for the Court, Justice Scalia reviewed the applicable standards for granting asylum under § 208(a). First, he noted, the fear of persecution had to be such that a reasonable factfinder would conclude that it existed. He reasoned that, in this case, the political opinion in question was not that of the applicant, but rather, that of the guerrilla organization (the persecutor). In response, Elias–Zacarias argued that failure to join the guerrillas was itself tantamount to expressing a political opinion, but the Court was not persuaded, holding instead that Elias–Zacarias had failed to show evidence which compelled a reversal of the BIA decision.

In a dissenting opinion, Justice Stevens stated that "A political opinion can be expressed negatively as well as affirmatively," and that in these circumstances, expression led to a reasonable fear of persecution. It is not clear how far-reaching the *Elias–Zacarias* decision will be; whether the "forcible recruitment" theory can still prevail with the proper evidence; or whether the decision indicates greater Supreme Court deference for the asylum determinations of the BIA.

If the applicant had suffered past persecution, it is presumed that his/her life or freedom would be threatened upon return. This presumption can be rebutted if the INS established by a preponderance of evidence that conditions in the country have changed to an extent that it is no longer more likely than not that the applicant would face persecution. 8 C.F.R. § 208.13(1). Moreover, under the procedure discussed in § 10–2.2, the asylum officer must consider the fact that a national who leaves his/her country to seek asylum elsewhere may face increased danger if forced to return. 8 C.F.R. § 208.13(b)(2)(c).

§ 10–2.2 Basic Asylum Application Procedures

Asylum is not a right; rather it is granted at the discretion of the asylum officer or immigration judge in the district where the alien resides or enters the U.S. 8 C.F.R. § 208.1. The Refugee Act of 1980 established a new INA § 208 dealing with asylum. In 1990, regulations were promulgated to respond to the problems in adjudicating asylum cases.

a. Jurisdiction

The 1990 regulations take the determination of asylum applications out of the hands of the district director and shift them to the asylum officers in the Office of Refugees, Asylum, Parole (CORAP) in the INS. 8 C.F.R.

§ 208.2. Asylum officers receive special training in international law and relations under the joint direction of the Assistant Commissioner at CORAP and the Director of the Asylum Policy and Review Unit (APRU) of the Office of Policy Development at the Department of Justice.

Asylum officers have jurisdiction over all asylum applications except those filed by aliens in exclusion or deportation proceedings, which are evaluated by immigration judges. Interestingly, if the asylum officer denies the application for political asylum and deportation proceedings commence, the immigration judge will review the application *de novo*.

Prior to 1990, the INS district director, who was chiefly responsible for enforcing immigration laws, was also responsible for determining asylum cases. The 1990 regulations formally give the asylum officers bureaucratic independence from the INS.

b. The Application Process

The alien must submit an application for asylum, Form I–589, along with biographic information, Form G–325A, and an FD–258 fingerprint chart. 8 C.F.R. § 208.3. Provided the alien is not in deportation or exclusion proceedings, s/he files these materials with the district director who then forwards them to the asylum officer. The asylum officer then sends a copy of the application to CORAP and the State Department.

An alien who has a pending application for asylum or withholding of deportation is eligible to receive employment authorization. 8 C.F.R. § 208.7. The applicant must file an initial application for employment authorization (I–765) along with his/her application for asylum.

The authorization is good for one year, provided the application for asylum or withholding of deportation is not frivolous, and is renewable in one-year increments. The employment authorization remains valid until the end of the authorization period or sixty days after an asylum officer's denial of asylum, whichever is longer.

Under the 1990 regulations, each applicant for asylum shall be interviewed by the asylum officer in a non-adversarial manner, and not in public, if the applicant so requests. 8 C.F.R. § 208.9. The applicant may have counsel and may submit affidavits of witnesses. In making a determination, the asylum officer may rely on information and material provided by the State Department and CORAP, as well as other "credible" sources, such as international organizations. If such material is used to reach an adverse decision, the applicant can demand inspection, unless the information is classified. 8 C.F.R. § 208.12.

Prior to the new regulations, comments from the Bureau of Human Rights and Humanitarian Affairs (BHRHA) of the Department of State were required. Courts, however, were critical of the weight given to BHRHA opinions. The Second Circuit affirmed the admissibility of the State Department's opinions on the degree of persecution that exists in the country of prospective deportation. *Zamora v. INS* (2d Cir.1976). The advisory opinions are admissible provided the State Department reveals, so far as possible, the basis for its views and does not attempt to apply such knowledge to the particular case.

In *Arteaga v. INS* (9th Cir.1988), however, the Ninth Circuit overruled a BIA decision because the Board erred when it determined that guerrillas did not engage in forced recruitment. Under the new regulations, comment from the BHRHA is optional, and there is a 45–day period during which the agency must respond if it so intends. 8 C.F.R. § 208.11.

The decision to grant or deny asylum by an asylum officer shall be communicated in writing to the applicant, the district director, CORAP, and APRU at the Department of Justice. An adverse decision must state why asylum was denied. There is no right to appeal a decision of an asylum officer; however, the application can be renewed *de novo* in deportation or exclusion proceedings.

An applicant who leaves the United States is presumed to have abandoned his application for asylum or withholding of deportation. 8 C.F.R. § 208.6. Moreover, an unexcused failure to appear for a scheduled interview raises the presumption that the alien has abandoned his/her application. 8 C.F.R. § 208.10.

Asylum will be denied as a matter of statutory eligibility if (1) the alien fails to qualify as a refugee; (2) the alien has been firmly resettled in another country; (3) the alien participated in the persecution of any other person on account of race, religion, nationality, membership in a particular group, or political opinion; (4) the alien, having been convicted by a final judgment of a particularly serious crime, constitutes a danger to the community of the United States; (5) there are serious reasons for considering that the alien has committed a serious non-political crime outside the United States prior to the arrival of the alien in the United States; or (6) there are reasonable grounds for regarding the alien as a danger to the security of the United States. 8 C.F.R. §§ 208.14, 208.15. The 1990 Act disqualified "aggravated felons" from asylum and made all aggravated felonies "particularly serious crime[s]." INA §§ 208(d), 243(h)(2).

In addition to statutory ineligibility, asylum may be denied as a matter of discretion by either the asylum officer or the immigration judge with jurisdiction over the case. A common basis for discretionary denial of asylum, even though statutory eligibility has been proved, involves cases where the alien has fraudulently or grossly circumvented U.S. legal procedures to enter the U.S. and make an asylum claim. *See, e.g., Matter of Salim* (BIA 1982). In *Matter of Pula* (BIA 1987), however, the Board did not find the applicant's use of false documents to enter the U.S. such a disqualifying factor as to justify denial of asylum or the exercise of discretion. The negative factor of fraud had to be weighed against such positive factors as fear of persecution, lack of knowledge about procedures for seeking refugee status, family ties in the U.S., etc.

The Board of Immigration Appeals in *Matter of McMullen* (BIA 1984) concluded that the alien's effective membership in the Provisional Irish Republican Army (PIRA), a "clandestine, terrorist organization" engaged in the persecution of individuals opposed to the organization and its terrorist activities, constituted persecution of others on account of political opinion, making the alien ineligible for asylum. The Board also found that the organization's random bombing of civilian targets during the period of the alien's active membership provided "serious reasons for considering that the alien has committed a serious non-political crime outside the United States." The Board held that a crime is non-political if the crime is grossly out of proportion to the political objective or if it involves acts of an atrocious nature.

If asylum is denied, the alien will be placed under exclusion proceedings if the application was made at the border of the U.S., unless the alien withdraws the application. 8 C.F.R. § 208.8(f)(3). If asylum is denied for an alien already present in the U.S., regardless of whether the application was for an original grant of asylum or a renewal, the asylum officer shall either commence deportation proceedings or grant voluntary departure. 8 C.F.R. § 208.8(f)(4).

The courts have differed over whether excludable and deportable aliens must be informed of their right to apply for asylum. The court in *Nunez v. Boldin* (S.D.Tex.1982) decided that the Due Process protection of aliens within the borders of the United States requires that citizens of El Salvador and Guatemala held at an INS detention facility be informed of their right to apply for asylum. The United States has "by treaty, statute, and regulations, manifested its intention of hearing the pleas of aliens who come to this country claiming a fear of being persecuted in their homelands." The court stated that although no regulation specifically requires the INS to inform detainees of their right to apply for asylum, failure to do so may effectively render these treaties and statutes virtually nonexistent for the majority of aliens who would otherwise claim their benefits.

The court in *Jean v. Nelson* (11th Cir.1984) took an opposing view. The court concluded that "too many asylum applications may only bury the truth by straining INS resources and preventing careful assessment of individual claims. If the volume of asylum claims rises significantly, the INS may feel compelled to rely more and more on group profiles and less on individual evidence and credibility." The court held that although aliens have a protected statutory and regulatory right to apply for asylum, the Constitution, the Refugee Act, and its regulations do not require the INS to inform aliens of this right.

The decision in *Orantes–Hernandez v. Thornburg* (9th Cir.1990) and the settlement in *American Baptist Churches v. Thornburg* (N.D.Cal.1991) imply that aliens must be notified of their right to apply for political asylum and the right to be represented by counsel at no cost to the government. In *Orantes–Hernandez,* the court held that the INS had to advise the Salvadorans seeking entry of their rights in English and Spanish. The INS must tell them orally that they are being detained by the INS, that they will be given written notice of their rights prior to their deciding whether to return voluntarily to El Salvador, and that they will have to acknowledge that they received the written notice of their rights (called an "*Orantes* advisal").

The written notice advises the alien that s/he has the right to counsel, the right to a deportation hearing, the right to apply for political asylum, and the right to request a voluntary departure. In addition, each alien must be given a list of organizations that provide free legal services in the area. The *ABC* settlement, discussed in greater detail below, reiterates these requirements. Moreover, 8 C.F.R. § 236.3 requires the immigration judge presiding over an exclusion or deportation proceeding to advise the alien that s/he may apply for asylum in the U.S. if the alien expresses a fear of persecution or harm upon returning to his/her country of origin.

An alien who has been found deportable and requests a reopening of deportation proceedings to enable her/him to apply for asylum may be denied that opportunity if s/he has not reasonably explained his/her failure to apply for asylum prior to completion of the initial deportation proceedings. *INS v. Abudu* (Sup.Ct.1988). Abudu, a citizen of Ghana, had expressly declined to seek asylum during deportation proceedings. Upon motion to reopen, Abudu alleged that a surprise visit from a former acquaintance, who had become a high official in the government of Ghana, was aimed at enticing Abudu to return to Ghana in order to force him to disclose the whereabouts of his brother and other enemies of the government. All the other facts upon which Abudu based his claim were available at the time of the deportation hearing. The Supreme Court held that the Board of Immigration Appeals did not abuse its discretion in holding that the alien had not reasonably explained his failure to request asylum during the initial deportation proceedings as required by 8 C.F.R. § 3.2. If Abudu had made a timely application for asylum, supported by the same factual allegations and evidence set forth in his motion to reopen, the immigration judge would have been required to grant him an evidentiary hearing. But an "alien who has already been found deportable has a much heavier burden when he first advances his request for asylum in a motion to reopen."

If the application for asylum is approved, asylum status is granted for an indefinite period. 8 C.F.R. § 208.20. Employment authorization is automatically granted as well. In addition, a spouse or children may be granted asylum. CORAP can revoke asylum only if the INS proves by a preponderance of the evidence that conditions have changed in the alien's country of origin, that the alien was guilty of fraud in the application process, or that the alien had committed any act that would have been grounds for denial. 8 C.F.R. § 208.24. The alien can then reassert his/her claims in any subsequent exclusion or deportation proceedings. 8 C.F.R. § 208.15. After asylum status is terminated, the alien is placed in deportation proceedings if s/he was in the United States at the time asylum was granted or exclusion proceedings if the alien was an applicant for admission to the United States at the time asylum was granted. 8 C.F.R. § 208.16.

An alien who has been granted asylum and who remains in the U.S. for one year may apply for adjustment of status to that of a permanent resident alien. 8 C.F.R. § 209.1. The applicant for asylum must generally meet the normal admission requirements of any immigrant with the exceptions that an applicant for asylum does not require labor certification, proof of self-sufficiency, a valid visa, or proof of literacy. The acceptance of unauthorized employment by the asylee will not bar his/her adjustment of status as it would under INA § 245(c). The alien also must continue to be a refugee within the meaning of INA § 101(a)(42) and not have been firmly resettled in a foreign country. 8 C.F.R. § 209.2(a)(iii). Further, there must be a number available from the admission allowance for refugees in general, as provided by INA § 207(a), and there is an annual numerical limitation of 10,000 on the number of adjustments for asylees. 8 C.F.R. § 209.2(a); INA § 209(b). If that number is exceeded, a waiting list is established. Such a numerical limitation on the number of aliens whose status may be adjusted under section 209(b) shall not apply to an alien who: (a) was granted asylum before November 29, 1990; (b) is no longer a refugee due to a change in circumstances in a foreign state; and (c) meets other requirements for adjustment of status under this section.

The asylum officer's decision is reviewed by the Assistant Commissioner of CORAP, and the Deputy Attorney General, assisted by APRU, in designated cases. There is, however, no right of appeal to any of these offices, nor do parties have any right to appear before these offices. 8 C.F.R. § 208.18. Any motion to reopen or reconsider, for proper cause, may be filed with the asylum officer or immigration judge, whichever had jurisdiction for the prior determination. 8 C.F.R. § 208.19. Again, the denial of an application for adjustment of status is without prejudice to the alien's right to renew the application in deportation or exclusion proceedings. 8 C.F.R. § 209.2(f).

If the application is granted, the date of admission as a permanent resident alien is recorded as one year prior to the actual date of approval. INA § 209(b). The date on which the alien becomes a permanent resident will determine when the alien may apply for citizenship. The existence of a waiting list for asylee adjustment of status is significant since the alien must frequently wait several years before actually qualifying for permanent residence.

§ 10–2.3 Asylum and Withholding of Deportation

The provisions of INA § 243(h) governing withholding of deportation are closely connected to those of INA § 208(a) governing asylum. Section 243(h) provides that the Attorney General shall not deport an alien, with certain exceptions, if the alien's "life or freedom would be threatened ... on account of race, religion, nationality, membership in a particular social group, or political opinion." An alien most often will apply for asylum as relief in deportation proceedings along with a request for withholding of deportation under § 243(h). If an undocumented alien, residing in the United States and not under deportation proceedings, applies for asylum, the INS will become aware of that alien's undocumented status and will force the alien to return to the country of alleged persecution if his/her asylum application is denied and a request for a *de novo* review before an immigration judge is unsuccessful. In light of the small percentage of aliens actually granted asylum, many aliens do not risk exposure to the INS, but bring the asylum claim along with a request for a withholding of deportation if subjected to deportation proceedings.

Asylum or withholding may be revoked upon motion of the Assistant Commissioner for changed country conditions, fraud, or commission of an act which is grounds for denial under § 208.14(c), after a hearing before an asylum officer. 8 C.F.R. § 208.24. Asylum is a discretionary matter, however, § 243(h) relief is mandatory if the Attorney General determines that the alien is qualified. An alien, therefore, having established the requisite likelihood of persecution, must be granted a withholding of deportation to the country of persecution, but may be denied asylum at the discretion of the INS asylum officer or immigration judge. The alien in *Matter of Salim* (BIA 1982), for example, established the requisite probability of persecution in Afghanistan, but was denied asylum as a matter of discretion because of his arrival in the United States with a fraudulently obtained passport. The court ordered the alien's deportation to Pakistan. The standard for reviewing withholding of deportation or asylum is slightly stricter than the clear error standard. The appellate court will reverse only "if we conclude that the Board's evaluation is not supported by substantial evidence. This standard requires only that the Board's conclusions based on the evidence presented is substantially reasonable." *Arriaga–Barrientos v. INS* (9th Cir.1991).

§ 10–2.4 Extended Voluntary Departure

Rather than grant asylum which can mature into permanent residence, the INS may give temporary relief from deportation known as "extended voluntary departure." Extended voluntary departure is granted to aliens who cannot return to their country of origin because of a civil war or a similar crisis. It reflects the volatile nature of the political or armed conflict situation which can change with unpredictable world events. Extended Voluntary Departure (EVD) is an ad hoc process in which the Attorney General and the INS grant blanket temporary relief to nationals of designated countries. Beneficiaries receive unrestricted employment authorization. 8 C.F.R. § 274.12(a)(11). Under EVD, there are no standards for adjustment to lawful permanent status, nor any guidelines as to what federal programs a beneficiary may be entitled.

EVD status was extended to the Ugandans who suffered under the rule of Idi Amin, and to Nicaraguans and Iranians who faced the consequences of revolution in their respective countries. Critics have charged that EVD is too political. For example, in 1989, when the Chinese government suppressed dissident activity in the

wake of the Tiananmen Square massacre, the State
Department halted forceful deportations but did not
grant EVD.   Later, Chinese nationals in the United
States were given a "deferred departure" status, ensuring their ability to remain in the U.S. through 1994.
Extended Voluntary Departure could also be considered
as a form of relief from deportation.

§ 10–2.5 Temporary Protected Status

Extended Voluntary Departure was devised by the
executive branch to respond to changing world events;
it was not, however, codified in the INA or other statute.   The 1990 Act contained a program that is quite
similar to EVD and designed to replace it: Temporary
Protected Status (TPS).   INA § 244A.   Under TPS, the
Attorney General may designate a country or region as
too unstable for aliens to return.   One of the three
conditions must be met before the Attorney General can
grant TPS: 1) ongoing war or armed conflict would pose
a serious threat to an alien who sought to return to that
country; 2) earthquake, flood, drought, or other environ-
mental disaster has caused the country to seek TPS
designation because it temporarily cannot handle the
return of its nationals; 3) the safe return of aliens is
prevented by "extraordinary and temporary conditions"
and the national interest is not compromised by allowing their temporary stay.   INA § 244A(b)(1).   TPS may
be granted for up to eighteen months, and the Attorney
General's decision to do so is not subject to review.   INA
§§ 244A(b)(2), 244A(b)(5)(A).

A national of a designated country should apply to the
INS district director, even if exclusion or deportation
proceedings were underway before the country was so

designated. 8 C.F.R. § 240.7(a) & (d). If, however, facts proved in those prior proceedings are sufficient to deny the alien eligibility under TPS, the immigration judge or the BIA must make a final determination. 8 C.F.R. § 240.7(d).

The 1990 Act provides eligibility for Salvadorans who were in this country as of September 19, 1990, and applied for TPS between January 1 and June 30, 1991. Salvadorans meeting § 303 of the 1990 Act requirements receive protected status for 18 months. Soon after the 1990 Act, Kuwait, Liberia, and Lebanon received TPS designations as well. 56 Fed.Reg. 12745–47. Somalia has also received TPS designation and Yugoslavia was under consideration as this book went to press. In the future, TPS status may be given to other groups in need of temporary protection.

The benefit of TPS is freedom from deportation during the period of protection and an authorization for employment. The alien is restricted, however, in her/his ability to travel abroad and in her/his ability to receive welfare. As soon as the alien's TPS terminates, deportation proceedings may begin. The *ABC* settlement discussed below, however, requires that each Salvadoran be given the opportunity for a new asylum interview and adjudication.

a. The ABC Settlement

In *American Baptist Church v. Thornburg* (N.D.Cal. 1991) the INS and ABC reached a settlement in a class action suit against the Service for discriminatory handling of asylum cases involving Guatemalans and Salvadorans. In this landmark settlement, all Salvadorans in the U.S. as of September 19, 1990, and all Guatemalans in the U.S. as of October 1, 1990, who had previously been denied asylum can have their cases reopened and reheard before an asylum officer. This benefit also extends to all class members who had not previously filed for asylum. Only aggravated felons are excluded from the settlement.

Deportation is stayed during the pendency of their *de novo* asylum adjudications; deportation and exclusion proceedings are closed until the new adjudications have been made. If, however, deportation is based on criminal conduct or the proceedings were commenced after November 30, 1990, the applicant must make an affirmative request for closure of exclusion or deportation proceedings. All members of the class are entitled to employment authorization in the meantime and the "non-frivolous" standard does not apply.

A significant aspect of the settlement is that the government is barred from considering the following factors in making asylum determinations: (1) U.S. foreign policy as regards the applicant's country of origin; (2) border enforcement considerations; (3) the U.S. support of the applicant's country of origin; and (4) the applicant's political or ideological beliefs. All Salvadorans and Guatemalans in detention were to be released, advised of their "*ABC* rights," and given the appropriate forms for complying with formal procedures.

b. Procedures

Under TPS, the Salvadoran must have been continuously physically present in the United States since September 19, 1990; any departure precludes eligibility. The alien must be admissible as an immigrant, not have committed a felony or two misdemeanors, not have

engaged in activities prejudicial to the interests of the
U.S., and not have been involved in the persecution of
any group of people.

To register for TPS, the alien must complete an I–104
registration form, an I–765 work authorization form, an
I–263W Record of Sworn Statement with Addendum
Questionnaire, and a fingerprint card. An interview is
scheduled and a work authorization issued. If the applicant fails to appear for the interview, s/he will be
presumed to have abandoned her/his application. Also,
an alien subject to deportation proceedings may raise
eligibility for TPS as a defense.

CHAPTER 11

INTERNATIONAL LAW ISSUES RELATED TO IMMIGRATION

§ 11–1 FREEDOM OF MOVEMENT

§ 11–1.1 Freedom of Exit

The right of an individual to leave a nation first was mentioned in the Magna Carta of 1215, which stated that everyone had the right to leave England, subject to feudal obligations. In the following centuries, a common law writ of Ne Exeat Regno developed in England, conferring on the King the right to refuse exit to specific persons without special authorization. Everyone else enjoyed freedom of exit and even this royal prerogative gradually lost its importance. Blackstone stated that there was an absolute right to leave England, subject to an injunction to remain, but he also advocated the common law doctrine of perpetual allegiance, or citizenship.

In Medieval Germany, free departure was recognized as release from the feudal structure. Peasants and townspeople, who were "freemen," normally had the right to leave, but they had to pay a tribute for the privilege. Serfs, however, could not claim this right until they had bought themselves free from their bondage. In 1555 the Edict of Augsburg conferred the right to leave Germany for religious reasons. The Peace of Westphalia of 1648 also contained the right of departure. During the subsequent period, however, emigration from Germany was permitted only in exceptional situations.

The right to leave a nation was further recognized near the end of the Eighteenth Century. The U.S. Declaration of Independence and the Bill of Rights, and the French Declaration des Droits de l'Homme et du Citoyen of 1789 did not mention the right of exit, but were, of course, an important foundation of human rights. The French Constitution of 1791 specifically proclaimed the right to leave a nation. By the middle of the Nineteenth Century, most European nations in practice allowed individuals to leave freely, though no generally accepted right to emigrate existed.

The right to leave a nation became more generally recognized after World War II, with the adoption of several international instruments. The Charter of the United Nations, which came into force on December 24, 1945, is the most prominent international document dealing with human rights. The Charter announces a duty of states to promote and respect human rights; it does not specifically mention the right to leave. The Universal Declaration of Human Rights, adopted by the General Assembly on December 10, 1948, provides an authoritative interpretation of the human rights proclaimed by the Charter and states that "everyone has the right to leave any country, including his own...." Article 12(2) of the International Covenant on Civil and Political Rights contains almost identical language that is binding on the more than 100 nations which have ratified the Covenant. The Fourth Protocol, Article 2(2), of the European Convention on Human Rights also contains nearly identical wording. Further, the right to leave is recognized in Article 22(2) of the American

Convention on Human Rights and in Article 12(2) of the African Charter on Human and Peoples' Rights. These documents mention only the right to leave a nation, but one may infer that this right also includes the right to renounce one's citizenship.

§ 11–1.2   Right to Return

An individual may leave her/his home state, only to find that the home state will not allow her/his return. This problem may occur especially when an unpopular individual temporarily leaves the country to travel abroad. Article 13(2) of the Universal Declaration of Human Rights, Article 12(4) of the International Covenant on Civil and Political Rights, the Fourth Protocol to the European Convention on Human Rights, Article 22(5) of the American Convention on Human Rights, and Article 12(2) of the African Charter recognize the right of an individual to return to her/his home state. The U.N. Sub–Commission on Prevention of Discrimination and Protection of Minorities is considering a draft declaration on freedom and non-discrimination in respect to the right of everyone to leave any country, including her/his own, and to return to her/his country.

§ 11–1.3   Right to Enter

There is no corresponding right to enter any nation of which the individual is not a citizen. Based on the theory of sovereignty, both Blackstone and Vattel recognized the right of every nation to exclude aliens, or to place upon their entrance whatever restrictions the nation may want. Most nations place the greatest restrictions on immigration. Nations regularly admit aliens if there is a treaty of commerce, establishment, and navigation between the alien's home state and the admitting state. Parties to these treaties usually retain the right to exclude individuals who are deemed physically, medically, morally, or socially undesirable. The international human rights treaties do not grant individuals the right to enter any nation other than their own, but the Convention and Protocol relating to the Status of Refugees protect a refugee from being expelled or returned to a country where her/his life or freedom will be threatened. See § 11–3; ch. 10.

§ 11–1.4 Right to Travel

No general international right to travel between nations exists. While an individual has a right to leave any nation, the individual does not have a right to enter another nation. Special travel rights are, however, given to stateless persons and to refugees. These groups will be considered in the sections below. Nations do, however, admit aliens more readily for temporary travel than for immigration, especially if the nation is a party to a treaty of commerce, establishment, and navigation. The Helsinki Accord, which is a European/North American regional agreement adopted in 1975 at the European Conference on Security and Cooperation in Europe (CSCE), provides for freer movement of individuals between the signatories. In particular, the agreement provides for freer movement on the basis of family ties, family reunification, proposed marriages, and personal or professional travel. In addition, further agreements in the CSCE context, changes in Eastern Europe and the Confederation of Independent States (former Soviet Union), as well as the European unification in 1992 indicate a trend of away from obstacles to free travel.

In *Haig v. Agee* (Sup.Ct.1981), the Supreme Court upheld a regulation granting the Secretary of State broad discretion to revoke or withhold passports for reasons of national security or foreign policy. In so doing, the Court expressly limited the right to travel abroad, first announced by the Court in *Kent v. Dulles* (Sup.Ct.1958). Chief Justice Burger reasoned in *Agee* that Congress had implicitly authorized passport denials and revocations in the Passport Act of 1926 by remaining inactive in the years during which that act has been construed. Under *Agee,* the Secretary of State can deny or revoke a passport only if s/he finds that "serious damage" has been done to U.S. foreign policy or national security.

The Universal Declaration of Human Rights (Art. 13(1)), the International Covenant on Civil and Political Rights (Art. 12(1)), the Fourth Protocol to the European Convention on Human Rights (Art. 2(1)), the American Convention on Human Rights (Art. 22(1)), and the African Charter (Art. 12(1)) do not provide for travel between nations, but they do provide for freedom of movement within a state. The Convention and Protocol relating to the Status of Refugees as well as the Convention relating to the Status of Stateless Persons also provide for freer movement within a state for these groups. These last three instruments subject the right of free movement to any regulations generally applicable to aliens in the same circumstances.

§ 11-2   THE RIGHTS OF STATELESS PERSONS

Traditionally, states had full authority to determine who could be citizens. This authority led to dual nationalities for some, and statelessness for others. State-lessness also can occur through denationalization, voluntary renunciation of citizenship, or territorial transfer. Citizenship can also be lost because of a conflict of nationality laws. For example, statelessness can arise at birth when the state in which the child is born only recognizes the child as receiving the nationality of the parents, while the parent's home state recognizes only the nationality of the state where the child is born.

Stateless persons had no right under traditional principles of international law, because they had no home state to protect them. Stateless persons were therefore totally at the mercy of the nation in which they lived.

The traditional law regarding stateless persons began to change after World War I. Little effort was made to address the issue before World War I because the problem of statelessness had not occurred on a large scale. Most of the progress, however, was made after World War II in connection with two types of international instruments.

The first type of agreement gives rights to stateless persons. The leading document is the Convention relating to the Status of Stateless Persons. This treaty grants three types of rights. First, stateless persons are given rights at least as favorable as aliens in the particular nation where they live, for activities such as the acquisition of property. Second, stateless persons have the same rights as citizens in regard to government services such as elementary public education and public relief. Third, stateless persons are given special rights with respect to identity papers and travel documents for the purpose of travelling outside the host state.

The second type of instrument tries to prevent statelessness. Article 15 of the Universal Declaration of Human Rights says "1. Everyone has a right to a nationality. 2. No one shall be arbitrarily deprived of his nationality nor denied the right to change his nationality." Article 32 of the Convention relating to the Status of Stateless Persons provides that "the Contracting States shall as far as possible facilitate the assimilation and naturalization of stateless persons." The Convention on the Nationality of Married Women provides that a woman's nationality is not dependent on her husband's nationality. The Convention on the Reduction of Statelessness similarly deals with the problem of statelessness at birth. A state may not deprive a person of her/his nationality under this Convention if the deprivation would render the person stateless. Finally, this Convention provides that no person shall become stateless as a result of a transfer of territory. None of these instruments does much to gain citizenship for people who are already stateless. Granting these people the citizenship of the nation where they live may be the only adequate way to solve this problem. Most nations, however, have not gone that far yet.

§ 11–3 THE RIGHTS OF REFUGEES

Refugees have problems concerning travel, social and political rights, as well as resettlement. In 1922 the High Commissioner for Russian Refugees, in conjunction with the League of Nations, created the Nansen passport. This document, which was a certificate of identity in the form of a passport, was intended to permit the bearer to travel abroad during the period of its validity, and, if specifically stated, to permit the bearer to return to the issuing country. The state where the refugee was located issued the passport, not the League of Nations.

The 1951 Convention relating to the Status of Refugees and the 1967 Protocol relating to the Status of Refugees define a refugee as:

"Any person who owing to well-founded fear of being persecuted for reasons of race, religion, nationality, membership of a particular social group or political opinion, is outside the country of his nationality and is unable or, owing to such fear, is unwilling to avail himself of the protection of that country; or who, not having a nationality and being outside the country, of his former habitual residence is unable or, owing to such fear, is unwilling to return to it."

The Convention applies to persons affected by events in Europe occurring prior to January 1, 1951. The Protocol extends the protections of the Convention without the geographic and date limitations. For the 110 nations which have ratified either the Convention or the Protocol, those treaties establish the basic norm of *non-refoulement* that prohibits states from expelling or returning refugees to frontiers or territories where they would be threatened on account of race, religion, nationality, membership of a particular social group, or political opinion. These instruments also prohibit a state from expelling a refugee lawfully in its territory without Due Process of law. If a refugee is found to be excludable, s/he should be given an opportunity to find another country which will grant refuge.

In addition, the Refugee Convention of 1951 and the Protocol of 1967 give refugees certain travel rights. Article 26 of the Convention affords refugees the same right as aliens, in the same circumstances, to travel within a state. Article 27 provides that states "shall issue identity papers to any refugee in the territory who does not possess a valid travel document." Furthermore, Article 28 provides that states shall issue travel documents to refugees lawfully staying in their territory for the purpose of travelling outside their territory.

The Refugee Convention of 1951 and 1967 Protocol also give rights to refugees almost identical to the rights given stateless persons in the Convention relating to the Status of Stateless Persons. Under the 1951 Convention, refugees have rights at least as great as other aliens in the same state in regard to such subjects as the acquisition of property. The Universal Declaration of Human Rights and the two International Covenants on Human Rights provide civil, political, economic, social, and cultural rights to all people, including refugees. The rights of people displaced by armed conflicts are also protected by the Fourth Geneva Convention of 1949, as extended by the two Additional Protocols of 1977.

The Organization of African Unity Convention Governing the Specific Aspects of Refugee Problems in Africa of 1969 broadens the definition and thus the protection of refugees to include as refugees:

". . . every person who, owing to external aggression, occupation, foreign domination or events seriously disturbing public order in either part or the whole of his country of origin or nationality, is compelled to leave his place of habitual residence in order to seek refuge in another place outside his country of origin or nationality."

A similarly broad definition of refugee was also accepted by the Organization of American States General Assembly in its Cartegena Declaration of 1985 to include persons who have fled their country because their lives, safety, or freedom have been threatened by generalized violence, foreign aggression, internal conflicts, massive violations of human rights, or other circumstances which have seriously disturbed public order.

There are several international organizations which protect and provide assistance to refugees. There are estimated to be about 18 million refugees in the world. The United Nations High Commissioner for Refugees (UNHCR) provides "for the protection of refugees falling under the competence of his office." The UNHCR also helps to house; feed; and resettle, repatriate, or integrate refugees. The International Committee for Migration and many voluntary agencies assist the UNHCR in these tasks. The International Committee of the Red Cross and the Red Cross/Red Crescent Societies around the world assist victims of armed conflicts. Unfortunately, international law and international organizations have not been able to give significant protection or assistance to the 20 million persons who are internally displaced within their own countries. More attention is expected to be focused on helping internally displaced persons.

§ 11–4 ASYLUM

§ 11–4.1 The Right to Grant Asylum

A nation may grant either asylum within its territory ("territorial asylum") or within its embassies, consular offices, military ships, or other such locations. The idea of asylum developed before the Middle Ages when churches granted a refuge in holy places where persons fleeing from danger could be free from seizure. As the power of governments grew, asylum in churches became less prevalent.

European governments began granting territorial asylum as the Reformation divided the continent. An increase in the granting of territorial asylum occurred in the Eighteenth Century. Legal writers in the Eighteenth Century began invoking asylum for those persons guilty of political crimes and for victims of religious persecution. Grotius went so far as to view asylum as both a state's right and duty. Most other writers, however, did not go so far as saying that states had a duty to grant political asylum. During and after the French Revolution, this notion was transformed into a juridical principle. The Revolution considered it a duty of countries to help the oppressed. The French Constitution of 1793 provided asylum for foreigners who were exiled from their home state in the cause of human rights and liberty.

The right to grant asylum is reflected in several international instruments. Article 14 of the Universal Declaration of Human Rights provides the right to "seek and enjoy" asylum. This right, however, "may not be invoked in the case of prosecutions genuinely arising from non-political crimes or from acts contrary to the purposes and principles of the United Nations." U.N. General Assembly Resolution 2312 (XXII) on Territorial Asylum, 1967, reaffirmed the right to grant asylum contained in Article 14 of the Universal Declaration of Human Rights.

§ 11–4.2 The Right to Receive Asylum

While it is generally agreed that nations have the right to grant asylum, there is no similar agreement on the right of an individual to demand asylum. Article 14 of the Universal Declaration of Human Rights provides a "right to seek and to enjoy in other countries asylum from persecution." There is no right, however, to be granted asylum. An earlier draft provided for a right to "seek and be granted" asylum. This language was amended to make clear that states were not willing to accept an obligation to open their borders in advance to an unascertainable and possibly large number of refugees.

Even though an individual may not have a right to asylum, the emerging international law forbids a nation from forcibly returning a refugee who is fleeing from a neighboring state. The admitting nation is then free to force the individual to go to another nation. This right is reflected in U.N. General Assembly Resolution 2312 (XXII) on Territorial Asylum of 1967. Article 3, paragraph 1 states that "no person referred to in Article 1, paragraph 1, shall be subjected to measures such as rejection at the frontier or, if he has already entered the territory in which he seeks asylum, expulsion or compulsory return to any state where he may be subjected to persecution." Paragraph 2 provides an exception in the case of national security, public safety, or massive influx of persons.

The U.N. High Commissioner for Refugees (UNHCR) attempted in 1977 to establish a treaty on territorial asylum along the same lines as the Declaration on Territorial Asylum by convening a Conference of Plenipotentaries in Geneva. The participating states, however, were unable to agree; the UNHCR adjourned the conference indefinitely because of the concern that the states would diminish the international protections for those persons who seek asylum.

The Executive Committee of the UNHCR in 1981 adopted non-binding recommendations regarding the protection of asylum seekers particularly in the context of massive movements of population. The Executive Committee recommended that asylum seekers be admitted to the state where they first seek entry, so that they may be afforded protection and assistance, even for a temporary period. The recommendations also state that asylum seekers should not be punished for illegal entry, should enjoy the rights established in the Universal Declaration of Human Rights, should be granted all the necessary facilities to enable them to obtain a satisfactory durable solution, etc.

In 1981 the U.N. Human Rights Commission initiated a study by the former U.N. High Commissioner for Refugees, Mr. Sadruddin Aga Khan, as to how the world community should respond to massive exodus situations. The U.N. General Assembly also has set up a Group of Governmental Experts on International Co-operation to Avert New Flows of Refugees. There seems to be a growing recognition that the Convention on Refugees, the related Protocol, and national asylum procedures do not establish a satisfactory legal framework for dealing with the recent large influxes of asylum seekers. The Convention, the Protocol, and the national procedures which they inspired are premised upon the need for an individual determination of eligibility for asylum. Massive population movements in which many claim asylum do not permit such individual determinations.

Also, intended immigrants claim asylum in many countries knowing that the procedures for individual adjudication are so overloaded that they effectively will be able to remain indefinitely. Governments have begun to respond by detaining large numbers of asylum seekers and by developing expedited asylum procedures.

While there is a need for a new legal structure, there is concern that such a structure may be less protective of the rights of asylum seekers than the present approach. Rather than seek a new legal structure, the UNHCR has used ad hoc approaches in which, for example, a prima facie determination of eligibility for asylum is made for whole groups at a time. Nonetheless, there is little doubt that the problem of mass exodus and asylum represents a continuing challenge for both domestic and international legal systems.

§ 11–5 THE RIGHTS OF MIGRANT WORKERS

The International Labour Organization (I.L.O.) in 1949 promulgated Convention No. 97 concerning Migration for Employment and the related Recommendation No. 86 concerning Migration for Employment. These two instruments provide:

1. Safeguards against misleading information relating to emigration and immigration;

2. assurance of medical services for migrants;

3. a prohibition against discrimination in regard to conditions of employment, trade union membership, social security, and taxes;

4. a prohibition against returning a migrant to her/his country of origin after s/he was admitted on a

permanent basis, but is no longer able to work by reason of illness; and

5. similar protections for migrants.

The Migrant Workers (Supplementary Provisions) Convention of 1975 (No. 143) and the Migrant Workers Recommendations of 1975 (No. 151) supplement these legal protections by providing that governments should not only repeal discriminatory legislation, but enact promotional legislation to guarantee equality of opportunity and treatment in respect of employment, occupation, social security, trade union and cultural rights, as well as individual and collective freedoms of migrant workers. The I.L.O. also has adopted a convention supporting the rights of migrant workers to social security.

Thirty-eight countries have ratified Convention No. 97, including Belgium, France, the Federal Republic of Germany, Italy, Netherlands, Portugal, Spain, and the United Kingdom. The United States is conspicuously absent from this list. Only 15 countries have, so far, ratified the supplementary Convention No. 143; of the countries just mentioned, only Italy and Portugal have ratified this instrument.

There is also a European Convention on the Legal Status of Migrant Workers. This convention came into force on 1 May 1983. It has been ratified by France, Netherlands, Norway, Portugal, Spain, Sweden, and Turkey.

After eleven years of drafting, the U.N. General Assembly on December 18, 1990, adopted the International Convention on the Protection of the Rights of All Migrant Workers and Members of Their Families. The

Convention provides further protection for the rights of all migrant workers and their families, including frontier workers, seasonal workers, itinerant workers, and project-tied workers. The Convention does not apply to investors, students, trainees, refugees, and stateless persons. Furthermore, Article 35 of the Convention provides that none of its provisions shall be interpreted to imply the regularization of nondocumented migrant workers.

With regard to certain rights the U.N. Convention is broader and more specific than the existing I.L.O. instruments. Articles 43 and 45 of the U.N. Convention provide for equality of treatment for migrant workers and their families in access to educational institutions, vocational training, social and health services, and to cultural life. Furthermore, the migrant worker is guaranteed equality of treatment in access to co-operatives and self-management enterprises without change in migration status, and to housing. Further rights provided in the Convention include: the right to equality of treatment with nationals of the state concerned before courts and tribunals (Article 18); the prohibition of collective expulsion (Article 22); equal treatment with nationals as regards remuneration (Article 25); trade union rights and freedom of association (Articles 26 and 40); the facilitation of reunification of migrant workers with their families (Article 44); and the right to transfer earnings, particularly for the support of their families, to the country of origin (Article 47).

Further, the Convention establishes a Committee on the Protection of the Rights of All Migrant Workers and Members of Their Families to examine government reports to be submitted every five years on their laws and practices with regard to the rights recognized in the Convention. This Committee will also consider complaints made by one state party concerning the laws and practices of another state party and will consider individual complaints if that individual's government declares that it is willing to authorize the Committee to receive such complaints.

§ 11–6 RIGHTS OF NON–CITIZENS

In 1985, the U.N. General Assembly adopted by consensus a declaration on the human rights of individuals who are not citizens of the country in which they live. The declaration covers all individuals who are not nationals of the state in which they are present. The declaration provides for the respect of basic fundamental human rights of aliens (Article 5—right to life; right to privacy; equality before the courts and tribunals; freedom of opinion and religion; and retention of language, culture, and tradition). Subject to certain national restrictions, aliens shall also be guaranteed the right to leave the country, to freedom of expression, to peaceful assembly, and to own property alone or collectively.

Articles 7 and 8 provide rights for aliens lawfully in the country. Article 7 prohibits individual or collective expulsion on discriminatory grounds. Article 8 provides for trade union rights as well as the right to safe and healthy working conditions and the right to medical care, social security, and education.

The rights of aliens are also set forth in the General Comments of the Human Rights Committee issued in 1986 to interpret the relevant provisions of the International Covenant on Civil and Political Rights.

CHAPTER 12

CITIZENSHIP

§ 12–1 CONCEPTS OF CITIZENSHIP

§ 12–1.1 Citizenship and Alienage

Citizenship connotes membership in a political society to which a duty of permanent allegiance is implied. The United States Supreme Court in *United States v. Cruikshank* (1875), stated:

> Citizens are the members of the political community to which they belong. They are the people who compose the community, and who, in their associated capacity, have established or submitted themselves to the dominion of a government for the promotion of their general welfare and the protection of their individual as well as collective rights.

Alienage has the opposite meaning and signifies a condition of not belonging to the nation. The allegiance required of aliens is temporary and consists of willingness to comply with the nation's laws while residing in its territory.

The status of citizens in the United States carries with it all the rights and privileges embodied in the Constitution. Although aliens also enjoy certain constitutional protections, some provisions protect only "citizens," such as the Privileges and Immunities Clause of Article IV and the Fourteenth Amendment. Moreover, only citizens have the right to vote and to hold office; a citizen cannot be barred or expelled from the United States.

With the additional rights of citizenship come added responsibilities, such as the obligation to perform military service, required of able-bodied adults. 50 U.S.C.A. §§ 453, 454. Aliens have served in the armed forces (which is one means by which an alien may expedite the acquisition of citizenship), but they have traditionally been exempt from military conscription—at least until they become permanent residents. Citizenship also imposes the obligation to accept jury duty when called. 28 U.S.C.A. § 1861. In contrast, aliens are disqualified from serving on a jury, and an alien's presence on the jury in a felony trial has served as grounds to vacate a conviction.

The degree of connections one must have with the nation to be a citizen varies with the manner by which citizenship is acquired. Almost all persons born in the United States, for example, acquire citizenship automatically and cannot lose it involuntarily, even if they leave the United States immediately after birth and never return. Aliens seeking citizenship by naturalization, however, generally must reside in the United States for five years after having been granted permanent residence and demonstrate their good moral character, attachment to the United States, as well as their understanding of United States history and principles of government. INA § 316(a).

When the United States acquired outlying territorial possessions near the turn of the century, native populations were not considered citizens, though their allegiance to the United States was expected. The Supreme Court held in the "Insular Cases" that these territories were not "incorporated" into the United States, and hence, local populations were to be accorded a reduced level of constitutional protection. *See Balzac v. Pörto Rico* (1922). The continued vitality of the incorporation doctrine is unclear. *See, e.g., Torres v. Puerto Rico* (1978).

This chapter examines the two major methods by which citizenship may be acquired—birth and naturalization. It describes the substantive requirements of naturalization and the procedures involved in seeking citizenship under the naturalization laws. The final section focuses on loss of nationality through either denaturalization or expatriation. As a preliminary matter, however, the discussion first considers the two rules for determining citizenship—the principles of *jus soli* and *jus sanguinis.*

§ 12–1.2 The Principles of Jus Soli and Jus Sanguinis

Citizenship at birth is conferred automatically—the person's volition plays no part. Such automatic acquisition of citizenship assures that each person will have a nationality in the United States. In light of experience such a result appears reasonable, as people have traditionally remained loyal and committed to the citizenship they acquire at birth. There exists no universal nationality rule, however. While some nations adhere to the principle of *jus soli*—citizenship by the place of one's birth, others embrace the principle of *jus sanguinis*—citizenship by descent, or literally, blood relationship. Moreover, a number of nations, including the United States and Great Britain, have adopted a combination of the two principles.

The principle of *jus soli* was a tenet of the common law of England. Although it has its roots in feudalism, it still serves well as a basic rule of citizenship in many parts of the world. *Jus sanguinis* was the rule of civil law in Europe which determined an individual's citizenship at birth by the citizenship of her/his parents. The concept of nationality based upon blood took hold in Europe during the French Revolution, which had created a spirit of patriotism and fraternity for the French as a distinct people, and this sort of nationalistic fervor eventually spread to other peoples of Europe.

Jus soli continued to establish the citizenship of people born in England even after feudalism no longer existed. The rule's primary advantage as the criterion for citizenship lay in the certainty it provided each person's political status. In Great Britain the principle of *jus soli* remains the basis of nationality law. Nonetheless, the development of the British Empire, resulting foreign trade, and travel led to statutory provisions which followed the approach of *jus sanguinis*—granting citizenship to children born abroad of British parents.

Similarly, in the United States the principle of *jus soli* generally was accepted as part and parcel of the common law inherited from England. *See United States v. Wong Kim Ark* (Sup.Ct.1898). Hence, citizenship was conferred ordinarily upon the native born, although large groups of native born persons—American Indians, blacks, and Asians—did not enjoy citizenship status for many years after the formation of the republic. *See Elk v. Wilkins* (Sup.Ct.1884). The principle of *jus sanguinis* in United States nationality law was first established by the Act of 1790, which provided that children born abroad of United States citizens who had resided in the

United States "shall be considered as natural-born citizens." 1 Stat. 103. Every subsequent statute has precluded acquisition of United States citizenship by a child born abroad unless the citizen parent or parents have resided in the United States. *See* INA § 301.

§ 12–1.3 Dual Nationality

The problem of dual nationality directly results from the existence of two different rules for conferring citizenship. For example, an individual born of alien parents in the United States ordinarily obtains U.S. citizenship at birth yet s/he also may be vested with the citizenship of her/his parents by the laws of the foreign state. *See, e.g., Mandoli v. Acheson* (Sup.Ct.1952). Such dual nationality is generally regarded as undesirable, as it inevitably leads to conflicts of loyalty which are inconsistent with the unitary allegiance normally required for citizenship.

These conflicts become particularly serious in times of war, as the case of *Kawakita v. United States* (Sup.Ct. 1952) demonstrated. Tomoya Kawakita was born in the United States of Japanese parents and obtained dual citizenship by virtue of the nationality laws of each country. He lived in the United States until 1939, when at age seventeen he went to Japan and undertook studies at the Meiji University. After December 7, 1941, the United States and Japan were engaged in war but Kawakita remained in Japan to continue his studies. In March 1943, he registered in the Koseki, a family census register, after being told by the Japanese police that he must make a choice of citizenship. He never served in the armed forces of Japan. Rather, he obtained employment as an interpreter with the Oeyama

Nickel Industry Co., Ltd., where he worked until Japan's surrender. He was hired to interpret communications between the Japanese and the prisoners of war who were assigned to work at the mine and in the factory of the company. During his employment he allegedly committed acts of brutality against United States prisoners.

In December 1945, Kawakita went to the United States consul at Yokohama and applied for registration as a U.S. citizen, stating under oath that he was a citizen of the United States and had not done any acts amounting to expatriation. He obtained a passport and returned to the United States in 1946. Shortly thereafter he was recognized by one of the former prisoners of war; Kawakita was arrested, charged, and tried for treason.

At his trial Kawakita argued that he had terminated his United States citizenship in 1943 before the alleged acts of brutality, and thus could not be guilty of treason. The trial court submitted the issue as to whether he had expatriated himself to the jury, and charged that upon finding Kawakita had lost his citizenship prior to the time specified in the indictment, they must acquit him, since his duty of allegiance would have ceased with the termination of his United States citizenship. The jury found that Kawakita had not expatriated himself under any of the methods prescribed by Congress, and he was found guilty of treason and sentenced to death. The Court of Appeals for the Ninth Circuit affirmed in 1951.

On writ of certiorari the United States Supreme Court (by a 4–3 majority) affirmed the conviction and death sentence, upholding the jury's findings of fact. The Court further stated: "He cannot turn (his United

States citizenship) into a fair-weather citizenship, retaining it for possible contingent benefits but meanwhile playing the part of the traitor. An American citizen owes allegiance to the United States wherever he may reside." President Eisenhower later commuted Kawakita's death sentence to life imprisonment. In 1963 he obtained his release and returned to Japan.

Partly in response to the problems *Kawakita* and similar cases present, many nations have attempted to eliminate dual nationality by statute. A typical solution is to require the individual, who has acquired two citizenships while a minor, to choose a single nationality upon reaching the age of majority. Section 349(a)(1) of the INA provides that a U.S. citizen will lose her/his nationality by voluntarily obtaining naturalization in a foreign state upon her/his own application, or upon an application filed by a duly authorized agent, after having obtained the age of eighteen years. INA § 349(a)(1). See § 12–3.3, *infra*. Nonetheless, the statute does not address the issue of the individual obtaining dual nationality at birth or before the age of eighteen. So long as different national rules for conferring citizenship exist, dual nationality and its attendant problems will remain an issue for the law of citizenship.

§ 12–2 METHODS OF OBTAINING CITIZENSHIP

§ 12–2.1 Citizenship at Birth

a. *Birth Within the United States*

There are four ways to obtain citizenship: by birth in the United States or its territories, by birth outside the U.S. to a U.S. parent, by naturalization, or by naturalization of a parent while a child is under 18 years old.

All persons born in the United States and subject to its jurisdiction automatically acquire citizenship. INA § 301(a). This principle of common law was codified by the Fourteenth Amendment to the Constitution, adopted in 1868:

All persons born or naturalized in the United States, and subject to the jurisdiction thereof, are citizens of the United States and of the State wherein they reside.

The Citizenship Clause was intended to go further than the common law and included all African–Americans born in the United States. Before the amendment, African–Americans—whether slaves or free—had been denied the status of American citizen. The Supreme Court in *Scott v. Sanford* (1857) had declared that Dred Scott was not a "citizen" but a "Negro" of African descent, whose ancestors were slaves. He was thus barred from filing suit in U.S. District Court to obtain recognition of the freedom he had gained by entering and residing in free territory. The resulting Civil War led to the abolition of slavery. Because of the *Dred Scott* decision, however, proponents of the Fourteenth Amendment argued that while the Emancipation Proclamation had freed African–Americans, they could not become citizens without a constitutional amendment. The Fourteenth Amendment was thus adopted.

The Fourteenth Amendment also eliminated any doubt that persons born in the United States of alien parents were citizens. Such a proposition was confirmed by the Court in *United States v. Wong Kim Ark* (1898). Wong Kim Ark was born in San Francisco in 1873. His parents were native-born Chinese merchants who lived in this country as resident aliens. They left the United States in 1890 and returned to China permanently. Wong Kim Ark made a temporary visit to his parents in 1894, but upon return the following year to the United States, was not permitted to land at San Francisco. The government claimed Wong Kim Ark was not an American citizen but a Chinese laborer, and was properly barred entrance under the Chinese Exclusion Act. 22 Stat. 58. He challenged his exclusion in federal court, claiming citizenship under the Fourteenth Amendment. Justice Gray, in delivering the opinion of the United States Supreme Court, rejected the government's contention that the rule of *jus sanguinis*—citizenship by blood relationship—determined nationality in the United States. To the contrary, both the Fourteenth Amendment and the Civil Rights Act of 1866 (14 Stat. 27) had explicitly reaffirmed "the fundamental principle of citizenship by birth within the dominion." *Wong Kim Ark.* Hence, children born in this country were citizens without regard to the nationality of their parents. Wong Kim Ark won readmission to the United States.

The words "subject to the jurisdiction thereof" suggest exceptions to the general rule of *jus soli* or citizenship by birth within the dominion. For example, where a child was born in the United States to parents in the diplomatic service of the French government, the child was subject to the jurisdiction of the French Republic, not that of the United States. The physical fact of birth in this country did not alone confer citizenship in the *In re Thenault* (D.D.C.1942) case.

A second exception concerned Native Americans, illustrated by the case of *Elk v. Wilkins* (Sup.Ct.1884). John Elk was born a member of a Native American tribe. He severed his tribal relations and moved to Omaha, Nebraska. He asked to be registered and permitted to vote in local elections, but registrar Wilkins refused him, claiming Elk—as a Native American—was not a citizen of the United States and thus not qualified to vote. Elk claimed citizenship under the Fourteenth Amendment in his suit against the registrar. The Supreme Court held that the Fourteenth Amendment failed to confer citizenship upon Elk, who was born subject to the jurisdiction of his tribe rather than that of the United States. His subsequent renunciation of his tribal allegiance was irrelevant. He only would become a U.S. citizen by being "naturalized in the United States."

The Citizenship Act of 1924, however, established the citizenship status of Native Americans born after its enactment in the United States. 43 Stat. 253. The Nationality Act of 1940 reconfirmed the citizenship of all Native Americans born in the U.S. 54 Stat. 1137. INA § 289 also recognized the right of many "American Indians born in Canada" to pass the border of the United States. INA § 301(b) provides:

The following shall be nationals and citizens of the United States at birth:

(b) A person born in the United States to a member of an Indian, Eskimo, Aleutian, or other aboriginal tribe: *provided,* that the granting of citizenship under this subsection shall not in any manner impair or otherwise affect the right of such person to tribal or other property.

By its proviso expressly excepting tribal property rights, Congress emphasized its intention to impose all other obligations of citizenship, or so found the Second

Circuit in *Ex parte Green* (2d Cir.1941). Accordingly, appellant Green, a member of the Onondaga Tribe, was a citizen within the meaning of § 3(a) of the Selective Service Act of 1940, and subject to military service.

Two additional exceptions to the general rule of *jus soli* merit mention. Children born on foreign public ships while such vessels sit in the territorial waters of the United States, are not subject to U.S. jurisdiction and thus do not receive American citizenship. *United States v. Wong Kim Ark* (Sup.Ct.1898). Persons born in private vessels within the territorial sovereignty of the United States, however, would acquire United States citizenship. Finally, children born to alien enemies in hostile occupation of United States territory would not be subject to United States jurisdiction and would not gain citizenship upon their birth.

b. Birth in the Territories of the United States

Near the end of the nineteenth century the United States began to acquire territories and possessions beyond its mainland. The issue of how and whether to grant the peoples of these territories United States citizenship generated much debate. Congress has passed several statutes granting nationality to the residents of some but not all territories and possessions of the United States.

(1) *Hawaii*—The Hawaiian Islands became part of the United States on July 7, 1898, and persons born in Hawaii after that date are United States citizens. 30 Stat. 750. A person who was a citizen of the Republic of Hawaii on August 12, 1898, obtained United States citizenship as of April 30, 1900, the date Congress enacted a statute incorporating Hawaii into the Union as a

territory. 31 Stat. 141. Hawaii became a state on August 21, 1959. 73 Stat. 4.

(2) *Alaska*—Russia owned Alaska until 1867 when it sold the territory to the United States. 15 Stat. 539. All persons born in Alaska after March 30, 1867, except noncitizen Native Americans acquired United States citizenship. A Native American living or born in Alaska as of June 2, 1924, is a citizen of the United States. 43 Stat. 253. Alaska gained statehood on January 3, 1959. 72 Stat. 339.

(3) *Puerto Rico*—In 1899, the island of Puerto Rico was ceded to the United States by Spain in the treaty concluding the Spanish–American War. 30 Stat. 1154. Persons born in Puerto Rico from the date of cession to January 13, 1941, did not acquire citizenship at birth. With the Nationality Act of 1940, persons born there after January 13, 1941, and subject to the jurisdiction of the United States became United States citizens. 54 Stat. 1137. Persons born between April 11, 1899, and January 12, 1941, gained U.S. citizenship as of January 13, 1941, if they were residing in territory over which the United States exercised sovereignty.

(4) *Canal Zone and Panama*—The United States acquired the Canal Zone by treaty with Panama in 1904, to lease it in perpetuity. 33 Stat. 1234. By legislation first enacted in 1937 (50 Stat. 558), children born in the Canal Zone after February 25, 1904, became U.S. citizens if either the father or mother was a U.S. citizen. INA § 303(a). A child born in the Republic of Panama also received U.S. citizenship if either parent was a citizen employed by the United States, by the Panama Railroad Company, or by its successor in title. INA § 303(b).

In 1977, a treaty was negotiated returning sovereignty over the Canal Zone to Panama which Congress ratified in 1979. 93 Stat. 452. Citizenship acquired under the statute prior to the transfer is unaffected; but since the Canal Zone no longer constitutes U.S. territory, children born in the region of United States citizens are subject to the general rules applicable to children born outside the United States.

(5) *Virgin Islands*—The United States purchased the Virgin Islands from Denmark pursuant to an Act of January 25, 1917. 39 Stat. 1706. The Act of 1952 (66 Stat. 237) grants citizenship to all persons born in the Virgin Islands after January 17, 1917, and to any former Danish citizens who (1) did not declare an intent to preserve their Danish citizenship as provided under the treaty of purchase or (2) had subsequently renounced the declaration. INA § 306(a)(1). Several other categories of Virgin Island residents also became U.S. citizens after 1917.

(6) *Guam*—The island of Guam was acquired from Spain in settlement of the Spanish–American War. Persons living in Guam on April 11, 1899, and their children born on or after that date were declared citizens of the United States as of August 1, 1950, if on this date they were residing in Guam or in other territory over which the United States exercises sovereignty and had taken no steps to retain or acquire a different nationality. All persons born in Guam on or after April 11, 1899, are citizens of the United States as of the date of their birth, provided that if the person was born before August 1, 1950, s/he has taken no steps to retain or acquire a different nationality. INA § 307.

(7) *The Philippines*—The United States acquired the Philippines as a result of the Spanish–American War. Filipinos never collectively obtained the status of American citizens, instead being designated "noncitizen nationals." INA § 308. They owed allegiance to the United States, but received none of the privileges of citizenship. In 1946, the Philippines obtained independence (61 Stat. 1174); Filipinos thus acquired a new nationality and the status of aliens in regard to the United States.

c. Birth Outside the United States

Individuals born abroad of United States citizen parents can acquire United States citizenship. This acquired form of citizenship is controlled by statute, rather than by the Constitution or the Fourteenth Amendment. Each statute dating from the original 1790 Act has required the citizen parent or parents to have lived in the United States prior to the child's birth. 1 Stat. 103. The statutes conferring citizenship by *jus sanguinis* (blood relationship) underwent substantive changes in 1934, 1940, and 1952. Hence, in order to determine whether an individual obtained citizenship at birth outside the United States, it must be determined which statutory period is applicable. See 66 Interp.Rel. 444 (1989) (containing a reprinted chart illustrating the rules that apply to legitimate and illegitimate children born at various time periods).

(1) PERSONS BORN ABROAD BEFORE MAY 24, 1934

The first Congress exercised its constitutionally granted power to "establish an Uniform Rule of Naturalization" by enacting the Act of March 26, 1790, which provided: "And the children of citizens of the United States, that may be born beyond sea, or out of the limits of the United States, shall be considered as natural born citizens: *Provided*, That the right of citizenship shall not descend to persons whose fathers have never been resident in the United States." 1 Stat. 103. This provision, with minor phrasing changes and with the same emphasis on paternal residence, was retained by three subsequently enacted naturalization statutes. 1 Stat. 415, 2 Stat. 155, 10 Stat. 604.

(2) Birth Abroad Between May 24, 1934, and January 12, 1941

The Act of May 24, 1934, extended acquired citizenship to persons whose *mothers* were citizens and past residents of the United States. 48 Stat. 797. Consequently, in cases where one parent is an alien and the other a citizen, a foreign-born child could acquire citizenship through the citizen parent, whether it be a father or mother. To have retained citizenship, however, the child must have resided continuously in the United States during the period immediately prior to the child's eighteenth birthday. Persons born abroad between May 24, 1934, and January 12, 1941, were governed by the 1934 statute. Congress later passed retroactive legislation which abolished the retention requirement for any person under age 26 as of October 10, 1978.

(3) Birth Abroad Between January 13, 1941, and December 23, 1952

The Nationality Act of 1940 conferred citizenship at birth to children of parents who were both United

States citizens, or of which one was a citizen and the other a national, as long as a citizen parent had previously resided in the United States or its outlying possessions. 54 Stat. 1138. If only one parent was a citizen and the other an alien, the citizen parent was required to have resided previously in the United States or its outlying possessions for ten years, at least five of which were after attaining the age of sixteen. Moreover, a child lost her/his acquired citizenship by failure to take up residence in the United States for a period or periods totaling five years between the ages of thirteen and twenty-one. This residency requirement did not apply to a child born abroad whose U.S. citizen parent was, at the time of the child's birth, residing abroad solely or principally in the employment of the United States government, certain U.S. organizations having their principal place of business in the United States, or an international agency in which the United States participates. Persons born between January 13, 1941, and December 23, 1952, are covered by the provisions of the 1940 Act.

(4) Persons Born Abroad After December 23, 1952

Under the Immigration and Nationality Act of 1952 (66 Stat. 163), where both parents of a foreign-born child are United States citizens, the child inherits citizenship in the same manner as provided by the 1940 Act. If one parent is a citizen and the other a U.S. "national" (*see, e.g.,* § 12–2.1(b)(7)), the citizen parent must have been physically present in the United States or its outlying possessions for one year prior to the child's birth. INA § 301(d). If one parent is a citizen and the other an alien, the 1952 statute provided that the citizen parent must have been physically present in the United States or its outlying possessions for a period of ten years, at least five of which were after attaining the age of fourteen. INA § 301(g). In 1986 this physical presence requirement was reduced to five years, at least two of which were after attaining the age of fourteen.

(5) Amendments to the 1952 Act

(i) *Exemption for Foreign Service.* In 1966 Congress passed an amendment to section 301(g) of the 1952 Act (80 Stat. 1322) attaching a proviso which allowed periods of overseas service in the armed forces, in the employment of the United States government, or in the employment of an international organization to which the United States is a member, as counting towards satisfaction of the ten year physical presence requirement. INA § 301(g). Congress retained this provision when it reduced the physical residence requirement to five years in 1986. In addition, any period during which the citizen parent was physically present abroad as an unmarried dependent of a person in such service counts towards satisfying the requirement.

The amendment specifically was designed to alleviate the hardship of the children of parents in foreign civilian service who, if they were to marry a foreign national, were precluded by law from transmitting their United States citizenship to their foreign-born children, because they lacked the requisite years of physical presence in the United States. As the State Department wrote in its letter to then Vice–President Humphrey, requesting the legislation:

It is not uncommon for the children of a foreign service officer to spend most of their youthful years abroad accompanying the parents from one assignment to another. The proposed amendment, in effect, would treat the time spent abroad in such cases as constructive physical presence in the United States for the purpose of transmitting U.S. citizenship.

(ii) *Elimination of Retention Requirement for Children Born Abroad.* Until 1972, INA § 301(b) required that the citizen child born abroad of parents, one of whom was a citizen and the other an alien, had to reside in the United States for five consecutive years after attaining the age of fourteen but before reaching age twenty-four. Congress decided in 1972 that the intent of the law could be met by a lesser period of residence, "thereby alleviating the hardship that is often caused by the separation of children or young adults from their families and the attendant financial burden imposed by such separation." Therefore, Congress reduced the residence requirement to two years of physical presence in the United States for a continuous period between the ages of fourteen and twenty-eight, further providing that absence of less than sixty days in the aggregate would not break the continuity of such physical presence. Finally, the legislation provided that these residence requirements would not apply in the case of a child whose alien parent was naturalized while the child was under age eighteen.

Despite the liberalized residence requirement of the 1972 amendment, 693 citizens lost their citizenship for failure to comply between 1972 and 1977. This unhappy result prompted Congress in 1978 to eliminate altogether the residence requirement for children born of one citizen parent and one alien parent. In its report accompanying the bill the House Judiciary Committee stated: "The Committee believes that section 301(b) of the Immigration and Nationality Act currently creates an inconsistency in our citizenship laws, in that this is the only class of United States citizens who are subject to any residence requirement in order to retain their citizenship."

The Judiciary Committee felt that repeal of section 301(b) would best redress the inequity. While some members of Congress expressed concern that repeal of section 301(b) would create the possibility of "generations of citizens residing with little or no connection with the United States," such fears were groundless. Until 1986, section 301(g) continued to provide that in order for a United States citizen to transmit citizenship to her/his child born abroad of the citizen parent and an alien parent, the citizen parent must have resided in the United States for ten years at least five of which were after attaining the age of fourteen. In 1986, this residency requirement was reduced to five years, at least two of which were after attaining the age of fourteen.

§ 12–2.2 Citizenship by Naturalization

a. *Historical Development*

Naturalization is the process by which persons not acquiring citizenship at birth may obtain citizen status. The power to confer citizenship in this manner derives from Article I, section 8 of the Constitution which authorized Congress "to establish a uniform Rule of Naturalization." Since the initial naturalization statute of 1790 (1 Stat. 103), Congress has exclusively exercised the power to establish the conditions upon which aliens might be naturalized. *See Collet v. Collet* (1792).

In the original statute of 1790 Congress prescribed that a "free white alien" who had resided in the United States for two years might be naturalized in a court proceeding, provided s/he was of good moral character and took an oath to support the Constitution. 1 Stat. 103. The Act of 1795 lengthened the residency requirement to five years and enacted additional conditions that the applicant for naturalization declare formal intent to seek citizenship three years before actual admission; that the applicant renounce any former allegiance and swear allegiance to the United States; that the applicant satisfy the court s/he "has behaved as a man [sic] of good moral character, attached to the principles of the Constitution of the United States, and [be] well disposed to the good order and happiness of the same." 1 Stat. 414.

An unfortunate period (1798–1802) of hysteria against foreigners produced the Alien and Sedition Acts and much more restrictive naturalization requirements (residence requirement increased to fourteen years, declaration of intent period increased to five years). 1 Stat. 566. The hysteria soon dissipated, however, and Congress enacted the more lenient provisions of the 1795 Act in the Act of April 14, 1802. 2 Stat. 153. The substantive provisions of 1795 closely resemble the general requirements of the present law, notwithstanding several refinements discussed *infra*.

Congress established substantive requirements for naturalization in the first years of the republic, but failed to provide uniform procedures and administration until passage of the Naturalization Act of 1906. 34 Stat. 596. The statute vested responsibility for administrative supervision of naturalization in the federal Bureau of Immigration and Naturalization within the Department of Commerce and Labor; it prescribed uniform naturalization forms; required that each petitioner for naturalization obtain an official certificate of lawful admission and attach it to the petition for naturalization; required uniform naturalization fees; established time limitations for the courts to hear and grant petitions (minimum of 90 days after filing, no hearings permitted within 30 days of a general election); and finally, required that each petition be supported by two citizen witnesses who would testify to the petitioner's qualifications for citizenship.

Subsequent procedural revisions included permitting heretofore excluded "alien enemies" to petition for naturalization and the establishment of court-appointed naturalization examiners who would hear the evidence in naturalization cases and recommend dispositions to the federal courts. 44 Stat. 709. Congress added several substantive revisions in the Nationality Act of 1940. 54 Stat. 1137. Most significantly, the act eased racial restrictions on naturalization. Persons from races indigenous to the Western Hemisphere became eligible for naturalization. Up until that time only white persons and persons of African nativity or descent had been eligible. 1 Stat. 414; 16 Stat. 254. In 1943 Congress added Chinese immigrants as a fourth class of eligible persons, (57 Stat. 600) while at the same time repealing the Chinese Exclusion Act (22 Stat. 58) which had specifically prohibited naturalization of Chinese persons.

The Immigration and Nationality Act of 1952 provided comprehensive codification of the law governing citizenship. 66 Stat. 163. Among the most significant changes enacted by the 1952 law was elimination of all racial and gender qualifications for naturalization. The statute finally ended the blatantly racist formulations of previous naturalization provisions. INA § 311. The statute did, however, preclude naturalization (1) of persons belonging to certain subversive groups (INA § 313), (2) of persons who had sought relief from United States military services on the ground of their alienage (INA § 315), or who had deserted from the armed forces during wartime (INA § 314), and (3) of aliens against whom a deportation proceeding or order was outstanding. INA § 318. Congress also enacted provisions to facilitate naturalization of aliens who had actively served in the armed forces during World War I, World War II, the Korean hostilities, the Vietnam Conflict, or later conflicts. INA § 329.

The 1990 Act and the 1991 Act made the INS the sole decisionmaker in naturalization cases, but the court should administer the oath of allegiance within 45 days or the district director will give the oath.

b. *Requirements of Naturalization*

(1) RESIDENCE AND PHYSICAL PRESENCE

Section 316(a) of the Immigration and Nationality Act requires that, except as otherwise provided, no person shall become a U.S. citizen by being naturalized unless (1) s/he has resided continuously in the United States for five years as a lawfully admitted permanent resident, (2) during the five years immediately prior to filing the petition for naturalization s/he has been physically present in the United States for at least half of the time, and (3) s/he has resided within the district in which s/he filed the petition for at least three months.

The applicant need not reside continuously within the United States from the date of the petition up to the time of admission to citizenship. INA § 316. The purpose of the residency requirements is to create a reasonable period of "probation" that will enable candidates to discard their foreign attachments, to learn the principles of the U.S. system of government, and to develop an identification with the national community.

To comply with the statute a legal residence is necessary; a valid statutory residence prior to naturalization cannot be founded on an illegal entry into the country. Congress has defined "residence" under the 1952 Act to mean "the place of general abode ... [a person's] principal, actual dwelling place in fact, without regard to intent." INA § 101(a)(33). The question of residence thus turns on a determination of where an applicant has held the status of lawful permanent resident alien, not on declarations of where s/he intends to live.

An applicant for citizenship need not show that s/he stayed at the claimed residence each day of the five year statutory period. Temporary absences from the place of abode—even from the United States—do not alone break the continuity of an applicant's residence. Absence from the United States for less than six months during the statutory period do not affect continuous residence, while an absence of more than six months but less than one year presumptively breaks the continuity. INA § 316(b). The applicant can overcome the presumption by "establish[ing] to the satisfaction of the Attorney General that he did not in fact abandon his residence in the United States during such period." An absence from the United States for one year or more will as a matter of law break the continuity of residence; the applicant will be required to complete a new period of residence after s/he returns to the United States.

As an exception to the physical residency requirement, persons who expect to be away from the United States for a year or more in service of the United States government, a recognized U.S. institution of research, a U.S. corporation engaged in foreign trade and commerce, a public international organization of which the United States is a member by treaty or statute, or a religious organization, may apply for permission to be absent without breaking their residence for purposes of naturalization. Before seeking such exception with Form N–470, an applicant must continuously reside in the United States—following lawful admission—for one year or more. INA §§ 316(b), 317. The applicant must establish to the satisfaction of the Immigration and Naturalization Service that her/his absence from the United States for such period is in service of the government, for the purpose of conducting scientific research, for the purpose of developing trade or commerce necessary to protect property rights in a foreign country, or as a member of a public international organization. INA § 316(b)(1). A 1981 amendment provides that dependent unmarried sons and daughters of a person who qualifies for benefits under this provision shall also be entitled to such benefits during the period for which they were residing abroad as dependent members of the person's household. INA § 316(b).

Recognizing the peculiar difficulties individuals employed on seagoing vessels face in meeting the normal residency requirements, Congress has traditionally relaxed those requirements for persons serving on certain

United States vessels. 40 Stat. 542; 54 Stat. 1137. Under current law the benefit of "constructive residence" is granted to aliens lawfully admitted for permanent residence who thereafter serve with good conduct, in any capacity other than as a member of the armed forces, on board (a) a vessel owned and operated by the United States government, or (b) a vessel whose "home port" is in the United States. INA § 330. Such service is deemed residence *and* physical presence for the purpose of satisfying the residency requirements of section 316(a). Similarly, INA § 317 preserves both the residence and physical presence of ordained persons who are sent outside the U.S. by a recognized U.S. religious institution.

The exemption to the one year absence limitation concerning continuity of residence, which is provided for certain applicants (INA § 316(b)(1)), does not relieve such persons from the requirement of physical presence within the United States for one-half of the statutory five year period. INA § 316(c). Persons employed by the United States government, however, are exempted completely from the physical presence requirements of section 316(a). INA § 316(c).

Where an alien's absence from the United States is involuntary, courts have excused the absence for the purpose of residence and physical presence requirements. In the case of *In re Yarina* (N.D.Ohio 1947), a Czech immigrant, who had spent his entire childhood in the United States, was employed by an American company at Wake Island, a United States territory in the South Pacific. In December 1941, the Japanese captured the island and took petitioner Yarina and many others prisoner. He remained a captive in a Japanese prisoner of war camp until September 1945. He filed his petition for naturalization in the year following his liberation and return to the United States. The court held that the provision depriving an alien of the right to naturalization, in case of absence from the United States for a year or more during the statutory period preceding the application, contemplated a voluntary departure from this country. Since the forces of the enemy transported Yarina from Wake Island to the prison camp, petitioner "never left his residence in the United States within the purview of the statute." He was thus granted his naturalization petition.

Nonetheless, if a petitioner departs the United States voluntarily but is prevented from returning by events beyond her/his control, the absence is unexcused. Mary Holzer, an Israeli national, was a lawfully admitted permanent resident alien who left the United States to visit Israel in October 1952. She cited financial reasons for her inability to return to the United States within the one year period. The court found that her extended absence barred the petition for naturalization, stating "the rule applies even where the absence from the United States beyond the statutory period was involuntary." *Petition of Holzer* (S.D.N.Y.1956).

(2) AGE

To apply for naturalization an applicant must generally have attained the age of eighteen years. INA § 334(b)(1). A parent or adoptive parent, however, can file an application on behalf of a child under age eighteen, if the parent is a citizen—either by birth or naturalization—at the time the petition is filed. The child must be residing with the citizen parent in the United

States as a lawful permanent resident.   INA § 322.
Most children acquire citizenship at the time their parents are naturalized;   they are not subject to the five
year waiting period.   Their naturalization is by operation of law;   hence, no application or proceeding is
necessary.   The child's status is called derivative citizenship.

(3) LITERACY AND EDUCATIONAL REQUIREMENTS

Unless s/he is physically unable to do so through
blindness or deafness, an applicant for naturalization
must be able to speak and understand simple English,
as well as read and write it.   INA § 312(1).   Before
1978, the Act provided an exemption to the literacy
requirement for persons who, on the effective date of
this chapter (1952), were over fifty years of age and had
been living in the United States for periods totalling at
least twenty years.   In 1978 Congress amended the
provision to exempt any person who was over the age of
fifty years *at the time of filing their petition,* and who
had been lawfully admitted for permanent residence for
periods totalling twenty years.   92 Stat. 2474.   The
legislative history to this amendment pointed to the
original exemption's lack of flexibility in addressing the
language problems of persons who were slightly under
fifty years of age as of December 24, 1952.   In addition,
the 1990 Act provided an exemption from the literacy
requirement for any person who had been a permanent
resident for 15 years and who is over 55 years of age as
of the date of application for naturalization.

The statute further requires "a knowledge and understanding of the fundamentals of the history, and of the
principles and form of government, of the United

States." INA § 312(2). Each person applying for naturalization, including the older persons mentioned above, must pass an examination demonstrating the requisite knowledge of the United States. An interpreter or sign language may be used to test the applicant's knowledge of United States history, principles, and form of government, if s/he is exempt from the literacy requirement. 8 C.F.R. § 332.11(b). The Immigration Service generally applies the educational requirements in a lenient manner with due consideration given to such factors as the extent of the applicant's education, background, age, and length of residence in the United States. 8 C.F.R. § 312.2. Moreover, the regulations provide for second and third opportunities to pass the examinations. 8 C.F.R. § 312.3.

The power of Congress to establish these literacy requirements has withstood constitutional challenge. In *Trujillo–Hernandez v. Farrell* (5th Cir.1974), petitioner brought a class action, attacking the statute on equal protection grounds. The Court of Appeals for the Fifth Circuit held that a direct attack on Congress' exercise of its naturalization power was foreclosed and nonjusticiable, as such power was part of the foreign relations responsibilities committed to Congress.

(4) GOOD MORAL CHARACTER

An applicant for naturalization must show that, during the five year statutory period before filing and up until the final hearing of the naturalization petition, s/he "has been and still is a person of good moral character. ..." INA § 316(a). The burden of establishing good moral character falls upon the petitioner, as an applicant must prove her/his eligibility for citizenship in every respect. *Berenyi v. INS* (Sup.Ct.1967).

Courts have struggled with the issue of what constitutes good moral character. Judge Learned Hand stated that it is a "test, incapable of exact definition; the best we can do is to improvise the response that the 'ordinary' man or woman would make, if the question were put whether the conduct was consistent with a 'good moral character'." *Posusta v. United States* (2d Cir.1961). Prior to 1952, no attempt had been made to define good moral character by statute. Then, in the 1952 Act, Congress chose to define by enumerated exclusions what would *preclude* a finding of good moral character. 66 Stat. 166. A person could not be considered of good moral character if s/he was at any time during the five year period:

(1) a habitual drunkard;

(2) one who during this period has committed adultery;

(3) a polygamist or a person illegally connected with prostitution, narcotics, or the unlawful entry of other aliens;

(4) one whose income is principally from illegal gambling activities;

(5) convicted of two or more gambling offenses committed during this period, or one whose income is derived principally from illegal gambling activities;

(6) one who has given false testimony for the purpose of obtaining any benefits under the Act;

(7) convicted and jailed for 180 days or more, regardless of whether the offense was committed within this period;

(8) one who *at any time* has been convicted of the crime of murder. INA § 101(f) (emphasis added). (The 1990 Act changed the words "the crime of murder" to "an aggravated felony.")

The fact that a person is not within the classes enumerated does not preclude a finding for other reasons that s/he lacks the requisite good moral character.

Congress hoped by this provision to establish some nationally uniform standards for determining good moral character. This objective was not fully realized, however, at least with respect to one of the most controversial bars to citizenship—adultery. For example, the Immigration and Naturalization Service took the position that what constituted adultery was to be determined under the law of the state where the act was committed. Laws concerning adultery varied considerably from state to state, raising the obvious question: what about the goal of uniformity? The Board of Immigration Appeals, which reviews the administrative decisions, sought to rationalize the Service's interpretation in *In re Pitzoff* (1962):

> Congress' desire that there be uniformity related not to the methods to be used in determining whether adultery had been committed but related rather to the desire that *all* who had committed adultery should be barred from the prizes of the law. (emphasis added).

The Service's position was followed by some but not all courts. In *Moon Ho Kim v. INS* (D.C.Cir.1975), the U.S. Court of Appeals for the District of Columbia Circuit held that the definition of "adultery," as the term is used in the act, is not that definition which applies in the state where the extramarital act took place; rather, the appropriate approach is the application of a uniform federal definition, namely, "extramarital intercourse which tends to destroy an existing, viable marriage, and which would represent a threat to public morality."

If a person committed "technical adultery" but acted in good faith, as where petitioner obtained a Mexican divorce from his first wife and remarried, unaware of the invalidity of the divorce, he did not fall within the sanction of the act concerning adultery. *Dickhoff v. Shaughnessy* (S.D.N.Y.1956). In addition, the existence of extenuating circumstances were generally deemed relevant in determining whether an alien had established good moral character despite the commission of adultery. Hence, in *Wadman v. Immigration & Naturalization Service* (9th Cir.1964), petitioner's isolated acts of sexual intercourse with another, after his wife had willfully and permanently abandoned him, did not preclude him from establishing good moral character. But some courts insisted upon a stricter application of the statutory provision, such as the U.S. District Court for the Southern District of New York in *Petition for Naturalization of O_____ N_____* (1964), which refused to consider as extenuating circumstances that the cohabiting petitioners were recent immigrants who wanted to marry but were unfamiliar with American divorce procedure. Referring to the legislative history, the court stated, "[T]he two Senate reports ... support the view that Section 1101(f)(2) [INA § 101(f)(2)] was an attempt to tighten the law and exclude the relevance of extenuating circumstances ...."

Ultimately, in 1981, Congress acknowledged the problems that the adultery classification had created for the courts in evaluating moral character on the individual facts of each case. It therefore repealed the adultery provision. 95 Stat. 1611. A person can still be found to lack good moral character under the discretionary provision that permits a finding of a lack of good moral character "for other reasons." INA § 101(f). Adultery, however, is no longer a mandatory bar to citizenship. Congress stated its rationale for repeal in the report accompanying the legislation:

With respect to adultery, the Committee believes that the Immigration Service should not be required to inquire into the sex lives of applicants for naturalization. Such questions clearly represent an invasion of privacy. Furthermore, in testimony before the 96th Congress witnesses concurred in the view that the adultery bar was merely "window dressing" in the law; INS estimated that "7 out of 10 persons today who would admit to that conduct would fall within one or more of the judicial interpretations which excuse that conduct for purposes of naturalization."

INA § 316(e) provides that, in determining whether the applying alien is of good moral value character, "the Attorney General shall not be limited to the applicant's conduct during the five years preceding the filing of the application, but may take into consideration ... the applicant's conduct and acts at any time prior to that period." The U.S. Court of Appeals for the Second Circuit in *Tieri v. INS* (2d Cir.1972) held that in evaluating petitioner's application for naturalization in 1966, the district court properly considered evidence of the petitioner's six arrests between 1922 and 1959, two of which resulted in convictions of robbery and bookmaking. The Second Circuit concluded that "petitioner persistently attempted to obscure any past conduct which he feared might prove suspicious or embarrassing to his cause, and that, accordingly, the district court was not mistaken in discerning a pattern of deception in the whole mosaic of petitioner's testimony."

The Third Circuit Court of Appeals held that INA § 101(f)(6), regarding the giving of false testimony for the purpose of obtaining benefits under the act, is mandatory in its terms and not subject to a distinction between material and immaterial matters. *In re Haniatakis* (3d Cir.1967). Haniatakis falsely stated on her naturalization application that she was unmarried for fear that her naturalization would be delayed for 5 more years if the INS knew of her marriage to another alien. The petitioner also misrepresented her prior places of residence.

The INS declared that her marriage to another alien would not have affected her application. The district court concluded that the false testimony did not affirmatively demonstrate the absence of good moral character because the misrepresentations were immaterial and the facts concealed would not have been a barrier to her naturalization. In reversing the judgment of the district court, the Third Circuit reasoned that naturalization is denied whenever false testimony is given for a practical reason, and in addition that one who gives false testimony to deceive the government is unworthy of citizenship. A false answer which appears immaterial may nevertheless cut off a line of inquiry which might have revealed facts material to the applicant's eligibility for citizenship. The court distinguished *Chaunt v. United States* (Sup.Ct.1960), in which the Supreme Court refused to denaturalize a citizen who had twenty years before failed to reveal on his naturalization application that he had previously been arrested. The provision of the act involved in *Chaunt,* INA § 340(a), specifically required that the fact concealed be "material." The government was attempting to deny the privileges of citizenship to one who had already been granted them.

(5) Attachment to Constitutional Principles

An applicant must show that s/he is "attached to the principles of the Constitution of the United States, and well disposed to the good order and happiness of the United States." INA § 316(a). The purpose behind this requirement is the admission to citizenship of only those persons who are in general accord with the basic principles of the community. *Petition of Sittler* (S.D.N.Y. 1961). Courts have defined attachment to the Constitution as a belief in representative democracy, a commitment to the ideals embodied in the Bill of Rights, and a willingness to accept the basic social premise that political change only be effected in an orderly manner. Similarly, a favorable disposition to the good order and happiness of the United States has been characterized as a belief in the political processes of the United States, a general satisfaction with life in the United States, and a hope for future progress and prosperity. Neither requirement is thought to preclude a belief that change in our form of government within constitutional limits is desirable.

Whether an applicant for citizenship is attached to the principles of the Constitution depends on her/his state of mind, which must be determined on the basis of the applicant's conduct and expressions over a period of time. The INS cannot safely base its judgment on isolated statements of the applicant. Hence, the federal court in *In re Kullman* (W.D.Mo.1949) found that petitioner's isolated statement made before America's involvement in World War II expressing sympathy for the German people and praise for Adolf Hitler would not deny him citizenship, in light of his thirty-seven years of law-abiding residence in the United States and his aid to United States armed forces during World War I.

Although the general requirements of attachment to the Constitution allow discretion in evaluating a case on its own facts, several statutes enacted in 1952 specifically and automatically preclude naturalization of certain persons. Individuals belonging to the Communist Party or other totalitarian groups (INA § 101(a)(37)), and persons who—irrespective of membership in any organization—advocate the overthrow of the United States government by force or violence or other unconstitutional means may not obtain naturalization. INA § 313(a)(4). An applicant is not disqualified, however, if s/he can show that the membership in the prescribed organization is or was involuntary. INA § 313(d). Moreover, if the applicant can establish that such membership or affiliation occurred and terminated prior to the alien's attaining sixteen years of age, or such membership or affiliation was by operation of law or for purposes of obtaining employment, food, or other essentials, he or she may yet qualify for naturalization. In *Grzymala–Siedlecki v. United States* (5th Cir.1961), therefore, petitioner's enrollment in the Polish Naval Academy, which automatically conferred Communist Party membership, did not disqualify him from naturalization where the college education was necessary to the applicant's earning a livelihood in Poland.

A few courts have added another exception to the disqualification for Communist membership. Such membership or affiliation does not disqualify an applicant unless it is or was a "meaningful association." The Supreme Court had held, in the context of deportation proceedings, that a "meaningful association" signifies at minimum "[an] awareness of the Party's political aspect." *Rowoldt v. Perfetto* (Sup.Ct.1957). The federal district court of Puerto Rico applied the same analysis in *In re Pruna* (D.Puerto Rico 1968) holding that where petitioner's membership in an organization supporting Fidel Castro's revolution in Cuba in 1958 resulted from a belief that the organization's objective was to restore to the Cuban people a representative democracy, and where he was unaware that the organization was connected with the Communist Party, his participation did not constitute a "meaningful association" with a subversive group. His membership thus did not preclude him from naturalization.

An applicant may escape the preclusion statute if more than ten years have passed, between her/his membership in the subversive organization or the act of advocating overthrow of the government, and the filing of the petition for naturalization. INA § 313(c).

Section 314 of the INA permanently precludes the naturalization of anyone who, during the time that the U.S. "has been or shall be at war," deserts the U.S. armed forces or leaves the country with the intent of avoiding the military draft, and is convicted of that offense by a court-martial or a court of competent jurisdiction. INA § 314. The provision also specifically prohibits such people from ever holding an official position of the United States. Uncertainty remains whether the term "at war" includes hostilities lacking a formal declaration of war—such as the Korean, Vietnam, and Persian Gulf conflicts of recent years. The Immigration Service has stated that the Korean conflict constituted a "time of war" within the meaning of the 1940 version of this provision. To the date of this writing, no reported judicial determinations exist.

INA § 315(a) provides that an alien who seeks or obtains exemption from service in the armed forces on the ground that s/he is an alien becomes permanently ineligible for citizenship, unless the alien had served in the military of a country having a treaty with the U.S. INA § 315(a). Selective Service records are conclusive on the issue of whether an alien secured the exemption because of alienage. INA § 315(b).

(6) OATH OF ALLEGIANCE TO THE UNITED STATES

Related to the requirement that an applicant be attached to the Constitution of the United States, s/he also must take an oath of renunciation and allegiance in open court. Section 337(a) of the INA requires that the applicant pledge (1) to support and bear true faith and allegiance to the Constitution of the United States; (2) to renounce all allegiance to any foreign state or sovereign; (3) to support and defend the Constitution and laws of the United States against all enemies, foreign and domestic; (4) to bear arms on behalf of the United States when required by law, or to perform noncombatant service in the armed forces, or to perform civilian work of national importance when required by law. INA § 337.

If an applicant can show by clear and convincing evidence, that s/he is opposed to the bearing of arms, the applicant may revise the pledge to perform only noncombatant services in the armed forces. Similarly, if the applicant can show by the same standard of proof that s/he opposes any type of service in the armed forces by reason of "religious training and belief," s/he may pledge merely to perform important civilian work. INA § 337(a).

The present statute was designed to codify judicial decisions relieving conscientious objectors of naturalization requirements to bear arms. The moral stand taken by conscientious objectors frequently resulted in the denial of their naturalization petitions between the world wars—a result the Supreme Court affirmed in *United States v. Schwimmer* (Sup.Ct.1929) and *United States v. MacIntosh* (Sup.Ct.1931). In the 1946 case of *Girouard v. United States* (Sup.Ct.1946), however, the Court overruled these prior cases and held that religious objection to bearing arms was not of itself incompatible with allegiance to the United States. Congress adopted the Supreme Court's holding by enacting the statute currently in effect.

Congress followed *United States v. Seeger* (Sup.Ct. 1965), a later Supreme Court decision on conscientious objection to military service, in defining the phrase "religious training and belief" as "an individual's belief in a relation to a Supreme Being involving duties superior to those arising from any human relation, but does not include essentially political, sociological, or philosophical views or a merely personal moral code...." INA § 337(a). The Supreme Court, however, has construed this language in *Seeger* to apply to persons who, while not believing in a personalized God, possess a sincere and meaningful belief which occupies in the life of the believer a place "parallel" to that filled by the God of persons who clearly qualify for the exemption. Hence, the applicant need not found a claim of conscientious objector status upon the precepts of an organized religion or a belief in a Supreme Being. *In re Weitzman* (8th Cir.1970).

c. *Relaxed Requirements for Particular Persons*

Although the naturalization requirements discussed in the preceding subsections apply to most applicants for citizenship, Congress has chosen for various policy reasons to relax the requirements with respect to particular persons. The most significant special classes are: persons serving in the armed forces, spouses of United States citizens, and minor children of U.S. citizens.

(1) PERSONS SERVING IN THE ARMED FORCES

A lawful permanent resident alien who has served honorably in the armed forces of the United States for periods totaling three years may apply for naturalization without meeting the standard residence and physical presence requirements, provided such application is filed while the applicant is still in the service or within six months of discharge. INA § 328(a). If the applicant's service was continuous, a certificate of honorable service establishes compliance with the requirements of good moral character. INA § 328(e). Where the service was not continuous, the applicant must establish good moral character by the standards applicable to other naturalization applicants. INA § 328(c).

The statute further provides that an alien whose service in the armed forces terminated more than six months prior to filing of the application is not exempted from the standard residence and physical presence requirements. INA § 328(d). Nonetheless, the period of time served in the military, if within five years immediately preceding the date of filing, shall constitute residence and physical presence for the purpose of meeting the standard requirements.

Another statute provides even broader exemptions for aliens who have actively and honorably served in the armed forces for at least one day during periods of hostilities—from World War I to the Grenada conflict or during any periods which the President designates involving armed conflict with a hostile foreign force. INA § 329. Such persons may be naturalized without having been lawfully admitted to the United States if they were in the United States or specified territories at the time of induction. INA § 329(a). If an applicant was not within these territories when enlistment occurred, s/he must subsequently obtain lawful admission to qualify under the provision.

An applicant seeking naturalization through active duty service in the armed forces is exempt from the standard age requirement; the generally prescribed residence and physical presence requirements; and the provision precluding the naturalization of persons subject to an outstanding deportation order. INA § 329(b).

(2) SPOUSES OF UNITED STATES CITIZENS

Section 319 of the Immigration and Nationality Act relaxes the naturalization requirements for spouses of United States citizens. The applicant spouse must have resided continuously in the United States for three years—instead of five—immediately before filing the petition for naturalization. INA § 319(a). The residence must follow lawful admission, and the applicant must live "in marital union" with the citizen spouse throughout this period. The phrase "living in marital union" is not interpreted so strictly as to require that one spouse refrain from seeking a temporary separation from the other in situations of domestic violence. Hence, in *Petition of Omar* (S.D.N.Y.1957) the court ordered a separation of petitioner from his citizen spouse for two weeks as a "cooling off" period, following the petitioner's arrest (at his wife's request) for allegedly striking her. The judicially enforced separation did not preclude compliance with the statute.

Although a short separation, such as the two weeks involved in *Omar,* will not operate to destroy the marital union for purposes of the statute, an extended estrangement produces a different result. The rationale behind section 319(a), said the federal court in *Petition of Kostas* (D.Del.1958), was "the congressional expectation that a non-citizen spouse who lived in close association with a citizen spouse for three years would more speedily absorb the basic concepts of citizenship than one not so situated." In *Kostas* the facts showed an "uneasy union marked by frequent separations of substantial duration," to the extent that it appeared the couple spent more time apart than together during the three year statutory period. On that record the court determined that petitioner fell far short of the "marital union" requirement.

The statute does not relieve the spouse applicant of the burden of establishing good moral character and attachment to the principles of the Constitution.

If the citizen spouse is an employee of the United States government, a U.S. firm engaged in foreign commerce, a recognized U.S. institution of research, a public international organization in which the United States participates by treaty or statute, or s/he performs qualified religious functions abroad, and is regularly stationed abroad in such activity, the applying spouse may be naturalized without any prior residence in the United States. The applying spouse, however, must declare to the Immigration Service in good faith an intention to take up residence in the United States immediately upon the termination of such employment abroad of the citizen spouse. INA § 319(b). The applicant also must comply with all other requirements for naturalization.

Further, the surviving spouse of a citizen, whose citizen spouse dies while serving honorably in the armed forces, may be naturalized without any prior residence or physical presence in the United States. INA § 319(d).

(3) CHILDREN OF CITIZENS

A minor child born outside of the United States may be naturalized upon the petition of a natural parent who, at the time of application is a citizen of the United States either by birth or naturalization. INA § 322(a). Residence and physical presence requirements do not apply under this provision. Good moral character and attachment to the principles of the Constitution will be presumed for a child of tender years.

A citizen parent may apply for the naturalization of her/his adopted minor child. The child must be lawfully admitted to the United States for permanent residence, but no specified period of residence is required. INA § 322(b)–(c). A prior statute prescribing a minimum of two years residence before an adopted child could be naturalized was repealed in 1978. Children adopted by two U.S. citizen parents can also derive citizenship under INA § 341(c).

d. Naturalization Procedures

(1) JURISDICTION TO NATURALIZE

Exclusive authority to naturalize is conferred upon the Attorney General. INA § 310(a). Prior to the 1990 Act, the court decided whether a petitioner had complied with statutory conditions for citizenship. An INS designated examiner recommended whether naturalization should be granted, but the court could decide regardless of the INS recommendation. The 1990 Act shifted both the decision on naturalization and the principal responsibility for administration of the oath of allegiance to the INS. The 1990 Act authorized the federal district court to review *de novo* denials of naturalization and determine the matter if the INS fails to decide within 120 days after hearing. INA §§ 210(d), 336(b). The 1991 Technical Amendments returned principal responsibility for administration of oaths to the federal district courts, but left the substantive determination with the INS. Title I of the Technical Amendments Act gives the courts 45 days to administer the oath of naturalization, after which an applicant can choose to have the oath administered by the INS. This compromise gives the courts an important role in naturalization, without creating backlogs due to crowded court dockets. INA § 310 *et seq.* State courts of record are also authorized, but not required, to aid in the administration of oaths of allegiance.

(2) APPLICATION

An applicant for naturalization first must file an application to enable the Immigration and Naturalization Service to conduct an investigation of the applicant's qualifications. INA § 334(a). The application (Form N–400) consists of several pages wherein the applicant must provide background information regarding family history, periods of residence in the United States, and the names of witnesses who will support the petition for naturalization.

A 1981 amendment removed the two-witness requirement (95 Stat. 1619) because the rule had become too time consuming and unproductive. Moreover, the INS should be sufficiently thorough in its investigation to determine the applicant's fitness for citizenship. The INS can still seek witnesses as part of the investigation.

An applicant may also file a formal declaration of intention to naturalize, but such declaration is no longer mandatory. INA § 334(g). Several documents and pieces of information must accompany the application, including three identical photographs of the applicant to be affixed to the naturalization certificates and application form (INA § 333(a)), a record of the applicant's fingerprints, alien registration number, biographical information, and the date of arrival in the United States.

(3) EXAMINATION

The applicant and witnesses who can testify to the applicant's qualifications for citizenship appear before a naturalization examiner. INA § 335(b). Each applicant and witness is interrogated separately, during which questioning the applicant's attorney or representative may be present (provided the attorney or representative has filed a notice of appearance) to observe without taking part. The proceeding may be videotaped or tape recorded; the hearing is not formal and the rules of evidence do not apply. The record of the examination is admissible in any subsequent hearing under INA § 336(a).

If after completion of the questioning, the examiner determines that the application lacks any necessary qualifications, s/he advises the applicant of that determination. An applicant is not bound, however, by the examiner's findings, and may as a matter of right file a request for a hearing before an immigration officer and then may seek *de novo* review by the federal district court. INA §§ 310(c), 336.

(4) HEARING ON DENIAL OF APPLICATION

If the application is initially denied, a new hearing takes place before another immigration officer. INA § 336(a). The applicant's attorney may take an active part in this hearing, present evidence, subpoena witnesses, make objections, and conduct cross-examination of the government's witnesses. The hearing is scheduled within 180 days after a request is filed; it is tape recorded or videotaped for purposes of judicial review. Upon consideration of the testimony and review of all documents properly submitted in support or opposition, the immigration officer decides whether the application for naturalization should be granted or denied. If the immigration officer fails to decide the matter within 120 days after the examination, the federal district court may determine the naturalization or remand the matter to the INS with instructions. INA § 336(b).

(5) ADMINISTRATION OF OATH

If the examiner approves the naturalization, the applicant will be granted citizenship at a hearing in open court after s/he takes the oath of allegiance to the United States. INA § 337. In the case of verified illness or disability of the applicant, the court may excuse her/his attendance at the final hearing. INA § 337(c). As provided under the technical amendments to the 1990 Act, if the court cannot administer the oath within 45 days, the applicant may choose to have the oath administered by the INS.

If the INS denies the application, the applicant can seek judicial review in federal district court. Upon request by the applicant, the court can consider all issues *de novo*. If the INS does not act upon the application within 120 days, the applicant can request a hearing in federal district court. These procedures have been designed and modified to expedite the naturalization process, which, given the benefits that naturalization confers, is significant to the applicant.

(6) CERTIFICATE OF NATURALIZATION

Upon granting the citizenship, the INS issues a certificate of naturalization. INA § 338. The certificate itself does not convey citizenship, but simply serves as evidence that the INS has granted citizenship. The statute prescribes the information that the naturalization certificate will contain, including the number of the petition and the certificate; date of naturalization; the name, signature, place of residence, signed photograph, and personal description of the naturalized person (including age, sex, marital status, and country of former nationality); and a statement that the INS has found the application in full compliance with the requirements of the naturalization laws and has ordered the applicant be admitted to citizenship. INA § 338.

Minor clerical errors do not affect the evidentiary value of the certificate nor do informalities in the certificate—such as the misspelling of names or the misnaming of the applicant. *Brassert v. Biddle* (2d Cir.1945).

The date on the certificate of naturalization is determined by the date of the oath. If the oath is waived for children under six, the date is the day on which the application is granted. If the court administers the oath, it may also grant a name change.

A naturalization order is subject to *direct* attack in independent denaturalization proceedings as prescribed by the Congress. INA § 340(a). Revocation of naturalization is discussed below.

§ 12–3 LOSS OF NATIONALITY

§ 12–3.1 Introduction

There are two ways by which a citizen may lose citizenship: denaturalization and expatriation. Denaturalization involves the judicial revocation of the naturalization order based on a finding that the naturalization was illegally or fraudulently procured. INA § 340(a). Obviously, denaturalization applies only to naturalized citizens. Expatriation, however, applies to both naturalized and all other citizens, and does not assume a defect in the original acquisition of citizenship. Rather, expatriation results from certain actions enumerated in the statute (INA § 349) by which the citizen voluntarily relinquished her/his citizenship.

§ 12–3.2   Denaturalization

a. *Congress' Power to Denaturalize*

The authority of Congress to provide for cancellation of wrongfully procured naturalization certificates is derived from the constitutional power of Congress to establish a uniform rule of naturalization under Article I, section 8, and the "Necessary and Proper" clause.

The Supreme Court in *Costello v. United States* (Sup. Ct.1961) sustained the constitutionality of the 1952 version of the denaturalization statute with respect to Congress' powers to cancel certificates procured "by concealment of a material fact or by willful misrepresentation." But while the power of Congress to prescribe grounds for revoking naturalization has been repeatedly upheld, the Supreme Court has stricken those provisions it deemed arbitrary or discriminatory. Hence, in *Schneider v. Rusk* (Sup.Ct.1964) the Court invalidated the provision prescribing loss of nationality by a naturalized citizen who resided in a foreign state for three years or more. Native-born citizens faced no such punishment. Justice Douglas wrote:

This statute proceeds on the impermissible assumption that naturalized citizens as a class are less reliable and bear less allegiance to this country than do the native born. This is an assumption that is impossible for us to make. Moreover, while the Fifth Amendment contains no equal protection clause, it does forbid discrimination that is "so unjustifiable as to be violative of due process"....

The court thus held that the provision discriminated against naturalized citizens in violation of Due Process, creating a "second-class citizenship" without a rational justification.

The revocation statute empowers United States district attorneys, upon an affidavit showing good cause, to institute proceedings in equity to cancel the naturalization certificate. INA § 340(a). The original naturalization order has no res judicata effect against this independent attack by the United States, *Johannessen v. United States* (Sup.Ct.1912), in contrast to the immunity it enjoys from collateral attack. *Tutun v. United States* (Sup.Ct.1926).

b. Grounds for Denaturalization

(1) CONCEALMENT OF MATERIAL FACT OR WILLFUL MISREPRESENTATION

Naturalization may be revoked if the certificate of naturalization was "procured by concealment of a material fact or by willful misrepresentation" or was "illegally procured." INA § 340(a). Fraud and illegal procurement as grounds for denaturalization date back to the original 1906 statute. 34 Stat. 596. The introduction of the term "concealment of a material fact by willful misrepresentation" was intended to assure that both "extrinsic fraud" (outside of the proceedings—like concealment of witnesses) and "intrinsic fraud" (perjured testimony) would serve as grounds for denaturalization. *Costello v. United States* (Sup.Ct.1961).

Clearly, facts suppressed or concealed in a naturalization proceeding are "material" if disclosure of those facts alone would justify denial of citizenship. But the scope of materiality also includes concealed facts which, if disclosed, would have led to the investigation and discovery of other facts bearing on the applicant's eligibility for naturalization. In *Chaunt v. United States* (1960), the Supreme Court considered the materiality of Chaunt's failure to disclose three prior arrests for petty offenses in his naturalization application. The government argued that the arrests were material because, if disclosed, the Immigration Service would have investigated and *might* have discovered that Chaunt was (as one witness testified) an active member of the Communist Party. The Court established a two part test for materiality, by which it concluded on the facts before it that "the government failed to show by 'clear, unequivocal, and convincing' evidence *either* (1) that facts were suppressed which, if known, would have warranted denial of citizenship, or (2) that their disclosure *might* have been useful in an investigation *possibly* leading to the discovery of other facts *warranting* denial of citizenship." (emphasis added).

Confusion has ensued as to the second part of the *Chaunt* test—that "disclosure might have been useful in an investigation possibly leading to the discovery of other facts warranting denial of citizenship." The Ninth Circuit in *United States v. Rossi* (9th Cir.1962) held that a concealed or suppressed fact is material only "if disclosure of the true facts would have justified a refusal to issue a visa." The Sixth Circuit, however, took a different view in *Kassab v. Immigration and Naturalization Service* (6th Cir.1966), holding it sufficient if the suppressed fact, if revealed, "*might* have led to further action and the discovery of facts which would have justified the refusal of the visa" (emphasis in original).

More recently, the Southern District Court of Florida in *United States v. Fedorenko* (S.D.Fla.1978) ruled that the government must *prove the existence* of the facts which would have warranted denial of naturalization, although it need only show that an investigation leading to discovery of these facts *possibly* would have taken place. The court found the government had failed to establish that the defendant had voluntarily served as a guard and committed atrocities at a German death camp while a prisoner of war during World War II, which the government contended it might have discovered through investigation, had the defendant disclosed on his visa application that he had resided at the particular concentration camp. The Fifth Circuit reversed, stating that the government need only prove "that disclosure of the true facts would have [prompted] an inquiry that might have uncovered other factors warranting denial of citizenship." The government would not be burdened with the overwhelming task of conducting an investigation into the past, discovering ultimate facts warranting disqualification, and proving those facts in court by clear and convincing evidence.

The Supreme Court affirmed the Fifth Circuit, but on other grounds, not addressing the materiality question. The U.S. Court of Appeals for the Tenth Circuit, however, in *United States v. Sheshtawy* (10th Cir.1983), adopted Justice Blackmun's views expressed in his concurring opinion to the *Fedorenko* case. The court concluded that the *Chaunt* test "requires that the government demonstrate the existence of actual disqualifying facts—facts that themselves would have warranted denial of petitioner's citizenship." Since the government had not claimed to have established facts that would have warranted denial of citizenship, it had not met the rigorous *Chaunt* test, and revocation of naturalization under INA § 340(a) was not justified.

In *Kungys v. United States* (Sup.Ct.1988), the Supreme Court attempted to clarify the *Chaunt* holding. The Court held that the test of whether concealments or misrepresentations are "material" under INA § 340(a) is whether they can be shown by clear, unequivocal, and convincing evidence to have been predictably capable of affecting the decisions of the INS, *i.e.,* to have "had a natural tendency to influence the decisions of the INS." Of the seven other participating justices, four joined this part of Justice Scalia's opinion.

Kungys was admitted to the United States for permanent residence in 1948 and became a naturalized citizen in 1954. In 1982 the United States commenced denaturalization proceedings. The government alleged that Kungys had participated in executing over 2,000 Lithuanians, most of them Jewish, in Kedainiai, Lithuania, between July and August 1941. The government also demonstrated that, in his visa application and in his naturalization petition, Kungys misrepresented his date and place of birth, as well as his occupation and residence during World War II.

In determining whether Kungys' misrepresentations met the Court's new standard of materiality, the Court held that § 340(a) is limited to falsehoods or deceptions in the naturalization proceedings and not misrepresentations made in the visa process, because it is the former falsehoods which "procure" the naturalization. The

Court concluded that Kungys' misrepresentations of the date and place of his birth in his naturalization petition were not material. There was no suggestion that the facts were themselves relevant to Kungys' qualifications for citizenship. Likewise, there was no showing that the true date and place of birth would have disclosed other facts relevant to his qualifications and would have resulted either in outright denial or an investigation resulting in denial of the naturalization application. Hence, the government failed to establish clearly, unequivocally, and convincingly that Kungys' misrepresentations had a natural tendency to influence the decision of the INS. Only two justices joined Justice Scalia in this part of the opinion.

As an alternative basis for upholding denaturalization, the government argued that Kungys' naturalization had been "illegally procured" because, at the time of his naturalization, he lacked the good moral character required under INA § 316(a). (Illegal procurement of naturalization is discussed further in the following section of this chapter.) In the government's view, Kungys' misrepresentations, whether material or not, constituted false testimony given for the purpose of obtaining benefits in both the visa and naturalization proceedings, which indicates a lack of good moral character under INA § 101(f)(6).

The Court decided in favor of the government on this issue, holding that § 101(f)(6) does not contain a materiality requirement for false testimony for the purposes of determining whether naturalization was "illegally procured" because of a lack of good moral character. In the Court's view, lack of good moral character is present to some degree whenever there is subjective intent to deceive, no matter how immaterial the deception. The Court pointed out, however, that "testimony" is limited to oral statements made under oath and that the false testimony provisions do not apply to "concealments." Section 101(f)(6) applies to only those misrepresentations made with the subjective intent of obtaining immigration benefits, and this intent must be proven by clear, unequivocal, and convincing evidence. The Court concluded that it would be "relatively rare that the Government will be able to prove that a misrepresentation that does not have the natural tendency to influence the decision regarding immigration or naturalization benefits was nonetheless made with subjective intent of obtaining those benefits." A majority of the justices joined this part of the opinion.

Although a majority of the justices agreed that § 101(f)(6) contains no materiality requirement, only three of the justices concurred in Justice Scalia's opinion holding that denaturalization could not be affirmed under that provision. The question whether Kungys' misrepresentations constituted false testimony for the purpose of obtaining immigration or naturalization benefits cannot be answered without first resolving two issues: (1) whether Kungys' misrepresentations constituted "testimony" and (2) whether in making the misrepresentations, Kungys possessed the subjective intent to obtain immigration or naturalization benefits. The latter question is one of fact to be resolved by the trier of fact. Since the case had to be remanded in any event, the Court chose not to resolve the former question of law.

Five separate opinions were filed in the *Kungys* case and there was no clear majority holding on many of the issues presented in the majority opinion. Hence, *Kungys* did little to dispel the uncertainty about the *Chaunt* standard of materiality.

In addition to being material, the misrepresentation must be intentional. Hence, where the defendant in *Maisenberg v. United States* (Sup.Ct.1958) had answered "no" to a question on her preliminary application for naturalization asking whether she belonged to or was associated with any organization which teaches or advocates anarchy or overthrow of the existing government, she did not conceal a material fact or commit willful misrepresentation. Although she was at the time a member of the Communist Party, the question was ambiguous and she could reasonably have interpreted it as relating solely to anarchy, and not as calling for disclosure of membership in nonanarchistic organizations advocating violent overthrow of the government. Moreover, an applicant does not "conceal" a material fact, within the meaning of the statute, if s/he merely fails to *volunteer* facts which might have a bearing on eligibility. In *Cufari v. United States* (1st Cir.1954) the First Circuit held that a naturalized citizen could not be denaturalized for failing to disclose his criminal record at the time of naturalization, unless the government could prove that he had been asked during the proceedings whether he had a criminal record and that he had answered in the negative.

Specific concealments and misrepresentations which courts have found sufficient to warrant denaturalization include: deliberate suppression of criminal records where there is a duty to disclose (*United States v. Oddo* (2d Cir.1963))—unlike the situation in *Cufari, supra;* knowingly false statements concerning marital or family status (*United States v. D'Agostino* (2d Cir.1964)); and deliberate misstatement concerning an applicant's fulfillment of the residence requirements. *Rosenberg v. United States* (3d Cir.1932).

(2) Illegal Procurement of Naturalization

Illegal procurement provides an independent ground for revoking naturalization. The term has been held to convey something wider in scope than fraud, not restricted to intentional deception. It has encompassed naturalizations procured when prescribed requirements—for example, attachment to the principles of the Constitution or lack of good moral character—had no existence in fact. *United States v. Ginsberg* (Sup.Ct. 1917). In *Kungys v. United States* (Sup.Ct.1988), the Supreme Court held that false testimony given for the purpose of obtaining benefits in a naturalization proceeding indicates a lack of good moral character under INA § 101(f)(6) and may render the naturalization "illegally procured," even though the misrepresentations may not have been material. This case is discussed in more detail in the immediately preceding section. The term also connotes affirmative misconduct by the applicant to induce the court or governmental agents to act in a manner not authorized by law; it encompasses the granting of certificates upon an error of law, for example, as to jurisdiction or procedural irregularities such as denying the government the opportunity to question the applicant in open court or to introduce evidence.

To justify denaturalization, however, the error must be substantial. Hence, clerical mistakes in connection with the issuance of a naturalization certificate will not constitute grounds for revocation and errors of judgment in granting citizenship against the preponderance of the evidence are better corrected on appeal in the original naturalization proceeding than in an action to revoke naturalization.

(3) RESIDENCE IN FOREIGN COUNTRY WITHIN ONE YEAR AFTER NATURALIZATION

Section 340 provides that if a naturalized citizen takes up permanent residence in a foreign country within one year after naturalization, it shall be considered prima facie evidence of a lack of intention to establish permanent residence in the United States at the time of the application for citizenship. In the absence of countervailing evidence, this prima facie evidence shall be sufficient to justify revocation of naturalization, as having been obtained by concealment of a material fact or by willful misrepresentation. INA § 340(d). The naturalized person may rebut the presumption by testimony that s/he intended in good faith to establish permanent residence in the United States. The court, not wishing to cancel lightly the valuable right of citizenship, will grant the defendant every reasonable doubt, and show great receptiveness to consideration of extenuating circumstances. For example, in *United States v. Delmendo* (9th Cir.1974), the Ninth Circuit held that a naturalized citizen's years of residence in the Philippines did not show intent to establish permanent residence in the Philippines or an intent not to reside permanently in the United States at the time he applied for naturalization, because the citizen was very ill, poor, and had been given erroneous legal advice by the State Department that his three-year residence abroad had automatically deprived him of citizenship.

(4) OTHER GROUNDS FOR DENATURALIZATION

The denaturalization statute provides two additional grounds for revoking naturalization: (1) Refusal on the part of the naturalized citizen, within ten years following her/his naturalization, to testify as a witness before a congressional committee concerning her/his subversive activities, will be a ground for revocation of naturalization, if such refusal resulted in a conviction for contempt. INA § 340(a). The refusal to testify establishes as a matter of law that naturalization was procured by concealment of a material fact or by willful misrepresentation and the naturalized citizen is not granted an opportunity within this provision to present countervailing evidence. (2) If within five years of naturalization a naturalized citizen becomes a member of any of the proscribed subversive organizations, of which membership would have precluded naturalization in the first place, it shall constitute prima facie evidence that such person was not attached to the principles of the Constitution at the time of naturalization. INA § 340(c). In the absence of countervailing evidence it will be sufficient to revoke the person's citizenship as having been obtained by concealment of a material fact or by willful misrepresentation. Neither ground has been invoked in any naturalization proceeding to date and the constitutionality of these provisions may be in doubt because of the discrimination they impose on naturalized citizens. *Cf. Schneider v. Rusk* (Sup.Ct. 1964).

§ 12–3.3 Expatriation

a. Introduction

Expatriation provides the second means for loss of nationality, to which both naturalized and all other citizens are subject. INA § 349(a). The term is defined as the *voluntary* act of abandoning one's country and becoming the citizen or subject of another. Under current Supreme Court jurisprudence, the specific intent of the alleged expatriate to renounce citizenship must accompany the expatriating act, in order to constitute relinquishment of citizenship. In 1986, Congress amended INA § 349(a) to conform to the rulings of the Supreme Court, by providing that a person will lose her/his U.S. citizenship only by "voluntarily performing any of the following acts with the intention of relinquishing United States nationality."

b. Development of the Law of Expatriation

The Constitution makes no mention of expatriation. Courts were reluctant in the early days of the United States to acknowledge expatriation of a citizen without express consent of the government. The right of a citizen to voluntary expatriation notwithstanding lack of the sovereign's consent was first recognized by Congress in 1868. 15 Stat. 223. The 1868 Act proclaimed that "the right of expatriation is a natural and inherent right of all people, indispensable to the enjoyment of the rights of life, liberty and the pursuit of happiness." Although intended to protect naturalized United States citizens from claims of allegiance by their former sovereigns, the Attorney General construed the statute to permit U.S. citizens to abandon their citizenship. 14 Ops. Att'y Gen. 295. Also in 1868 the United States initiated a series of treaties—named the Bancroft Treaties for George Bancroft, a United States diplomat who negotiated the first of these treaties with the North German Confederation (15 Stat. 615)—which provided that each country would regard as citizens of the other, those of its own subjects who became naturalized by the other.

Although the right of expatriation was thus established, Congress did not first define the manner by which a citizen may lose citizenship until the Expatriation Act of 1907. 34 Stat. 1228. The statute provided that a citizen was deemed expatriated if s/he was naturalized in any foreign state in conformity with its laws or took the oath of allegiance to any foreign state; a female citizen who married an alien assumed the nationality of her husband; and a naturalized citizen returning to the country of her/his origin and living there for two years was presumed to have effected expatriation. 34 Stat. 1228. Marriage to a foreigner ceased to be an expatriating act in 1922. 42 Stat. 1022.

The Nationality Act of 1940 expanded the grounds for expatriation, to include: service in the military or government of a foreign state, voting in a political election in a foreign state, formal renunciation of United States citizenship, court martial conviction and discharge from the armed services for desertion in wartime, conviction for treason against the United States, and failure for nationals born abroad to take up permanent residence in the United States before attaining 16 years of age. 54 Stat. 1137. In addition, naturalized citizens could be expatriated for three years continuous residence in the state of their birth, or for five years continuous residence in any other foreign state. Many of these provisions reflected the trying economic times and the security consciousness resulting from the onset of World War II. The Immigration and Nationality Act of 1952 essentially re-enacted the expatriation provisions of the 1940 statute, with some minor additions. INA § 349 (examined in section 12–3.3d, *infra*).

c. *The Power of Congress to Prescribe Grounds for Expatriation*

The 1907 statute prescribed specific methods of expatriation. 34 Stat. 1228. Certain provisions appeared to mandate loss of nationality without regard to intent, most notably, marriage of a female citizen to an alien. In *MacKenzie v. Hare* (Sup.Ct.1915), the petitioner challenged this provision, which withdrew her citizenship upon her marriage to a British national. She argued that expatriation required not merely the act of marrying a foreign national, but a subjective intent to "permanently reside elsewhere [and] to throw off the former allegiance, and become a citizen or subject of a foreign power." The Court determined that Mrs. MacKenzie had voluntarily relinquished her citizenship because her marriage was voluntary, and she had notice of the consequences.

The Court further held that Congress had authority to prescribe grounds for expatriation, based on powers "implied, necessary or incidental" to its expressed power over nationality and foreign relations. The Court viewed the law in controversy as a reasonable exercise of government power for the prevention of potential international controversies arising out of dual nationality.

Subsequent cases over the next forty years reinforced an "objective intent" standard for determining relinquishment of citizenship. In *Savorgnan v. United States* (Sup.Ct.1950), the petitioner was a native-born U.S. citizen who was engaged to an Italian government official. To obtain royal approval of her marriage, she was informed she would have to become naturalized as an Italian citizen, recite an oath of allegiance to Italy, and sign a document renouncing her United States citizenship. She believed her signing was only a technical requirement, and she asserted that she never intended to renounce her United States citizenship. The Court held that under the statute one who obtained citizenship in a foreign country loses United States citizenship, regardless of her/his subjective intent:

> [T]he acts upon which the statutes expressly condition the consent of our Government to the expatriation of its citizens are stated objectively. There is no suggestion in the statutory language that the effect of the specified overt acts, when voluntarily done, is conditioned upon the undisclosed intent of the person doing them.

The Supreme Court's attitude, heretofore one of deference to Congress regarding laws of expatriation, began to change in 1958. In *Perez v. Brownell* (Sup.Ct.1958), the Court upheld the constitutionality of the provision prescribing loss of nationality for voting in a foreign political election. 54 Stat. 1137. Justice Frankfurter, speaking for the majority, ruled that a "rational nexus" existed between the congressional power to regulate foreign affairs and the withdrawal of citizenship for voting in a foreign election. The power of Congress to terminate citizenship did not depend on consent of the citizen but the voluntary performance of the expatriating act. The holding thus reaffirmed the power of

Congress to prescribe acts which would constitute loss of nationality, but the Court was closely divided, five justices to four. Chief Justice Warren wrote a vigorous dissent, maintaining that Congress did not have the power to take away the "most basic right" of citizenship. Congress could only acquiesce in the wishes of the citizen to abandon her/his nationality.

On the same day, March 31, 1958, the Court for the first time held an expatriation provision unconstitutional; Chief Justice Warren wrote the plurality opinion in another five to four decision, *Trop v. Dulles* (Sup.Ct. 1958). The suit challenged section 401(g) of the Nationality Act of 1940, which provided for expatriation upon conviction by court martial and dishonorable discharge for desertion in time of war. 54 Stat. 1137. Private Trop, serving abroad in the United States army, escaped from a stockade where he had been confined for disciplinary reasons. He turned himself in several hours later, but for his offense he was court martialed and convicted of desertion, sentenced to three years of hard labor and dishonorably discharged. Chief Justice Warren concluded that section 401(g) was a penal statute, violative of the Eighth Amendment's prohibition against cruel and unusual punishment, as it stripped the individual of any nationality, leaving him stateless. (In 1978 Congress repealed the statute. 92 Stat. 1046.)

A second expatriation provision was invalidated in *Kennedy v. Mendoza–Martinez* (Sup.Ct.1963). The challenged statute provided loss of citizenship for those persons who had left the United States in time of war to evade military service. 58 Stat. 746. In 1942, Mendoza–Martinez (a native born U.S. citizen with dual Mexican nationality) went to Mexico solely, as he admitted, for the purpose of evading service in the armed forces. He further conceded that he remained there for that purpose until November 1946, when he voluntarily returned to the United States. In 1947, he pleaded guilty to and was convicted of, evasion of his service obligation, and sentenced to imprisonment of a year and one day. He served his sentence and upon his release lived undisturbed until 1953 when, after a lapse of five years, he was arrested and subjected to deportation proceedings. The government asserted that Mendoza–Martinez was deportable as he had expatriated himself by committing the act specified in the provision. Justice Goldberg wrote for the majority, holding that the statute's automatic deprivation of nationality for the offense of evading military service was an unconstitutional punishment, in violation of rights to Due Process and trial by jury.

In 1964, the Court again limited the power of Congress to expatriate in *Schneider v. Rusk* (Sup.Ct.1964). It decided that the statute expatriating a naturalized citizen for three years continuous residence in the state of their former nationality was an invalid discrimination against naturalized citizens.

In *Trop, Mendoza–Martinez,* and *Schneider,* the Court utilized an *ad hoc* approach for restricting congressional power to expatriate, by invalidating several provisions as violative of specific constitutional rights. The issue of the requisite intent for finding a voluntary relinquishment of citizenship had not been addressed since *Perez v. Brownell, supra.* In *Afroyim v. Rusk* (Sup.Ct. 1967), the Supreme Court overruled its 1958 decision in *Perez,* holding that Congress had no general power, express or implied, to expatriate without the citizen's

assent. Afroyim was a naturalized citizen who went to
Israel and while in that country voted in an Israeli
election. The State Department subsequently refused
to renew his passport, asserting Afroyim's loss of citizenship under section 401(e) of the Nationality Act of 1940.
54 Stat. 1137. Afroyim contended that neither the
Fourteenth Amendment nor any other provision of the
Constitution allowed Congress to extinguish his citizenship without his voluntary renunciation. Writing for
the majority, Justice Black agreed, and held that the
Fourteenth Amendment "can most reasonably be read
as defining a citizenship which a citizen keeps unless he
voluntarily relinquishes it. Once acquired, this Fourteenth Amendment citizenship was not to be shifted,
canceled, or diluted at the will of the Federal Government, the States or any other governmental unit."

The expansive language of Justice Black's majority
opinion caused speculation as to its meaning. Some
reasoned that *Afroyim* had invalidated all expatriation
statutes, leaving the decision as to one's nationality at
all times with the individual. With the right of citizenship judicially defined as absolute, it was not necessary
for the allegedly expatriated individual to do more than
assert her/his claim to citizenship in order to recover it.
Others believed that *Afroyim* had reinstated a subjective
intent test, which required for expatriation a finding
that not only did the citizen commit the expatriating
act, but s/he did so with the specific intent of relinquishing citizenship.

The Court's next opportunity to consider the scope
and vitality of the *Afroyim* holding occurred in *Rogers v.
Bellei* (Sup.Ct.1971). Bellei acquired citizenship by
birth outside the United States to an American mother

and Italian father. He lived abroad, although he visited the United States several times on a United States passport. He was warned shortly before his twenty-third birthday that the statute conferring his citizenship required him to remain in the United States for five years in order to preserve his citizenship. Bellei left the United States one year later and was notified that he had lost his citizenship. He sought to enjoin the statute, claiming it was violative of Due Process, and constituted cruel and unusual punishment. The district court ruled the statute unconstitutional, citing *Afroyim* and *Schneider.* The Supreme Court reversed in another five to four decision, holding that Bellei's citizenship acquired upon birth abroad was not constitutionally conferred, nor was it protected under the Fourteenth Amendment, which referred in its first sentence to "persons born or naturalized *in the United States.*" (emphasis added). As a mere creation of statute his citizenship was subject to congressional restrictions, and it was perfectly reasonable for Congress to impose a "condition subsequent" to the grant of citizenship. In dissent, Justice Black saw no distinction between the various forms of citizenship which justified the second class treatment afforded citizens born abroad. "I cannot accept the Court's conclusion that the Fourteenth Amendment protects the citizenship of some Americans and not others." (Congress has since repealed the statute at issue in *Bellei.* 92 Stat. 1046.)

The Supreme Court's 1980 pronouncement on the issue of congressional power to expatriate, *Vance v. Terrazas* (Sup.Ct.1980), went in two directions. Terrazas was born in the United States of Mexican parents, thus acquiring dual nationality. He obtained a certificate of Mexican nationality while in Mexico in 1970, which included renunciation of all other nationalities. He claimed it was not his intent to relinquish U.S. citizenship. On the one hand, the Court unanimously reaffirmed the basic holding of *Afroyim*—that expatriation required a showing of specific intent to relinquish citizenship voluntarily, in addition to proof that the expatriating act itself was committed voluntarily. The specific intent could be expressed in words or fairly inferred from proven conduct. On the other hand, the Court upheld a statute providing that the government must prove merely by "a preponderance of the evidence" that citizenship was voluntarily relinquished. The Court of Appeals had declared the statute unconstitutional, believing a "clear and convincing" standard of proof was required. In reversing, Justice White stated "[We do not] agree with the Court of Appeals that, because under *Afroyim* Congress is constitutionally devoid of power to impose expatriation on a citizen, it is also without power to prescribe the evidentiary standard to govern expatriation proceedings." The "preponderance of the evidence" standard was held to apply, for both the government's burden of proving voluntary relinquishment, and for the citizen's burden of rebutting the presumption that the expatriating act, which the government proved to have been committed, was voluntary.

d. Methods of Expatriation

(1) OBTAINING NATURALIZATION IN A FOREIGN STATE

Subject to the constitutional and statutory requirement of voluntariness, INA § 349 provides that a person who is a citizen may lose her/his nationality by obtaining naturalization in a foreign state, either upon personal application or that of a parent or duly authorized agent, after having obtained the age of eighteen years.

(2) Oath of Allegiance to a Foreign State

If a citizen, having obtained the age of eighteen years, takes an oath or other formal declaration of allegiance to a foreign state, s/he is expatriated under the current statute. INA §. 349(a)(2). Under *Vance v. Terrazas* (Sup.Ct.1980) the courts again will inquire if the person taking the oath actually intended to abandon United States citizenship. If the oath is taken in circumstances indicating lack of voluntariness, such as military conscription, the requisite intent to transfer allegiance may not be found. *Riccio v. Dulles* (D.D.C.1953).

(3) Military Service in a Foreign State

If a citizen enters the armed forces of a foreign country, s/he is expatriated if such armed forces are engaged in hostilities against the United States or s/he served as a commissioned or noncommissioned officer. INA § 349(a)(3). Again, the requirement that the expatriating act be done with the intention of relinquishing United States nationality applies to service in foreign armed forces. INA § 349(a).

(4) Foreign Government Employment

Employment in the government of a foreign state coupled with (as a condition of employment) acquisition of nationality in or declaration of allegiance to the foreign state will serve as grounds for expatriation. INA § 349(a)(4). This broad language has, however, been restricted by the courts. For example, in *Kenji Kamada v. Dulles* (N.D.Cal.1956) petitioner had taught public school in Japan during and after World War II, for which the United States government claimed she was expatriated. A federal district court disagreed, focusing not only on the voluntariness question but upon the nature of the government service. Teaching school, reasoned the district judge, was not the type of foreign government employment envisioned by the act; rather, the law was intended to encompass service to a foreign government the performance of which required absolute allegiance to the foreign government. Teaching, as such, did not come within this category.

(5) FORMAL RENUNCIATION OF NATIONALITY

Making a formal renunciation of nationality before a diplomatic or consular officer of the United States in a foreign country will lead to expatriation, if performed in a manner prescribed by the Secretary of State. INA § 349(a)(5). Informal renunciations of citizenship are ineffective, however, as are other methods not meeting the State Department regulations. *Vance v. Terrazas* (Sup.Ct.1980).

Davis v. District Director (D.D.C.1979) is, perhaps, the most dramatic case in which a citizen's renunciation was held to be effective. In 1948 Davis, a native born citizen, voluntarily signed an oath of renunciation before the U.S. Consul in Paris, on the form provided by the Consul. Davis indicated at the time that he wanted to become "a citizen of the world." He set up a "World Service Authority" and issued himself a passport. The Immigration Service refused to permit Davis to enter the U.S. in 1977 on the ground that he was not a U.S.

citizen and lacked a visa to enter as an alien. Even though Davis failed to obtain another citizenship when he renounced his U.S. citizenship, the federal district court sustained the Immigration Service's decision to exclude Davis from this country.

If renunciation occurs in the United States, it must be in writing and during time of war to take effect. INA § 349(a)(6). The Attorney General is empowered to designate the officer to receive such renunciations and to promulgate procedures for accepting them. The current statute has not been invoked, although a prior version was used to expatriate several citizens of Japanese descent during World War II.

(6) ACTS OF TREASON AND SUBVERSION

A citizen shall lose nationality, if convicted of committing any act of treason against the United States, of attempting to overthrow the government of the United States, or of conspiring to incite insurrection against the government. INA § 349(a)(7). The constitutionality of this provision has not been tested in the courts.

(7) REPEALED EXPATRIATION PROVISIONS; BURDEN OF PROOF; AND AGE OF MATURITY

Several expatriation provisions have been repealed as a result of Supreme Court decisions declaring them unconstitutional. Specifically, they are: (1) residence abroad by naturalized citizen in excess of three years (in the country of former nationality) or five years (in another foreign state), declared unconstitutional by *Schneider v. Rusk* (Sup.Ct.1964); (2) voting in a foreign political election, declared invalid by *Afroyim v. Rusk*

(Sup.Ct.1967); (3) desertion from the United States armed forces in time of war, struck down in *Trop v. Dulles* (Sup.Ct.1958); and (4) departing from the United States to avoid military service, declared unconstitutional by *Kennedy v. Mendoza–Martinez* (Sup.Ct.1963).

Regarding the burden of proof, the statute places the initial burden on the proponent of expatriation, requiring proof by a "preponderance of the evidence" that the expatriating act occurred. INA § 349(c). The act shall be presumed to have been done voluntarily, but such presumption may be rebutted upon a showing by a preponderance of the evidence that the act was not committed voluntarily. The Supreme Court upheld the constitutionality of this provision in *Vance v. Terrazas* (Sup.Ct.1980).

A second general restriction applicable to most expatriating acts is the requirement that the citizen (at the time of the act) must have attained the age of legal maturity. The statute sets the age of maturity at eighteen years for performance of several expatriating acts—obtaining foreign naturalization, oath of foreign allegiance, military service in a foreign state, renunciation of nationality, and employment in a foreign government. INA § 351(b).

CHAPTER 13

THE RIGHTS OF ALIENS IN THE UNITED STATES

§ 13–1 INTRODUCTION

Generally, persons seeking to enter the United States have virtually no rights recognizable under American law. The judiciary is very reluctant to interfere with Congress' authority over immigration matters. As a result, Congress and immigration officials lawfully exercise a great deal of discretion in establishing and applying immigration law; they control the hopeful immigrant's application for entry. Far from having any right to enter this country, an individual's admission is granted exclusively by Congress under whatever terms it chooses. In determining who shall be admitted, Congress has the authority to discriminate with impunity; it has done so on the basis of national origin and race, and currently employs a system of priorities that excludes, among others, persons with undesirable political beliefs, moral character, and mental or physical disability. INA § 212(a). Special preference is granted to certain relatives of U.S. residents, and to persons possessing work skills needed in the U.S. economy. INA §§ 201, 203. The Supreme Court has unwaveringly held that the decisions to exclude or expel certain aliens are within the exclusive province of Congress. *Chae Chan Ping v. United States* (Sup.Ct.1889); *Fiallo v. Bell* (Sup.Ct.1977).

349

Aliens who are admitted, however, can claim certain general protections under the Constitution. Almost all constitutional guarantees of individual freedom have no personal designation and are extended by terms to "persons." Only the rights to hold federal elective office is reserved for citizens, as is the entitlement to the "privileges and immunities of citizens." Therefore, all aliens in the U.S. appear to be guaranteed the rights secured by the Bill of Rights including the freedoms of speech, association, religion, and the press; the rights to be free from unreasonable searches and seizures as well as self-incrimination; and other criminal procedure protections. In expulsion proceedings, resident aliens are entitled to the safeguards of Due Process as guaranteed by the Fifth Amendment.

This chapter sets forth the rights enjoyed by aliens once they reside in the United States, the limitations imposed on those rights, and their theoretical rationale. The first section briefly reminds the student of immigration law about the often hostile social reality faced by immigrants to this country. The second section concentrates on official discrimination against aliens. Third, specific rights and liabilities are discussed with regard to use of the courts, welfare, education, military service, payment of taxes, property ownership, and other areas of concern to the alien living in the United States.

§ 13–2 THE EXPERIENCE OF BEING AN ALIEN IN THE UNITED STATES

Despite legal guarantees of equal treatment and the image of the Statue of Liberty welcoming distressed immigrants, resident aliens have experienced difficulties with adjustment and assimilation. Official hostility, expressed in immigration law and other restrictive legislation, has been especially flagrant in periods of war, racial animosity, and high unemployment. At various times, some academics theorized that certain racial and ethnic groups were unfit or unacceptable for "Americanization." Many U.S. citizens readily adopted such justifications for their own prejudice. Thousands of immigrants, historically poor, were faced with social stigma, language barriers, unfamiliar customs, and a complete lack of political representation.

Certainly some improvement in official and popular thought has been won since the great waves of immigration occurred in the 19th and early 20th centuries. Immigrants to the United States today still, however, encounter discrimination sanctioned by state and federal governments as well as the racial and ethnic prejudice of many U.S. citizens. A recognition of the immigrant's difficult experience in adjusting to life in the United States is essential to an understanding of the full impact of U.S. law and policy.

§ 13–3 DISCRIMINATION ON THE BASIS OF ALIENAGE

§ 13–3.1 Introduction

For purposes of immigration and other law affecting aliens, four broad classes of aliens can be identified: (1) persons seeking entry to the United States; (2) persons admitted as immigrants or permanent resident aliens; (3) persons admitted as nonimmigrants or temporary visitors; and (4) undocumented persons or "illegal" aliens who are present in the country without the official knowledge or permission of the federal government.

Most of the law involving discrimination on the basis of alienage has developed in cases concerning resident aliens. These individuals are most like citizens of the United States: this country is their permanent home; they pay taxes, are subject to military service, contribute to the economic and cultural life of their communities, and generally have a stake in the country that a nonimmigrant alien cannot ordinarily claim.

The immigrant or permanent resident alien is entitled to protection under the Equal Protection guarantees of the Fifth and Fourteenth Amendments. The judicial review of discrimination on the basis of alienage, however, varies with the particular restriction and whether the state or federal government has imposed it. In *Plyler v. Doe* (Sup.Ct.1982) the United States Supreme Court decided that even undocumented aliens are entitled to Equal Protection—at least in so far as the children of undocumented aliens have the right to attend public schools.

This section will discuss the historical and modern treatment of discrimination against aliens. Because of the distinct governmental interests involved and because of markedly different judicial treatment, state and federal discrimination will be considered separately.

§ 13–3.2 State Discrimination

a. Historical Treatment: Pre–Graham v. Richardson

In 1886 the Supreme Court declared in *Yick Wo v. Hopkins* (Sup.Ct.1886) that the guarantees of the Fourteenth Amendment extended universally to all persons within the territorial jurisdiction of the United States, without regard to race, color, or nationality. *Yick Wo* invalidated the discriminatory application of a San Francisco ordinance, effectively prohibiting Chinese residents from operating laundry facilities, while allowing white citizens under similar circumstances to own laundries. In *Yick Wo*, the Court definitively established that aliens must be treated on a basis equal to citizens and that the state had no authority to restrict arbitrarily an alien's "life, or the means of living, or any material right essential to the enjoyment of life...."

In practice, however, the strictures of *Yick Wo* have not been followed. The Supreme Court for many years applied an extremely lax standard of review in alienage discrimination cases, upholding severe restrictions on resident aliens. Only in recent years has the alien enjoyed a degree of the protection guaranteed by the Equal Protection Clause of the Fourteenth Amendment so clearly enunciated in *Yick Wo*.

Throughout the late 19th and early 20th centuries, when massive immigration to the United States was occurring, states imposed a wide variety of restrictions on the activities of resident aliens. Most of these discriminatory measures easily withstood Equal Protection challenges. Several theories justified state discrimination:

(1) If a public resource or "special public interest" was involved, public monies could properly be reserved for citizens and withheld from aliens. On this ground, the Court in 1915 upheld New York's exclusion of aliens from employment on public works and other public employment. *Heim v. McCall* (Sup.Ct.1915).

(2) If the resource in question was viewed as "common property" of the citizens of the state, non-citizens could be prohibited from enjoying it. Therefore, Pennsylvania could limit permission to hunt wildlife and carry firearms to citizens (*Patsone v. Pennsylvania* (Sup.Ct. 1914)), and Virginia could reserve for its citizens the right to plant oysters in a stream bed within its boundaries. *McCready v. Virginia* (Sup.Ct.1876).

(3) If the limitation constituted a valid exercise of police power, the alien could be barred from activities routinely allowed citizens, including certain forms of private employment. Such reasoning perhaps was stretched the furthest in *Clarke v. Deckebach* (Sup.Ct. 1927), in which the Court upheld the requirement of citizenship for licensing of pool hall operators as a valid exercise of police power. The Court's rationale was that pool halls often attracted criminals and other undesirable people and that non-citizens were less familiar with American laws and customs than native-born or naturalized citizens. The Court held that it was in the interest of the public welfare to limit pool hall operators to citizens.

(4) If the particular benefit was characterized as a "privilege" not a "right," it could be withheld from the alien who was not entitled to the privileges and immunities guaranteed to citizens by the Constitution. On this ground and because of the states' traditionally broad power over the regulation of property ownership, the Court approved prohibitions against the inheritance and ownership of land by aliens in the absence of a treaty to the contrary. *Hauenstein v. Lynham* (Sup.Ct.1879); *Terrace v. Thompson* (Sup.Ct.1923). It was not until 1948 that doubt was cast on the validity of such restric-

tions on property rights. *Oyama v. California* (Sup.Ct. 1948).

In this tradition, the Court gave short shrift to most resident aliens' claims under the Equal Protection Clause. The standard of review was not very severe, indicating the Court's unwillingness to interfere with the judgments of local governments. The ordinance was affirmed where "the possibility of a rational basis for the legislative judgment" was not "preclud[ed]," and where the Court had "no such knowledge of local conditions ... to say it is wrong." *Clarke v. Deckebach* (Sup.Ct.1927).

Despite this deference to state discriminatory actions, the Court in *Truax v. Raich* (Sup.Ct.1915) struck down an Arizona law which required private employers of more than five persons to employ at least 80% "qualified electors or native-born citizens." Noting that the discrimination in *Truax* was imposed on private enterprise, reaching broadly across all industries, the Court found no special public interest or public resource involved that could justify the restriction. The Court held that the discrimination was "an end in itself" and inimical to the Fourteenth Amendment's guarantee of personal freedom and opportunity. Significantly, the Court also found that the state's attempt to deny aliens the opportunity to work collided with the federal government's exclusive power to permit aliens to enter and reside in the United States. The Court reasoned that the privilege of living in the U.S., granted by Congress, would be destroyed if the state could severely restrict employment solely on the basis of alienage and that the privilege to reside here carried with it "the right to work for a living in the common occupations of the community." Arizona's attempt virtually to take away from resident aliens the opportunity to earn a livelihood impinged on the authority of Congress over immigration.

Truax v. Raich (Sup.Ct.1915) was a significant decision because it laid the foundation for the Court's later repudiation of the line of cases in which state discriminatory actions had been almost routinely upheld. It was not until 1948, however, that an alien was again successful in an Equal Protection challenge. In *Takahashi v. Fish and Game Commission* (Sup.Ct.1948), the Supreme Court considered a California statute which forbade the granting of commercial fishing licenses to persons "ineligible to citizenship." Federal law at that time provided that Japanese nationals were ineligible for United States citizenship. The Court quoted extensively from *Truax,* rejecting California's assertion that because the state owned the fish off the coast as trustee for its citizens, it had a "special public interest" in conserving fish for the benefit of its citizens. In holding that this ground was inadequate for discriminating against Japanese residents, the Court implicitly overruled its earlier line of cases. Justice Murphy's concurring opinion in *Takahashi* argued vigorously that California's action was racially motivated; he cited impressive historical evidence and claimed that the statute was invalid for that reason. The majority, however, did not address the race question. *Takahashi* represented a departure from traditional Equal Protection analysis in alien discrimination cases. In refusing to approve a state's citizenship requirement in a case that involved public interests as strong as many in earlier cases, the Court signalled that it would more carefully review such discrimination in the future.

b. Modern Treatment

Takahashi made clear that states would not be allowed to discriminate casually on the basis of alienage: "the power of a state to apply its laws exclusively to its alien inhabitants as a class is confined within narrow limits." Such language suggested that aliens should be protected more diligently than the traditional rational basis standard of review would demand. Finally in 1971, the Supreme Court explicitly held in *Graham v. Richardson* (Sup.Ct.1971) that aliens as a group constitute a "discrete and insular minority" deserving of heightened judicial protection, and that alienage is a "suspect classification" prompting strict scrutiny of state discrimination under the Equal Protection Clause.

Graham involved the denial of state welfare benefits to aliens. The state argued that the receipt of welfare benefits was a privilege, a share in the state's wealth, which could properly be reserved for members of the body politic. In rejecting this assertion, the Court laid to rest the special public interest doctrine and the right-privilege distinction which had justified many earlier restrictions on aliens. As it had in *Truax* and *Takahashi,* the Court also objected to the statute as an impermissible state interference with the exclusive federal power to regulate immigration.

For several years following *Graham,* the Court analyzed cases of alienage discrimination by using the same Equal Protection mode that it had developed in racial discrimination and other cases: if a personal fundamental interest is at stake or if a suspect class is found, state laws invariably fall when submitted to strict judicial scrutiny. To sustain its burden, the state must show that its purpose or interest justifying the classification

is "substantial" and that the classification is " 'necessary . . . to the accomplishment' of its purpose or the
safeguarding of its interest." *Application of Griffiths*
(Sup.Ct.1973). Many state restrictions on aliens were
overturned by the lower courts.

Following this approach the Supreme Court in *Sugarman v. Dougall* (Sup.Ct.1973) struck down a New York
statute that barred all aliens from competitive civil
service employment. The state asserted that its interest in assuring the loyalty of its employees who implement government policy justified the bar. While recognizing a state's interest in limiting government participation to those persons who are within the "basic
conception of a political community," and the state's
authority to define that political community, the Court
found that the statute swept far too broadly. Within
New York's statutory framework, menial competitive
civil service positions were subject to the citizenship
requirement while other elective and high appointive
offices were not. The Court declared that despite a
valid state interest, the means employed were too im-
precisely drawn to survive strict scrutiny.

Sugarman did recognize a state's prerogative to define
a class of positions requiring citizenship in some situations: the power of the state to define the political
community applied to persons holding state elective or
important non-elective legislative and judicial positions,
for officers who participate directly in the formulation,
execution, or review of broad public policy perform
functions that go to the heart of representative government.

Decided the same day as *Sugarman,* the Court in
Application of Griffiths invalidated a Connecticut law

which limited to U.S. citizens licenses to practice law. The Court rejected the state's argument that because lawyers are officers of the Court, the state must be assured of undivided allegiance by requiring citizenship. Furthermore, in spite of their access to courts and their traditional leadership role in government, the Court found that a lawyer is not "so close to the core of the political process as to make him a formulator of government policy." In so ruling the Court appeared to confine narrowly the reaches of the political function exception mentioned in *Sugarman.*

In similar fashion, the Court struck down a Puerto Rican statute which denied engineering licenses to virtually all aliens in *Examining Board v. Flores de Otero* (Sup.Ct.1976), and a New York statute which denied higher education financial assistance to certain resident aliens in *Nyquist v. Mauclet* (Sup.Ct.1977). In *Mauclet* the Court held that a suspect class existed, even though non-citizens were eligible for assistance if they applied for citizenship or filed statements of intent to become citizens. New York's stated interest in encouraging naturalization was held, first, to be related insufficiently to preservation of the political community and, second, an interference with the federal government's power over immigration and naturalization, since only the national government was properly concerned with encouraging naturalization. Furthermore, the Court found that while the state has a legitimate interest in enhancing the educational level of the electorate, allowing aliens to participate in financial aid programs would not defeat that goal. By way of *dicta,* the Court explained that the political function exception to which the Court had alluded in *Sugarman* was very narrow, limited to the states' historical or constitutional powers to define such characteristics as the qualifications of voters or of government officers who directly participate in the formulation, execution, or review of broad public policy.

Despite the purported narrowness of the "political function" exception extracted from *Sugarman,* the Court has retreated from its suspect classification-strict scrutiny approach to alienage cases. In 1978 the Court read "political function" expansively in *Foley v. Connelie* (Sup.Ct.1978) to uphold a New York statute which allows only citizens to compete for the job of state trooper. In a clear withdrawal from the Court's previous position, Chief Justice Burger's majority opinion cited his own dissenting opinion in *Mauclet* to pronounce that every statutory restriction on aliens does not demand strict scrutiny. The Court theorized that as only citizens are entitled to participate in the political process, the right to govern thereby could be properly reserved to citizens; as states have the authority to delimit the political community, a state could permissibly exclude aliens from positions relating to "the right of the people to be governed by their citizen peers." If the position under review involves discretionary decision-making or execution of policy, "which substantially affects members of the political community," a lesser standard of review would be proper. The Court then held that police officers have considerable discretionary powers, exercise a high degree of judgment in executing state policy, and affect the public significantly. Therefore, the state may assume that citizens are "more familiar with and sympathetic to American traditions," which presumably the Court found important if citizens were to submit to such police powers as arrest, search, and seizure.

In *Ambach v. Norwick* (Sup.Ct.1979), the political function exception also was used as the basis for upholding New York's denial of permanent certification as public school teachers to any non-citizen unless that person declared an intention to become a citizen. The State Commissioner of Education was authorized to certify aliens provisionally only in certain narrowly prescribed situations. The Court first emphasized the importance of education in preparing students for participation as citizens, in preserving societal values and instilling civic virtues. Second, the Court held that the role of teachers was critical in developing students' attitudes toward government and the political process. In order to place a teacher within the governmental function principle, the Court cited a teacher's discretion over communication of course material and position as a role model. The Court then held that (1) the state has a valid interest in furthering its educational goals and (2) in pursuit of that interest, it could rationally conclude that non-citizens or permanent residents who did not want to become citizens were inappropriate candidates for teachers. Strong dissenting opinions in both *Foley* and *Norwick* protested the Court's opinions as unjustified departures from Equal Protection precedents and as an unwarranted expansion of the *Sugarman dicta*.

Despite *Foley* and *Norwick* most lower courts have continued to apply *Graham* after deciding that a political function is not involved. For example, in striking down a statute that required citizenship for appointment as a notary public, the Florida Supreme Court determined that notaries public do not perform political functions as described in *Foley;* instead, they are more like public employees performing routine ministerial duties. The court applied strict scrutiny and ruled that the statute violated the Equal Protection Clause. Applying *Graham* outright, a district court struck down New Mexico State University's attempt to deny admission to Iranian students until their government released American hostages. *Tayyari v. New Mexico State University* (D.N.M.1980). The Supreme Court of Connecticut, however, held that a criminal defendant was not entitled to a jury selected from a panel which included resident aliens. Under *Foley* and *Norwick*, the court classified jury service as a political function from which aliens rationally could be excluded. *Connecticut v. Thigpen* (Conn.Super.1978).

In 1982, the Supreme Court upheld a California statute that limits positions classified as "peace officers" to citizens. Plaintiffs were resident aliens seeking employment as deputy probation officers, positions within the statutory classification of "peace officers." The district court twice had held the statute unconstitutional both on its face and as applied, the latter decision rendered after consideration in light of *Foley*. In *Cabell v. Chavez–Salido* (Sup.Ct.1982), a 5–4 majority read *Sugarman, Foley,* and *Norwick* to require strict review of state restrictions on resident aliens only where an alien's *economic interests* were affected; here the restriction served a political function, a far less stringent standard of review was appropriate. The Court set out a two-step evaluation process to determine the character of the restriction. First, the specificity of the classification would be considered; substantial under- or over-inclusiveness would tend to negate the claim that the classification is intended to serve a political function. Second, even if "sufficiently tailored," the classification as applied must affect only persons who "perform functions that go to the heart of representative government."

The Court would look at the extent of discretionary decision-making or policy execution that affects members of the political community.

The statutory scheme in *Chavez–Salido* defined about 70 positions as peace officers, including toll service employees, cemetery sextons, and livestock identification inspectors. The Court found, however, that such over-inclusiveness is not fatal: "the classifications used need not be precise; there need only be a *substantial fit*" in order to support the state's claim that an important government function is involved. The Court held that nearly all peace officers shared a law enforcement function primarily because they had the power to arrest and must undergo training in arrest and the use of firearms. Such an exercise of the sovereign's "coercive police powers" could be limited to members of the political community under *Foley*.

In considering the statute as applied, the Court characterized the work of a probation officer as involving a great deal of discretion, because their decisions must be made in the first instance without supervision. Alluding to the "educational function" of probation officers, the Court also asserted that the position symbolized the state's sovereign power and the political community's control over the juvenile offender.

In a forceful dissent, Justice Blackmun reviewed the history of the challenged statute. No legislative rationale or common purpose behind the peace officer classification and citizenship requirement had been articulated. Justice Blackmun asserted that the majority distorted *Sugarman* by employing a weak standard of review and by approving a mere "substantial fit" between the classification and justifications asserted by the state. The dissenters would have found the statute to be fatally under- and over-inclusive as it limited to citizens some jobs which were not even rationally related to the political community, while in other areas failed to bar aliens from jobs which arguably encompassed a political function. In the view of the dissent, even *Foley* and *Norwick* required a substantial showing by the state. By abolishing a strict standard of review, Justice Blackmun stated, "*Sugarman*'s exception swallows *Sugarman*'s rule."

Justice Blackmun also took issue with the majority's "coercive power" characterization of the position of all peace officers, pointing out that probation officers are not allowed to carry guns, can arrest only probationers under their jurisdiction, and then only for the purpose of bringing them before a court to decide on detention or release. Further, their discretion is limited by judicial supervision and is extensively regulated by statute. After setting out compelling statutory inconsistencies which allow aliens to play integral roles in the criminal justice system and the considerable qualifications of the plaintiffs, the dissent concluded that the state discrimination "stems solely from state parochialism and hostility toward foreigners who have come to this country lawfully."

The Supreme Court, however, returned to its suspect classification—strict scrutiny approach to alienage cases in *Bernal v. Fainter* (1984). By a vote of 8–to–1, the Court struck down as a violation of the Equal Protection Clause a Texas statute requiring a notary public to be a U.S. citizen. Applying strict scrutiny, the Court found no legitimate political function to support a citizenship requirement. Because the functions of a notary public are primarily clerical and ministerial, the position is not one "such that the office holder would necessarily exercise broad discretionary power over the formulation or execution of public policies importantly affecting the citizen population, power of a sort that a self-governing community could properly entrust only to full-fledged members of that community." In contrast to the state troopers in *Foley,* notaries public do not routinely exercise the state's monopoly of "legitimate coercive force," nor do they "exercise the wide discretion typically enjoyed by public school teachers" as in *Norwick.*

Foley, Norwick, and *Chavez–Salido* indicate that the Court has increasingly been willing to find a political function which invokes only a minimal rationality standard of review. In contrast to *Sugarman* 's 8–1 majority, however, the Court in *Chavez–Salido* was sharply divided, with the dissent in vehement opposition to the majority's approach. Perhaps this sharp division, along with the Court's decision in *Bernal,* portends an eventual re-examination of the political function exception, or, at the least, signals that the outer limits of the exception have been reached. Certainly, the Court has changed directions without repudiating its holding in *Graham* that classifications on the basis of alienage are suspect. Commentators object that the Court has not set out a forthright or disciplined judicial analysis, although several alternative theories are available.

In cases involving a political function, the Court could have maintained its strict scrutiny review of alienage restrictions by finding a compelling state interest that justified the classification, if precisely drawn. The significance of citizenship in the political process cannot be dismissed: in certain situations the public or political character of the position in question may justify the requirement. In that way, the Court would have remained consistent with *Graham* and its progeny.

Alternatively, the Court could have straightforwardly re-evaluated the suspect classification rubric and concluded that aliens, indeed, do not exhibit the range of disabilities that requires the judicial vigilance evident in racial classifications. Significantly, alienage is not an immutable characteristic, nor is it always evident. Certainly important state and federal interests are connected with citizenship which in some cases may warrant different treatment. But aliens comprise a class which is in many ways prototypic of a discrete and insular minority group which needs judicial protection against a political process which is often oblivious or hostile to its interests. Historically, aliens have been discriminated against, socially stigmatized, and ostracized, though arguably their experience has not been as severe as that of racial minorities. Deprived of political rights, aliens have no representative voice and thus need the protection of courts which must protect minority and underrepresented interests. In any case, it undermines the integrity of the suspect classification approach to Equal Protection to hold that alienage is suspect for some purposes, but not for others.

Other commentators suggest that Equal Protection analysis is inappropriate in this area; that those cases which strike down state restrictions under the Equal Protection Clause are expounding an unarticulated pre-emption theory. In each case, the Court either specifically indicated or consistently could have indicated, that the state provision in question interfered with the federal government's exclusive authority over immigration and naturalization. *Truax* and *Takahashi* expressly held that a state's restriction on the alien's opportunity to earn a living conflicted with congressional power to set the terms and conditions of continued residence. Other cases involving employment could be similarly considered. Burdens on aliens other than those related to employment could also be overturned if they have an adverse effect on the conditions of residence as determined by Congress. Consistent with this preemption theory, those activities truly related to the political process, could withstand challenge if not in conflict with federal policy.

Many lower courts have considered and decided the preemption issue, raised by plaintiffs as the alternative to an Equal Protection claim. For example, Louisiana's statute requiring citizenship for the granting of a license to practice dentistry was invalidated as a denial of Equal Protection under *Graham*'s strict scrutiny standard, but was held not to be an interference with immigration and naturalization. *Szeto v. Louisiana State Board of Dentistry* (E.D.La.1981). At least one state court apparently has adopted the preemption theory as the most logical approach to alienage discrimination cases. *Matter of Adoption of a Child by L.C.* (N.J.1981).

A clearly articulated approach to state restrictions on resident aliens is needed to assure minimally uniform treatment. The Supreme Court must re-examine its departures from Equal Protection analysis and provide more forthright guidance for lower courts and prospective litigants. Resident aliens at least are entitled to consistently reasoned judgments when challenging discrimination under a constitution which promises equal treatment to all persons.

§ 13–3.3 Federal Discrimination

a. Introduction

In contrast to state discrimination, actions by the federal government which classify individuals on the basis of alienage touch upon policies and interests traditionally immune from searching judicial review. This section will examine the deferential judicial approach to alienage discrimination by the federal government and the special federal interests grounded in congressional power over immigration that are asserted in its defense.

b. Judicial Deference to the Political Branches: Special Federal Interests

The Court has long held that immigration and naturalization, like foreign policy generally, encompass an area over which Congress maintains almost plenary power and the judiciary has a very limited responsibility. *E.g., Fong Yue Ting v. United States* (Sup.Ct.1893). Immigration matters raise complex and sensitive questions of national policy, calling for informed political judgments. This country's treatment of prospective immigrants or temporary foreign visitors is intertwined with U.S. foreign policy. It may be a factor in treaty negotiations, contribute to this country's influence abroad, and influence how other governments treat U.S. citizens traveling abroad. In some cases, national security matters may be implicated. The Supreme Court considers itself an inappropriate forum, and judges inexpert, for the weighing of policy choices presumably done by Congress in setting immigration and naturalization priorities.

In fact, in reviewing immigration legislation, the Court has stopped just short of applying the political question doctrine which is grounded in the separation of government powers and in effect would render challenges to congressional authority in this area nonjusticiable. Historically, the Court has thus upheld discrimination on whatever basis Congress may choose in deciding what groups shall be admitted to this country and under what terms. Constitutional challenges to such exclusion and expulsion laws repeatedly have failed.

Although the Court has admitted to misgivings about the extent of congressional plenary power and its own virtual abdication of review, the strength of long-standing precedent has thus far prevented any effective reconsideration: As Justice Frankfurter explained,

> In light of the expansion of the concept of substantive Due Process as a limitation upon all powers of Congress, even the war power, ... much can be said for the view, were we writing on a clean slate, that the Due Process Clause qualifies the scope of political distinction heretofore recognized as belonging to Congress in regulating the entry and deportation of aliens.... But the slate is not clean. As to the extent of the power of Congress under review, there is not merely "a page of history," ... but a whole volume. Policies pertaining to the entry of aliens and their right to remain here are peculiarly concerned with the political conduct of government. In the enforcement of these policies, the Executive Branch of the Government must respect the procedural safeguards of Due Process.... But that the formulation of these policies is entrusted exclusively to Congress has become about as firmly embedded in the legisla-

tive and judicial tissues of our body politic as any aspect of our government. *Galvan v. Press* (Sup.Ct. 1954).

Quoting the above passage, the Court declined again to expand the scope of judicial review in *Fiallo v. Bell* (Sup.Ct.1977), a case in which substantive constitutional rights of U.S. citizens and permanent resident aliens were compromised by provisions of the Immigration and Nationality Act. In *Fiallo,* the statutes in question granted special preference immigration status to aliens qualified as "children" or "parents" of American citizens or permanent resident aliens. The INA's definition of "child" excluded illegitimate children whose claim to preferential status was based on their relationship with their natural fathers, while including those who claimed through their mothers. Further, a natural father was ineligible to claim a preference status for his illegitimate child, while a natural mother was eligible.

Plaintiffs were natural fathers and their illegitimate children who sought to be reunited under the special preference provisions, claiming, among other things, that the INA discriminated against them on the basis of gender, marital status, and illegitimacy. Despite the statute's clear detrimental impact on the rights of citizens and resident aliens, the Court refused to expand the scope of judicial review of immigration matters. In rather parrot-like fashion the Court reiterated that it had a limited role to play in such policy decisions, and applied an extremely lax minimum rationality standard of review to uphold the restrictions. (The Immigration Reform and Control Act of 1986 amended INA § 101(b)(1) to allow an illegitimate child to claim preferential status through its natural father "if the father has or had a bona fide parent-child relationship with" the child. INA § 101(b)(1)(D).)

The federal government regulates the lives of aliens in a myriad of ways, however, other than directly through its immigration and naturalization policies. Historically, federal, like state restrictions on the activities of resident aliens have been substantial and severe. Because congressional power is viewed as broadly encompassing "regula[tion] of the relationship between the United States and our alien visitors," *Mathews v. Diaz* (Sup.Ct.1976), those justifications for deferring to Congress and the Executive on matters of immigration, foreign policy, national security, etc. have apparently been extended to any federal actions which affect aliens. Consequently, the guarantee of Equal Protection of the law inferred from the Due Process Clause of the Fifth Amendment has had little meaning for resident aliens.

c. Protection Under the Fifth Amendment

The Court's treatment of federal discrimination on the basis of alienage departs sharply from Equal Protection jurisprudence in the areas of discrimination on the basis of race, national origin, and religion. Classification on these bases is immediately suspect, invokes strict judicial scrutiny, and virtually never survives an Equal Protection challenge. The federal government has been required to abide by the same stringent standards under the Fifth Amendment as have the states under the Fourteenth Amendment.

Where the classification is on the basis of alienage, however, the Court has declared that the Equal Protection component of the Fifth Amendment is not always co-extensive with that of the Fourteenth although the analysis is much the same:

> Not only does the language of the two Amendments differ, but more importantly, there may be overriding national interests which justify selective federal legislation that would be unacceptable for an individual State. *Hampton v. Mow Sun Wong* (Sup.Ct.1976) (fn. omitted).

Only where the federal government acts very much like a state, must it adhere to standards applicable to the states:

> [W]hen a federal rule is applicable to only a limited territory, such as the District of Columbia, or an insular possession, and when there is no special national interest involved, the Due Process Clause has been construed as having the same significance as the Equal Protection Clause. *Hampton v. Mow Sun Wong* (fn. omitted).

Therefore, stepping outside its precedent in *Graham v. Richardson* (Sup.Ct.1971), the state discrimination case in which aliens' "discrete and insular minority" status prompted "heightened judicial solicitude," the Supreme Court has refused to scrutinize closely nationwide federal actions which burden aliens. Two leading cases (*Hampton* and *Diaz*), neither directly involving immigration or naturalization, firmly establish the Court's refusal to restrain the federal government in any area relating to aliens. Unfortunately, the Court's deference to Congress overshadows the significant deprivation of individual rights involved in those cases.

In *Hampton v. Mow Sun Wong* (Sup.Ct.1976), the Supreme Court considered a U.S. Civil Service Commission regulation which excluded non-citizens from employment in the competitive federal civil service. The resident alien plaintiffs argued that they had been deprived of Equal Protection of the laws. On that ground the Ninth Circuit Court of Appeals invalidated the regulation; the Supreme Court relied on rather narrow *procedural* Due Process grounds to affirm the lower court.

In *Hampton* the Supreme Court first refused to use the same approach for federal as for state discrimination: "the paramount federal power over immigration and naturalization forecloses a simple extension of the holding in *Sugarman v. Dougall* (Sup.Ct.1973), in which New York's bar of non-citizen employment in state competitive civil service was held to be a violation of the Equal Protection Clause of the 14th Amendment." The Court did concede, however, that some judicial interference may be proper, noting that plenary federal power does not allow *any* agent of the federal government to discriminate between aliens and citizens. Writing for the Court, Justice Stevens recited the disabilities suffered by aliens due to lack of political rights and unfamiliarity with language and customs, holding that the inability to be employed by the federal civil service was a deprivation of a liberty interest which entitled the plaintiff aliens to Due Process of law. The Court set out the standard under which the deprivation was reviewable:

When the Federal Government asserts an overriding national interest as justification for a discriminatory rule which would violate the Equal Protection Clause if adopted by a State, Due Process requires that there be a legitimate basis for presuming that the rule was actually intended to serve that interest. If the agency which promulgates the rule has direct responsibility for fostering or protecting that interest, it may reasonably be presumed that the asserted interest was the actual predicate for the rule. That presumption would, of course, be fortified by an appropriate statement of reasons identifying the relevant interest. Alternatively, if the rule were expressly mandated by the Congress or the President, we might presume that any interest which might rationally be served by the rule did in fact give rise to its adoption.

Applying such presumptions, the Court found that the Civil Service Commission was not authorized or required by Congress or the President to promulgate the citizenship requirement. Although legitimate national interests could be asserted, only the interest in administrative convenience was within the concern of the Civil Service Commission. In the absence of specified reasons, the Court was unwilling to presume that the Commission was attempting to further national interests outside of its responsibility. Therefore, the regulation as promulgated deprived plaintiffs of procedural Due Process. The Court strongly suggested, however, that had the President or Congress expressly adopted the rule or had the agency done so with justifications that were within its scope of concern, the rule would not have been invalid.

Indeed, within three months of the Court's decision in *Hampton*, President Ford issued an Executive Order which in effect restored the invalidated Commission rule barring aliens from competitive civil service. 5 C.F.R. § 7.4. He did not specify, as the Court had implied was important, the national interests to be furthered by this rule. The Ninth Circuit Court of Appeals later held the new Executive Order to be constitutional in *Mow Sun Wong v. Campbell* (9th Cir.1980); the Supreme Court denied certiorari. The Court of Appeals found the order to be within the President's constitutional and statutory authority. Under the standards set forth in *Hampton v. Mow Sun Wong* (Sup.Ct. 1976), the national interest in creating an incentive for aliens to be naturalized was sufficient to justify the rule.

The Supreme Court did not hesitate to decide plaintiff's Equal Protection claim in *Mathews v. Diaz* (Sup.Ct. 1976), which was issued the same day as the Court's decision in *Hampton*. *Diaz* challenged the constitutionality of a statute limiting eligibility for certain Medicare benefits to citizens and resident aliens who have resided in the United States for at least five years. A unanimous Court held that such a classification was constitutional because it was not "wholly irrational." The Court invoked both the plenary power of Congress over immigration and naturalization as well as the political question doctrine to justify such an extremely lax standard of review:

> Any rule of constitutional law that would inhibit the flexibility of the political branches of government to respond to changing world conditions should be adopted only with the greatest caution. The reasons that preclude judicial review of political questions also dictate a narrow standard of review of decisions made by the Congress or the President in the area of immigration and naturalization.

Although the Court conceded that the five year residency requirement is longer than necessary to protect the fiscal integrity of the program and that unnecessary hardship is incurred by some persons, the Court found that the restriction reasonably insured that those qualified for the benefits have a greater affinity with the United States; accordingly, the classification was not "wholly irrational." The Court did not state why affinity with the United States is somehow significant in relation to Medicare; nor did it examine how well the classification furthered that end. The *Diaz* court distinguished *Graham v. Richardson* (Sup.Ct.1971), which had invalidated a similar restriction on state welfare benefits on the ground that a state's relationship with aliens differs substantially from that of the federal government.

The message from *Diaz* and *Hampton* appears clear: virtually no federal limitation on aliens would fail under the Fifth Amendment. Under the minimum rationality standard of *Diaz* no real evaluation of the asserted government interest nor the necessity of the means employed to further that interest would be undertaken. Although *Hampton* spoke in terms of an "overriding national interest," that case in effect requires only that an administrative agency, which is not officially concerned with national interests involving aliens, must spell out its reasons for imposing a restriction based on alienage. Where Congress or the President acts, or presumably the Immigration and Naturalization Service, virtually any national interest would sustain the restriction against an Equal Protection challenge.

Following *Diaz* and *Hampton,* Equal Protection challenges to federal legislation concerning resident aliens have failed in such diverse areas as employment in federal non-competitive civil service, eligibility for farm operating loans, licensure as commercial radio operators, and eligibility for certain Social Security benefits. In most cases plaintiffs were long time permanent resident aliens qualified in every way for the benefit in question except for their alienage. Courts usually applied minimum rational basis review, resulting in ready acceptance of the government interest asserted. One lower court has read *Hampton* as requiring an intermediate standard of review, at least where a liberty interest is involved and the statute in question is not directly related to the admission, exclusion, or expulsion of aliens. *Yuen v. IRS* (2d Cir.1981). In that case, however, the government nevertheless prevailed.

d. Implications of the Current Approach

Resident aliens can expect to be afforded more judicial protection when the state discriminates against them than when the federal government does so. This discrepancy may be entirely defensible in immigration or other areas which directly involve questions of foreign policy and where refined political judgments are crucial to maintaining consistency and strength as an international power. Unquestionably, the national government requires a degree of flexibility that a state does not in order to pursue the international affairs of the country.

Important national interests, however, should not obscure the impact of discrimination on the individual rights of aliens who have been lawfully admitted and have taken up permanent residence here. The Supreme Court has mechanically extended its deference to congressional plenary power and its restraint in the face of the political question implications of immigration to all other areas of federal control over aliens. This unfounded extrapolation subordinates constitutional rights to the interests of the national government regardless of the substantive area involved or the relative importance of the interest asserted.

Rational basis review may be particularly misplaced in cases of alienage discrimination. Professor Rosberg in his article, *The Protection of Aliens From Discriminatory Treatment by the National Government,* argues that aliens are in as much need of protection from state-sponsored discrimination as are members of the more traditional suspect classifications. Like other groups given suspect classification status, aliens have suffered a history of discriminatory treatment. Although alienage is not an immutable characteristic, as is race, before an alien fulfills the five year residency requirement, her/his status is inescapable. Political powerlessness, however, is the alien's most obvious and significant debilitating condition. While other protected minorities may have seriously weakened political voices, an alien has no voice or vote. The suspect classification doctrine is at least partially based on the understanding that judicial vigilance is necessary because the political process does not adequately represent the interests of oppressed groups. In Rosberg's words,

Where a group is systematically shut out of the political process, ... and is denied an opportunity to form alliances with any other group, it may well lose on every issue. At that point the proper functioning of the majoritarian political process is very much in question. In such case, the Court begins to fear that the injury to the members of the disadvantaged class, far from being an unintended by-product of the state's effort to serve a legitimate interest, was in fact the very purpose of the classification. And the likelihood increases that the classification was based on a stereo-typical and erroneous view of the characteristics of the members of the group.

It would seem that the suspect classification rubric fits perfectly the particular needs of aliens for extra protection. In fact, the applicability of the political question doctrine is ironic: The Court's refusal to inter-fere with any congressional judgment regarding aliens assumes that debate and political reflection are essen-tial. Yet the political powerlessness of aliens guaran-tees a one-sided debate.

Of course, broad use of the suspect classification doc-trine and strict scrutiny would make it very difficult for the federal government to carry out any legitimate immigration or foreign policy objectives with the use of alienage classifications. The Court's fear of imposing constitutional rigidity in an area in which flexibility is important would be justified. While adherence to strict scrutiny may hamstring the federal government, the current rational basis review virtually ignores the legit-imate interests of resident aliens.

Unfortunately, the strict/rational dichotomy causes an all or nothing situation; the Court should explore alternative methods of analysis in which asserted government interests and the means employed to fur-ther them are balanced against the severity of the burden on resident aliens. At least three approaches provide for such balancing. First, within Equal Protec-tion analysis, an intermediate standard of review could be applied. *See Reed v. Reed* (Sup.Ct.1971). Less severe than strict scrutiny, intermediate judicial review would nonetheless substitute more exacting justification than the weak rational basis standard.

Second, analysis under the Due Process Clause affords another alternative. The Court already has been innovative in this area. In *Hampton v. Mow Sun Wong* (Sup.Ct.1976), the Court looked at the process of decision-making to declare invalid an administrative rule that discriminated against aliens. While in that case, the Court's intervention proved very short-lived, a more aggressive track could similarly examine the process of congressional decision-making.

To alleviate the concern that questions of national policy as to aliens must be left to Congress, the Court could first determine whether such issues are, in fact, raised by the particular classification. If so, the Court could examine the statute and legislative history to assess whether Congress indeed considered the national interest which is to be served by the alienage classification. Such an approach would necessarily abandon any presumption that Congress made an informed policy judgment simply because the legislation relates to aliens. At the least, this approach would force the political branches to evaluate and justify discrimination against resident aliens. Depending on the vigor of the Court's review, it could succeed in weeding out arbitrary and very harmful discrimination that contributes little or nothing to U.S. immigration or foreign policies.

Third, focusing on fairness to the individual, cases of alienage discrimination by the federal government could be reviewed under the conclusive presumption doctrine. In essence, that doctrine requires that if an individual is disadvantaged by a classification which is premised on a congressional presumption, for a particular purpose, s/he must be given an opportunity to prove that the presumption is untrue. A restriction which *conclusively presumes* a characteristic or fact without allowing rebuttal would be a deprivation of Due Process. On the one hand, this approach to alienage discrimination cases would avoid the rigidity of an Equal Protection holding because even if struck down, a restriction could be re-instituted with a provision allowing for a rebuttable presumption. On the other hand, substantive review of congressional presumptions would assure greater protection of individual rights. Only some similar type of analysis which recognizes and investigates competing interests will result in fairness to both the individual alien and the federal government.

The real question that the federal government, including both the political and judicial branches, needs to answer is whether fairness is a goal in its treatment of aliens. The rationales advanced by the Court for its hands-off approach do not justify the poor treatment resident aliens sometimes suffer. Less laudable reasons probably explain it.

At the least, much legislation appears to be the effect of stereotypic thinking about foreigners, unwarranted assumptions about loyalty and the importance of "affinity" to the United States, and in some situations outright racial prejudice. The Court has ignored or avoided any significant curtailment of this abuse although such bases for law-making are repugnant to the American system.

Hundreds of lawful classifications are embodied in the immigration laws that set preferences for admittance and establish conditions under which an alien may remain in this country. In characterizing all legislation that burdens aliens after they have been admitted as part of an ongoing scheme with foreign policy overtones, the government may simply extend the prejudices expressed in the immigration laws. The U.S. government apparently prefers affluent immigrants who will not need Medicare for at least five years; immigrants who will seek only private or state civil service employment, while refraining from certain private employment; who will not request government farm loans, but who will nevertheless pay taxes, contribute to the community, and if necessary, serve in the military. A prospective immigrant could not know the true terms of entry without checking all federal legislation for restrictions as to citizenship.

In any case, unprincipled discrimination against resident aliens creates an image of the United States in the eyes of the world as being hypocritical and unfair. If, indeed, treatment of aliens is a crucial element in foreign relations, then the government has the opportunity to improve its international image by treating resident aliens fairly.

§ 13–3.4 Conclusion

Resident aliens can expect to suffer discrimination after immigration to this country. While technically the law guarantees treatment equal to that of citizens, such has never been the case. Historically, as waves of immigrants came to the United States to escape economic and political difficulties in their native countries, social stigma and official discrimination have been commonplace. While significant steps were taken during the early and middle 1970's to halt discrimination by states on the basis of alienage, the Supreme Court has since the late 1970's retreated from its briefly active role in that area.

Vis-a-vis the federal government, aliens have never been found to be deserving of significant protection and apparently can be disadvantaged with little or no justification.

§ 13–4 OTHER RIGHTS AND DUTIES OF ALIENS

§ 13–4.1 Right to Vote

The Constitution reserves for citizens only the right to vote, and no state presently allows aliens to vote in elections. Throughout much of the nineteenth and part of the twentieth century, however, aliens were able to vote in many states. In 1928, Arkansas was the last state to end alien suffrage. The progressive disenfranchising of aliens in the early part of the twentieth century was due primarily to increased hostility to and distrust for foreigners. Anti-alien sentiment was fueled in part by the assassination of President McKinley, a large influx of immigrants who did not have Anglo–Saxon origins, and the outbreak of World War I.

When an opportunity arose for the Supreme Court to decide whether a state could deny aliens the right to vote, the Court declined to hear the case for failure to present a substantial federal question. *Skafte v. Rorex* (Sup.Ct.1977). (The Colorado Supreme Court had sustained a Colorado statute which denied aliens the right to vote in school elections.) While the Supreme Court has stated that citizenship is a permissible criterion for determining who may vote, the Court has not explained the basis for requiring voters to be citizens. *See, e.g., Sugarman v. Dougall* (Sup.Ct.1973). Many arguments have been suggested to preserve the citizenship requirement. Voting is seen by many as the quintessential right of citizenship. Others claim that aliens are unable to vote intelligently in elections because of unfamiliarity with U.S. institutions and values. Still others argue that aliens may be incapable of voting responsibly because they lack loyalty, due to strong ties with their native country.

Although aliens are a protected class in the eyes of the Supreme Court, it is unlikely that the Court would acknowledge a right to vote. But as a suspect class, aliens are provided some degree of protection in the courts without being held to the political responsibilities which accompany participation in the political processes.

§ 13–4.2 Capacity to Use the Courts

The Supreme Court held, in *Ex parte Kawato* (Sup.Ct. 1942), that lawful resident aliens have a full capacity to sue and be sued in state courts. This principle does not apply to nonresident aliens, who will usually be allowed to bring suit in state courts only where it is necessary to avoid injustice or to serve the interests of international comity.

Any alien may bring suit in federal court if the alien can claim federal question jurisdiction. This jurisdiction specifically covers cases where the alien's constitutional, treaty, or federal statutory rights have been violated. The Second Circuit in *Filartiga v. Peña–Irala* (2d Cir.1980), permitted the Paraguayan relatives of a Paraguayan youth who had been tortured to death in Paraguay by a police officer acting under the authority of the Paraguayan government to maintain an action in federal district court against the Paraguayan police officer, who was visiting the United States. Torture was held to violate the law of nations, which is part of the law of the land. 28 U.S.C.A. § 1350. The Court of Appeals did not, however, decide the difficult issues related to choice of laws to be applied and as to the doctrine of *forum non conveniens*. The trial court on remand applied Paraguayan law and awarded damages. *Filartiga v. Peña–Irala* (E.D.N.Y.1984).

In *Tel–Oren v. Libyan Arab Republic* (D.C.Cir.1984), however, the D.C. Circuit Court dismissed for lack of subject matter jurisdiction an action brought by Israeli citizens who were survivors and representatives of persons murdered in a terrorist attack on a civilian bus in Israel. The Israeli citizens sought compensatory and punitive damages from the Libyan Arab Republic, the Palestine Liberation Organization, and various other organizations for tortious acts in violation of the law of nations, treaties and criminal law of the United States, and the common law. The plaintiffs asserted that, as in *Filartiga*, the district court had power to hear their claim under the Alien Tort Claims Act, 28 U.S.C.A. § 1350, which provides that "[t]he district courts shall have original jurisdiction of any civil action by an alien for a tort only, committed in violation of the law of nations or a treaty of the United States."

The D.C. Circuit Court affirmed per curiam the district court's ruling that it lacked jurisdiction over the claim. The judges could not agree on a single opinion, but unanimously concurred that the case should not be heard in the U.S. federal courts. Judge Edwards indicated that he agreed with the Second Circuit's decision in *Filartiga*, but distinguished *Filartiga* by noting that the terrorist organizations did not qualify as governments and that there existed no international customary law prohibiting the terrorist acts alleged in the suit. Judge Bork disagreed with the interpretation of § 1350 adopted in *Filartiga,* theorizing that in order for § 1350 to establish jurisdiction, not only must there be a violation of international law, but international law must expressly create a domestic cause of action in tort. Since it is unclear whether there exists any such international law, Judge Bork's opinion would essentially turn § 1350 into a nullity. Judge Robb's opinion suggested that the court should not take jurisdiction because the case raised political questions.

The right of an alien to bring suit in federal court based on federal question jurisdiction was also limited in *Sanchez–Espinoza v. Reagan* (D.C.Cir.1985). Nicaraguan citizens sought damages from the President of the United States and other federal defendants for tortious injuries caused by the U.S.-backed contra forces. The court found that no treaty made it unlawful for executive officials, in their private capacity, to support forces bearing arms against the government of Nicaragua, and absent a waiver of sovereign immunity, such officials were immune in their official capacity from actions for monetary damages. The court held that the Alien Tort Claims Act, 28 U.S.C.A. § 1350, is not a waiver of sovereign immunity, but "may conceivably have been meant to cover only private, nongovernmental acts that are contrary to treaty or the law of nations—the most prominent examples being privacy and assaults upon ambassadors." The Court also held that it would be an abuse of discretion to award discretionary, nonmonetary relief because the support for military operations was approved by the President, the Secretary of State, the Secretary of Defense, and the Director of the CIA, and involved the conduct of diplomatic relations with at least four foreign states. Furthermore, the court found that "[t]he danger of foreign citizens using the courts in situations such as this to obstruct the foreign policy of our government is sufficiently acute that we must leave to Congress the judgment whether a damage remedy should exist."

An alien may be able to claim jurisdiction in a suit against a foreign state under the Foreign Sovereign Immunities Act, 28 U.S.C.A. § 1330(a). In *Verlinden B.V. v. Central Bank of Nigeria* (Sup.Ct.1983), the Supreme Court held that a nonresident alien could sue a foreign state in a federal district court on any nonjury civil action under the Foreign Sovereign Immunities Act of 1976 (FSIA), 28 U.S.C.A. § 1330(a). In *Verlinden,* a Dutch corporation brought suit against an instrumentality of Nigeria in a U.S. district court, alleging anticipatory breach of a letter of credit. The Court held that, under the FSIA, a foreign sovereign is immune to suits involving the foreign sovereign's public acts, but such immunity does not extend to cases arising out of its strictly commercial acts. If one of the exceptions to sovereign immunity specified under 28 U.S.C.A. §§ 1605–07 or under any applicable international agreement applies, a federal district court may exercise subject-matter jurisdiction under § 1330(a), and the FSIA contains no limitation based on the plaintiff's citizenship.

Any alien also may sue the U.S. in the Court of Claims if U.S. citizens are granted reciprocal rights by the alien's country and subject matter jurisdiction would otherwise exist. 28 U.S.C.A. § 2502.

Aliens may sue or be sued in federal court based on diversity of citizenship, but the Constitution limits such

suits to those between U.S. citizens and subjects of a
foreign state. U.S. Const. Art. III, § 2. Hence, an alien
may not sue another alien based on diversity jurisdiction, even if a U.S. citizen is party to the suit. 28
U.S.C.A. § 1332. An alien may bring suit against a
citizen, however, even if the alien resides in the same
state as the citizen. The alien thus has greater jurisdic-
tional rights in this respect than a similarly situated
citizen would have. *Breedlove v. Nicolet* (Sup.Ct.1833).
Stateless aliens, though, can never meet diversity jurisdiction requirements, because they are not subjects of a
foreign state.

Aliens, who are enemies during times of war, may
also bring suit. Resident enemy aliens have full access
to all courts. *Ex parte Kawato* (Sup.Ct.1942). Nonresident enemy aliens may also bring suit, but are subject to
greater restrictions, especially if the judgment would
hamper the war effort. The court may still deliver
judgment, but the amount of the claim may be withheld
pending termination of hostilities.

§ 13–4.3 Education

An alien's right to education depends both on the
status of the alien in the U.S. and on the level of
education sought. In general, an alien must apply for
nonimmigrant visa status in order to study in the United States. The F visa for academic students, the J visa
for exchange students, and the M visa for vocational
students are discussed above in the Nonimmigrant Visa
chapter six. See also chapter 7 (academic student visas), *supra*. Nevertheless, the Supreme Court has rendered decisions delineating the limits of a state's power
in relation to aliens and education.

The first of these decisions, *Plyler v. Doe* (Sup.Ct. 1982), considered the right of undocumented or illegal alien children to receive elementary education. The Court noted that undocumented aliens do not constitute a "suspect class," so that any statute on this subject would not be subject to "strict scrutiny." The Court then described the unique and lifelong effect that elementary education has on a person. The Court feared that denying these children an education might create a nearly permanent underclass of illegal aliens who probably would remain in the U.S. for the rest of their lives. Furthermore, any statute which discriminated against the illegal alien children would punish them for the acts of their parents, since the children had no choice in coming to the U.S. Accordingly, the Court held that any state statute which created special burdens for undocumented alien children to receive an elementary education would be voided unless it could be shown that the statute furthered some substantial state interest. No such interest was found in the *Plyler* case.

The second decision of the Supreme Court on aliens and education was *Toll v. Moreno* (1982). This case concerned the right of the children of aliens who are international organization employees (G–4 nonimmigrants) domiciled in a state to pay the lower in-state tuition rate at the state university. The Court noted that G–4 nonimmigrants were a special group of aliens to which Congress had granted the right of acquiring domicile in the U.S. If the state then required the children of a domiciled G–4 nonimmigrant to pay a higher out-of-state tuition, the state would be creating a burden on them not contemplated by Congress. The Court held that the imposition of such a burden would be impermissible, since it would frustrate the federal policy. Although the case only dealt with G–4 nonimmigrants, presumably other classes of nonimmigrants would also be covered by this decision if they, too, were not required to maintain their domicile outside the U.S. Hence, the reasoning of *Toll* might extend to the children of holders of other nonimmigrant visas.

§ 13–4.4 Eligibility for Federal Benefit Programs

An alien's eligibility for federal benefit programs is largely determined by the alien's status in the United States. This status will generally fall into one of four classifications: permanent resident alien, alien permanently residing under color of law, nonimmigrant alien, and undocumented alien. The classification "permanently residing under color of law" includes refugees and parolees and has been liberally construed to mean any alien permitted to remain in the U.S. indefinitely. *Holley v. Lavine* (2d Cir.1977). The first two classifications are generally eligible for federal benefits, while the last two are not. Each benefit program must be examined to determine which aliens are eligible.

The largest group of federal benefits are authorized under the Social Security Act. Old Age, Survivors and Disability Insurance (OASDI) is available to holders of social security numbers. In order to obtain a social security number for work purposes, a person must be a citizen, permanent resident alien, or an alien who, under authority of law, is permitted to work in the United States. 20 C.F.R. § 422.104. Where the alien already holds a security number, regardless of the alien's status, the alien will be eligible to receive OASDI, assuming other qualifications are met. This coverage can be suspended, however, regardless of the alien's status, if

the alien leaves the U.S. for more than six months, 42
U.S.C.A. § 402(t). The coverage can also be suspended
if the alien is deported for certain reasons. 42 U.S.C.A.
§ 402(n). This suspension is not a violation of Due
Process. *Flemming v. Nestor* (Sup.Ct.1960). These conditions for OASDI also apply to hospital insurance benefits. 42 U.S.C.A. § 426. For the uninsured alien, Medicare is available, but this coverage is restricted to permanent resident aliens who have resided in the U.S. for
five or more years. 42 C.F.R. § 405.205. The Supreme
Court unanimously upheld this restriction as within the
authority of Congress in *Mathews v. Diaz* (Sup.Ct.1976).

Aliens also may qualify for a variety of public assistance programs. These include Aid For Dependent Children (AFDC), General Assistance, Food Stamps, Supplemental Security Income (SSI), Medicaid, and Refugee
Assistance. The states administer AFDC under plans
which, when approved, receive federal funding. These
plans must include permanent resident aliens and
aliens residing under color of law to meet federal regulations. 42 C.F.R. § 233.50. General Assistance is also
a state program, which has no federal requirements, but
which cannot discriminate between citizens and permanent resident aliens. *Graham v. Richardson* (Sup.Ct.
1971).

Food Stamps (7 C.F.R. § 273.4), SSI (20 C.F.R. § 416.-
202(b)), and Medicaid (42 C.F.R. §§ 435.402, 436.402) are
all federal programs, and so are not restricted by *Graham v. Richardson*, as discussed in *Mathews v. Diaz*.
Nonetheless, these programs are all available to permanent resident aliens and aliens residing under color of
law. Congress has, however, established greater restrictions, so these eligibility requirements for aliens must

be checked regularly. Specifically, SSI benefits are now restricted during the first three years because the income of the alien's sponsor is attributed to the alien. 42 U.S.C.A. § 1382(j). The same is true with regard to AFDC benefits for aliens applying after September 1981. 45 C.F.R. § 233.51. There is also a danger in this area for the alien who actually receives benefits. If the alien leaves the U.S. and then tries to re-enter, the INS may exclude the alien as one likely to become a public charge, based on the alien's previous welfare history. There also may be an adverse effect if the alien applies for an adjustment of status to permanent resident. Finally, in the extreme, an alien who becomes a public charge within five years after entry may be deported, unless the causes arise after entry. INA § 241(a)(8).

Temporary resident aliens who receive benefits for which they are not qualified, either through agency inadvertence or "grandfathering," will not necessarily be denied permanent residency. The INS applies two tests to determine whether an alien legalized under IRCA is excludable as "likely to become a public charge." 8 C.F.R. § 245a.3(g)(4). The first test examines the alien's current earnings, job history, skills, education, and past receipt of welfare. The second test, deemed the "special rule," considers only whether the alien has maintained a consistent job history without receiving public cash assistance. Often, however, only AFDC is considered a "cash assistance" program; hence, an alien with a consistent job history can receive other forms of assistance without fear that permanent residency will later be denied.

Formerly undocumented aliens who were legalized under the Immigration Reform and Control Act of 1986 are disqualified for a period of five years after the date of legalization from receiving "programs of financial assistance furnished under Federal law ... as such programs are identified by the Attorney General," including AFDC, SSI, Medicaid, and Food Stamp benefits. INA § 245A(h)(2). This five year waiting period does not apply to Cuban and Haitian aliens, and except for AFDC benefits, to the aged, blind, or disabled. INA § 245A(h)(2).

The purpose of these restrictions was to minimize the financial burden that newly legalized aliens might place on U.S. taxpayers by ensuring that the legalized aliens would not draw on welfare or other cash-based subsistence programs. It is unclear whether the provision of IRCA that made aliens ineligible for "public welfare assistance" for a five-year period excludes aliens from receiving public legal services. One court held that Congress did not intend legal services to be considered as a "program of financial assistance." *California Rural Legal Assistance, Inc. v. Legal Services Corporation* (N.D.Cal.1989). This decision is consistent with the congressional hope that the amnesty program would bring illegal aliens out of the shadows of society, so they could assert their legal rights.

Refugee aliens, as defined by INA § 207(c)(2), may qualify for Refugee Assistance, a program through which the federal government makes grants to, and contracts with, public or private nonprofit agencies for initial resettlement of refugees in the United States. INA § 412. The goals of the program are to (i) make available sufficient resources for employment training and placement in order to achieve economic self-sufficiency among refugees as quickly as possible, (ii) provide refugees with the opportunity to acquire sufficient English language training to enable them to be resettled effectively as quickly as possible, (iii) insure that cash assistance is made available to refugees in such a manner as not to discourage their economic self-sufficiency, and (iv) insure that women have the same opportunity as men to participate in training and instruction. INA § 412(a)(1)(A). Through the Refugee Medical Assistance program, refugees who do not qualify for Medicaid may receive free health care.

Aliens may also receive unemployment compensation based on state law. The Secretary of Labor must approve these laws, but under the Unemployment Compensation Amendments of 1976, the Secretary must approve any state law that limits the availability of benefits to permanent resident aliens or those residing under color of law, if the state law also meets the other requirements of 26 U.S.C.A. § 3304(a). 26 U.S.C.A. § 3304(a)(14)(A). States failing to adopt these amendments are denied certification. Similarly, very few state workers' compensation laws contain alien restrictions on eligibility, and thus, even undocumented aliens are generally eligible for workers' compensation and disability benefits.

Aliens also may find limitations in a number of lesser used programs. These programs include loans for farm purchases (7 C.F.R. § 1822), housing financial assistance (42 U.S.C.A. § 1436a), student financial aid, or student eligibility for state resident tuition. *See Nyquist v. Mauclet* (Sup.Ct.1977). These programs are usually limited to permanent resident aliens, but other restrictions may exist, and they may change from time to time.

§ 13–4.5 Freedom of Speech

The Supreme Court decided in *Schneider v. New Jersey* (Sup.Ct.1939) that aliens present in the U.S. are entitled to the same right of freedom of speech as any citizen. Nonetheless, any alien may be deported if s/he has engaged at any time since entry in terrorism or in any activity a purpose of which is the overthrow of the U.S. government by force or other unconstitutional means. INA § 241(a)(4). An alien's statements could also be used to attack the alien's good moral character or attachment to the principles of the Constitution, which are both required for naturalization. INA § 313.

One federal court declared portions of § 241 unconstitutional on their face as being "substantially overbroad," but the U.S. Court of Appeals reversed for lack of standing and ripeness. *American–Arab Anti–Discrimination Committee v. Thornburgh* (9th Cir.1991). These provisions stated that nonresident aliens should be deported if they advocate the doctrines of world communism; advocate unlawful damage of property; write, publish, etc., material advocating world communism or the establishment of totalitarian dictatorship in the United States; and if they affiliate with any organization that writes, circulates, etc., material advocating world communism or establishment of a totalitarian dictatorship in the U.S. The court reasoned that the provisions are applicable to both constitutionally permissible and impermissible activities. The statutes prohibit a range of conduct, including the teaching of organizational viewpoints, advocacy of imminent lawless violence, and even an alien's wearing of an organization's button. The court noted that resident aliens have First Amendment rights generally and these rights cannot be infringed despite the plenary power of Congress over immigration matters. The 1990 Act modified § 241 considerably, restricting its application in this respect to an alien's activities after entry and removing the offending provisions.

An unadmitted nonresident alien has no right of free speech. The Supreme Court stated in *Kleindienst v. Mandel* (Sup.Ct.1972), that aliens could be excluded for views held or opinions expressed because aliens have no constitutional right of entry to the U.S. Additionally, the Court held that U.S. citizens have no right to have aliens enter the country so that ideas may be exchanged. The plenary power of Congress to control admission of aliens overrides a citizen's right to receive information under the First Amendment.

§ 13–4.6 Right to Own Land

Land ownership laws in the United States originally developed from English land laws. England prohibited aliens from owning land because all land grants required an oath of loyalty to the King; that oath conflicted with the alien's allegiance to another sovereign. This prohibition, however, inhibited territorial expansion and was even a subject of complaint in the Declaration of Independence. Yet, after the U.S. gained independence, the common law restrictions against alien ownership remained intact; states relaxed them slowly over the next century as the needs of territorial growth and foreign investment dictated. By the end of the 1800's, however, when unlimited territorial expansion was no longer possible, both state and federal legislatures began re-establishing restrictions on alien landholding. Many of the federal enactments from this era are still in effect, although few of the state restrictions are.

Alien land ownership law is primarily a state concern, and there are only three principal areas of federal restriction. First, the federal government has been concerned in time of war when enemy aliens hold land; second, the federal government is concerned with safeguarding of natural resources for citizens or permanent residents; third, the federal government has an interest in seeing that foreigners are treated equitably and in a manner consistent with national policies regarding immigration and foreign affairs.

As to the *first* area of federal concern, the Trading with the Enemy Act, 50 U.S.C.A.App. § 1, empowers the government to control land transactions during times of *declared* war. The Foreign Assets Control Regulations limit land transactions for aliens of certain listed countries, such as Cuba and the Democratic People's Republic of Korea at present. The International Emergency Economic Powers Act, 50 U.S.C.A. § 1701, grants the President broad authority to control alien property during a time of declared national emergency. President Carter used this authority during the Iranian hostage crisis to freeze all Iranian assets, including land. Similarly, President Bush froze Iraqi and Kuwaiti assets in 1991 after Iraq invaded Kuwait.

Second, federal laws restrict alien exploitation of agricultural, grazing, mineral, or timber land. Foreigners are required to notify the Department of Agriculture if they own agricultural land. 7 U.S.C.A. § 3501. The Taylor Grazing Act, 43 U.S.C.A. § 315, restricts grazing rights on public lands to citizens or immigrants who have applied for citizenship. The Mining Law of 1882 and the Mineral Lands Leasing Act of 1920 (41 Stat. 437) create restrictions on alien ownership of mineral rights, including petroleum. 30 U.S.C.A. § 181. More recent laws restrict alien development of off-shore oil deposits and geothermal resources. Finally, the Forest Service places some restrictions on standing timber sales to aliens, using a national preference system.

The *third* area of federal concern is founded upon constitutional protections and treaty rights. The Equal Protection Clause of the Fourteenth Amendment invalidates state laws which forbid resident aliens from owning land. Furthermore, in *Zschernig v. Miller* (Sup.Ct. 1968), the Supreme Court relied on the constitutional grant of the foreign affairs power to the federal government to invalidate state laws which restrict inheritance by nationals of totalitarian countries. The reasoning of this decision conceivably could be used to void any state restriction on alien investment as an infringement on the federal foreign affairs power. Finally, if the federal government has granted another nation's citizens land ownership rights by treaty, the state cannot abridge these rights, since treaties are part of the "supreme law of the land."

In state law, there is a wide diversity of statutes which control alien land ownership. All states permit resident aliens who have applied for citizenship to purchase and inherit land, but the uniformity ends there. A few states prohibit nonresident alien ownership; a few others limit the duration of land ownership; and some place acreage limits on ownership in order to inhibit aliens from owning agricultural land. Some states have restricted ownership by "enemies" in times of war. Other states limit land ownership to those who are eligible for citizenship. Minor restrictions abound: For example, South Carolina restricts ownership to ½ million acres; other states will not sell state-owned property or mineral rights to aliens. States generally do not restrict inheritance of land by aliens, except that some states insist upon reciprocity by the foreign country, permitting inheritance by U.S. citizens and receipt of the land by the heir. A few states require that the land inherited by an alien be sold within a statutory period after inheritance. About a dozen states also place restrictions on alien corporate landholding.

In general, the practitioner must examine the laws of each state with regard to both the type of land transaction and the identity of the alien individual or corporation involved. These laws must also be examined for constitutionality, because alien land ownership or usage is still an unsettled area of law.

§ 13–4.7 Military Service

The United States currently has a Selective Service registration requirement, 50 U.S.C.A.App. § 453, even though there is no longer any military draft, 50 U.S.C.A.App. § 467. This registration requirement applies to all male persons between the ages of 18 and 26 who reside in the U.S. except for lawfully admitted nonimmigrant aliens (50 U.S.C.A.App. § 453), and aliens who have resided in the U.S. less than one year, 50 U.S.C.A.App. § 455(a)(1)(3). The U.S. also has treaties with a number of other countries granting exemption from military service on a reciprocal basis. A resident alien from one of these countries may apply for a classification of exemption from the Selective Service. 32 C.F.R. § 1630.42. If the alien is granted the exemption based on alienage, however, the alien is barred from becoming a citizen, unless the alien is covered by a treaty. INA § 315. Any alien permanently ineligible for citizenship is excludable from entry into the U.S. except as a nonimmigrant. INA § 212(a)(22). Therefore, a permanent resident alien who obtains an exemption from military service and then leaves the U.S. may be excluded from re-entering. An alien in this category may apply to the Attorney General for an authorization for admission, but such authorizations are discretionary. INA § 212(c). Aliens who have departed the U.S. in order to avoid military service are also excluded from re-entry and may only apply to the Attorney General for discretionary admission.

An alien who does enter the military service will receive the benefit of reduced residency requirements when applying for naturalization. INA § 328(a). If the service is during a time of hostilities, additional benefits are granted, including waiver of any age and residency requirement. INA § 329(b). Aliens in the military are ineligible to become commissioned officers and if the alien deserts the service, s/he is permanently barred from naturalization. INA § 314.

§ 13–4.8 Taxation of Aliens

The liability of an alien in the United States to pay taxes will depend on the alien's status as a resident or a nonresident. This status for tax purposes is determined by the Internal Revenue Code (26 U.S.C.A. § 1 *et seq.*) and not by the Immigration and Naturalization Act. Under 26 U.S.C.A. § 7701(b)(1)(A), an alien is treated as a U.S. resident with respect to any calendar year if s/he is either a lawful permanent resident at any time during that year or s/he meets a "substantial presence" test. With certain exceptions, an alien meets the substantial presence test if s/he is present in the U.S. on at least 31 days during the current year, and on at least 183 days within the last three years, with each day present in the current year counting as a full day, each day in the first preceding year as one-third of a day, and each day in the second preceding year as one-sixth of a day. Qualified aliens may also make a special election to be taxed as U.S. residents. 26 U.S.C.A. § 7701(b)(1)(A).

A resident alien is generally taxed in the same way as a U.S. citizen. A resident is thus taxed on income derived from all sources, including sources outside the U.S., and this income is subject to the graduated tax rates that apply to U.S. citizens. An individual who was a resident alien for the entire tax year may also claim the same deductions allowed for U.S. citizens. 26 C.F.R. § 1.871–1. Certain tax laws, however, may have a greater impact on resident aliens than on citizens; examples include: (1) a taxpayer may claim as a dependent only a citizen, national, or resident of the United States, a resident of Canada or Mexico, or an alien child adopted by and living with the U.S. citizen or national taxpayer (26 U.S.C.A. § 152(b)(3), 26 C.F.R. § 1.152–2(a)(2)); (2) a qualified individual may elect to exclude from gross income up to $70,000 of income earned in a foreign country and a limited amount based on housing costs paid or incurred as a result of foreign employment (26 U.S.C.A. § 911); and (3) a tax credit or deduction may be taken for certain foreign tax paid (26 U.S.C.A. § 901, 26 C.F.R. §§ 1.901–1, 1.901–2).

The situation of a nonresident alien is considerably more complicated. Any income derived from U.S. sources is taxed at the same graduated rates as for a U.S. citizen, if the income is effectively connected with the alien's trade or business in the United States. 26 U.S.C.A. §§ 871, 872. Other income, not effectively connected with a trade or business in the United States, such as an annuity or the income from the sale of a capital asset, is taxed at either a flat 30% rate, or a lower rate if a separate treaty exists with the alien's country. 26 C.F.R. § 1.871–8.

Nonresident aliens engaged in a trade or business in the United States may be able to exclude certain U.S. income from their effectively connected gross income. Nonresident aliens whose U.S. business is performing personal services in the United States may exclude compensation from a foreign employer, if the nonresident was admitted to the U.S. under INA §§ 101(a)(15)(F), (J), or (M) (as a nonimmigrant student or exchange visitor), income from certain annuities, and income exempt by treaty.

In general, deductions for nonresident aliens are allowed only if they are effectively connected with a trade or business. The following deductions, however, are allowed whether or not the nonresident's income was effectively connected with a U.S. trade or business: (1) deductions for casualty and theft losses on property located within the U.S.; (2) deductions for charitable contributions; and (3) deductions for personal exemptions. 26 U.S.C.A. § 873. Nonresident aliens who receive income effectively connected with their U.S. trade or business may deduct certain itemized deductions, including state and local income taxes, charitable contributions to U.S. organizations, casualty and theft losses on property located in the U.S., moving expenses, and miscellaneous deductions.

Nonresident aliens may also claim credits against U.S. income tax liability for certain taxes paid, including certain foreign tax paid. With limited exceptions, nonresident aliens engaged in a trade or business in the U.S. are allowed only one personal exemption. A fuller discussion, complete with examples, is available in Publication 519, U.S. Tax Guide for Aliens, from the local office of the Internal Revenue Service (IRS). This guide includes an updated list of tax treaties in effect.

In order to ensure that all taxes owed are paid, the departing alien is required to obtain a Certificate of Compliance from the IRS. Also known as a Sailing Permit or Exit Permit, this document shows that either the taxes have been paid or an adequate bond has been posted to cover taxes owed. Diplomats, certain employees of foreign governments and international organizations, aliens present in the U.S. for a short term with no taxable income, commuting residents of Canada or Mexico, and some students or trainees do not have to obtain a Sailing Permit before departing. 26 C.F.R. § 1.6851–2(a)(2).

An alien who has obtained a social security number for work purposes also will pay social security taxes for work performed in the U.S. 26 U.S.C.A. § 3101. The United States has bilateral social security agreements with many foreign countries to coordinate social security coverage and generally to make sure that social security taxes are paid only to one country. Agreements are in effect with Austria, Belgium, Canada, France, Germany, Italy, Netherlands, Norway, Portugal, Spain, Sweden, Switzerland, and the United Kingdom. Under these agreements, aliens are generally subject to social security tax only in the country where they are working.

Resident aliens, like U.S. citizens, are subject to gift tax no matter where the gift property is situated and whether it is tangible or intangible property. 26 U.S.C.A. § 2501(a), 26 C.F.R. § 25.2501–1(a). Nonresident aliens are generally liable for gift tax only with respect to gifts of real property or tangible personal property situated in the U.S. when the alien made the gift. 26 U.S.C.A. §§ 2501(a), 2511(a). A marital deduction is not allowed for gifts made to a spouse who is not a U.S. citizen. 26 U.S.C.A. § 2523(i). The law, however, raises the tax exclusion to the first $100,000 of the value of the gift from the previous $10,000. Federal estate taxes are also applied to aliens and citizens on a similar basis, with a separate rate table for nonresidents. 26 U.S.C.A. § 2101. A marital deduction, however, is not allowed for bequests made to a surviving spouse who is not a U.S. citizen. 26 U.S.C.A. § 2056(d). In addition, aliens normally will be required to pay state taxes; states vary in their taxation of citizens and aliens, but ordinarily citizen and alien taxpayers are treated alike.

CHAPTER 14

CRIMINAL ASPECTS OF IMMIGRATION

§ 14–1 INTRODUCTION

In addition to the harsh penalties of deportation and exclusion, aliens may incur actual criminal penalties for misconduct related to immigration. Criminal sanctions for aliens are found under both the Immigration and Nationality Act and portions of the U.S. Criminal Code. This chapter describes immigration-related conduct which may result in criminal penalties for aliens and citizens, including unlawful entry, bringing aliens into the U.S. without inspection, transporting or concealing an alien who entered unlawfully, encouraging an alien to enter unlawfully, misrepresentation or fraud in obtaining immigration status, failure to comply with deportation regulations, and unlawful employment of aliens. The chapter also discusses the immigration consequences of an alien's criminal activity, including exclusion, deportation, and denial of asylum.

§ 14–2 CRIMINAL PROVISIONS RELATED TO IMMIGRATION

§ 14–2.1 Unlawful Entry

a. Entry of Alien at Improper Time or Place; Avoidance of Examination or Inspection; Misrepresentation and Concealment of Facts

Unlawful entry into the United States became a criminal offense in 1929. 45 Stat. 1551. Today, INA § 275 penalizes all aliens who enter or attempt to enter this country improperly—at any time or place other than as designated by immigration officials—by eluding examination or inspection or by a willfully false or misleading representation or the willful concealment of a material fact. An alien who enters the country unlawfully can be fined not more than $2,000 (or the amount provided under 18 U.S.C.A.) or imprisoned not more than 6 months, or both, for a first offense in violation of § 275. For a subsequent conviction the prison sentence increases to a maximum of two years. Note that in order for a felony sentence to be imposed under INA § 275, the alien must have previously been convicted of the offense. Mere proof that the alien entered the country unlawfully is insufficient. *United States v. Arambula–Alvarado* (9th Cir.1982). This fact is significant because prosecution under the misdemeanor provision of § 275 is not a high priority for prosecutors and is therefore fairly unusual. Prosecution is more often used as a threat by INS officers to get aliens to accept prompt deportation. In addition, the 1990 Act proscribes an individual from establishing a commercial enterprise for the purpose of evading immigration law. If convicted, such a person is subject to a fine in accordance with 18

U.S.C.A., a prison term of not more than five years, or both.

This statute does not reach attempted entries. *United States v. Oscar* (9th Cir.1974). In *Oscar,* the aliens had crossed the border into the United States but were held not guilty of an "entry" under § 275 because they were never free of official restraint by customs officials. *United States v. Martin–Plascencia* (9th Cir.1976) distinguished *Oscar* in holding that an alien only 50 yards into the United States, within the confines of a port of entry, was guilty of illegal entry on the ground that he was under no official restraint until the time of his arrest.

b. Re-entry of Deported Alien

Under INA § 276, an alien who has been deported and who re-enters or attempts to re-enter the United States without permission of the Attorney General is guilty of a felony. The penalty for this felony is imprisonment up to two years, a fine under 18 U.S.C.A., or both.

Theoretically, when an alien re-enters the United States after deportation without permission, s/he is subject to criminal penalties under both § 275 and § 276. In *United States v. Ortiz–Martinez* (9th Cir. 1977), however, the Ninth Circuit Court of Appeals held that since one single act of reentering is involved, a person convicted of violating both statutes cannot be subjected to consecutive terms of imprisonment.

Specific intent to reenter the country illegally is not required for a conviction under § 276. Hence, the government need not prove that the alien knew s/he was not entitled to reenter the United States without permission of the Attorney General. *Pena–Cabanillas v. United States* (9th Cir.1968); *United States v. Hernandez* (10th Cir.1982). In *United States v. Anton* (7th Cir.1982), however, the Seventh Circuit Court of Appeals held that an alien's reasonable belief that he had the consent of the Attorney General to re-enter the country constitutes a viable mistake-of-law defense to a § 276 charge.

An alien prosecuted for unlawful entry after deportation may be able to challenge collaterally the validity of the underlying deportation order. In *United States v. Mendoza–Lopez* (Sup.Ct.1987), the Supreme Court held that although the language of § 276 does not require the deportation to have been lawful and there is no evidence that Congress intended to permit a challenge to the validity of the prior deportation order, "[i]f the statute envisions that a court may impose a criminal penalty for reentry after *any* deportation, regardless of how violative of the rights of the alien the deportation proceedings may have been, such a statute does not comport with the constitutional requirement of due process." The Court further held that where the deportation proceeding effectively eliminates the right of the alien to obtain judicial review, that review must be made available in any subsequent proceeding in which the result of the deportation proceeding is used to establish an element of a criminal offense.

Since the exclusion provisions of INA §§ 212(a)(6)(A) and (B) provide that an alien who has been excluded and deported is barred from admission for one year, an alien who has been arrested and deported for five years, and an alien convicted of an aggravated felony for 20 years, one might conclude that an alien is not punishable under § 276 for an unlawful entry committed after the applicable time period has passed. In *United States v. Bernal–Gallegos* (5th Cir.1984), however, an alien was convicted under § 276 for an unlawful entry committed more than five years after deportation.

An alien may argue before the Court of Appeals that he was compelled to incriminate himself, even if that argument was not made before the immigration judge. *Navia–Duran v. INS* (1st Cir.1977). If INS agents arrest an alien without a warrant, they must comply with regulations requiring that the alien be advised of certain rights. *Id.* Moreover, an alien in INS custody must be advised of her/his rights under *Miranda v. Arizona* (Sup.Ct.1966). The 1990 Act provides that an officer or employee of the INS may arrest an alien without a warrant, if that officer or employee has reasonable grounds to believe the individual has committed or is committing a felony. Again, failure to give *Miranda* warnings may invalidate any confessions obtained during the custodial interrogations of the alien.

c. *Deportation Consequences of Unlawful Entry*

In addition to the criminal penalties imposed by INA §§ 1325 and 275 and 276, an alien who enters or re-enters the United States unlawfully may also be subject to deportation. INA § 241(a)(1)(B) provides that an alien shall be deported if s/he "entered into the United States without inspection or at any time or place other than as designated by the Attorney General or is in the United States in violation of this chapter or in violation of any other law of the United States." The alien's guilty plea to a § 275 or § 276 charge will establish the alien's unlawful entry or re-entry for purposes of deportation proceedings under § 241(a)(2). *See, e.g., Marro-*

quin–Manriquez v. INS (3d Cir.1983). The Fifth Circuit Court of Appeals in *Garcia–Trigo v. United States* (5th Cir.1982) held that the alien need not be informed of the collateral immigration consequences of her/his conviction under § 275.

Although deportation, rather than criminal penalties, is more often enforced in cases of unlawful entry, an alien held deportable under § 241(a)(1)(B) may still be subject to criminal prosecution. During the deportation proceeding, once the INS has established that the respondent is an alien, the alien has the burden of proof to show the time, place, and manner of her/his entry into the United States. If this burden is not sustained, the alien will be presumed to be in the U.S. in violation of law and thereby subject to criminal prosecution. INA § 291. Generally, since a deportation hearing is not a criminal proceeding, there is no presumption of innocence, and therefore, no abridgement of the alien's Fifth Amendment rights in requiring the alien to demonstrate the time, place, and manner of her/his entry into the United States. *Chavez–Raya v. INS* (7th Cir.1975); *Cabral–Avila v. INS* (9th Cir.1978).

Because of potential criminal liability for unlawful entry under § 275 or § 276, however, the right to remain silent is available in deportation proceedings under § 241(a)(1)(B). In *Cabral–Avila* the Ninth Circuit Court of Appeals held that the alien's decision to remain silent during deportation proceedings is an appropriate exercise of the alien's Fifth Amendment privilege, but by doing so, the alien is not shielded from the inference that s/he is not legally in the country, and the alien's silence cannot be relied upon to carry forward her/his duty to rebut the government's prima facie case.

§ 14–2.2   Crimes Related to Facilitating An Alien's Unlawful Entry or Continued Unlawful Presence in the United States

a.   *Bringing in an Alien*

The INA contains two sections which impose criminal penalties upon persons who unlawfully bring aliens into the U.S. The first, INA § 274(a)(1)(A), applies to any person who brings or attempts to bring an alien into the country without inspection, even if the alien had received prior official authorization to enter or reside in the United States. The penalties imposed for this violation include a fine, imprisonment up to five years, or both, for each alien in respect to whom the violation occurred. The second section, INA § 274(a)(2), applies to any person who, knowing or in reckless disregard of the fact that an alien has not received prior official authorization to enter or reside in the United States, brings or attempts to bring that alien into the country, although not necessarily without inspection. The penalties under this section include a fine, imprisonment up to one year, or both, for each transaction constituting a violation of this section, regardless of the number of aliens involved. The fine is increased and the possible prison sentence lengthened to five years, however, in the case of a second or subsequent offense, an offense done for the purpose of commercial advantage or private financial gain, or an offense in which, upon arrival, the alien is not immediately presented to an appropriate immigration officer at a designated port of entry.

Under either section, the penalty is imposed regardless of any further official action which may be taken with respect to the alien, and no consideration is given to the manner in which the offender brought or attempted to bring the alien into the United States. While §§ 274(a)(1)(A) and (a)(2) apply to attempts, there is no violation of the statute unless the alien is brought within the territorial jurisdiction of the United States. For example, in *Yenkichi Ito v. United States* (9th Cir.1933), a ship carrying Japanese citizens was seized approximately forty miles off the California coast. The Court of Appeals held that for the purpose of jurisdiction over offenses, the territorial domain of the United States extends three miles from its shores, and thus, the statute is inapplicable to an attempt committed outside the three-mile boundary. Defendants in such a case, however, may still be subject to prosecution on charges of conspiracy to unlawfully bring an alien into the United States. (See § 14-2.4, *infra.*)

It is interesting to note that the 1986 amendments to INA § 274(a)(1)(A) were expressly intended to correct "shortcomings and ambiguities" identified in *United States v. Anaya* (S.D.Fla.1980) and *United States v. Zayas–Morales* (11th Cir.1982). In those cases, the defendants had made no effort to land undocumented Cubans surreptitiously or evasively, but instead brought them directly into immigration officers in Key West, Florida, to apply for asylum. In House Report No. 99–682(1) to the Immigration Reform and Control Act of 1986, this perceived "gap" in the law was intentionally closed. Hence, an individual may be charged and convicted under INA § 274(a)(1)(A) even if s/he is merely bringing an undocumented alien to the border for purposes of applying for asylum.

Problems may arise in a criminal prosecution under § 274(a)(1)(A) or (a)(2) if, prior to trial, the government deports the alien witnesses who allegedly were brought into the U.S. unlawfully. The defendant may claim that her/his Sixth Amendment right to compulsory process has been violated by the deportation of these witnesses. In *United States v. Valenzuela–Bernal* (Sup. Ct.1982), the Supreme Court held that in order to show a denial of Due Process through the deportation of alien witnesses, the defendant must show that the testimony of the deported witnesses would have been material and favorable to her/his defense in ways not merely cumulative to the testimony of available witnesses.

b. Transporting an Alien Within the United States

INA § 274(a)(1)(B) imposes a criminal penalty on any person who "knowing or in reckless disregard of the fact that an alien has come to, entered, or remains in the United States in violation of law, transports, or moves or attempts to transport or move such alien within the United States by means of transportation or otherwise, in furtherance of such violation of law." To support a conviction for this offense, the government must prove that (1) the defendant transported or attempted to transport an alien within the United States; (2) the alien was in the United States in violation of the law; (3) the defendant knew the alien was in the United States in violation of the law or acted in reckless disregard of this fact; and (4) the defendant acted willfully in furtherance of the alien's violation of the law. The 1986 amendment to this section eliminated an earlier requirement that the defendant know or have reasonable grounds to believe that the alien's last entry into the United States occurred less than three years before. The penalties imposed under this section include a fine, imprisonment up to five years, or both, for each alien in respect to whom the violation occurred.

The mere transportation of a person known to be an alien unlawfully in the country is not a violation of this provision. The transportation must be "in furtherance of [the alien's] violation of law." The statute does not delineate the specific circumstances under which transportation of an alien will constitute transportation "in furtherance of such violation of law." In *United States v. Moreno* (9th Cir.1977), the Ninth Circuit Court of Appeals held that "there must be a direct or substantial relationship between [the] transportation and its furtherance of the alien's presence in the United States." If the act of transporting the alien is "only incidentally connected to the furtherance of the violation of law" it is "too attenuated to come within the boundaries of § 274(a)(1)(B)." *Moreno* involved the transportation of undocumented aliens by a foreman of a reforestation company who was required to transport employees from one job site to another. The court concluded that "his transportation of aliens was only incidentally connected with the furtherance of the violation of the law, if at all," and noted that the foreman's employer was not charged with any offense.

The Fifth Circuit Court of Appeals held, in *United States v. Merkt* (5th Cir.1985), that by definition, a person intending to assist an alien in obtaining legal status, such as by transporting the alien to an INS office, is not acting in furtherance of the alien's illegal presence in the U.S. within the meaning of § 274(a)(1)(B). In *United States v. Shaddix* (1982), however, the Fifth Circuit held that the fact that the alien's ultimate purpose in being transported within the United States was a lawful one, *i.e.* to find work, does not provide a defense to one whose guilt has been established under the elements of the statutory provision.

Although the defendant employer in this case was not implicated in the aliens' illegal entry into the country, his offer of employment and voluntary transportation of the aliens to the place of employment were held to have furthered the aliens' illegal presence in this country sufficiently to constitute a violation of § 274(a)(1)(B). Similarly, in *United States v. Pereira–Pineda* (5th Cir. 1983) and in *United States v. Aguilar* (9th Cir.1989) the courts of appeal held that the possibility that aliens might apply for asylum, allowing them to remain at liberty while their rights were determined, did not mean that the aliens resided lawfully in the United States before applying for asylum. In *Aguilar* the court sustained the conviction of several individuals who had helped Arizona churches give sanctuary to Central Americans.

While a mistake of fact may constitute a valid defense to the crime of unlawfully transporting an alien, a mistake of law will not. In *Merkt,* the defendant's belief that the aliens' genuine qualifications for political asylum entitled them to legal status even though they had not yet filed an asylum claim was held to be based on a mistake of law and therefore did not constitute a defense.

c. *Concealing, Harboring, or Shielding an Alien*

Under § 274(a)(1)(C), criminal penalties are imposed upon any person who "knowing or in reckless disregard of the fact that an alien has come to, entered, or remains in the United States in violation of law, conceals, harbors, or shields from detection or attempts to conceal, harbor, or shield from detection, such alien in any place, including any buildings or any means of transportation." A violation will subject the defendant to a fine, imprisonment up to five years, or both, for each alien in respect to whom the violation occurred.

Because this section is aimed at preventing undocumented aliens from remaining in the United States, as well as preventing them from entering, the harboring need not be directly connected with the alien's illegal entry to be prohibited. The activity need only substantially facilitate the alien's continued unlawful presence in the U.S. *United States v. Lopez* (2d Cir.1975); *United States v. Cantu* (5th Cir.1977).

Persons who warn aliens of the presence of immigration officers have been held to fall within this section. *United States v. Rubio–Gonzalez* (5th Cir.1982). § 274(a) previously had contained a clause providing "[t]hat for the purposes of this section, employment (including the usual and normal practices incident to employment) shall not be deemed to constitute harboring." This exception was eliminated by the 1986 amendment to § 274(a).

d. Inducing an Alien to Enter

Under § 274(a)(1)(D), it is a crime to "encourage or induce an alien to come to, enter, or reside in the United States, knowing or in reckless disregard of the fact that such coming to, entry or residence is or will be in violation of law." Persons convicted of this crime are punishable by a fine, imprisonment up to five years, or both, for each alien in respect to whom the violation occurred.

Unlike the crime of bringing an alien into the United States, it is not necessary for a criminal inducement conviction that the induced alien have entered the country. There need only be, at minimum, a contemplated entry. *United States v. Kavazanjian* (1st Cir. 1980). Defendants in *Kavazanjian* operated a scheme in which they arranged for aliens to enter the country under the travel-without-visa privilege, which permits an alien traveling from one foreign country to another with a stopover in the U.S. to proceed in "immediate and continuous transit" through the country without passport or visa. Once at a U.S. airport, defendants would take or direct the aliens to the INS so that the aliens could apply for parole, a temporary status available to those persons seeking asylum in the United States. The First Circuit overturned the conviction of the defendants under § 274(a)(1)(D) on the ground that the defendants had not encouraged the aliens to "enter" the United States. The court construed "entry" to require freedom from restraint. The court reasoned that aliens entering under the travel-without-visa privilege are in custody of the transportation company until they are paroled and that parole status entails restraint and has been held not to constitute "entry." The offense could not be predicated upon the possibility that the alien might ultimately be granted asylum and thus have "entered" the country, because the possibility of asylum is too speculative.

The defendant in *United States v. Hanna* (5th Cir. 1981) petitioned for a rehearing of his § 274(a)(1)(D) conviction on the basis of *Kavazanjian,* claiming that he also did not violate the statute because his passengers were paroled and thus were under restraint and never "entered the country." The Fifth Circuit Court of Appeals denied the rehearing, holding that parole "is simply a device through which needless confinement is avoided while administrative proceedings are conducted" and that parole "was never intended to affect an alien's status . . . ." The court concluded that "[i]t would be a misuse of the parole concept to conclude that one who physically transports into the United States persons not otherwise entitled to come in cannot be guilty under [§ 274(a)(1)(D)] if the United States grants parole to those brought in while it determines whether they should be given asylum."

The act of inducement or encouragement need not have been committed in the United States. The Ninth Circuit Court of Appeals in *United States v. Castillo–Felix* (9th Cir.1976) reasoned that acts of inducement committed outside the United States may constitute crimes in view of the fact that such acts "have no purpose unless they are intended to facilitate the unlawful entry of an alien or his continued illegal presence in the United States." The effect of such crimes committed outside of the United States takes place in the United States and "in terms of the regulation of immigration, it is unimportant where acts constituting the crime occur."

e. Aiding or Assisting a Subversive Alien to Enter the U.S.

Any person who knowingly aids or assists any criminal or subversive alien excludable under INA § 212(a)(2) (an aggravated felony) or § 212(a)(3) to enter the United States, or who connives or conspires with any person to permit any such alien to enter the United States, can be fined under 18 U.S.C.A., or imprisoned not more than 10 years, or both.

f. Importing an Alien for an Immoral Purpose

Under INA § 278, it is a felony offense to import, directly or indirectly, any alien for the purpose of prostitution or for any other immoral purpose. Attempts to import an alien for such purposes are also covered by the statute. Similarly, it is an offense "to hold any alien for any such purpose in pursuance of such illegal importation" or to "keep, maintain, control, support, employ, or harbor in any house or other place, for the purpose of prostitution or for any other immoral purpose, any alien, in pursuance of such illegal importation." Persons convicted of this offense may be punished by a fine under 18 U.S.C., imprisonment up to ten years, or both.

g. Related Civil Penalties

In addition to the criminal penalties discussed above, several sections of the Immigration and Nationality Act provide civil penalties for certain acts related to bringing in aliens. A fine of $3,000, for example, may be imposed upon any person who improperly brings to the United States an alien (other than an alien crewman) who is excludable under INA § 212(a)(1).

INA § 271 imposes a duty upon "every person, including the owners, masters, officers, and agents of vessels, aircraft, transportation lines or international bridges or toll roads" (Other than transportation lines which have entered into contracts with the Attorney General under INA § 238), bringing an alien to, or providing a means for an alien to come to the United States, to prevent the unauthorized landing of aliens. Violators are subject to a $3,000 fine. An owner or operator of a railroad line, international bridge, or toll road, however, may escape liability by establishing that it acted diligently and reasonably to prevent unauthorized landings, even though such a landing occurred. INA § 271(c)(1). Any owner or operator of a railroad line, international bridge, or toll road may request that the Attorney

General inspect any facility or method used at a point of entry to the United States to comply with this provision. If the Attorney General has approved the facility or method, proof that the individual has diligently maintained the approved facility or used the approved method is prima facie evidence that the individual acted diligently and reasonably to fulfill the duty to prevent unauthorized landings. INA § 271(c).

The Act contains several other provisions which impose civil fines upon carriers. INA § 239 provides a $2000 penalty for failure of an aircraft to land at a designated port of entry or for violating regulations related to such ports of entry. The failure or refusal of a transportation line to receive and deport an excluded alien or to pay deportation expenses, as ordered by the Attorney General, will subject the carrier to a $300 fine under INA § 243(e). A civil penalty also is imposed upon persons, including transportation lines and other vessel operators, who bring in aliens who do not have valid passports and unexpired visas, if a visa is required for such alien, or who fail to detain or deport a stowaway or deportable crewmember. The penalty consists of a $3,000 fine per alien, and in the case of an alien without an unexpired visa who is not admitted or permitted to land temporarily, an additional amount equal to that amount paid by the alien for his transportation from the initial point of departure. This additional amount paid is then returned to the alien. Any amounts paid as a penalty for bringing in an alien without an unexpired visa may be refunded if the Attorney General is convinced that the violator did not know, and could not have ascertained by the exercise of reasonable diligence, that the individual transported was an alien and that a visa was required. INA § 273.

§ 14–2.3 Failure to Comply With Registration Requirements

INA § 262 provides that every alien who remains in the United States for thirty days or more must be registered and fingerprinted. Any alien who "willfully fails or refuses" to register may be fined up to $1,000, imprisoned up to six months, or both. INA § 266(a). Similarly, this provision provides that every alien required to be registered must also give written notice of each change of address and provide other such information as the Attorney General may require. Violators of this provision may be subject to a $200 fine, imprisonment up to thirty days, or both. After registering and being fingerprinted, the alien is issued a certificate of alien registration or an alien registration receipt card. Aliens eighteen years old or older must "at all times carry with him and have in his personal possession" the certificate or card issued to him/her. INA § 264(e). Aliens who fail to comply with this requirement may be subject to a fine of $100, imprisonment up to thirty days, or both.

In actual practice, however, these registration requirements are not generally enforced. The INS has stopped reminding aliens that they ought to notify the INS of their address and effectively has ceased administering the address notification requirement. Although failure to give the written notice of address required by § 265 is a deportable offense under INA § 241(a)(3), Operating Instruction 265.1(a) provides that failure of an alien to comply with the § 265 requirements regarding notification of address "shall not normally serve as the sole basis for initiating prosecution or deportation proceedings." Hence, an alien ordinarily will not be prosecuted under this section unless the alien also is deportable for some other reason. Similarly, Operating Instruction 265.1(b) implies that an alien will not normally be prosecuted solely under § 264(e): "[a]ny alien not in possession of an alien registration card shall be advised of the requirements and sanctions of section 264 of the Act and shall be furnished an application for a replacement or duplicate card."

Any alien who files an application for registration containing statements known by him/her to be false or who registers or attempts to register through fraud is guilty of a misdemeanor. Upon conviction, such person may be fined up to $1,000, imprisoned up to six months, or both. Conviction will also render the alien deportable under INA § 241(a)(3). INA § 266(c). Other statutes dealing with conspiracy to defraud the United States also may penalize fraud or falsification in registration. See § 14–2.4, *infra.* Counterfeiting a certificate of alien registration or an alien registration receipt card is an offense punishable by a fine of up to $5,000, imprisonment up to five years, or both. INA § 266(d). Persons who manufacture and sell counterfeit cards also are punishable under 18 U.S.C.A. § 1426.

§ 14–2.4 Misrepresentation, False Statements, and Fraud

a. Perjury

Several statutes apply to perjury in immigration proceedings. These statutes overlap to some extent, and depending on the situation, a prosecution can be brought under any of them.

The perjury provision of the Immigration and Nationality Act is contained in INA § 287(b). This statute empowers INS vice officers and employees to administer oaths, and provides that:

[A]ny person to whom such oath has been administered (or who has executed an unsworn declaration, certificate, verification, or statement under penalty of perjury ...), ... who shall knowingly or willfully give false evidence or swear ... to any false statement concerning any matter referred to in this subsection shall be guilty of perjury and shall be punished as provided by section 1621 of Title 18.

18 U.S.C.A. § 1621 is the general perjury provision of the United States Code. § 1621 provides:

Whoever—(1) having taken an oath before a competent tribunal, officer, or person, in any case in which a law of the United States authorizes an oath to be administered, that he will testify, declare, depose, or certify truly, or that any written testimony, declaration, deposition, or certificate by him subscribed, is true, . . . states or subscribes any material matter which he does not believe to be true; is guilty of perjury, and shall, except as otherwise expressly provided by law, be fined not more than $2,000 or imprisoned not more than five years, or both.

A third statute related to perjury in immigration proceedings is 22 U.S.C.A. § 4221. This statute authorizes certain embassy officials and consular officers to administer oaths, and directs that any person who "willfully and corruptly" commits perjury or "by any means procure[s] any person to commit perjury" before such officers may be prosecuted in any United States district court in the same manner as if the offense had been committed in the United States.

The fact that false statements made under oath may constitute perjury does not preclude prosecution under other applicable statutes. Because of the demanding requirements for proof of perjury, prosecutors often proceed under other statutes whose requirements are less stringent, such as laws dealing with false statements, fraud, misuse of documents, or conspiracy. See §§ 14–2.4c.–e.

b. False Claim to Citizenship

Under 18 U.S.C.A. § 911, any person who falsely and willfully represents her/himself to be a United States citizen may be fined up to $1,000, imprisoned for not more than three years, or both. The misrepresentation of citizenship must be willful, in addition to being false. The Ninth Circuit Court of Appeals in *Chow Bing Kew v. United States* (9th Cir.1957) held that "willfully" means only that the misrepresentation was made voluntarily and deliberately and, therefore, the prosecution need not show that the misrepresentation was made for a fraudulent purpose. In reaching this conclusion, the court pointed out that § 911 was an amendment to a prior statute (35 Stat. 1088, 1103) which, in contrast, specifically required a fraudulent purpose. *See also De Pratu v. United States* (9th Cir.1948); *United States v. Franklin* (7th Cir.1951).

The statute reaches misrepresentations of citizenship in numerous contexts, including statements made to private employers, to unions, in voting, in applying for a U.S. passport, in an immigration or naturalization proceeding, in a selective service questionnaire, in applying for a license, and in responding to questions of arresting police officers. Under some circumstances, the false representation of citizenship may constitute perjury. See § 14–2.4a. The false citizenship claim also may be punishable under 18 U.S.C.A. § 1001, which deals with false statements made to government officers, or under 18 U.S.C.A. § 1546, concerning fraud and misuse of visas and other documents. See §§ 14–2.4c. and d.

c. *False or Fraudulent Statements and Representations*

18 U.S.C.A. § 1001 establishes a broad foundation for criminal penalties against false statements and misrepresentations in general. The statute provides:

> Whoever, in any matter within the jurisdiction of any department or agency of the United States knowingly and willfully falsifies, conceals or covers up by any trick, scheme, or device a material fact, or makes any false, fictitious or fraudulent statements or representations, or makes or uses any false writing or document knowing the same to contain any false, fictitious or fraudulent statement or entry, shall be fined not more than $10,000 or imprisoned not more than five years, or both.

§ 1001 imposes a penalty for false statements or misrepresentations made to any officer, department, or agency of the United States and thus covers false statements and misrepresentations made to immigration and consular officers in a broad variety of immigration contexts. False statements made in application for or use of a passport are specifically punishable under 8 U.S.C.A. § 1542.

d. *Fraud and Misuse of Visas, Permits, and Other Documents*

18 U.S.C.A. § 1546 criminalizes a wide variety of acts involving misuse of a visa, permit, or other document

required for entry into the United States or as evidence of authorized stay or employment in the United States. The following offenses are subject to criminal sanctions:

a.   Knowingly forging, counterfeiting, altering, or falsely making any immigrant or nonimmigrant visa, permit, or other document required for entry into or as evidence of authorized stay in the United States, or using, possessing, obtaining, etc., such document knowing it to be fraudulently or unlawfully obtained;

b.   Unauthorized possession of any blank permit; unauthorized creation, sale, transport, control, or possession of any plate in the likeness of a plate designed for printing permits; unauthorized making of any print, photograph, or impression in the likeness of any visa, permit, or other document required for entry into the United States; or unauthorized possession of the distinctive paper used for printing these documents; (Note: commonly used forms such as the I–94 are routinely photocopied; because this proscription reaches all documents, however, photocopies should not be sent to the I.N.S.)

c.   Assuming a false identity when applying for a visa, permit, or other document required for entry into or admission to the United States;

d.   Selling or offering to sell or dispose of a visa, permit, or other document to a person not authorized to receive such document;

e.   Knowingly making under oath or penalty of perjury any false statement with respect to a material fact in any application, affidavit, or other document required by the immigration laws or regulations; or knowingly presenting any such document containing a false statement.

f. Using an identification document, knowing or having reason to know that the document was not lawfully issued for the use of the possessor or that the document was false, or using a false attestation, for the purpose of satisfying the requirements of the employment verification system under INA § 274A(b).

Persons who violate any of the first five offenses in § 1546 (a.–e., above) may be fined in accordance with Title 18, imprisoned for up to five years, or both. Commission of the sixth offense (f.) subjects the violator to a fine, imprisonment up to two years, or both. Similarly, 18 U.S.C.A. §§ 1543, 1544 provide for a fine of up to $2,000, imprisonment up to five years, or both, for forgery or misuse of a passport.

e. *Conspiracy*

The general conspiracy statute, 18 U.S.C.A. § 371, provides yet another means of penalizing false statements, misrepresentations, and other fraud in immigration matters. This statute provides:

If two or more persons conspire either to commit any offense against the United States, or to defraud the United States, or any agency thereof in any manner or for any purpose, and one or more of such persons do any act to effect the object of the conspiracy, each shall be fined not more than $10,000 or imprisoned not more than five years, or both.

If, however, the conspired offense is a misdemeanor only, the punishment for the conspiracy must not exceed the maximum punishment provided for the misdemeanor. 18 U.S.C.A. § 371.

Because the commission of a substantive offense and a conspiracy to commit the offense are distinct crimes, an individual may be convicted under both § 371 and the statute relating to the substantive offense. *Pereira v. United States* (Sup.Ct.1954). Often, however, the charge of conspiracy is brought alone because it is easier to show participation in a conspiracy than it is to prove the substantive crime.

f. Marriage Fraud

The Immigration Marriage Fraud Amendments of 1986 intended to deter aliens from seeking immigration benefits through a fraudulent marriage to a U.S. citizen or permanent resident alien. Those amendments, for example, impose a two-year conditional residency requirement on alien spouses before they may obtain permanent resident status on the basis of a "qualifying marriage" to a U.S. citizen or permanent resident alien. The Fraud Amendments also provide a criminal penalty for marriage fraud. INA § 275 states, "[a]ny individual who knowingly enters into a marriage for the purpose of evading any provision of the immigration laws shall be imprisoned for not more than five years, or fined not more than $250,000, or both." The statute applies to the U.S. citizen or permanent resident alien as well as to the nonresident alien involved in the fraudulent marriage. See § 5–2.1 for a discussion of the Immigration Marriage Fraud Amendments of 1986.

§ 14–2.5 Failure to Comply With Deportation Proceedings

a. Failure to Comply With Supervision Regulations

The Attorney General has a period of six months from the date of an alien's final deportation order within which to effect the alien's departure from the United States. INA § 242(c). If the alien is not deported within this six month period, the alien is subject to supervision under regulations prescribed by the Attorney General. These regulations include requirements of periodic reporting; submission, if necessary, to medical and psychiatric examination; testimony as to the alien's "nationality, circumstances, habits, associations, and activities" and other such information as the Attorney General deems proper; as well as conformity to other written restrictions. Any alien who willfully fails to comply with these requirements may be fined up to $1,000, imprisoned for up to one year, or both. INA § 242(d). If a criminal proceeding is brought against an alien for a violation of § 242(d) and the validity of the underlying deportation order was never judicially determined, the validity of the deportation order may be challenged in the same proceeding, but only by separate motion for judicial review before trial. INA § 106(a)(6).

b. *Failure to Depart*

INA § 242(e) penalizes numerous categories of aliens who willfully fail to depart the United States within six months of the date of a final order of deportation. The statute applies to any alien found deportable by reason of being a member of any of the classes described in INA §§ 241(a)(2)–(4). Included in this list are subversive aliens, narcotic drug addicts, aliens associated with Nazi Germany, aliens who have violated registration requirements, aliens convicted of crimes involving moral turpitude or unlawful possession of certain weapons, and aliens convicted of any of an extensive list of misdeeds relating to national security. In addition to willfully failing to depart, the statute penalizes aliens of the above-listed classes who do the following:

1. Willfully fail or refuse to make timely application in good faith for travel or other documents necessary for departure;

2. Connive, conspire, or take any other action with the purpose of preventing or hampering the alien's departure; or

3. Willfully fail or refuse to present him or herself for deportation at the time and place required by the Attorney General.

Before an alien can be convicted of a willful failure to depart, the country willing to receive the alien must be identified. *Heikkinen v. United States* (Sup.Ct.1958). In *Heikkinen*, an alien had been convicted under § 242(e) for willful failure to depart. Because the government had not shown that any country would have admitted the alien, the Supreme Court reversed, holding the evidence insufficient to support conviction.

Violation of the statute constitutes a felony, punishable by imprisonment up to ten years. The statute provides, however, that it is not illegal for an alien "to take any proper steps for the purpose of securing cancellation of or exemption from such order of deportation or for the purpose of securing his release from incarceration or custody...."

As with proceedings under INA § 242(c) for failure to comply with supervision regulations, if criminal proceedings are brought against an alien for violation of § 242(e) and the validity of the underlying deportation order was never judicially determined, the validity of the deportation order may be challenged in the same proceeding, by separate motion for judicial review before trial.   INA § 106a(a)(6).

§ 14–2.6   Unlawful Employment of Aliens

The Immigration Reform and Control Act (IRCA) in 1986 was enacted as a response to growing concern that the United States had lost control over the influx of undocumented aliens to the country.   IRCA attempts to control immigration by creating sanctions for the employment of unauthorized aliens.

IRCA makes it unlawful for any person or entity to hire, recruit, or refer for a fee for employment in the United States, an alien, knowing that the alien is unauthorized with respect to such employment, or any individual without complying with the employment verification system established under INA § 274a.   INA § 274a.2.   It is also unlawful for a person or entity to continue employing an alien, knowing that the alien is or has become unauthorized.   INA § 274a.3.

In addition to civil fines, which increase with multiple offenses, IRCA imposes criminal penalties upon persons and entities engaging in a "pattern or practice of violations."   These penalties include a fine of up to $3,000 for each unauthorized alien, imprisonment up to six months for the entire pattern or practice, or both.   INA § 274a.10.   The term "pattern or practice" means "regular, repeated and intentional activities, but does not include isolated, sporadic or accidental acts."   *United States v. Mayton* (5th Cir.1964), *International Brotherhood of Teamsters v. United States* (Sup.Ct.1977), and *United States v. International Association of Iron Workers Local No. 1* (7th Cir.1971).   These interpretations were incorporated expressly into the legislative history accompanying the Immigration Reform and Control Act of 1986 by House Report No. 99–682(I).

Although IRCA imposes no penalties upon unauthorized aliens merely for working illegally, an individual seeking employment in the United States must attest under penalty of perjury, that s/he is a citizen or national of the U.S., a permanent resident alien, or an alien authorized to be hired, recruited, or referred for employment. INA § 274a.2. Similarly, the employer must attest under penalty of perjury that it has verified that the individual is not an unauthorized alien by examining documents which establish employment authorization and the identity of the individual.

The employer sanctions do not apply to individuals who were hired, recruited, or referred prior to November 6, 1986. An employer also may establish an affirmative defense to an allegation of unlawful employment by showing that it has complied in good faith with the requirements of the employment verification system. INA § 274a.4. Although the employer sanctions do not apply to continuing employment of an alien who was hired before November 6, 1986, the felony provisions of INA § 274, which penalize the concealing, harboring, or shielding of undocumented aliens, may still apply. IRCA § 112(a) removed from § 274 an earlier clause providing that employment does not constitute harboring of an undocumented alien. The removal from § 274 of the so-called "Texas Proviso" was a considerable departure from prior law, which had excepted mere employment from conduct constituting a harboring offense.

§ 14–3 IMMIGRATION CONSEQUENCES OF CRIMINAL ACTIVITY

An alien convicted of a crime generally will suffer the penalties prescribed by statute. A criminal conviction, however, may have a direct effect on the alien's immigration status as well. The effect of the conviction may be felt almost immediately, as when conviction of the crime constitutes a ground for deportation, or the impact of the conviction may not occur for several years, as when conviction of the crime precludes the showing of good moral character necessary for naturalization.

§ 14–3.1   Exclusion

An alien seeking to enter the United States may be excluded on the basis of prior criminal activity. INA § 212 provides several categories of aliens who are ineligible to receive visas and are excluded from the United States as a result of criminal activity. These grounds of exclusion apply equally to aliens who seek entry to the United States for the first time and to aliens who, after residing in the United States for a period of time, seek re-entry after a temporary departure.

Aliens convicted of a crime involving moral turpitude (other than a purely political offense), aliens who admit having committed such a crime, and aliens who admit committing acts which constitute the essential elements of a crime involving moral turpitude are excludable. INA § 212(a)(2)(A). An exception is made under certain circumstances for aliens who have committed only one such crime while under the age of eighteen, provided the crime was committed and the alien has been released "from any confinement to a prison or correctional institution imposed for the crime" more than five years before the date of application for a visa and for admission to the United States. An exception also is made for aliens who committed only one crime involving moral turpitude in which "the maximum penalty possible for the crime of which the alien was convicted (or which the alien admits having committed . . .) did not exceed imprisonment for one year and, if the alien was convicted of such crime, the alien was not sentenced to a term of imprisonment in excess of 6 months (regardless of the extent to which the sentence was ultimately executed)."

In ascertaining whether an alien is entitled to this exception, one should look to the sentence imposed by the court. When the alien admits committing an offense, though s/he has not been convicted, one should look to the maximum penalty for that crime. If convicted by a foreign court, comparison to a similar crime under U.S. law is irrelevant.

The courts generally agree that crimes of moral turpitude "include elements which necessarily demonstrate the baseness, vileness, and depravity of the perpetrator." *Tutrone v. Shaughnessy* (S.D.N.Y.1958). The following criminal offenses have been held to involve moral turpitude: offenses in which either an intent to defraud (*e.g.*, counterfeiting, forgery fraud) or an intent to steal is an element; offenses (usually felonies) in which great bodily harm is caused or threatened by an intentional or willful act (*e.g.*, homicide, aggravated assault, assault with a deadly weapon, assault with intent to kill) or by recklessness (*e.g.*, vehicular homicide, driving while intoxicated resulting in personal injury to another); offenses in which "malice" is an essential element; sex offenses in which some "lewd" intent is required.

INA § 212(h) allows the Attorney General to waive the exclusion of an alien who has committed a crime involving moral turpitude if the alien is the spouse, parent, or child of a United States citizen or lawfully admitted permanent resident, provided the alien is excludable for activities that occurred more than 15 years before the alien's application for an immigration benefit; the alien's admission would not be contrary to the national welfare, safety, or security; and the alien has been rehabilitated. No waiver can be granted if the crime was murder or involved torture.

An alien is excluded if s/he has been convicted of two or more offenses (other than purely political offenses) for which the aggregate sentences to confinement actually imposed were five years or more. INA § 212(a)(2)(B). This provision applies regardless of whether the conviction was in a single trial or whether the offenses arose from a single scheme of misconduct and regardless of whether the offenses involved moral turpitude. The Attorney General may issue a waiver upon finding the same circumstances required for a waiver of a crime involving moral turpitude, *i.e.*, cases in which the alien is the spouse, parent, son, or daughter of a citizen of the United States or lawfully admitted permanent resident. INA § 212(h).

INA § 212(a)(2)(A)(i)(II) excludes any alien convicted of a violation of, or a conspiracy to violate, any law or regulation of a state, the United States, or a foreign country relating to a controlled substance (as defined in 21 U.S.C.A. § 802). INA § 212(h) allows the Attorney General to waive applicability of § 212(a)(2)(A)(i)(II) in so far as it relates to a single offense of simple posses-sion of 30 grams or less of marijuana, provided the alien meets the same criteria for a waiver of crimes involving moral turpitude.   Moreover, § 212(a)(2)(C) excludes "[a]ny alien who the consular or immigration officer knows or has reason to believe is or has been an illicit trafficker in any such controlled substances or is or has been a knowing assister, abettor, conspirator, or collu-der with others in the illicit trafficking in any such controlled substance."   No waiver is available for this ground of exclusion.   INA § 212(a)(6)(E) also excludes any alien who at any time, knowingly and for gain, encouraged or assisted any other alien to enter the United States in violation of law.   This section elimi-nates the "for gain" requirement under the previous law.   INA § 212(d)(11) provides the Attorney General with the discretionary power to waive this ground of exclusion "for humanitarian purposes, to assure family unity, or when it is otherwise in the public interest." Other grounds of exclusion related to criminal activity include polygamy (INA § 212(a)(9)(A)), involvement in prostitution (INA § 212(a)(2)(D)), and aliens coming to the United States to engage in any other unlawful commercialized vice, whether or not related to prostitu-tion (INA § 212(a)(2)(D)(iii)), terrorists (INA 212(a)(3)), and international child abductors (INA § 212(a)(9)(C)).

§ 14–3.2 Deportation

Deportation also may be a direct result of an alien's involvement in criminal activity.   INA § 241 lists sever-al grounds for deportation related to criminal activity. For a discussion of these grounds, see § 8–2.   An alien who has committed an "aggravated felony" is presump-tively deportable and subject to special expedited depor-

tation proceedings. INA § 242A. See §§ 8–2.3, 8–3.1.
A full pardon by the President or the governor of the
state of conviction would have the effect of removing
convictions for offenses, not involving controlled substances or firearms, as the grounds for deportation.
INA § 241(a)(2)(A)(iv); *see also* § 8–2.3. If an alien is
convicted of an offense for which there is no pardoning
authority under state or federal law, the conviction
cannot be used to deport the alien. Under the Technical Amendments Act of 1991, an alien is not only
deportable for the commission of certain crimes, but for
the attempt or conspiracy to commit these crimes as
well.

Many jurisdictions have statutes permitting the expungement or sealing of criminal records, which also
has the effect of eliminating some convictions as a
ground for deportation. Expungement of a conviction
involving narcotics, however, cannot defeat deportability. *See Tsimbidy–Rochu v. INS* (9th Cir.1969). Even if
a conviction is expunged, the conduct which resulted in
the conviction, may be a subject of inquiry if the alien
applies for United States citizenship. *See Petition of De
La Cruz* (S.D.N.Y.1983). It may be possible for the alien
to escape criminal charges by participating in various
programs such as community service work or rehabilita-
tion, thereby avoiding the immigration consequences of
some convictions. If an alien pleads guilty to a deportable crime without being aware of the immigration consequences of that plea, it may be possible to vacate the
guilty plea or to obtain a writ of error coram nobis.
Many states now require defense attorneys to advise
non-citizen defendants as to the immigration consequences of their pleas. *See, e.g., People v. Soriano* (Cal.
1987). Some courts have allowed the withdrawal of a

guilty plea upon a showing of ineffective assistance of counsel, for failure to research the immigration consequences of the plea. *See, e.g., State v. Lopez* (Minn.App. 1986).

§ 14–3.3 Failure to Establish Good Moral Character

Conviction of a crime may prevent an alien from establishing good moral character, which is a statutory prerequisite to a number of immigration benefits. These benefits include naturalization (INA § 316), voluntary departure (INA § 244(e)), suspension of deportation (INA § 244(a)), and registry (INA § 249). A petitioner for naturalization or voluntary departure must establish good moral character during the five years prior to application. An alien seeking suspension of deportation must show that s/he has been of good moral character during her/his continuous presence in the United States of at least seven years. An applicant for registry need only show that s/he is presently of good moral character. For a discussion of what constitutes "good moral character," see § 12–2.2b(4).

§ 14–3.4 Denial of Asylum

Another possible consequence of an alien's criminal activity is denial of the alien's application for asylum or termination of the alien's asylum status. An immigration judge or asylum officer must deny a request for asylum or withholding of deportation if it is determined that the alien, "having been convicted by a final judgment of a particularly serious crime, constitutes a danger to the community of the United States...." 8 C.F.R. §§ 208.16(c)(2)(ii)&.14(c)(1). Further, even if the alien has not been convicted of a crime, asylum or withholding of deportation will be denied if there are "serious reasons for considering that the alien has committed a serious non-political crime outside the United States prior to the arrival of the alien in the United States...."   8 C.F.R. § 208.16(c)(2)(iii).

Similarly, once granted asylum, an alien's asylum status will be terminated if the alien poses a danger to the United States community because of conviction of a serious crime, as described in 8 C.F.R. § 208.16(c)(2). 8 C.F.R. § 208.24(b)(3). Asylum status also will be terminated if it appears that the alien was not, in fact, eligible for asylum at the time of application for either of the reasons specified in the previous paragraph. 8 C.F.R. 208.24.

Once an alien's asylum status is terminated, the alien, unless eligible for other immigration benefits, will be subject to either deportation or exclusion proceedings. The alien will be placed under deportation proceedings if s/he was in the United States at the time asylum status was granted. The alien will be subject to exclusion proceedings if s/he was an applicant for admission to the U.S. at the time asylum status was granted.

CHAPTER 15

ETHICAL DIMENSIONS
OF IMMIGRATION
PRACTICE

Immigration lawyers are confronted by ethical issues probably more often than other practitioners. The alien clients of the immigration lawyer are often suspicious about the fairness of United States laws and administrative practices and are usually unfamiliar with them. Some aliens may try to suggest or pursue courses of conduct from their culture, which might be inappropriate or, perhaps, unethical for a lawyer in the United States. Hence, the student of immigration law should be aware of the ethical dimensions of an immigration practice.

This chapter analyzes four typical ethical problems encountered by the immigration lawyer from the perspective of both the Model Code of Professional Responsibility and the Model Rules of Professional Conduct. The four problems deal with common situations faced by immigration lawyers:

(1) The alien is in violation of her/his immigration status, or has fraudulently married to gain permanent resident status. Must the lawyer report her/his client to the INS?

(2) An alien consults the lawyer about admission to the United States. The client is qualified for a nonimmigrant visa, but in discussing the alien's ultimate

objectives, the lawyer learns that the client may want eventually to become an immigrant and a United States citizen. If the alien has a present intent to immigrate to the United States, s/he would be ineligible for the nonimmigrant visa. What should the lawyer tell the client?

(3) The INS has ordered the client deported. The client wishes to stay in the United States as long as possible. Filing a petition for review stays the actual deportation for at least several months, if not years, while the review is pending. When can the lawyer ethically file a petition?

(4) An immigration lawyer is paid by a company to obtain a visa for an employee or potential employee. In the course of the representation the lawyer learns facts—such as the employee's career plans—which may be adverse to the new employer's interest. What should the lawyer do? Can s/he tell the employer? Whom does the lawyer actually represent?

While each problem will be examined in some detail, this chapter does not attempt to provide definitive answers but merely raises the ethical issues.

This chapter discusses four sources of ethical constraint on the immigration lawyer. First, there are the ethical considerations from the Model Code of Professional Responsibility. Ethical considerations are aspirational objectives which the lawyer strives to achieve. Should the lawyer fail to abide by ethical considerations, however, there are theoretically no sanctions in most states. Second, the Model Code contains disciplinary rules which mandate a minimum level of conduct for the lawyer. Should the attorney's conduct fall below this minimum level s/he may be subject to disbarment, suspension, or other sanction. A third source of ethical rules for the lawyer is the Model Rules of Professional Conduct adopted in 1983. The Model Rules are the replacement for the Model Code. Thirty-nine states and the District of Columbia have revised their rules to follow substantially the Model Rules. Because the drafting committee concluded that in practical effect ethical considerations were no longer merely aspirational goals, the Model Rules abandon the distinction between ethical considerations and disciplinary rules in favor of only rules. Finally, the immigration lawyer must adhere to the regulations governing the conduct of lawyers who appear before the Immigration and Naturalization Service. The Code of Federal Regulations lists fourteen non-exclusive reasons for suspending or disbarring the immigration lawyer, some of which overlap the Model Code and Model Rules and some of which are unique to immigration practice. 8 C.F.R. § 292.3.

§ 15–1 MUST THE LAWYER REPORT HIS/HER CLIENT TO THE IMMIGRATION SERVICE?

A situation which frequently confronts the immigration lawyer occurs when the attorney becomes aware—through discussions with the client, independent investigation, or other outside sources—that the client is not observing her/his visa conditions. For example, a student-client with an F–1 visa accepts employment outside the educational institution without the requisite permission. Under these circumstances, what is the lawyer's obligation to (a) report the client's violation of immigration status to the INS and/or (b) advise the client as to the possible consequences of accepting employment?

Similarly, an immigration attorney is frequently confronted with an alien who seeks permanent resident status after marrying a U.S. citizen. Preliminary results of an INS pilot study suggest fraud in as many as 30% of the spouse petitions that were intensively reviewed. What if the attorney becomes aware that her/his client is involved in a sham marriage solely to attain permanent resident status? Does the attorney have an obligation to report her/his client's fraudulent marriage to the INS? Would disclosure violate lawyer-client confidentiality requirements?

§ 15–1.1   Reporting the Client's Activities

Under the provisions of both the Model Code and the Model Rules the lawyer appears to face competing mandates concerning whether to report the client. On the one hand, the lawyer has a duty to preserve the client's confidences and secrets. DR 4–101(B) of the Model Code provides that the lawyer shall not reveal confidences and secrets obtained in the course of representation. In addition, the rule prohibits any use of the confidence which disadvantages the client. The Model Rules also require the attorney not to reveal a confidence except in a limited number of circumstances. Model Rules of Professional Conduct Rule 1.6 (1983). In the F–1 student example, the information about the student's employment is a client confidence or secret because it was obtained in the course of representing the client. Similarly, information regarding a client's fraudulent marriage received in the course of representing that client is also a client confidence or secret. In the former case, if the attorney informed the INS of the client's employment, the client could be deprived of the student visa and possibly deported. Likewise, if the attorney informed the INS of her/his client's fraudulent marriage, that client could be denied resident status, prosecuted, fined, and/or deported. Hence, it appears the lawyer cannot disclose the information to the INS without violating either the Model Code or the Model Rules.

The Model Code, the Model Rules, and the applicable C.F.R. provision, however, prohibit the lawyer from making false statements to the INS. According to DR 7–102(A) of the Model Code, the lawyer "shall not . . . (3) conceal or knowingly fail to disclose that which he is required by law to reveal." Likewise, the Model Rules provide that the lawyer shall not "knowingly . . . make a false statement of material fact or law to a third person." Model Rules of Professional Conduct Rule 4.1(a) (1983). The Code of Federal Regulations contains similar language. 8 C.F.R. § 292.3(a)(3). At times, the lawyer is required by law to reveal information about her/his client. For example, INS Form I–539, Application to Extend/Change Nonimmigrant Status, requires the lawyer to respond to questions concerning whether the client has worked. If the lawyer knowingly makes a false statement on these forms, s/he is subject to substantial penalties. *See, e.g., United States v. Lew* (9th Cir.1989) (immigration attorney convicted of making false statements to Department of Labor).

In these circumstances, the lawyer would be faced with either violating the mandate regarding client confidences or violating the mandate regarding false statements. The immigration lawyer's dilemma, however, is not without resolution. The lawyer is charged with preserving client confidences only within the bounds of the law. Hence, while a lawyer cannot volunteer information about the client's activities to the INS, s/he must advise the client to answer truthfully. The lawyer does not violate a client confidence when s/he truthfully answers a direct question because to make a false statement would violate the law.

§ 15–1.2   Advising the Client

Under the circumstances of this problem both the Model Code and the Model Rules apparently require the lawyer to discuss the probable consequences of the client's actions with the client. EC 7–8 of the Model Code provides:

> A lawyer should exert his best efforts to insure that decisions of his client are made only after the client has been informed of relevant considerations. A lawyer ought to initiate this decision-making process if the client does not do so.

In addition, EC 7–5 of the Model Code notes that "[a] lawyer as advisor furthers the interest of his client by giving his professional opinion" about the consequences of her/his client's decision. The Model Rules translated the ethical considerations of the Model Code into rules with essentially the same substance. Rule 2.1 requires the lawyer to render candid advice in her/his role as advisor to the client. In a comment to the rules, the Committee notes:

> (W)hen a lawyer knows that a client proposes a course of action that is likely to result in substantial adverse legal consequences to the client, duty to the client ... may require that the lawyer act [give advice]....

In the case of the F–1 student, the client may suffer the adverse consequences such as loss of visa and deportation. If the client later qualifies for an immigrant visa, the client, at minimum, may be required to process the alien's immigrant status outside the United States.

The client may not have realized the adverse consequences of her/his decision to accept employment at the time it was made. Therefore, the lawyer's obligation to her/his client is to inform the client of the negative consequences of violating the visa conditions. As there may be criminal as well as civil penalties for working without proper authorization, the information is essential. The strength of the obligation may depend on whether the lawyer learns of the student's employment before or after the work commences. If the lawyer learns of the student's intention before the employment begins, the duty to act is stronger because the lawyer can prevent the adverse consequences by rendering the correct legal advice. If the lawyer learns afterwards, the duty to act is not as great because the legal consequences (loss of visa, deportation, and ineligibility to adjust status in the United States) would have already become applicable. Nevertheless, a lawyer might advise the client against continued employment because the INS might take more severe enforcement action against a client who has been illegally employed for a longer period.

§ 15–2 SHOULD THE LAWYER TELL THE CLIENT ABOUT A FIXED INTENT TO IMMIGRATE?

Different sorts of ethical problems are raised in advising the client regarding her/his fixed intent to immigrate to the United States. The problem arises when a client otherwise eligible for a nonimmigrant visa informs the lawyer that s/he wants to immigrate to the

United States. The client would be ineligible for most nonimmigrant visas, however, if s/he has a present intent to immigrate. What should the lawyer tell the client to do? If the lawyer tells the client not to form a present intent to immigrate, would the lawyer be assisting the client in perpetrating a fraud?

Both the Model Code and the Model Rules have sections dealing with client fraud and the lawyer's duty, none of which provide any clear solutions to this problem. According to DR 7–102(A) of the Model Code:

> (A) . . . a lawyer shall not:
>
> . . .
>
> (6) Participate in the creation or preservation of evidence when he knows or it is obvious that the evidence is false.
>
> (7) Counsel or assist his client in conduct that the lawyer knows to be illegal or fraudulent.

In addition, EC 7–6 of the Model Code discusses the lawyer's position in assisting the client in developing state of mind evidence. It provides:

> [The lawyer] may properly assist his client in the development and preservation of evidence of existing motive, intent, or desire; obviously, he may not do anything furthering the creation or preservation of false evidence.

The Model Rules contain similar prohibitions. Rule 1.2(d) refers most directly to this situation: "a lawyer shall not counsel to engage, or assist a client in conduct that the lawyer knows is criminal or fraudulent. . . ." See also the similar language in 8 C.F.R. § 292.3(a)(3). Those provisions, however, do not resolve whether the client commits a fraud in declaring that s/he has no present intent to immigrate. It is not clear that the lawyer would assist the client in committing a fraud or in preserving false evidence by discussing the effect of the client's intent on her/his immigration status. The situation is made more complex because only the client knows her/his own intent. An attorney, however, can advise the client as to the consequences of pursuing a specific course of conduct, as separate from the question of the client's intent.

Other sections of the Model Code and the Model Rules imply that the lawyer has an obligation to discuss the probable consequences of alternate courses of action with the client. EC 7–8 Model Code provides that "[a] lawyer should advise his client of the possible effect of each legal alternative." While Rule 1.2 of the Model Rules prohibits the lawyer from assisting the client in fraudulent conduct, "a lawyer may discuss the legal consequences of any proposed course of conduct with a client and may counsel or assist a client to make a good faith effort to determine the validity, scope, meaning or application of the law." Model Rule 1.2(d). In this situation, the lawyer is not urging the client to adopt one course of action over another. Rather, s/he is merely discussing the client's two legal alternatives—to form a present intent to become an immigrant or a nonimmigrant—and the legal effects of each. The lawyer explains the consequences and the client makes the decision about her/his present intent. Such advice does not appear to be the kind of fraud contemplated by the drafters of the Model Code and the Model Rules.

In addition, one might draw inferences from the drafting history of the Model Rules. In an earlier discussion draft of the Model Rules, Rule 2.3(a)(2) mandated that a lawyer could not give advice that s/he "could reasonably foresee would ... aid the client in contriving false testimony." No counterpart to this draft Rule 2.3 appears in the Model Rules adopted in 1983. From this omission one could infer (1) that the drafting committee did not consider this advice an ethical violation, (2) that in a criminal law context this draft provision would be inappropriate, or (3) possibly that Rule 1.2 already covered this situation. In any case, even if draft Rule 2.3(a)(2) had appeared in the final version, the lawyer's advice would be unethical only in the unlikely event that it aided the client in contriving false testimony. Hence, the immigration lawyer probably can explain the consequences of the client's present intent to immigrate or her/his eligibility for a nonimmigrant visa without ethical violation, so long as the lawyer does not suggest which course of action the client should actually adopt.

The 1990 Act addressed this dilemma to an extent by recognizing the "dual intent" of many aliens seeking nonimmigrant visa status under the H and L categories. See §§ 6–8, 6–12, *supra*. Under the 1990 Act, a temporary worker with an H visa or a transferee with an L visa is not precluded from eventually seeking an adjustment of her/his status to that of a permanent resident. The problem still exists, however, with regard to several other nonimmigrant statuses, such as B, F, and J.

§ 15–3 WHEN CAN THE LAWYER ETHI-CALLY APPEAL A DECISION OF THE IMMIGRATION SERVICE?

Another problem involves the filing of a petition for review of deportation. In this case, the alien-client has already had a deportation hearing and the client has been ordered to leave the country. The client wishes to stay in the United States as long as possible. Filing a petition for review with the Board of Immigration Appeals stays the actual deportation during the time the review is pending. 8 C.F.R. § 3.6(a). The lawyer realizes, however, that the appeal has little substantive merit, although there is a slight chance the Board would overturn the deportation order. Can the lawyer file the appeal?

To decide whether to file the appeal, the lawyer must weigh the duty to represent the client effectively against the duty not to engage in frivolous litigation. EC 7–1 of the Model Code says that the lawyer has a duty "to represent his client zealously within the bounds of the law." The Code's corresponding disciplinary rule, DR 7–101(A)(1) provides, "A lawyer shall not intentionally fail to seek the lawful objectives of his client through reasonably available means permitted by law...."

In *Anders v. California* (Sup.Ct.1967) the Supreme Court emphasized the attorney's duty to act as a vigorous advocate for her/his client when appealing a criminal conviction. If the attorney believes her/his client's position on appeal is frivolous, the attorney must advise the court which then makes the final decision about the appeal's merits.

Nonetheless, both the Model Code and the Model Rules condemn frivolous litigation clearly and directly.

Under DR 1–102(A)(5) of the Model Code, a lawyer cannot engage in conduct which is "prejudicial to the administration of justice." DR 7–102(A)(2) forbids frivolous litigation when it provides that "[i]n his representation of a client, a lawyer shall not ... [k]nowingly advance a claim or defense that is unwarranted under existing law...." Equally blunt, the Model Rules denounce frivolous litigation in Rule 3.1: "[a] lawyer shall not bring or defend a proceeding, or assert or controvert an issue therein, unless there is a reasonable basis for doing so...." The Code of Federal Regulations covers this situation also, although in a broader manner. It provides for the suspension or disbarment of a lawyer "who engages in contumelious or otherwise obnoxious conduct...." 8 C.F.R. § 292.3(a)(11). (From Black's Law Dictionary one can infer that "contumelious" means disdainful or contemptuous.) The lawyer clearly cannot ethically file a wholly frivolous petition for review. In this case, while proposed mainly to stay deportation, the appeal could conceivably succeed on the merits. Hence, the lawyer must determine whether this particular appeal is "frivolous" within the meaning of the ethical codes and the immigration law. INA § 242B(d) authorizes the Attorney General to develop a definition of frivolous behavior for which attorneys may be sanctioned. *Cf.* INA § 274B(j)(4) (attorney's fees in regard to unfair immigration-related employment discrimination.)

The courts have addressed the issue of when a petition for review is frivolous. Courts should, and do, give every reasonable deference to the lawyer's role as an advocate. Hence, only in the most extreme case will the court find an ethical violation in appealing a case. In one such case, *In re Bithoney* (1st Cir.1973), the court suspended an immigration lawyer who filed nine petitions for review, all of which the court found totally lacking in any substantive merit and four of which were not even pursued beyond the filing of the petition. The court made clear, however, that it regarded the lawyer's failure to pursue diligently the appeals, rather than their total lack of merit, as the more serious violation of ethics and the major reason for disciplinary action.

In a similar case, the court sanctioned a lawyer who filed a petition for review which the court found utterly frivolous and completely lacking in any merit. The court concluded that the petition was interposed solely as a delaying tactic and therefore imposed double costs on the attorney. *Acevedo v. Immigration and Naturalization Service* (2d Cir.1976). The opinions in both cases suggest that an attorney can file a petition for review only if there is some reasonable basis for appeal and only if the review is diligently pursued by the lawyer. Using the petition solely as a delaying tactic is not ethical. An attorney may file an appeal even if precedent is against her/his client's case, provided that the attorney seeks to reverse that precedent. Before filing an appeal, the lawyer should satisfy her/himself that there is more to the appeal than simply delaying deportation.

§ 15–4 WHOM DOES THE LAWYER REPRESENT?

Another problem concerns the lawyer who is retained by an employer to secure the proper work authorization for a present or prospective alien employee. For example, an engineering firm hires the lawyer to obtain an L–1 visa for an alien-engineer. In discussing the alien's ultimate career goals, the lawyer learns that the alien plans eventually to open her/his own engineering firm. When the alien's interest in the visa is adverse to the employer's interest, can the lawyer disclose the alien's intent to the employer?

Client confidences are protected under both the Model Code and the Model Rules. DR 4–101(B) of the Model Code provides:

[A] lawyer shall not knowingly:

(1) Reveal a confidence or secret of his client.

(2) Use a confidence or secret of his client to the disadvantage of the client.

Rule 1.6 of the Model Rules provides that the "lawyer shall not reveal information relating to representation of a client" except in a limited number of circumstances such as to prevent the commission of a very serious crime. The solution to this problem turns on whether the client is the employer company, the alien prospective employee, or, in the case of joint representation, both. In all situations, the governing principle is early disclosure on the part of the lawyer to avoid even potential conflict.

If the alien is regarded as unrepresented, the lawyer may not offer to the alien advice that is adverse to the employer-client's interests. If the alien/employee is the client, however, the attorney may not use information acquired from the alien to the alien's disadvantage by revealing that information to the employer. Furthermore, if the attorney has a continuing relationship with the employer, violating the alien's confidence may be equivalent to using information acquired from the client for the lawyer's own purposes. Both uses of client information are prohibited under EC 4–5 of the Model Code which provides:

A lawyer should not use information acquired in the course of the representation of a client to the disadvantage of the client and a lawyer should not use, except with the consent of his client after full disclosure, such information for his own purposes.

The Model Rules adopt a similar position in Rule 1.7:

A lawyer shall not represent a client if the representation of that client may be materially limited by the lawyer's responsibilities to another client or to a third person, or by the lawyer's own interests,. . . .

The Model Code and the Model Rules recognize the practical difficulties inherent when the client's interest is adverse to that of the fee-paying employer. The lawyer naturally feels a certain amount of loyalty to the company that retains her/him. Should the lawyer's loyalty to the company interfere with the effective representation of the client, both the Model Code and the Model Rules provide for the lawyer's withdrawal from the case. See Model Code of Professional Responsibility, EC 5–21; Model Rules of Professional Conduct, Rule 1.16. The lawyer must, however, recognize that in doing so, s/he may jeopardize the client confidence anyway, since the employer may become suspicious of the client when the lawyer seeks to withdraw.

Where the lawyer has a continuing professional relationship with the employer, the lawyer's responsibility to the employer cannot be readily dismissed. The employer, not the alien, has selected the lawyer and defined the scope of her/his duties, and probably must also be considered a client. If both the employer and the alien are clients, EC 4–5 of the Model Code requires that care be exercised by the lawyer "to prevent the disclosure of the confidences and secrets of one client to another, and no employment should be accepted that might require such disclosure."

The Model Rules provide more guidance in this dilemma. Rule 1.7 allows a lawyer to represent clients with conflicting interests if the lawyer reasonably believes that the representation of each client will not adversely affect the relationship with the other and that each client consents to the arrangement after consultation. According to the Comment to Rule 1.7, the lawyer should consider "the likelihood that a conflict will eventuate and, if it does, whether it will materially interfere with the lawyer's independent professional judgment in considering alternatives or foreclose courses of action that reasonably should be pursued on behalf of the client." The lawyer also should consider whether each client is willing to accommodate the other interest involved.

The alien and the employer may thus be co-clients. Because of their common interest in allowing the alien to work for the employer, each may be willing to accommodate the other's interests. With full and early disclosure of the potential for conflict and the consent of the parties to the lawyer's role in representing them both, the lawyer can represent the alien and the employer, sharing relevant information between the two. It may, however, be impossible to disclose the information necessary to obtain consent. If the alien refuses to disclose her/his ultimate career goals to the employer, the employer will be unable to make an informed decision as to whether it should consent to the arrangement. In this situation, the lawyer cannot properly ask the employer to consent. Comment, Rule 1.7.

Another possible solution under the Model Rules would be for the lawyer to regard the alien as s/he would regard an employee of the employer organization. The ethical responsibilities of a lawyer retained by an organization are outlined in Rule 1.13. The client is the organization. While the employees are not clients, communications between an employee and the organization's lawyer are protected by Rule 1.6. Comment, Rule 1.13. Under Rule 1.13, however, the lawyer has discretion to reveal confidential information to the employer organization when the lawyer knows that an employee intends to violate a legal obligation to the organization (or the employee's actions are in violation of law and might reasonably be imputed to the organization, resulting in substantial injury). Hence, under this interpretation, the alien's plans eventually to open a competing firm would be protected from disclosure to the employer company under Rule 1.6 unless the alien's plans are in violation of the alien's legal obligation to the company. Rule 1.13, however, requires that, in dealing with an employee of the organization, the lawyer explain the identity of the client when it is apparent that the organization's interests are adverse to those of the employee. When a conflict of interest arises, care must be taken to assure that the employee understands the lawyer cannot represent her/him and that s/he may wish to obtain independent representation. Comment, Rule 1.13.

Upjohn Co. v. United States (Sup.Ct.1981) is instructive as to the confidentiality of employee communications. Counsel for Upjohn learned of questionable payments to foreign officials and initiated an internal investigation, sending questionnaires to all foreign managers and pursuing the matter further with interviews. Based on the results of this investigation, the company made a voluntary disclosure to the Internal Revenue Service. The IRS then began its own investigation and sought to discover the questionnaires and interview notes. The lower court rejected Upjohn's work product defense because the communications to officers and agents of the company were not to the client under the "control group test," which labels as clients only those who have authority to make decisions based on the lawyer's advice. The Supreme Court, however, regarded these employees as clients and held that the attorney-client privilege applied. The Court noted that the employees understood they were being questioned so that the corporation could obtain legal advice.

Unlike the Model Rules, the Supreme Court regards the employees as clients. The applicability of *Upjohn* is also limited by the fact that the employer and employees did not have clearly adverse interests. The case remains instructive, however, because the Court extended to employees the protection of communications. This extension of the evidentiary privilege of confidentiality (including the work product doctrine) is significant because the ethical privilege of confidentiality is even broader in scope. The Comment to Rule 1.6 states:

> The principle of confidentiality is given effect in two related bodies of law, the attorney-client privilege (which includes the work product doctrine) in the law of evidence and the rule of confidentiality established in professional ethics.

The evidentiary privilege generally applies in judicial proceedings, while the ethical privilege applies "in situations other than those where evidence is sought from the lawyer through compulsion of law." Comment, Rule 1.6. EC 4–4 of the Model Code states:

> The attorney-client privilege is more limited than the ethical obligation of a lawyer to guard the confidences and secrets of his client. The ethical precept, unlike the evidentiary privilege, exists without regard to the nature or source of information or the fact that others share the knowledge.

Under *Upjohn,* employee communications with an attorney retained by the employer may be privileged under the work product doctrine and not subject to discovery by people outside the corporation. Under Model Rule 1.13, employee communications with the employer's counsel may be privileged from disclosure to the employer under the ethical obligation of a lawyer to guard the confidences of the employee. Under the Model Rules, however, the employee is not regarded as a client and some information will not be protected, as described above.

Rule 1.13 has no direct counterpart in the Model Code. EC 5–18 of the Model Code states:

> A lawyer employed or retained by a corporation or similar entity owes his allegiance to the entity and not to a stockholder, director, officer, employee, representative, or other person connected with the entity. In advising the entity, a lawyer should keep paramount its interests and his professional judgment should not be influenced by the personal desires of any person or organization. Occasionally, a lawyer for an entity is requested by a stockholder, director,

officer, employee, representative, or other person connected with the entity to represent him in an individual capacity; in such a case the lawyer may serve the individual only if the lawyer is convinced that differing interests are not present.

DR 5–107(B) further provides that if a lawyer is hired by one person to render legal services for another, the lawyer must not permit the employer to direct or regulate her/his professional judgment in rendering such legal services for the other person.

As can be seen from the above discussion, there are several possible approaches to identifying the client and guarding the client's confidences. No simple consensus appears to be available for this problem.

CHAPTER 16

CONCLUSION

In reading through this volume, the student may get the impression that immigration law is comprised of a very stable set of administrative requirements for obtaining permission to enter and remain in this country. While that impression may be generally correct, the student should be aware that the immigration laws described in this Nutshell have changed significantly in the eight years since the publication of the first edition. Beyond landmark legislation like IRCA and the 1990 Act, the INS and the judiciary continually update and clarify the regulations that form the foundation for practicing immigration law. Furthermore, almost everyone involved even tangentially in the immigration process is aware that the Immigration Service is overworked, understaffed, and nearly overwhelmed by its statutory duties. Congress and the Administration have undertaken reforms to modernize the procedures of the INS, to resolve at least partially the very difficult problems created by the thousands—if not millions—of aliens who wish to live in the United States, and to decide which aliens should be encouraged to immigrate. Population analysts have noted that the U.S. may suffer a severe shortage of workers in coming decades and that immigration will be an important way of supplying workers for the U.S. economy. During periods of high unemployment and economic distress, however, immigration becomes particularly unpopular and the long-term needs of the U.S. economy may be ignored.

Hence, students should be aware that the target at which they are shooting is, indeed, moving and will require continued attention.

It seems appropriate to conclude this Nutshell by making a general observation about the nature of immigration law practice. Faced with all the detailed requirements for visas about which this volume says so much, some advocates, including attorneys, and their clients devote most of their attention to gathering the minimum information necessary to fulfill the various requirements. Unfortunately, some lawyers and almost all unrepresented aliens do not view the immigration process as an appropriate place for intelligent advocacy. This tendency has been addressed by groups such as the American Immigration Lawyers Association (AILA) which, through seminars and publications, has sought to raise the level of expertise in the practice of immigration law.

Ultimately, it is the duty of immigration lawyers to muster the relevant facts in such a way as to convince Immigration Service officers that the lawyers' clients should receive the appropriate immigration status. One should never forget when submitting an application that one has the power to establish the record on which the client's case will be won or lost. In addition, lawyers should remember that immigration officers are administrative decision-makers who ought to receive the same sort of attention and polite, effective advocacy as judges. Certainly, immigration laws and the multitude of immigration forms about which the student has read are not invitations to forget all the advocacy skills used in other contexts.

CHAPTER 17

BIBLIOGRAPHY

This chapter suggests some principal references for research in immigration law. Items which are starred might be found in the core immigration law library of an immigration practitioner or serious student.

§ 17–1 LAWS AND REGULATIONS

8 U.S.C.—Aliens and Nationality (Codification of the Immigration and Nationality Act, P.L. 414, ch. 477, 66 Stat. 163, June 27, 1952, and its subsequent amendments. This is the basic source of immigration law).*

22 U.S.C.—Foreign Affairs (Laws regulating the activities of U.S. consulates).*

8 C.F.R.—(Regulations governing immigration procedures).*

20 C.F.R.—(Labor Department regulations, including alien labor certification).*

22 C.F.R.—(Foreign relations regulations giving procedures and guidelines to U.S. consulates for issuing visas and passports).*

Bender's INS Regulations Service (Matthew Bender, 1989–) (1 vol. looseleaf updated bimonthly).

Bender's Immigration and Nationality Act Pamphlet: Including the Immigration Act of 1990. (Matthew

Bender, 1991) (Immigration and Nationality Act updated through January 1, 1991).

Extradition Laws and Treaties, United States (Igor I. Kavass & Adolf Sprudzs, comps., Buffalo, NY: W.S. Hein, 1980–) (2 vols. looseleaf).

Federal Immigration Laws, Regulations & Forms (West Pub. Co., 1991) (1 vol. containing the basic statutes and regulations).*

Federal Register (daily newspaper-style publication that updates the C.F.R. and provides notices of proposed rules).

Immigration Act of 1990, P.L. 101–649, 104 Stat. 4978, November 29, 1990.

Immigration Act of 1990 (New York, NY: Matthew Bender, 1991) (special supplement to *Immigration Law and Procedures* which contains the text of the 1990 Act with explanation and analysis by Charles Gordon and Stanley Mailman).

Immigration and Nationality Laws of the United States: Selected Statutes, Regulations, and Forms: As Amended to February 1, 1991 (including amendments effective October 1, 1991) (T. Alexander Aleinikoff & David A. Martin, selectors, St. Paul, MN: West Pub. Co., 1991).

Immigration and Naturalization Service, Code, Operations, Instructions, Regulations, and Interpretations (Internal policy guide covering the day-to-day operations of the INS).*

Immigration Law Service (Lawyers Co-operative Pub. Co., 1985–) (multivolume looseleaf service with statutes, regulations, and instructions).

Immigration Reform and Control Act of 1986, P.L. 99–603, 100 Stat. 3359, November 6, 1986.

United States Code Congressional and Administrative News (contains very recent statutes and legislative history of new statutes).

United States Department of State, *Foreign Affairs Manual* (vol. 9 contains State Department interpretations and regulations on immigration and citizenship) (reproduced in *Immigration Law Service, supra,* and Gordon & Gordon, *infra*).

The Whole Act: Immigration and Nationality Act, As Amended (Pravinchandra J. Patel, comp., East Meadow, NY: Legal Research Bureau, 1991, as of January 1, 1991).

§ 17–2 CASES AND DECISIONS

BIA Index Decisions Reporter (Washington, D.C.: American Immigration Lawyers Association, 1986–) (4 issues/year; annual from 1986–89).

Federal Immigration Law Reporter (Washington Service Bureau, 1983–) (contains selected court cases and administrative agency decisions).

Hein's Interim Decision Service (Buffalo, NY: W.S. Hein & Co., 1984–) (begins with # 2951, Dec. 12, 1983).

Immigration Labor Certification Reporter (Matthew Bender & Co., 1981–1985) (contains selected court cases and administrative agency decisions).

Immigration Law and Procedure Reporter (Matthew Bender & Co., 1985–) (contains selected court cases and administrative agency decisions).

United States Board of Immigration Appeals, *Administrative Decisions Under Immigration and Nationality Laws* (19 vols., U.S. Government Printing Office).*

United States Department of Labor, *Decisions of the Office of Administrative Law Judges and Office of Administrative Appeals* (U.S. Government Printing Office, 1987–) (contains decisions concerning labor certification).*

§ 17–3 HISTORY

Edward P. Hutchinson, *Legislative History of American Immigration Policy, 1798–1965* (University of Pennsylvania Press, 1981).

Nancy C. Montwieler, *The Immigration Reform Law of 1986: Analysis, Text, Legislative History* (Bureau of National Affairs, 1987).

Edward E. Proper, *Colonial Immigration Laws* (AMS Press, Inc., 1967).

Selected Legislative History of the Immigration Act of 1990 (Washington, D.C.: American Immigration Lawyers Assoc., 1991) (including text of the 1990 Act).

Selected Legislative History of the Immigration Reform and Control Act of 1986 (Washington, D.C.: American Immigration Lawyers Assoc., 1987).

Oscar Trelles & James Bailey, *Immigration and Nationality Acts Legislative Histories and Related Documents* (multivolume set with index; W.S. Hein Co., 1979).

Voices from Ellis Island: An Oral History of American Immigration (Frederick, MD: University Publications of America, 1989).

Peter H. Wang, *Legislating Normalcy: The Immigration Act of 1924* (R & E Research Associates, 1975).

§ 17–4　BOOKS, TREATISES, AND DIGESTS

1990 Hiring Foreign Personnel: Immigration Problems and Solutions; Expert Commentaries on Professionals, Executives and Managers; Employer Sanctions & Employment Authorization; Corporate Hiring Policies; Treaty Traders & Investors; Tax Consequences; Labor Certification Appeals (Sandra G. Levitt, Lawrence D. Bastone, & Amy R. Novick, eds., Washington, D.C.: American Immigration Lawyers Assoc., 1989).

1991–92 Immigration & Nationality Law Handbook (R. Patrick Murphy, ed., Washington, D.C.: American Immigration Lawyers Assoc., 1991) (vol. 1 Statutory Overview; vol. 2 Advanced Topics; vol. 3 Regulatory Overview; forthcoming supplement).

The AILA U.S. Consular Posts Handbook (Seymour Rosenberg & Richard S. Goldstein, 4th ed., Washington, D.C.: American Immigration Lawyers Assoc., 1991).

Thomas Alexander Aleinikoff & David Martin, *Immigration Process and Policy* (West Pub. Co., 2d ed. 1991).

American Immigration Lawyers Assoc., *1991 AILA Annual Conference* (Simi Valley, CA: Convention Seminar Cassettes, 1991) (sound cassettes).

American Immigration Lawyers Assoc., *1990 AILA Business Immigration Conference* (Simi Valley, CA: Convention Seminar Cassettes, 1991) (9 sound cassettes).

American Immigration Lawyers Assoc., *AILA's Comprehensive Seminar on the New Immigration Act of 1990* (Cheverly, MD: Audio Visual, 1991) (8 sound cassettes).

Deborah E. Anker, *The Law of Asylum in the United States: A Guide to Administrative Practice and Case Law* (2d ed., Washington, D.C.: American Immigration Lawyers Assoc., 1991).

BALCA Handbook (James Guill & Todd R. Smyth, comps., Washington, D.C.: American Immigration Lawyers Assoc., 1990–) (1 vol. looseleaf) (BALCA is the Board of Alien Labor Certification Appeals of the U.S. Employment Service).

Basic Guide to Naturalization and Citizenship (Washington, D.C.: U.S. Dept. of Justice, Immigration and Naturalization Service, Outreach Program, 1990).

Basic Law Manual: Asylum: A Training Manual for Immigration & Naturalization Officers (Washington, D.C.: American Immigration Lawyers Assoc., 1991) (reprints 2 manuals prepared by the INS' Asylum Branch, *Basic Law Manual: Asylum, Summary and Overview* and *Refugee/Asylum Law and Practice (RELAP): A Reference of Perspectives and Parameters on Selected Legal Issues*).

M. Cherif Bassiouni, *International Extradition: United States Law & Practice* (Oceana, 1983–).

Richard A. Boswell & Gilbert Paul Carrasco, *Immigration and Nationality Law: Cases and Materials* (Durham, NC: Carolina Academic Press, 1991–).

John L. Cable, *Decisive Decisions on United States Citizenship* (Michie Co., 1967).

David Carliner, *The Rights of Aliens* (Avon Books, 2d ed. 1990).

David W. Crosland, *Business Immigration Law Today: Course Manual* (Washington, D.C.: Federal Publications, 1990).

E Visa Form Book: Treaty Trader and Investor (E) Visa Questionnaires and Supplemental Information Forms Required by U.S. Consular Posts Abroad (Richard S. Goldstein, 2d ed., Washington, D.C.: American Immigration Lawyers Assoc., 1991).

Diana Elles, *International Provisions Protecting The Human Rights of Non–Citizens,* U.N. Doc. E/CN.4/Sub.2/392/Rev. 1 (1980).

Federal Procedural Forms, Lawyers Edition (Lawyers Co-operative Pub. Co., 1975–) (contains sample immigration law forms and includes references to statutes, court rules, administrative regulations, cases, law review articles, legal encyclopedia sections, and ALR annotations related to the subject matter of the forms).

A. Fragomen, A. Del Rey, & S. Bell, *Immigration Procedures Handbook* (Clark Boardman Co., 1985–) (annual kept up to date by supplements; 1992 is the most recent edition).

Hope M. Frye, & H. Ronald Klasko, *Immigration Compliance Guide* (Matthew Bender & Co., 1987).

Guy S. Goodwin–Gill, *The Refugee in International Law* (Oxford Univ. Press, 1985).

Charles Gordon & Stanley Mailman, *Immigration Law and Procedure* (2d rev. ed. 1991) (formerly C. Gordon

& S. Rosenfield) (multivolume looseleaf with case references, statutes, regulations, instructions, etc.).*

Hurst Hannum, *The Right to Leave and Return in International Law and Practice* (Martinus Nijhoff Publishers, 1987).

Bill Ong Hing, *Handling Immigration Cases* (Lawyers Co-operative Pub. Co., 1985 & Supp.1990).

Immigrant Investors: Creating Employment for U.S. Communities (Washington, D.C.: American Immigration Lawyers Assoc., 1991).

Immigrants' Rights Manual (Los Angeles, CA: National Immigration Law Center, 1990) (includes highlights of the Immigration Act of 1990).

Immigration and Nationality Law: 1990 Annual (Washington, D.C.: American Immigration Lawyers Assoc., 1990) (vol. 1 Fundamentals; vol. 2 Advanced Topics).

1991–2 Immigration & Nationality Law Handbook (R. Patrick Murphy, ed., Washington, D.C.: American Immigration Lawyers Assoc., 1991) (vol. 1 Statutory Overview; vol. 2 Advanced Topics; vol. 3 Regulatory Overview, forthcoming supplement).

Daniel J. Jacobs, *Political Asylum, Refuge and Sanctuary, (U.S., Foreign & International), A Selective Bibliography,* 42 Record 561 (1987).

Ira J. Kurzban, *Kurzban's Immigration Law Sourcebook: A Comprehensive Outline and Reference Tool* (2d ed., Washington, D.C.: American Immigration Law Foundation, 1991).

Stephen H. Legomsky, *Immigration Law and Policy: A Coursebook* (Westbury, NY: Foundation Press, Inc., 1992).

Richard Lillich, *The Human Rights of Aliens in Contemporary International Law* (Manchester University Press, 1984).

Manual on Labor Certification: Practice and Procedure (Robert E. Banta & Daryl R. Buffenstein, eds., Washington, D.C.: American Immigration Lawyers Assoc., 1990).

National Lawyers Guild, *Immigration Law and Defense* (3d ed. 1988–) (2 vols. looseleaf).

The New Immigration Act of 1990 (Minneapolis, MN: Minnesota Institute of Legal Education, 1991).

Amy Novick & Antoinette Rizzi, *Bibliography for Immigration Law and Practice,* in *Immigration and Nationality Law* (R. Juceam & E. Rubin, eds., American Immigration Lawyers Assoc., 1987).

Pravinchandra J. Patel, *Patel's Citations of Administrative Decisions Under Immigration and Nationality Laws* (Legal Research Bureau, 1982–).

Pravinchandra J. Patel, *Patel's Immigration Law Digest: Decisions from 1940* (Lawyers Co-operative Pub. Co., 1982–). (2 vols. looseleaf).

Records of the Immigration and Naturalization Service (Alan M. Kraut, ed., Bethesda, MD: United Publications of America, 1991–) (microfilm).

Alan Edward Schorr, *Refugee and Immigrant Resource Directory 1990–1991* (Juneau, AK: Denali Press, 1990).

Shepard's Immigration and Naturalization Citations (Shepard's/McGraw–Hill, 2d. ed. 1991–) (also on WESTLAW).

Helen Sklar & Stuart I. Folinsky, *The Immigration Act of 1990 Handbook: The Complete Practice Guide to the 1990 Act* (New York, NY: Clark Boardman, 1991).

Understanding the Immigration Act of 1990: AILA's New Law Handbook (Paul Wickham Schmidt, ed., Washington, D.C.: American Immigration Lawyers Assoc., 1991) (includes text of the Immigration Act of 1990).

United Nations High Commissioner For Refugees, *Collection of International Instruments Concerning Refugees* (1990), U.N. Doc. HCR/IP/1/Eng.

United Nations High Commissioner For Refugees, *Conclusions on the International Protection of Refugees* (1989–1 vol. looseleaf).

United Nations High Commissioner for Refugees, *Handbook on Procedures and Criteria for Determining Refugee Status* (1979).

United Nations High Commissioner for Refugees, *United Nations Resolutions and Decisions relating to the Office of the United Nations High Commissioner for Refugees,* U.N. Doc. HCR/INF.49 (1989–).

United States Congress, House Committee on the Judiciary, Subcommittee on Immigration, Refugees, and International Law, *Refugee Admissions for Fiscal Year 1990: Hearings Before the Subcommittee on Immigration, Refugees, and International Law of the Committee on the Judiciary, House of Representatives, 101st Congress, 1st Session, September 12 and 13, 1989* (Washington, D.C.: U.S. Government Printing Office, 1990).

United States Department of Labor, *Dictionary of Occupational Titles* (4th ed. rev. 1991).*

United States Immigration Commission, *Reports* (Washington, D.C.: U.S. Government Printing Office, 1911–). (41 vols.).

§ 17–5 PERIODICALS

For articles about immigration law, policy, and procedure, the Index to Legal Periodicals should be consulted under the following headings: Emigration & Immigration; Deportation, Citizens & Citizenship; and Aliens. The following periodicals are of continuing interest:

AILA Business Immigration News (Warren R. Leiden, ed.) Washington, D.C.: American Immigration Lawyers Assoc., 1990–) (4 issues/year).

The AILA U.S. Consular Posts Handbook (Seymour Rosenberg & Richard S. Goldstein, 4th ed., Washington, D.C.: American Immigration Lawyers Assoc., 1991) (4 issues/year).

Annual Immigration and Naturalization Institute (New York, NY: Practicing Law Institute, 1967–).

Georgetown Immigration Law Journal (Washington, D.C.: Georgetown University Law Center, 1985–) (4 issues/year).

Immigration Briefings (Washington, D.C.: Federal Publications, 1988–) (monthly).

Immigration Law Advisory (Rochester, NY: Lawyers Cooperative Pub. Co.; Bancroft Whitney Pub. Co.; 1985–) (published 8 times per year as part of the *Immigration Law Service*).

Immigration Law Report (New York, NY: New Clark Boardman Co., 1981–) (11 issues/year).

Immigration and Nationality Law Review (Buffalo, NY: W.S. Hein & Co., 1977–) (annual).

INS Reporter Immigration and Naturalization Service, Washington, D.C., (includes administrative decisions, C.F.R. changes, and statistics) (4 issues/year).

International Journal of Refugee Law (Oxford Univ. Press, 1989–) (4 issues/year).

International Migration Review (Staten Island, N.Y.: Center for Migration Studies, 1966–) (4 issues/year).

Interpreter Releases (New York, N.Y.: American Council for Nationalities Service, 1924–) (good for articles and analysis of new rules and decisions) (weekly).*

Journal of Refugee Studies (Oxford Univ. Press, 1988–) (4 issues/year).

Donatella Luca, *The 1951 Convention Relating to the Status of Refugees: A Selected Bibliography,* 3 International Journal of Refugee Law 633 (1991).

Refugee Abstracts (Centre for Documentation for Refugees, UNHCR, 1982–) (4 issues/year).

Refugees (Office of the United Nation's High Commissioner for Refugees, 1984–) (monthly).

San Diego Law Review Immigration Symposium (San Diego, CA: San Diego Law Review, 1975 (vol. 13)–) (annual).

Transnational Immigration Law Reporter (Palo Alto, CA: Immigration Common Law Exchange Society, 1979–) (covers international immigration problems) (monthly).

United States Immigration and Naturalization Service, *Annual Report* (Washington, D.C.: Immigration and Naturalization Service, 1946/47–).

Visa Bulletin (U.S. Dept. of State, Bureau of Consular Affairs, Washington, D.C., (lists availability of visas by country) (monthly).*

§ 17–6 DATABASES

LEGI–SLATE (database for proposed legislation on immigration).

LEXIS IMMIG Library (federal immigration statutes, court cases, administrative decisions, and regulations).

LEXIS IMMIG Library's BIA file (Board of Immigration Appeals decisions).

LEXIS IMMIG Library's REFORM file (text of Immigration Act of 1990).

WESTLAW FIM (federal immigration statutes, court cases, and regulations).

WESTLAW FIM–BIA (Board of Immigration Appeals decisions).

INDEX

IMMIGRANT VISAS—Cont'd
Procedures for immigrant visas, 117–27
Special immigrants, 115–16, 135
Visa chargeability, 109
Visas not subject to numerical limitations, 102–08
Visas subject to numerical limitations, 108–17

IMMIGRATION ACT OF 1990 (IMMACT 90)
In general, 32–43, 87
Worldwide limit, 33

IMMIGRATION AND NATURALIZATION SERVICE (INS)
See Executive Office of Immigration Review
Border patrol, 12, 14, 16, 19, 24–25, 76
History, 8, 10, 13, 19
Oversight by Congress, 86, 95–97
Regional offices, 75
Regional service centers, 76–77
Role in legalization, 25–27
Structure, 74–77

IMMIGRATION REFORM AND CONTROL ACT (IRCA), 22–32, 87

IMMIGRATION TECHNICAL AMENDMENTS OF 1991, pp. 43–44

INDIGENOUS PEOPLES, 1, 47

INSPECTION
See also Parole
In general, 175–76
Adjustment of status, inspection required, 215
Authority of INS, 8, 176–86
Avoiding inspection by false claim of citizenship, 168–69, 215
Deportation for failure, 168–69
History, 13–14, 17
Secondary inspection, 179

INTENT TO IMMIGRATE
See Nonimmigrant Visas, Nonimmigrant intent

INTERDICTION ON HIGH SEAS, 57, 73, 177–78, 232–34
See also Haiti; Refugees

INTERNATIONAL LABOR ORGANIZATION, 274–76

INTERNATIONAL LAW
See also Asylum; Refugees
In general, 50–55, 261–77
Asylum, 270–74
Freedom of exit, 261–63
Freedom of movement, 261–65

†